ECOLOGICAL POLICY AND POLITICS IN DEVELOPING COUNTRIES

SUNY Series in International Environmental Policy and Theory

Sheldon Kamieniecki, Editor

ECOLOGICAL POLICY AND POLITICS IN DEVELOPING COUNTRIES

ECONOMIC GROWTH, DEMOCRACY, AND ENVIRONMENT

EDITED BY
UDAY DESAI

STATE UNIVERSITY OF NEW YORK PRESS

Published by
State University of New York Press, Albany

For information, address State University of New York Press,
State University Plaza, Albany, N.Y. 12246

Production by M. R. Mulholland
Marketing by Anne M. Valentine

Library of Congress Cataloging-in-Publication Data

Ecological policy and politics in developing countries : economic
    growth, democracy, and environment / edited by Uday Desai.
        p.   cm. — (SUNY series in international environmental policy
    and theory)
      Includes bibliographical references and index.
      ISBN 0-7914-3779-5 (alk. paper). — ISBN 0-7914-3780-9 (pbk. alk.
    paper)
      1. Environmental policy—Developing countries.   I. Desai, Uday.
    II. Series.
    GE190.D44E36   1998
    363.7′009172′4—dc21   97-27167
                                                                                      CIP

10   9   8   7   6   5   4   3   2   1

FOR MY CHILDREN
MICHAEL, KAVITA, AND NEAL.
THEY ARE OUR FUTURE.

CONTENTS

TABLES AND FIGURES

MAPS

PREFACE

With the fall of communism, the struggle for ideological superiority is being replaced by worries over global warming and holes in the ozone layer. Along with ethnic conflict, concerns with the environment are the issues likely to dominate the international arena in decades to come. This is already being reflected in the proliferation of academic and popular writings, especially in the West, on environmental issues. The environment is likely to be for the next century what ideology was for this one.

Environmental problems, even global environmental problems such as global warming, are the result of thousands, even millions of individual local actions and decisions. An American middle-class professional's decision to live in a suburb and drive to work every day, a poor Brazilian farmer's decision to cut down a patch of rainforest to clear land for cultivation, and a poor African villager's desire to get rid of wild predator cats or elephants who destroy his livestock or his subsistence farm have enormous global environmental consequences when multiplied millions of times over. This is not to deny the critical importance of public policies in both creating and remedying environmental degradation. It is rather to recognize the extreme difficulty of dealing with environmental problems. Not only are the global problems intricately intertwined with local individual actions, they are also caught up in a vast web of social and economic networks. Problems of poverty and global environmental degradation are closely interconnected. And both are inseparable from issues of governance and public policy.

It is this complex web of interrelations among global and national governance and public policies and environmental and socio-economic issues that will require scholarly attention as the environment becomes the focus of international concern in the next century. This is indeed a tall order for academic study. The vast array of differences among the nations, in geography and climate, in history and culture, and in wealth and form of governance, makes it impossible for a single scholar or a single book to deal adequately with the subject. Perhaps a beginning can be made by bringing together, in one place, an overview of environmental issues, in the context of the history, economy, and public policies of key countries around the globe. Such a group of country studies would demonstrate the great diversity of conditions and practices that are so often lumped together simply as the environmental problem. It would also alert us to the many different histories, cultures, economies, and geographies in which these environmental problems have come to exist and within which milieus so many varied solutions will have to be designed.

This volume is a modest attempt to bring together such a group of country studies. It focuses on what is widely referred to as developing countries. It includes mostly poor countries such as India, China, Indonesia, Mexico, and Nigeria. But it also includes some not so poor countries such as Taiwan, Thailand, Venezuela, and the Czech Republic. Each chapter is authored by an established scholar of that country's environmental problems and policies, as well as its history, culture, and government. I have not attempted to force the authors to fit their country studies into a tightly-specified theoretical frame. Instead, each author was asked to address a common set of broad questions. These questions concerned the overview of major environmental problems and policies, the politics of environmental policies, and effectiveness of environmental policies in each country. This wide latitude was essential in view of diverse natural, historical, and political conditions in each country. Each country study, in a sense, stands on its own. Together, however, they are designed to provide a rich tapestry of common themes as well as distinct patterns. Only the readers can judge how well the book accomplishes that. A forthcoming volume will address the same questions in rich industrial countries.

This book has taken over four years and the help of many. The individual chapter authors have been the essential ingredient in the making of the book. Without their contributions, this book would not be. They have been prompt and patient through all the reviews, revisions, and drafts. Whatever merit the book has is because of them. Many others have assisted. Mrs. Mara Lou Howse carefully copyedited the draft chapters. I am grateful to her for her meticulous work. Several of my graduate research assistants have helped me over these four years on various book-related tasks. I would like to thank Ms. Christine Niesel, Lori Phan, Karen Schwander, and Mr. John Rutkowski for their help. I am most grateful to my secretary, Ms. Rhonda Musgrave for her untiring efforts in getting this manuscript ready through many drafts. My wife, Chris, has helped with all my writings in ways too numerous to mention.

Permissions

Pages 31 and 59 from *The Mexico Handbook: Economic and Demographic Maps and Statistics* by James B. Pick, and Edgar W. Butler. Copyright © 1994 by Westview Press. Reprinted by permission of Westview Press.

World Bank map of oilfields in Venezuela, map #1BRD 22154, March 1990. Copyright © 1990 by World Bank. Reprinted by permission of the World Bank.

Page 2 from *An Atlas of India* edited by S. Muthiah, R. Ramachandran, and P. Poovendran. Copyright © 1990 by Government of India. Reprinted by permission of TTK Pharma, Ltd.

1

Environment, Economic Growth, and Government in Developing Countries

Uday Desai

Introduction

Think globally, act locally is a popular environmental slogan. Nature is a seamless global whole. The world's natural environment is intricately interwoven. A small change in a faraway place may have major consequences on the amount of our rainfall or the severity of our summer storms. Destruction of Brazilian rainforests, deforestation in Thailand, air pollution in Mexico all have worldwide consequences: global warming, a hole in the ozone layer and the destruction of biodiversity. These, in turn, affect human health and well-being across the globe.

Our growing knowledge of the interconnectedness of the global environment inevitably leads to the study of environmental problems and policies in countries around the globe. While initially the focus of contemporary Western environmentalists' concern was the degradation of the environment in the industrialized West (Carson 1962), it has increasingly shifted to environmental pollution and degradation in the poor countries. Partly this is a reflection of the realization that life in the industrial countries is affected by the environmental degradation in the poor countries. Global warming and depletion of the ozone layer caused by the destruction of rainforests and use of chlorofluorocarbons (CFC) in the poor countries are going to jeopardize the lifestyles and comfort of the citizens of wealthy countries perhaps even more than those of the poor countries. It is in the self-interest of the wealthy industrial nations to be actively concerned about the state of the environment in the poor countries.

Another reason for the increasing concern with environmental destruction in the poor countries has been the heightened recognition that the earth's natural resources are finite and that the existence of modern industrial societies depends on the continuing availability of these resources. There has been steadily growing recognition by all but a few "true believers" in the magic of the market (Tucker 1982; Simon 1981, 1980; Beckerman 1974) that earth's resources and earth's ability to absorb pollution are already strained and that its ability to sustain our materially rich lifestyles is in serious jeopardy. Therefore, it is now widely conceded, especially in the industrial West, that the earth's natural resources must be considered in a "global" context. They must be utilized in a carefully planned and rational manner and must be protected from waste and overexploitation (Gamman 1994; Bennett and Chaloupka 1993; Porter and Brown 1991).

A small group of environmentalists, "deep" ecologists, have focused attention on the poor countries by developing a strong critique of the very basis of the political-economic system of wealthy industrial societies. They argue that the "commodification of relationships under capital and markets . . . are at the heart of current environmental problems" (Rogers 1994:2). They consider the "treadmill of production" and the "logic of competitive productivism" of the modern industrial society fundamentally incompatible with the planet's ecological well-being (Schnaiberg and Gould 1994; Sachs 1992). They consider global environmental degradation as a reflection of "a civilization impass—namely, that the level of productive performance already achieved turns out to be not viable in the North, let alone for the rest of the globe" (Sachs 1992:35–36). For these deep ecologists, the global environmental crisis is really a "civilizational crisis." The very foundations of modern industrial society—that is, science and technology, market capitalism and the idea of domination over nature—are challenged (Rogers 1994; Sikorski 1993; Sachs 1992; Evernden 1985; Leiss 1994). These critics bring attention to environmental policies and problems in poor countries by challenging the viability and even desirability of industrial civilization. They challenge the model of development based on the idea of domination over nature that has been followed by the West and is being aggressively pursued in the poor countries, often at the urging of the wealthy industrial countries.

A fourth reason for the increasing attention to environmental conditions in the poor countries is the recognition, often not explicitly or publicly articulated, that serious damage to the environment and thorough exploitation of natural resources have already taken place in the industrial countries. It is recognized that it is nearly impossible politically, if not ecologically, to reverse this environmental degradation. It is cheaper to prevent or reduce environmental degradation in poor countries than in the rich ones. This is reflected, for example, in increasing interest in debt for nature swaps.

Whether it is self-interest in maintaining a high material standard of living or self-doubt about its viability and desirability, or the genuine belief that the fate of all living things, including humans, is tied together on this spaceship earth, or some combination of all of these reasons, the problems of environmental pollution in a country are no longer the concern of that country alone. They have become the concern of many nations. The Rio Earth Summit is perhaps the most spectacular evidence of the internationalization of environmental concerns. This globalization of the environment has raised many difficult issues for the international community. The debates and disagreements surrounding the five Rio agreements, officially known as the United Nations Conference on Environment and Development (UNCED) agreements, concern many of the most contentious of these issues (Grubb et al. 1993).

There are two main concerns. First and central is a broad concern with the relationship between economic growth and environment. Second is concern with the roles of governments and markets and their consequences for the environment. There is a related concern about the relationship between democracy and environmental protection. These are overlapping and interrelated concerns. We discuss them in turn.

Environment and Economic Development

This is perhaps the central issue in the global environment debate. The dominant model of economic growth, based on neoclassical economics, does not consider the environment to be relevant to economics or economic development. It assumes that "there is not only an infinite supply of natural resources but also of 'sinks' for disposing of the waste from exploiting these resources— provided that the free market is operating" (Porter and Brown 1991:27). In this view, "the problems of raw materials exhaustion or pollution are minor diversions"; environmental pollution is an example of "negative externality" and only a matter of "minor resource misallocation" (Pearce 1986:15).

The environment is in an enduring conflict with this model of growth (Schnaiberg and Gould 1994). Economic growth requires exploitation of natural resources for expanding production of material goods and dumping of the waste products of this production into the environment. The modern "treadmill of production" inexorably degrades the environment (Schnaiberg and Gould 1994:v). In rich countries, mass production and consumption is a major cause of environmental degradation and destruction of natural resources. In poor countries, "the creation of value and access to subsistence are typically linked to *sacrificing* environmental quality for short-term economic gain" (Redclift and Goodman 1991:5). Poverty and subsistence do not always lead to environmental degradation. The poor often adopt sustainable use strategies, since their continuing survival depends on such strategies. However, among the multitude of poor and for most governments in poor countries, survival and reduction in poverty take precedence over concern for the environment. Questions of environmental quality are unlikely to receive careful hearing amid the overwhelming problems of poverty.

In addition, most of the poor countries, especially in Asia and Latin America, are now urbanized and semi-industrialized economies with sizable middle classes. These middle classes expect to achieve a relatively high material standard of living like their counterparts in the rich industrial countries. They are "oriented towards private consumer goods" (Redclift and Goodman 1991:13) and are unlikely to be enlisted in the cause of environmental protection at the expense of economic growth. The resistance of semi-industrialized countries, such as Malaysia, India, and Brazil, preceding the UN Conference on the Human Environment at Stockholm in 1972, to industrialized countries' focus on global environmental protection has continued. Developing countries, especially their governments and economic elites, consider environmental protection a luxury that can be considered only after the rising level of economic growth is secured (Grubb et al. 1993).

Long and hard bargaining preceding the Earth Summit in Rio focused on the developing countries' insistence on linkage between environmental protection and economic development. Poor countries demanded that the rich countries provide them with increased aid to compensate for their increased costs and for the adverse impact of environmental protection on their economic growth. The poor countries also demanded that the rich ones transfer advanced environmentally friendly technologies to them at low or no cost so that they can protect the environment without reducing their economic growth rate. Many developing countries refused to reduce their economic growth targets. China, for example, remains "committed to doubling its gross national product in twelve years at most" (Newhouse 1992:74).

However, it is not only the poor countries that resist sacrificing economic growth for environmental protection. Rich countries, especially the United States, have also generally refused to protect the environment at the expense of economic growth (Beckerman 1974). Richard Darman, a former director of the office of Management and Budget, expressed the sentiment shared by many when he said, in a lecture at Harvard University in 1990, "Americans did not fight and win the wars of the twentieth century to make the world safe for green vegetables" (quoted in Newhouse 1992:70). Recent legislations passed by the U.S. Congress in 1995, allowing oil drilling in Alaska's Arctic National Wildlife Refuge (not signed into law by President Clinton), reducing environmental regulations when they affect economic growth or jobs, generally reducing environmental regulation, and placing economic growth ahead of environmental protection, attest to the continuing priority of economic growth over environmental protection in the U.S. Even though there is increasing awareness of the need to protect the environment in the industrial countries, the pro-economic growth attitudes and mind-set are still dominant within "the most powerful institutions in the U.S. and elsewhere in the industrialized world" (Porter and Brown 1991:32).

Because pro-economic growth attitudes are held by the powerful elites and institutions as well as by a large section of the populace both in the rich industrial and in the poor industrializing countries, attempts have been made to reconcile economic growth with environmental protection. The poor countries' insistence that reducing poverty be the first goal has been the catalyst in developing approaches to reconcile economy and environment. The idea of "sustainable development" is the most widely accepted approach to reconciling economy and environment in a global context. The World Commission on Environment and Development (WCED) in its now famous report, "Our Common Future" (1987), developed the broad framework for what it called "sustainable development." It is a framework for the future of global human society. It is cautiously optimistic. It sees "the possibility for a new era of economic growth, one that must be based on policies that sustain and expand the environmental resource base." It also considers "such growth to be absolutely essential to relieve the great poverty that is deepening in much of the developing world" (1987:1) and declares that "Environment and development are not separate challenges; they are inexorably linked" (1987:37).

While sustainable development has become the dominant framework in discussions on global ecological preservation and international aid programs, questions about the wisdom of tying preservation of global ecology to economics have continued (International Union for Conservation of Nature and Natural Resources 1991; Wells, Brandon, and Hannah 1992; Pearce, Markandya, and Barbier 1989; Goodman and Redclift 1991; Redclift 1987, 1989). Some environmentalists have argued that economic growth is incompatible with ecological preservation. "The connotation of sustainable growth is that you can have development that is not detrimental to our environment, and that's where it becomes an oxymoron" (Robinson 1994:4). These environmentalists "fear that the new emphasis on human needs, . . . means a loss of commitment to the primary objective of conserving biological diversity" (Fuller 1994:2). They worry about the implicit threat that making "everything economic" poses to "reverence for life" on the planet (Wright 1994:3). Others suspect that "the ready adoption of sustainable development rhetoric implies a continuation of the present development models and policies" (Porter and Brown 1991:32).

While the difficulties of achieving economic growth without adversely affecting the environment are becoming increasingly apparent both in practice and in theory, it is also becoming abundantly clear that poverty exerts pressures that are equally perilous to the environment. A dominant current of thought addresses this paradox by stressing scientific knowledge and technological innovation as the key to reducing poverty through economic growth without degrading the environment. It places faith in human technological ingenuity and rational planning to enable us to escape the environmental costs of economic growth. Its advocates see earth as a store of resources that are limited, finite, and exhaustible. They argue for careful management of all earth's resources, its air, water, forests, minerals, biological diversity. In this perspective, humans must use their unparalleled rational powers, their science, and their technological prowess to manage judiciously the earth and its resources in the interest of human prosperity and ecological integrity. In this view the environmental crisis is "a crisis of will and rationality" (Caldwell 1990:7). Much of the writing on environmental problems and policies by economists, political scientists, and environmental policy experts takes this "resource management" perspective (McNeely 1988; Pearce, Markandya, and Barbier 1989; WCED 1987). In this view, economic incentives and penalties, as well as regulations when there is no properly functioning "market," would protect the environment and promote more efficient use of resources, thereby increasing overall economic efficiency. This view emphasizes efficiency. It does not pay much attention to "equity."

There is a small but persistent group who insist that equity considerations are vital to environmental protection, especially in the poor countries (Goodman and Redclift 1991; Hecht and Cockburn 1989; Schnaiberg, Watts, and Zimmerman 1986; Schnaiberg and Gould, 1994; Watts 1986; Shiva 1989). There are two types of equity considerations. One deals with the assessment of how environmental pollution and hazards are distributed, both within and between countries. There is growing evidence that the poor, in both rich and poor countries, bear a disproportionate share of the hazards of environmental pollution. Poor communities in the United States seem more frequently to be home to toxic dumps and more often have more degraded environmental quality (Bullard 1993, 1990; Bryant 1989). Most victims of the Union Carbide chemical plant disaster in Bhopal, India, were poor squatters in shanty towns around the plant. In recent years, rich countries also have tried to export their highly toxic wastes to poor countries. Areola for instance, points out in his chapter in this volume that there was a national scandal in 1987 when it was discovered that an Italian ship covertly brought in toxic waste to be buried in Nigeria. It was not long ago that the U.S. media reported a barge laden with garbage from an American city stranded at sea when it was not allowed to dump its "cargo" in a nearby nation. The growing concern about the export of toxic wastes was reflected in poor countries' demand for a total ban on exports of hazardous waste to their countries, in Agenda 21 at the Rio conference. Though this demand was not adopted, chapter 20 of the agenda calls for ratification and implementation of the global Basel Convention and African Bamako Convention regulating and restricting transboundary movement of hazardous wastes (Grubb et al. 1993:133–34).

There is a second type of equity concern that deals with distribution of the economic benefits and costs of growth. In poor countries reducing poverty by a more equitable distribution of the fruits of economic growth is not a minor element but the central necessity in protecting the environment (Redclift and Goodman 1991). Environmental protection policies have been shown to have regressive distributional effects on personal incomes (Zimmerman 1986). Thus, it would seem important to include equity considerations in all discussions of environmental policy. However, there is generally little attention given to these equity considerations and "little attempt has been made in policy to redress" the regressive effects of environmental policy (Watts 1986). Concern with the distributional consequences may grow, especially among the poor themselves, and especially if economic growth becomes anemic. A slow-down in growth is more likely to hinder than help policies to protect environment. It is more likely to lead to "a trend away from environmental protection altogether," rather than to "a development towards an equitable environmental policy" (Watts 1986:6), unless much greater attention is paid to equity in the distribution of the benefits of economic growth and of the costs of environmental protection policies.

Equity considerations at the global level, that is, distribution of the resources and benefits of economic growth among nations is equally critical in protecting global ecology. McNeely sums up the issue well in the context of conservation and sustainable use of global biodiversity: "A fundamental issue which remains to be solved is determining the optimal distribution of benefits from utilizing biological resources" (1988:iv). Most of the benefits flow to the global community while local, often poor, people bear the bulk of costs. McNeely's "global community" is, more often than not, the rich countries. Poor countries pay the price of protecting the environment and preserving biodiversity of the species, largely for the benefit and preferences of the rich countries. Environmental policy ultimately is an "inevitably distributive policy, and this applies as much to the global level as within individual countries." Given this, it is not possible to achieve sustainable development "without achieving greater global equality and more global responsibility" (Redclift and Goodman 1991:17).

Problems of poverty, its causes and its effects, are complex and seemingly intractable and inevitable. Environmental scholars and activists especially in the United States generally pay little or no attention to the connection between poverty and environmental degradation. They pay little attention to the adverse economic consequences of environmental policies on the poor. They generally do not concern themselves with the hardships that, for example, a ban on the use of forests or wilderness areas would impose on the subsistence of the poor who depend on them, except when these poor people engage in "illegal" activities to continue to eke out subsistence level living from these areas. (There are exceptions of course. For examples, see Hecht and Cockburn 1989; Goodman and Redclift 1991; Schnaiberg and Gould 1994.)

For some environmentalists poor countries are the major culprits for global environmental degradation. For them, poor countries with their burgeoning population of poor and illiterate people are not only incapable "of helping themselves" but are even beyond "being truly helped by other nations" (Caldwell 1990:19). For these Western environmentalists, the poor countries show by their actions that they "reject the social restraints." Instead, these countries have found an expedient solution to their difficulties in "the export of surplus poor people, chiefly to the industrialized countries" (Caldwell 1990:19).

From this perspective, one of the major problems is that there is no way "under the present disposition of national power and politics that nations may coerce one another into environmentally prudent policies"(Caldwell 1990:18). The idea of "national sovereignty" has become a problem for these environmentalists. They have even suggested that activities in one country that are detrimental to the environment of neighboring countries constitute "an international security issue" (Caldwell 1990:13). Presumably, such a situation would justify the affected countries' taking action to defend their "national security" by all necessary means, including coercion and intervention. Not surprisingly, many in the poor countries see the environment as "an excuse for political intervention" by the rich countries (Redclift and Goodman 1991:17; also Cleary 1991). One difficulty in considering another nation's environmental policies a national security issue is that "few developed countries would agree to intervention in their environments on the grounds of global necessity" (Redclift and Goodman 1991:17). Indeed, a great many of the U.S. government's objections to the Rio Earth Summit agreements were grounded in unwillingness to agree to anything that even remotely seemed to impinge on its sovereignty (Grubb et al. 1993; Newhouse 1992).

Environmentalists in the West, especially in the United States, find the ecological destruction in the poor countries alarming. They consider poor countries' unwillingness to give highest priority to environmental protection dangerous to the global environment. They find the poor countries' demand for monetary compensation for foregoing the use of their environmental resources offensive. And they find their inability to make poor countries protect their environment, for the present and future good of the world community, extremely frustrating. Poor countries, on the other hand, often consider Western environmentalism a disguise for neocolonialism. They see it as a program to perpetuate existing inequities between the rich and the poor, as a way to deny poor countries the opportunity to achieve the wealth and good life that the West enjoys (Porter and Brown 1991:127–28).

While economic growth seems to contribute to environmental problems, economic prosperity and security seem to contribute to environmental protection. Redclift and Goodman argue that increasing concern with environmental protection is part of the "quality-of-life" considerations which have surfaced in developed countries "precisely because of the success of industrial capitalism in delivering relatively high standards of living for the majority" (1991:4).

Paehlke believes that "the future success of environmentalism depends on a reasonable level of security and comfort for the majority in society" (1989:9). The basis of environmental activism in industrial countries has been the economically secure, college educated middle class. A study of the Green party in Germany found that "Green voters have tended to be under thirty-five years old, highly educated, new middle class (salaried white collar or professional), urban or university town residents" (Frankland and Schoonmaker 1992:2–3). Some Western environmentalists suggest that the highly educated, economically secure, white-collar, middle-class individuals are the post-materialist vanguard for a new society (Milbrath 1984). For these writers the future of environmentalism and the fate of the global ecology depend upon the transition to "a truly post-industrial era" (Paehlke 1989:9). Broad-based popular support for the protection of the global environment is possible only "in a society well beyond industrialism" (Paehlke 1989:9). Only post- (or advanced) industrial societies, in this view, could create the postmaterialist majorities necessary to protect the global environment. Inglehart has argued that the "values of Western publics have been shifting from an overwhelming emphasis on material well-being and physical security toward greater emphasis on the quality of life" (1990:5). The culture of Western publics, according to Inglehart, has shifted from materialist to postmaterialist (1990). And herein lies the hope, perhaps the only hope in the minds of many Western environmental scholars and activists, for the defense of the global environment.

We come full circle. Economic growth and environmental protection, some argue, are inherently incompatible (Schnaiberg and Gould 1994). Others argue that sustained economic development to relieve the poverty of the multitudes in poor countries is an essential precondition for the long-term protection of the global environment (WCED 1987). Some counter that poor countries are the major threat to the global environment (Caldwell 1990) and that long-term protection of the global environment depends on the economically secure, highly educated, young middle-class professionals in the advanced industrial societies (Frankland and Schoonmaker 1991; Paehlke 1989; Caldwell 1990; Milbrath 1984). Others argue that environmental policy is inevitably a "distributive policy" within individual countries but especially between rich and poor countries (Goodman and Redclift 1991). The fate of the global environment, they argue, depends on making the world more equitable and just. They believe protection of the environment, especially in the third world, rests on one word: *justice* (Hecht and Cockburn 1989). All seem to agree that environmental protection is inseparable from economic well-being.

Democracy, Markets and Environment

In popular thinking democracy is friendly to, and sometimes even necessary for, the protection of the environment. Political democracy allows citizens to influence public policy by participating, individually and collectively through "interest" groups, in their formulation and implementation. Fair periodic elections, freedom of speech, assembly and organization, and generally free press seem essential for citizens' ability to influence their government and keep it accountable. The vast scale of environmental destruction in the ex-Communist countries of Eastern Europe and the old Soviet Union has strengthened the idea that democracy is better able to protect the environment than authoritarian regimes (Albrecht 1987; Alcamo 1992; Bolan 1992; Feffer 1992; Singleton 1987; Ziegler 1987). The lack of freedom for citizens and the victims of pollution to openly organize and oppose environmental destruction in the ex-Communist countries has been considered a major reason for this unchecked destruction. The lack of political democracy in these countries contributed significantly to the lack of environmental protection (Debardeleben 1991; Jancar-Webster 1993; Singleton 1987; Ziegler 1987). Protests against environmental destruction became an important part of the general opposition to the Communist regimes in Eastern Europe that eventually resulted in their collapse (Desai and Snavely 1995; Jancar-Webster 1993).

Non-Communist authoritarian regimes seem to be equally unfriendly to the environment. In Nigeria and Indonesia, as Areola and Cribb point out in their chapters in this volume, the military dictatorships have paid little attention to the vast environmental destruction in their drive to exploit resources: oil and forests. The recent hanging of a Nigerian poet and playwright, Ken Saro-Wiwa, and eight other members of his Ogoni tribe underlined among other things the dangers of protest against environmental destruction in a military dictatorship. Lack of openness and lack of information about the government policies along with lack of freedom of speech and organization in authoritarian regimes make it very difficult to deal effectively with the problems of environmental pollution and destruction. Political democracy, with its freedoms and its openness and free flow of information, seems better designed and more likely to deal effectively with environmental problems.

The connection between political democracy and environmental protection appears less compelling when focus is on the rich industrial countries. Environmental pollution and ecological destruction have reached very high levels in the Western democracies. Most of the greenhouse gasses responsible for global warming, most of the chemicals responsible for the hole in the ozone layer, and most of the hazardous and toxic wastes are produced by the democratic industrial countries.

Democracy itself seems to be at least partly dependent on the level of a country's economic development (Lipset 1960). Lipset argued that "democracy is related to the state of economic development. The more well-to-do a nation, the greater the chances that it will sustain democracy" (Lipset 1960:31). The studies over the last three decades seem generally to support the causal relationship between economic development and democracy (Diamond 1992). As sustaining democracy is dependent on economic development, and since economic growth and prosperity generally result in environmental pollution and ecological destruction, democracy would not necessarily be protective of the environment. Freedoms associated with democracy perhaps provide a better potential for environmental protection, if (and only if) protection of the global environment becomes a highly desired value over a long and sustained period of time, for a large majority of the people. However, democracy's dependence on economic development means that for democracies to be friendly to the environment would require fundamental changes in the individual values and the dominant social paradigm that justify ever increasing material wealth and prosperity even at the expense of the environment. The historical record of ecological destruction in democracies does not inspire much confidence in their ability to protect the environment.

Notwithstanding the current popularity of the "market" as a solution for all social problems, much of the argument for the environmental regulations enacted over the last twenty-five years in market democracies is based on the need for government action to counter the limitations inherent in the working of the market (Hardin 1968; Hodge 1995; Tietenberg 1992). Problems of environmental pollution and destruction are, in neoclassical economics, a result of market failure (Samuelson 1983). In economic theory, environmental pollution in a market economy is a problem of externality, a result of the fact that not all the costs and benefits of the use of environment are reflected in market transactions (Hodge 1995; Andersen 1994). However, continued environmental pollution and ecological destruction in spite of environmental regulations have in recent years brought increasing attention to the failure of government regulations to protect the environment. Many explanations have been advanced for continuing ecological destruction and for inability of environmental regulations to stop it. Some environmentalists blame it on the continuing dominance of belief in perpetual economic growth and unchecked industrial expansion (Rogers 1994; Sachs 1992; Tokar 1987). However, believers in the superiority of the market have blamed it on the self-interested behavior of bureaucrats and the inherent inefficiency of administrative regulations (LeGrand 1991; Wilson 1980; Niskanen 1971). They argue that government regulations are not only ineffective and inefficient, but are also counterproductive. They believe that more extensive property rights to natural resources (including the natural environment) would protect more efficiently the environment people want to protect. They advocate "free market environ-mentalism" instead of environmental regulation (Andersen and Leal 1991).

Many of those between the true believers in the magic of an unfettered market and those who completely reject the market and the modern industrial order attribute the continuing environmental degradation both to market failure and to state failure (Janicke 1990; Cairncross 1994).

Many policy makers and academics, especially economists and political scientists, have increasingly advocated use of the "polluter pays" principle through market mechanisms such as green taxes and levies and tradeable pollution permits, as effective ways of dealing with market failure to protect the environment (Andersen 1994; Barde 1994; Baptist 1994; Mitnick 1980; Marcus 1982). While there have been relatively few empirical studies of the effectiveness of these economic instruments (Andersen 1994; Hidefumi 1990; OECD 1989; Hudson, Lake, and Grossman 1981) there is increasing evidence that such economic instruments in practice produce more mixed results than economics textbooks predict (Andersen 1994; OECD 1989; Majone 1989). Market-based instruments have serious limitations in protecting the environ-ment in practice. Their effectiveness depends on the institutional setting, including national policy style (Andersen 1994).

The willingness and capacity of governments in poor countries to enforce environmental policies and regulations are often questionable. Corruption among politicians as well as bureaucrats is widespread in many poor countries. Polluting industries and businesses fend off and ignore environmental regulations by routinely bribing or buying off government officials. Wang and Cribb in their chapters in this book provide examples of the corrupt nexus between businessmen and politicians in Taiwan and Indo-nesia respectively. In poor countries, there is often a general lack of scientific knowledge about the environment in the very agencies that are entrusted with protecting it. These agencies also often lack the professionalism, inde-pendence, and resources necessary to effectively enforce the regulations. In addition, the centralized nature of environmental protection agencies and policies reduce the government's capacity to control pollution and protect the environment. Some environmentalists and scholars suggest that grass-roots community and nongovernmental organizations provide a more effective alternative to government agencies in protecting the environment and in using natural resources wisely (Reilly 1993; Ostrom 1990; Ostrom, Schroder, and Wynne 1993).

This Book

The primary purpose of this book is to provide, under one cover, an overview of environmental problems, policies, and politics in industrializing countries. It discusses important environmental problems and public policies to deal with them in ten selected industrializing countries. It also explores some of the powerful interests and institutional forces that have created or contributed to the environmental problems and shaped the policies to deal with them in each of these countries. Each chapter, written by recognized scholar(s), discusses the increasingly international context of domestic environmental policies. The authors identify some of the major impediments both to well-designed environmental policies and to their effective implementation. The ten countries discussed here—Czech Republic and Slovakia, Nigeria, China, India, Indonesia, Taiwan, Thailand, Mexico, and Venezuela—represent all five continents, over half the world's population, and most of the major industrializing countries.

Considerations of cost as well as ease of use put constraints on the total number of pages that can be included in any single volume. This makes it necessary to limit the number of countries that can be discussed, if the depth of coverage of each country is not to be seriously compromised. Choosing any ten countries out of some one hundred fifty developing countries is inherently difficult. Any such list is going to leave out many countries worthy of our attention.

Several considerations guided the choice of the ten countries included in this volume. Size, location, and potential global as well as local ecological impacts of the developments were considered. Large and economically rapidly growing countries in Asia are especially important. Five of the ten countries included in this volume are in Asia. China, India, Indonesia, Taiwan, and Thailand are among the fastest growing developing nations in the world. Three, China, India, and Indonesia, are among the most populated in the world. Between them, these five contain about half of all humanity. The present rapid economic growth in these countries, especially in China, India, and Indonesia, is sure to have a most profound impact on global ecology in the next few decades (Brown 1995). Mexico and Nigeria are large, petroleum exporting, industrializing economies in two different continents. Their inclusion is important in any broad consideration of ecological issues in developing countries. We have developed summary tables of important demographic, economic and environmental statistics for each of the ten countries. They are included at the end of this chapter.

Including countries with different political systems was another important consideration. The highly authoritarian political regimes in China, Nigeria, and Indonesia; the democratic polities of India and Venezuela; the modestly open and democratic regimes of Mexico and Thailand; and Czech Republic and Slovakian regimes in transition provide a wide spectrum of political systems in developing countries. Including these countries with different political systems facilitates understanding of the interplay of politics, policy, and environmental pressures. It also points to the universality of environmental issues regardless of political system.

It was important to include at least one country from each continent to provide as comprehensive a global coverage as possible with only ten country chapters. The Czech Republic and Slovakia broadly represent what is happening ecologically in the former Communist states in Eastern and Central Europe. Venezuela provides a good case study of a medium size, moderate income, industrializing country in South America. A more practical concern was the availability of established scholars in the various countries to prepare a chapter; this played at least a minor role in selecting the countries.

A number of common themes emerge from these nine chapters. Desire for economic growth seems to be the central driving force in all of them. Rapid economic growth through industrialization and exploitation of natural resources appears to be the overriding national purpose and a guiding principle for all public policies. In a conflict between economic growth and environmental protection, the environment almost always loses. In the centrality of economic growth, there is little difference between the democracies, such as India, Venezuela, and Mexico, and the dictatorships, such as China, Nigeria, and Indonesia, included in this book. The desire of the elites to achieve higher material standards of living for themselves and sometimes for their countrymen, even at the expense of environmental degradation, is a common thread in all ten countries. In the Czech Republic and Slovakia, as Catherine Albrecht points out in her chapter, economic reform and privatization have become the top national priority. Public concern for environmental degradation has eroded. The public's attention has been focused on economic matters: entrepreneurial opportunities, the prospects for unemployment and inflation.

Stephen Mumme, in his chapter on Mexico, observes that Mexico's environmental problems are "rooted in an economic development strategy that favors rapid industrialization." A generally widespread acceptance of this economic development through industrialization strategy is reflected in the failure of Mexico's Ecology Party (PEM) to get even 1.5 percent of the national vote in 1991. Lack of green parties in the poor industrializing countries indicates a general popular acceptance of the primacy of economic growth. In Nigeria, Olusegun Areola points out in his chapter, environmental politics is basically the politics of natural resource allocation. Issues of environmental protection are only "residual considerations" in the struggle for natural resources. It is only recently that Nigeria has seen the beginnings of a change in the attitude that considers environmental protection and economic growth to be totally incompatible. Large-scale irrigation projects such as Tehri Dam and Sardar Sarovar, carried out in India, are justified on the basis of their contribution to economic growth. A large majority of people have supported these mega projects, even in the face of local and international protests. As R.

K. Sapru, in his chapter on India, shows, the desirability of economic growth is universally recognized in India. The basic question, for him, is not whether to choose development or environment. Economic development is essential. The issue is to select economic development patterns that also improve environmental quality. The story is the same in other industrializing countries. In Venezuela, mega projects in mining, oil, and heavy industry were developed in the 1960s and 1970s to create rapid economic growth. Economic crisis in recent years, Pablo Gutman observes in his chapter, has probably distracted Venezuela from environmental concerns.

Economic growth has been the primary public concern for decades in Taiwan. In Indonesia, as Robert Cribb shows in his chapter, the elites have emphasized economic growth at the expense of environment to enrich themselves and to improve the material standard of living for their supporters. In Thailand, the elites consider environmental protection "a luxury that the kingdom could ill afford," as Rigg and Stott point out in their chapter. Even in China, as Lester Ross shows in his chapter, economic growth has become the central concern of the ruling Communist party. Economy and environment are intimately intertwined in all ten countries. In all ten countries, economic growth takes precedence over environmental protection. In some, Indonesia and Nigeria for example, economic growth means exploitation of the country's natural resources. In others, Taiwan, China, Mexico, and India, for example, economic growth through rapid industrialization and consequent environmental pollution is the pattern. In democracies, economic growth is justified and pursued to relieve mass poverty. In a dictatorship, it is pursued largely to enrich the elites and their supporters. Nevertheless, it is pursued by all ten countries.

However, the adverse environmental consequences of industrialization and resource exploitation have become increasingly apparent. In the last twenty years, many laws and policies have been enacted in all the ten countries to protect the environment. The chapters following summarize the major laws and policies in each country. Environmental laws and policies have become more extensive over the years in all of them. However, powerful economic and political interests continue to influence these policies. In Taiwan a strong link exists between business and political elites as Wang illustrates in the golf course case. In Indonesia and Nigeria political elites use their power to secure enormous economic gains by exploiting their countries' vast natural resources in partnership with domestic and international businesses, with little regard for the environmental degradation. In China, the Czech Republic and Slovakia, India, Mexico, and Venezuela, state-owned industrial enterprises, along with private industries, represent powerful interests against environmental protection policies. In many of them heavily subsidized agriculturalists also exert considerable influence, through political parties, against policies designed to protect the environment by reducing subsidies or by increasing the prices of natural resources to fully reflect the environmental cost associated with their use. In democracies and in dictatorships, powerful economic and political interests, often working in symbiotic interdependence, determine the shape and the reach of environmental protection policies.

Increasing economic wealth and well-being and a growing middle class have increased awareness and demands for environmental protection in most of these countries. In China, as Lester Ross points out, environmental conditions are no longer ignored and "as the country is becoming wealthier and younger and better educated officials assume positions of responsibility." In almost all of these ten countries, except China, environmental groups have become an increasingly important voice in public debates. In many cases, for example in India and in Thailand, they have joined forces with other non-governmental organizations fighting for the rights of the poor, rural, or minority populations. Unlike in the industrial countries, the environmental movement in many poor industrializing countries is centered more in rural, poor, and minority community organizations. In the more industrialized and richer of these ten countries, Venezuela, Taiwan, and the Czech Republic, however, the environmental movement is centered more in the urban, educated middle class.

In all ten countries the international context and pressures for environmental protection have become an important force. In Mexico, Indonesia, India, the Czech Republic, Thailand, and even Nigeria and China international pressures to reduce air pollution, greenhouse gases, destruction of the forests, and displacement of indigenous peoples are often used by national environmental and other organizations to further pressure their governments to prevent or reduce ecological degradation. However, in Nigeria, and to a lesser extent in India, China, Venezuela, and most other developing countries, the international pressure for environmental protection often has led to resentment of the West and international environmental organizations. As Areola points out in his chapter, the concern for protecting the environment in Africa by Western powers and institutions has "long been viewed with apprehension by the Nigerian elite who perceive this concern as emanating from selfish economic and political motives." India, China, Mexico, and others also have often viewed Western concern with environmental protection similarly. Often this concern is viewed simply as a way to prevent these countries from acquiring the wealth and power that the West already possesses. Whether these industrializing countries welcome or resent international pressures for environmental protection, these pressures are real, and they play an increasingly important role in their environmental policy.

In all ten countries there are serious limitations to governments' capacity to implement effectively the already existing environmental policies and regulations. The management capabilities of government agencies entrusted with environmental policy implementation are found to be quite weak. There is a serious lack of resources, personnel, and expertise. The environmental ministries and agencies are generally weaker than the economic and industry ministries and agencies in the government. In addition, often there is lack of coordination among various official bodies responsible for environmental protection. Decision-making authority in environmental matters is often either too highly centralized or too fragmented. The issue of governmental capacity to implement environmental policies receives especially detailed attention in the chapters on India, Venezuela, Mexico, and Nigeria.

Market forces have very limited influence on environmental protection in these countries. There are some attempts being made now, for example in China and India, to use market mechanisms for environmental protection. The impact of middle-class-centered "postmaterialist" values on environmental protection in these industrializing countries is very modest, if any, although there may be some signs of it in Taiwan. There are indications, however, that in some of these countries there are indigenous nonmaterialist values, especially among some rural and tribal communities, that are fueling local environmental activism.

The central theme emerging from the chapters in this book is the centrality of economic growth and development. Powerful economic interests generally win over environmental concerns. However, international pressure and in some cases increasingly active nongovernmental organizations are becoming important forces in favor of environmental protection. Weak governmental capacity to implement environmental policies and enforce environmental regulations is a major constraint on effective environmental protection in most of these countries.

TABLE 1.1

Demographic and Environmental Statistics of China

Total population 1995[1]	1,221,462,000
Urban population[2]	30.3%
Average annual population increase 1990–1995[1]	1.1%
Average annual growth in labor force 1991–2000[1]	1.2%
Total area in square kilometers 1994[3]	9,596,961
Density per square kilometer[3]	126
GNP per capita[4]	$362
Life expectancy in years[5]	
male	67
female	69
Literacy rate[6]	81.5%

Access to safe drinking water[7]

    for rural population   68%

    for urban population   87%

Access to safe drinking water[7]	
for rural population	68%
for urban population	87%
Land use[8]	
arable land	10%
permanent crops	0%
meadows and pastures	31%
forest and woodland	14%
other	45%
Protected areas[9]	
in square miles	84,738
of total land area	2.3%
Deforestation in square miles per year[10]	0
Number of cars in 1991[11]	1,764,900
Carbon dioxide emissions (000 metric tons)[12]	2,667,982
Sulfur dioxide emissions (000 metric tons)[13]	
in 1980	13,370
in 1987	19,990
change between 1980–87	50%
Nitrous oxide emissions (000 metric tons)[14]	
in 1980	4,910
in 1987	7,370
change between 1980–87	50%
Greenhouse gases	
Methane (000 metric tons)[15]	47,000
Chlorofluorocarbons 1991 (metric tons)[16]	43,252
Halons 1991 (metric tons)[16]	19,569
Nonmethane volatile organic compounds[17]	NA

1. World Resources Institute (1996) 190–91.

2. Seager, et al. (1995) 92–99.

3. United Nations (1996) 126–33.

4. World Resources Institute (1994) 485.

5. Reddy (1994) 194.

6. United Nation's Educational, Scientific, and Cultural Organization (1995) 1–8 to 1–17.

7. World Resources Institute (1994). Figures dating generally from 1988 are supplied to the World Health Organization (WHO) by national governments and may represent optimistic assessments. *Urban population's* access to safe drinking water is defined as access to piped water or to a public standpipe within 650 feet of a dwelling or housing unit. *Rural population's* access to safe drinking water is defined as treated surface water or untreated water from protected springs, boreholes, and sanitary wells located such that a family member need not spend a disproportionate amount of the day fetching water (WHO, 485, 684).

8. Reddy (1994). Land use is human use of the land surface categorized as *arable land*—land cultivated for crops that are replanted after each harvest (wheat, maize, rice); *permanent crops*—land cultivated for crops that are not replanted after each harvest (citrus, coffee, rubber); *meadows and pastures*—land permanently used for herbaceous forage crops; *forest and woodland*—land under dense or open stands of trees; *other*—any land type not specifically mentioned above (urban areas, roads, deserts) (194, 1036).

9. World Resources Institute (1994). 1990 total protected areas (over 2,471 acres) under national protection in one of five World Conservation Union categories and where access is at least partially restricted: scientific reserves; national and provincial parks; natural monuments and natural landmarks; managed nature reserves and wildlife sanctuaries; and protected landscapes and seascapes. *Percent of total* is calculated on the basis of total land area (485, 683).

10. World Resources Institute (1992). *Deforestation* is defined as the permanent conversion of forest land to other uses. Areas that are logged are not counted as deforested if natural or artificial reforestation is planned (411, 591).

11. Seager, et al. (1995) 92–99.

12. World Resources Institute (1996) 326–27.

13. United Nation's Environment Programme (1993). Per capita emissions of SO_2 in 1990 are based on UN population statistics for 1990 unless otherwise indicated. The calculation of emissions of SO_2 per unit GDP is based on World Bank estimates of GDP in 1990 in US currency as reported in the World Development Report 1992. Emissions of SO_2 per unit GDP are given in kg a^{-1} per 10^3.

Note that emissions are given in units of 10^3 t a^{-1} as sulfur dioxide (SO_2); to convert to emissions in 10^3 t a^{-1} as sulfur (S) divide by 2.0.

Data presented in the above table generally represent official country emissions estimates as reported in "state of the environment"-type reports or as reported to the European Monitoring and Evaluation Program. As methods of estimation may vary between countries, intercountry comparisons should be made with caution. Trends observed within each country are more reliable than comparisons between countries (44–46).

14. United Nation's Environment Programme (1993). Per capita emissions of NO_x in 1990 are based on UN population statistics for 1990 unless otherwise indicated. The calculation of emissions of NO_x per unit GDP is based on World Bank estimates of GDP in 1990 in US currencys as reported in the World Development Report 1992. Emissions of NO_x per unit GDP are given in kg a^{-1} per 10^3 (47–48).

15. World Resources Institute (1996) 328–29.

16. United Nation's Environment Programme (1993). Chlorofluorocarbons (CFCs) refer to the Group I compounds: CFC-11, CFC-12, CFC-113, CFC-114, and CFC-115. Halons refer to the Group II compounds: Halon-1301, Halon-1211, and Halon-2402. Data on consumption of CFCs (Group I) and halons (Group II) are based on official reports submitted to the Ozone Secretariat, UNEP, under the terms of the Montreal Protocol (40–42).

17. Information not available.

TABLE 1.2

Demographic and Environmental Statistics of Indonesia

Total population 1995[1]	197,588,000
Urban population[2]	32.5%
Average annual population increase 1990–1995[1]	1.6%
Average annual growth in labor force 1991–2000[1]	2.1%
Total area in square kilometers 1994[3]	1,904,569
Density per square kilometer[3]	101
GNP per capita 1993[4]	$740
Life expectancy in years[5]	
male	59
female	63
Literacy rate[6]	83.8%
Access to safe drinking water[7]	
for rural population	33%
for urban population	35%
Land use[8]	
arable land	8%
permanent crops	3%
meadows and pastures	7%
forest and woodland	67%
other	15%
Protected areas[9]	
in square miles	68,725
of total land area	9.3%
Deforestation in square miles per year[10]	3,475
Number of cars in 1991[11]	1,416,200
Carbon dioxide emissions (000 metric tons)[12]	184,585
Sulfur dioxide emissions (000 metric tons)[13]	
in 1980	329
in 1987	485
change between 1980–87	47%
Nitrous oxide emissions (000 metric tons)[14]	
in 1980	465
in 1987	639
change between 1980–87	37%
Greenhouse gases	
Methane (000 metric tons) [15]	10,000
Chlorofluorocarbons 1986 (metric tons)[16]	2,489
Halons 1986 (metric tons)[16]	5
Nonmethane volatile organic compouds 1989[17]	NA

1. World Resources Institute (1996) 190–91.
2. Seager, et al. (1995) 92–99.
3. United Nations (1996) 126–33.
4. World Resources Institute (1996) 166–67.
5. Reddy (1994) 423.
6. United Nation's Educational, Scientific, and Cultural Organization (1995) 1–8 to 1–17.
7. World Resources Institute (1994). Figures dating generally from 1988 are supplied to the World Health Organization (WHO) by national governments and may represent optimistic assessments. *Urban population's* access to safe drinking water is defined as access to piped water or to a public standpipe within 650 feet of a dwelling or housing unit. *Rural population's* access to safe drinking water is defined as treated surface water or untreated water from protected springs, boreholes, and sanitary wells located such that a family member need not spend a disproportionate amount of the day fetching water (WHO, 491, 684).
8. Reddy (1994). Land use is human use of the land surface categorized as *arable land*—land cultivated for crops that are replanted after each harvest (wheat, maize, rice); *permanent crops*—land cultivated for crops that are not replanted after each harvest (citrus, coffee, rubber); *meadows and pastures*—land permanently used for herbaceous forage crops; *forest and woodland*—land under dense or open stands of trees; *other*—any land type not specifically mentioned above (urban areas, roads, deserts) (423, 1036).
9. World Resources Institute (1994). 1990 total protected areas (over 2,471 acres) under national protection in one of five World Conservation Union categories and where access is at least partially restricted: scientific reserves; national and provincial parks; natural monuments and natural landmarks; managed nature reserves and wildlife sanctuaries; and protected landscapes and seascapes. *Percent of total* is calculated on the basis of total land area (491, 683).
10. World Resources Institute (1992). *Deforestation* is defined as the permanent conversion of forest land to other uses. Areas that are logged are not counted as deforested if natural or artificial reforestation is planned (417, 591).
11. Seager, et al. (1995) 92–99.
12. World Resources Institute (1996) 326–27.
13. United Nation's Environment Programme (1993). Per capita emissions of SO_2 in 1990 are based on UN population statistics for 1990 unless otherwise indicated. The calculation of emissions of SO_2 per unit GDP is based on World Bank estimates of GDP in 1990 in U.S. currency as reported in the World Development Report 1992. Emissions of SO_2 per unit GDP are given in kg a^{-1} per 10^3.
Note that emissions are given in units of 10^3 t a^{-1} as sulfur dioxide (SO_2); to convert to emissions in 10^3 t a^{-1} as sulfur (S) divide by 2.0.
Data presented in the above table generally represent official country emissions estimates as reported in "state of the environment"-type of reports or as reported to the European Monitoring and Evaluation Program. As methods of estimation may vary between countries, intercountry comparisons should be made with caution. Trends observed within each country are more reliable than comparisons between countries. (44–46).

14. United Nation's Environment Programme (1993). Per capita emissions of NO_x in 1990 are based on UN population statistics for 1990 unless otherwise indicated. The calculation of emissions of NO_x per unit GDP is based on World Bank estimates of GDP in 1990 in US currency as reported in the World Development Report 1992. Emissions of NO_x per unit GDP are given in kg a^{-1} per 10^3 (47–48).

15. World Resources Institute (1996) 328–29.

16. United Nation's Environment Programme (1993). Chlorofluorocarbons (CFCs) refer to the Group I compounds: CFC-11, CFC-12, CFC-113, CFC-114, and CFC-115. Halons refer to the Group II compounds: Halon-1301, Halon-1211, and Halon-2402. Data on consumption of CFCs (Group I) and halons (Group II) are based on official reports submitted to the Ozone Secretariat, UNEP, under the terms of the Montreal Protocol (40–42).

17. Information not available.

TABLE 1.3

Demographic and Environmental Statistics of Thailand

Total population 1995[1]	58,791,000
Urban population[2]	35.4%
Average annual population increase 1990–1995[1]	1.1%
Average annual growth in labor force 1991–2000[1]	1.3%
Total area in square kilometers 1994[3]	513,115
Density per square kilometer[3]	116
GNP per capita 1993[4]	$2,110
Life expectancy in years[5]	
male	65
female	72
Literacy rate[6]	93.8%
Access to safe drinking water[7]	
for rural population	85%
for urban population	67%
Land use[8]	
arable land	34%
permanent crops	4%
meadows and pastures	1%
forest and woodland	30%
other	31%
Protected areas[9]	
in square miles	19,713
of total land area	10%
Deforestation in square miles per year[10]	610
Number of cars in 1991[11]	825,100

Carbon dioxide emissions (000 metric tons)[12]	112,477
Sulfur dioxide emissions (000 metric tons)[13]	
in 1980	420
in 1987	612
change between 1980–87	46%
Nitrous oxide emissions (000 metric tons)[14]	
in 1980	255
in 1987	384
change between 1980–87	51%
Greenhouse gases	
Methane (000 metric tons)[15]	5,500
Chlorofluorocarbons 1991 (metric tons)[16]	7,904
Halons 1990 (metric tons)[16]	420
Nonmethane volatile organic compounds[17]	NA

1. World Resources Institute (1996) 190–91.

2. Seager, et al. (1995) 92–99.

3. United Nations (1996) 126–33.

4. World Resources Institute (1996) 166–67.

5. Reddy (1994) 918.

6. United Nation's Educational, Scientific, and Cultural Organization (1995) 1–8 to 1–17.

7. World Resources Institute (1994). Figures dating generally from 1988 are supplied to the World Health Organization (WHO) by national governments and may represent optimistic assessments. *Urban population's* access to safe drinking water is defined as access to piped water or to a public standpipe within 650 feet of a dwelling or housing unit. *Rural population's* access to safe drinking water is defined as treated surface water or untreated water from protected springs, boreholes, and sanitary wells located such that a family member need not spend a disproportionate amount of the day fetching water (WHO, 533, 684.)

8. Reddy (1994). Land use is human use of the land surface categorized as *arable land*—land cultivated for crops that are replanted after each harvest (wheat, maize, rice); *permanent crops*—land cultivated for crops that are not replanted after each harvest (citrus, coffee, rubber); *meadows and pastures*—land permanently used for herbaceous forage crops; *forest and woodland*—land under dense or open stands of trees; *other*—any land type not specifically mentioned above (urban areas, roads, deserts) (918, 1036).

9. World Resources Institute (1994). 1990 total protected areas (over 2,471 acres) under national protection in one of five World Conservation Union categories and where access is at least partially restricted: scientific reserves; national and provincial parks; natural monuments and natural landmarks; managed nature reserves and wildlife sanctuaries; and protected landscapes and seascapes. *Percent of total* is calculated on the basis of total land area (533, 683).

10. World Resources Institute (1992). *Deforestation* is defined as the permanent conversion of forest land to other uses. Areas that are logged are not counted as deforested if natural or artificial reforestation is planned (461, 591).

11. Seager et al. (1995) 92–99.

12. World Resources Institute (1996) 326–27.

13. United Nation's Environment Programme (1993). Per capita emissions of SO_2 in 1990 are based on UN population statistics for 1990 unless otherwise indicated. The calculation of emissions of SO_2 per unit GDP is based on World Bank estimates of GDP in 1990 in US currency as reported in the World Development Report 1992. Emissions of SO_2 per unit GDP are given in kg a^{-1} per 10^3.

Note that emissions are given in units of 10^3 t a^{-1} as sulfur dioxide (SO_2); to convert to emissions in 10^3 t a^{-1} as sulfur (S) divide by 2.0.

Data presented in the above table generally represent official country emissions estimates as reported in "state of the environment"-type of reports or as reported to the European Monitoring and Evaluation Program. As methods of estimation may vary between countries, intercountry comparisons should be made with caution. Trends observed within each country are more reliable than comparisons between countries (44–46).

14. United Nation's Environment Programme (1993). Per capita emissions of NO_x in 1990 are based on UN population statistics for 1990 unless otherwise indicated. The calculation of emissions of NO_x per unit GDP is based on World Bank estimates of GDP in 1990 in US currency as reported in the World Development Report 1992. Emissions of NO_x per unit GDP are given in kg a^{-1} per 10^3 (47–48).

15. World Resources Institute (1996) 328–29.

16. United Nation's Environment Programme (1993). Chlorofluorocarbons (CFCs) refer top the Group I compounds: CFC-11, CFC-12, CFC-113, CFC-114, and CFC-115. Halons refer to the Group II compounds: Halon-1301, Halon-1211, and Halon-2402.

Data on consumption of CFCs (Group I) and halons (Group II) are based on official reports submitted to the Ozone Secretariat, UNEP, under the terms of the Montreal Protocol (40–42).

17. Information not available.

TABLE 1.4

Demographic and Environmental Statistics of Taiwan

Total population 1994[1]	21,299,000
Urban population[2]	NA
Average annual population increase 1990–1995[2]	NA
Average annual growth in labor force 1991–2000[2]	NA
Total area in square kilometers[3]	35,980
Density per square kilometer 1991[3]	1,659
GDP per capita 1993[4]	$10,600
Life expectancy in years[5]	
male	72
female	79
Literacy rate[2]	NA

Access to safe drinking water[2]
    for rural population   NA
    for urban population   NA

Land use[6]
    arable land   24%
    permanent crops   1%
    meadows and pastures   5%
    forest and woodland   55%
    other   15%
Protected areas[2]
    in square miles   NA
    of total land area   NA
Deforestation in square miles per year[2]   NA

Number of cars in 1991[7]   2,000,000
Carbon dioxide emissions (000 metric tons)[2]   NA
Sulfur dioxide emissions (000 metric tons)[8]
    in 1980   1,040
    in 1987   605
    change between 1980–87   -42%
Nitrous oxide emissions (000 metric tons)[9]
    in 1980   225
    in 1987   325
    change between 1980–1987   44%
Greenhouse gases
    Methane (000 metric tons)[2]   NA
    Chlorofluorocarbons 1990 (metric tons)[2]   NA
    Halons 1990 (metric tons)[2]   NA
Nonmethane volatile organic compounds[2]   NA

---

1. Reddy (1994) 901.

2. Information not available.

3. Reddy (1994). *Total area* is the sum of all land and water areas delimited by international boundaries and/or coastlines (901, 1036).

4. Wright (1995) 505.

5. Reddy (1994) 901.

6. Reddy (1994). Land use is human use of the land surface categorized as *arable land*—land cultivated for crops that are replanted after each harvest (wheat, maize, rice); *permanent crops*—land cultivated for crops that are not replanted after each harvest (citrus, coffee, rubber); *meadows and pastures*—land permanently used for herbaceous forage crops; forest and woodland—land under dense or open stands of trees; *other*—any land type not specifically mentioned above (urban areas, roads, deserts) (901, 1036).

7. Seager et al. (1995) 92–99.

8. United Nation's Environment Programme (1993). Per capita emissions of SO_2 in 1990 are based on UN population statistics for 1990 unless otherwise indicated. The calculation of emissions of SO_2 per unit GDP is based on World Bank estimates of GDP in 1990 in U.S. currency as reported in the World Development Report 1992. Emissions of SO_2 per unit GDP are given in kg a^{-1} per 10^3.

Note that emissions are given in units of 10^3 t a^{-1} as sulfur dioxide (SO_2); to convert to emissions in 10^3 t a^{-1} as sulfur (S) divide by 2.0.

Data presented in the above table generally represent official country emissions estimates as reported in "state of the environment"-type reports or as reported to the European Monitoring and Evaluation Program. As methods of estimation may vary between countries, intercountry comparisons should be made with caution. Trends observed within each country are more reliable than comparisons between countries (44–46).

9. United Nation's Environment Programme (1993). Per capita emissions of NO_x in 1990 are based on UN population statistics for 1990 unless otherwise indicated. The calculation of emissions of NO_x per unit GDP is based on World Bank estimates of GDP in 1990 in U.S. currency as reported in the World Development Report 1992. Emissions of NO_x per unit GDP are given in kg a^{-1} per 10^3 (47–48).

TABLE 1.5

Demographic and Environmental Statistics of India

Total population 1995[1]	935,744,000
Urban population[2]	26.8%
Average annual population increase 1990–1995[1]	1.9%
Average annual growth in labor force 1991–2000[1]	1.9%
Area in square kilometers 1994[3]	3,287,590
Density per square kilometer[3]	279
GNP per capita[4]	$300
Life expectancy in years[5]	
male	58
female	59
Literacy rate[6]	52%
Access to safe drinking water[7]	
for rural population	69%
for urban population	86%
Land use[8]	
arable land	55%
permanent crops	1%
meadows and pastures	4%
forest and woodland	23%
other	17%

Protected areas[9]	
in square miles	52,051
of total land area	4.1%
Deforestation in square miles per year[10]	185
Number of cars in 1991[11]	2,490,800
Carbon dioxide emissions (000 metric tons)[12]	769,440
Sulfur dioxide emissions (000 metric tons)[13]	
in 1980	2,010
in 1987	3,070
change between 1980–87	53%
Nitrous oxide emissions (000 metric tons)[14]	
in 1980	1,670
in 1987	2,560
change between 1980–87	53%
Greenhouse gases	
Methane (000 metric tons)[15]	33,000
Chlorofluorocarbons 1986 (metric tons)[16]	4,600
Halons 1986 (metric tons)[16]	700
Nonmethane volatile organic compounds 1989[17]	NA

1. World Resources Institute (1996) 190–91.
2. Seager, et al. (1995) 92–99.
3. United Nations (1996) 126–33.
4. World Resources Institute (1996) 166–67.
5. Reddy (1994) 417.
6. United Nation's Educational, Scientific, and Cultural Organization (1995) 1–8 to 1–17.
7. World Resources Institute (1994). Figures dating generally from 1988 are supplied to the World Health Organization (WHO) by national governments and may represent optimistic assessments. *Urban population's* access to safe drinking water is defined as access to piped water or to a public standpipe within 650 feet of a dwelling or housing unit. *Rural population's* access to safe drinking water is defined as treated surface water or untreated water from protected springs, boreholes, and sanitary wells located such that a family member need not spend a disproportionate amount of the day fetching water (WHO, 489, 684).
8. Reddy (1994). Land use is human use of the land surface categorized as *arable land*—land cultivated for crops that are replanted after each harvest (wheat, maize, rice); *permanent crops*—land cultivated for crops that are not replanted after each harvest (citrus, coffee, rubber); *meadows and pastures*—land permanently used for herbaceous forage crops; *forest and woodland*—land under dense or open stands of trees; *other*—any land type not specifically mentioned above (urban areas, roads, deserts) (417, 1036).
9. World Resources Institute (1994). 1990 total protected areas (over 2,471 acres) under national protection in one of five World Conservation Union categories and where access is at least partially restricted: scientific reserves; national and provincial parks;

natural monuments and natural landmarks; managed nature reserves and wildlife sanctuaries; and protected landscapes and seascapes. *Percent of total* is calculated on the basis of total land area (489, 683).

10. World Resources Institute (1992). *Deforestation* is defined as the permanent conversion of forest land to other uses. Areas that are logged are not counted as deforested if natural or artificial reforestation is planned (415, 591).

11. Seager, et al. (1995) 92–99.

12. World Resources Institute (1996) 326–27.

13. United Nation's Environment Programme (1993). Per capita emissions of SO_2 in 1990 are based on UN population statistics for 1990 unless otherwise indicated. The calculation of emissions of SO_2 per unit GDP is based on World Bank estimates of GDP in 1990 in U.S. currency as reported in the World Development Report 1992. Emissions of SO_2 per unit GDP are given in kg a^{-1} per 10^3.

Note that emissions are given in units of 10^3 t a^{-1} as sulfur dioxide (SO_2); to convert to emissions in 10^3 t a^{-1} as sulfur (S) divide by 2.0.

Data presented in the above table generally represent official country emissions estimates as reported in "state of the environment"-type reports or as reported to the European Monitoring and Evaluation Program. As methods of estimation may vary between countries, intercountry comparisons should be made with caution. Trends observed within each country are more reliable than comparisons between countries (44–46).

14. United Nation's Environment Programme (1993). Per capita emissions of NO_x in 1990 are based on UN population statistics for 1990 unless otherwise indicated. The calculation of emissions of NO_x per unit GDP is based on World Bank estimates of GDP in 1990 in U.S. currency as reported in the World Development Report 1992. Emissions of NO_x per unit GDP are given in kg a^{-1} per 10^3 (47–48).

15. World Resources Institute (1996) 328–29.

16. United Nation's Environment Programme (1993). Chloroflourocarbons (CFCs) refer to the Group I compounds: CFC-11, CFC-12, CFC-113, CFC-114, and CFC-115. Halons refer to the Group II compounds: Halon-1301, Halon-1211, and Halon-2402.

Data on consumption of CFCs (Group I) and halons (Group II) are based on official reports submitted to the Ozone Secretariat, UNEP, under the terms of the Montreal Protocol (40–42).

17. Information not available.

TABLE 1.6

Demographic and Environmental Statistics of Mexico

Total population 1995[1]	93,674,000
Urban population[2]	75.3%
Average annual population increase 1990–1995[1]	2.1%
Average annual growth in labor force 1991–2000[1]	2.6%
Total area in square kilometers 1994[3]	1,958,201
Density per square kilometer[3]	47

GNP per capita[4]	$3,610
Life expectancy in years[5]	
male	69
female	77
Literacy rate[6]	89.6%
Access to safe drinking water[7]	
for rural population	49%
for urban population	94%
Land use[8]	
arable land	12%
permanent crops	1%
meadows and pastures	39%
forest and woodland	24%
other	24%
Protected areas[9]	
in square miles	36,369
total land area	4.8%
Deforestation in square miles per year[10]	2,297
Number of cars in 1991[11]	7,400,000
Carbon dioxide emissions (000 metric tons)[12]	332,852
Sulfur dioxide emissions[13]	NA
Nitrous oxide emissions[14]	NA
Greenhouse gases	
Methane (000 metric tons)[15]	3,100
Chlorofluorocarbons 1990 (metric tons)[16]	11,117
Halons 1990 (metric tons)[16]	3,676
Nonmethane volatile organic compunds[17]	NA

1. World Resources Institute (1996) 190–91.

2. Seager, et al. (1995) 92–99.

3. United Nations (1996) 126–33.

4. World Resources Institute (1996) 166–67.

5. Reddy (1994) 613.

6. United Nation's Educational, Scientific, and Cultural Organization (1995) 1–8 to 1–17.

7. World Resources Institute (1994). Figures dating generally from 1988 are supplied to the World Health Organization (WHO) by national governments and may represent optimistic assessments. *Urban population's* access to safe drinking water is defined as access to piped water or to a public standpipe within 650 feet of a dwelling or housing unit. *Rural population's* access to safe drinking water is defined as treated surface water or untreated water from protected springs, boreholes, and sanitary wells located such that a family member need not spend a disproportionate amount of the day fetching water (WHO, 633, 684).

8. Reddy (1994). Land use is human use of the land surface categorized as *arable land*—land cultivated for crops that are replanted after each harvest (wheat, maize,

rice); *permanent crops*—land cultivated for crops that are not replanted after each harvest (citrus, coffee, rubber); *meadows and pastures*—land permanently used for herbaceous forage crops; *forest and woodland*—land under dense or open stands of trees; *other*—any land type not specifically mentioned above (urban areas, roads, deserts) (613, 1036).

9. World Resources Institute (1994). 1990 total protected areas (over 2,471 acres) under national protection in one of five World Conservation Union categories and where access is at least partially restricted: scientific reserves; national and provincial parks; natural monuments and natural landmarks; managed nature reserves and wildlife sanctuaries; and protected landscapes and seascapes. *Percent of total* is calculated on the basis of total land area (633, 683).

10. World Resources Institute (1992). *Deforestation* is defined as the permanent conversion of forest land to other uses. Areas that are logged are not counted as deforested if natural or artificial reforestation is planned (545, 591).

11. Seager, et al. (1995) 92–99.

12. World Resources Institute (1996) 326–27.

13. Information not available.

14. Information not available.

15. World Resources Institute (1996) 328–29.

16. United Nation's Environment Programme (1993). Chlorofluorocarbons (CFCs) refer top the Group I compounds: CFC-11, CFC-12, CFC-113, CFC-114, and CFC-115. Halons refer to the Group II compounds: Halon-1301, Halon-1211, and Halon-2402. Data on consumption of CFCs (Group I) and halons (Group II) are based on official reports submitted to the Ozone Secretariat, UNEP, under the terms of the Montreal Protocol (40–42).

17. Information not available.

TABLE 1.7

Demographic and Environmental Statistics of Venezuela

Total population 1995[1]	21,844,000
Urban population[2]	92.9%
Average annual population increase 1990–95[1]	2.3%
Average annual growth in labor force 1991–2000[1]	2.8%
Total area in square kilometers 1994[3]	912,050
Density per square kilometer[3]	23
GNP per capita[4]	$2,840
Life expectancy in years[5]	
male	70
female	76
Literacy rate[6]	91.1%
Access to safe drinking water[7]	
for rural population	36%
for urban population	89%

Land use[8]	
arable land	3%
permanent crops	1%
meadows and pastures	20%
forest and woodland	39%
other	37%
Protected areas[9]	
in square miles	78,245
of total land area	22.2%
Deforestation in square miles per year[10]	483
Number of cars in 1991[11]	1,590,000
Carbon dioxide emissions (000 metric tons)[12]	116,424
Sulfur dioxide emissions[13]	NA
Nitrous oxide emissions[14]	NA
Greenhouse gases	
Methane (000 metric tons)[15]	2,000
Chlorofluorocarbons 1991 (metric tons)[16]	3,037
Halons 1991 (metric tons)[16]	244
Nonmethane volatile organic compounds[17]	NA

1. World Resources Institute (1996) 190–91.

2. Seager, et al. (1995) 92–99.

3. United Nations (1996) 126–33.

4. World Resources Institute (1996) 166–67.

5. Reddy (1994) 996.

6. United Nation's Educational, Scientific, and Cultural Organization (1995) 1–8 to 1–17.

7. World Resources Institute (1994). Figures dating generally from 1988 are supplied to the World Health Organization (WHO) by national governments and may represent optimistic assessments. *Urban population's* access to safe drinking water is defined as access to piped water or to a public standpipe within 650 feet of a dwelling or housing unit. *Rural population's* access to safe drinking water is defined as treated surface water or untreated water from protected springs, boreholes, and sanitary wells located such that a family member need not spend a disproportionate amount of the day fetching water (WHO, 681, 684).

8. Reddy (1994). Land use is human use of the land surface categorized as *arable land*—land cultivated for crops that are replanted after each harvest (wheat, maize, rice); *permanent crops*—land cultivated for crops that are not replanted after each harvest (citrus, coffee, rubber); *meadows and pastures*—land permanently used for herbaceous forage crops; *forest and woodland*—land under dense or open stands of trees; *other*—any land type not specifically mentioned above (urban areas, roads, deserts) (996, 1036).

9. World Resources Institute (1994). 1990 total protected areas (over 2,471 acres) under national protection in one of five World Conservation Union categories and where access is at least partially restricted: scientific reserves; national and provincial parks;

natural monuments and natural landmarks; managed nature reserves and wildlife sanctuaries; and protected landscapes and seascapes. *Percent of total* is calculated on the basis of total land area (681, 683).

10. World Resources Institute (1992). *Deforestation* is defined as the permanent conversion of forest land to other uses. Areas that are logged are not counted as deforested if natural or artificial reforestation is planned (589, 591).

11. Seager, et al. (1995) 92–99.

12. World Resources Institute (1996) 326–27.

13. Information not available.

14. Information not available.

15. World Resources Institute (1996) 328–29.

16. United Nation's Environment Programme (1993). Chlorofluorocarbons (CFCs) refer to the Group I compounds: CFC-11, CFC-12, CFC-113, CFC-114, and CFC-115. Halons refer to the Group II compounds: Halon-1301, Halon-1211, and Halon-2402. Data on consumption of CFCs (Group I) and halons (Group II) are based on official reports submitted to the Ozone Secretariat, UNEP, under the terms of the Montreal Protocol (40–42).

17. Information not available.

TABLE 1.8

Demographic and Environmental Statistics of Nigeria

Total population 1995[1]	111,721,000
Urban population[2]	39.3%
Average annual population increase 1990–1995[1]	3.0%
Average annual growth in labor force 1991–2000[1]	2.4%
Total area in square kilometers 1994[3]	923,768
Density per square kilometer[3]	117
GNP per capita[4]	$300
Life expectancy in years[5]	
male	54
female	57
Literacy rate[6]	57.1%
Access to safe drinking water[7]	
for rural population	22%
for urban population	100%
Land use[8]	
arable land	31%
permanent crops	3%
meadows and pastures	23%
forest and woodland	15%
other	28%

Protected areas[9]
    in square miles   5,971
    of total land area   1.7%
Deforestation in square miles per year[10]   1,158

Number of cars in 1991[11]   785,000
Carbon dioxide emissions (000 metric tons)[12]   96,513
Sulfur dioxide emissions[13]   NA
Nitrous oxide emissions[14]   NA
Greenhouse gases
    Methane (000 metric tons)[15]   4,500
    Chlorofluorocarbons 1990 (metric tons)[16]   934
    Halons[17]   NA
Nonmethane volatile organic compounds[18]   NA

1. World Resources Institute (1996) 190–91.

2. Seager, et al. (1995) 92–99.

3. United Nations (1996) 126–33.

4. World Resources Institute (1996) 166–67.

5. Reddy (1994) 683.

6. United Nation's Educational, Scientific, and Cultural Organization (1995) 1–8 to 1–17.

7. World Resources Institute (1994). Figures dating generally from 1988 are supplied to the World Health Organization (WHO) by national governments and may represent optimistic assessments. *Urban population's* access to safe drinking water is defined as access to piped water or to a public standpipe within 650 feet of a dwelling or housing unit. *Rural population's* access to safe drinking water is defined as treated surface water or untreated water from protected springs, boreholes, and sanitary wells located such that a family member need not spend a disproportionate amount of the day fetching water (WHO, 437, 684).

8. Reddy (1994). Land use is human use of the land surface categorized as *arable land*—land cultivated for crops that are replanted after each harvest (wheat, maize, rice); *permanent crops*—land cultivated for crops that are not replanted after each harvest (citrus, coffee, rubber); *meadows and pastures*—land permanently used for herbaceous forage crops; *forest and woodland*—land under dense or open stands of trees; *other*—any land type not specifically mentioned above (urban areas, roads, deserts) (683, 1036).

9. World Resources Institute (1994). 1990 total protected areas (over 2,471 acres) under national protection in one of five World Conservation Union categories and where access is at least partially restricted: scientific reserves; national and provincial parks; natural monuments and natural landmarks; managed nature reserves and wildlife sanctuaries; and protected landscapes and seascapes. *Percent of total* is calculated on the basis of total land area (437, 683).

10. World Resources Institute (1992). *Deforestation* is defined as the permanent conversion of forest land to other uses. Areas that are logged are not counted as deforested if natural or artificial reforestation is planned (367, 591).

11. Seager, et al. (1995) 92–99.

12. World Resources Institute (1996) 326–27.

13. Information not available.

14. Information not available.

15. World Resources Institute (1996) 328–29.

16. United Nation's Environment Programme (1993). Chlorofluorocarbons (CFCs) refer to the Group I compounds: CFC-11, CFC-12, CFC-113, CFC-114, and CFC-115. Data on consumption of CFCs (Group I) is based on official reports submitted to the Ozone Secretariat, UNEP, under the terms of the Montreal Protocol (40–42).

17. Information not available.

18. Information not available.

TABLE 1.9

Demographic and Environmental Statistics of the Czech Republic

Total population 1995[1]	10,296,000
Urban population 1991[2]	75.3%
Average annual population increase 1990–1995[1]	0.0%
Average annual growth in labor force 1991–2000[1]	0.6%
Total area in square kilometers 1994[3]	78,864
Density per square kilometer[3]	131
GNP per capita[4]	$2,710
Life expectancy in years[5]	
male	69
female	77
Literacy rate[6]	NA
Access to safe drinking water (for Czechoslovakia)[7]	
for rural population	100%
for urban population	100%
Land use[8]	
cropland	43%
permanent pastures	11%
forest and woodland	34%
other land	12%
Protected areas (for Czechoslovakia)[9]	
in square miles	7,582
of total land area	15.4%
Deforestation in square miles per year (for Czechoslovakia)[10]	0
Number of cars in 1991[11]	NA
Carbon dioxide emissions (000 metric tons)[12]	135,608
Sulfur dioxide emissions (for Czechoslovakia) (000 metric tons)[13]	

in 1980	3,100
in 1989	2,564
change between 1980–1989	-17%
Nitrous oxide emissions (for Czechoslovakia) (000 metric tons)[14]	
in 1980	1,204
in 1989	1,122
change between 1980–1989	-7%
Greenhouse gases	
Methane (000 metric tons)[15]	380
Chlorofluorocarbons 1990 (for Czechoslovakia) (metric tons)[16]	5,870
Halons 1990 (for Czechoslovakia) (metric tons)[16]	160
Nonmethane volatile organic compounds 1989 (for Czechoslovakia)[17]	295

1. World Resources Institute (1996) 190–91.
2. United Nations (1996) 168.
3. United Nations (1996) 126–33.
4. World Resources Institute (1996) 166–67.
5. Reddy (1994) 247.
6. Information not available.
7. World Resources Institute (1994). Figures dating generally from 1988 are supplied to the World Health Organization (WHO) by national governments and may represent optimistic assessments. *Urban population's* access to safe drinking water is defined as access to piped water or to a public standpipe within 650 feet of a dwelling or housing unit. *Rural population's* access to safe drinking water is defined as treated surface water or untreated water from protected springs, boreholes, and sanitary wells located such that a family member need not spend a disproportionate amount of the day fetching water (WHO, 553, 684).
8. World Resources Institute (1996). Land use data is provided to the Food and Agriculture Organization of the United Nations (FAO) by national governments in response to annual questionnaires. FAO compiles data from national agricultural censuses. Because land use changes can reflect changes in data reporting, procedures along with actual land use changes, apparent trends should be interpreted with caution.
Cropland includes land under temporary and permanent crops, temporary meadows, market and kitchen gardens, and temporary fallow. Permanent crops are those that do not need to be replanted after each harvest, such as cocoa, coffee, fruit, rubber, and vines. It excludes land used to grow trees for wood or timber. *Permanent pasture* is land used for five or more years for forage, including natural crops and cultivated crops. This category is difficult for countries to assess because it includes wild land used for pasture. Grassland not used for forage is included in *other land. Forest and woodland* includes land under natural or planted stands of trees, as well as logged-over areas that will be reforested in the near future. *Other land* includes uncultivated land, grassland not used for pasture, built-on areas, wetlands, wastelands, and roads (216, 222).
9. World Resources Institute (1994). 1990 total protected areas (over 2,471 acres) under national protection in one of five World Conservation Union categories and where access is at least partially restricted: scientific reserves; national and provincial parks; natural monuments and natural landmarks; managed nature reserves and wildlife

sanctuaries; and protected landscapes and seascapes. *Percent of total* is calculated on the basis of total land area (553, 683).

10. World Resources Institute (1992). *Deforestation* is defined as the permanent conversion of forest land to other uses. Areas that are logged are not counted as deforested if natural or artificial reforestation is planned (479, 591).

11. Information not available.

12. World Resources Institute (1996) 326–27.

13. United Nation's Environment Programme (1993). Per capita emissions of SO_2 in 1990 are based on UN population statistics for 1990 unless otherwise indicated. The calculation of emissions of SO_2 per unit GDP is based on World Bank estimates of GDP in 1990 in U.S. currency as reported in the World Development Report 1992. Emissions of SO_2 per unit GDP are given in kg a^{-1} per 10^3.

Note that emissions are given in units of 10^3 t a^{-1} as sulfur dioxide (SO_2); to convert to emissions in 10^3 t a^{-1} as sulfur (S) divide by 2.0.

Data presented in the above table generally represent official country emissions estimates as reported in "state of the environment"-type reports or as reported to the European Monitoring and Evaluation Program. As methods of estimation may vary between countries, intercountry comparisons should be made with caution. Trends observed within each country are more reliable than comparisons between countries (44–46).

14. United Nation's Environment Programme (1993). Per capita emissions of NO_x in 1990 are based on UN population statistics for 1990 unless otherwise indicated. The calculation of emissions of NO_x per unit GDP is based on World Bank estimates of GDP in 1990 in U.S. currency as reported in the World Development Report 1992. Emissions of NO_x per unit GDP are given in kg a^{-1} per 10^3 (47–48).

15. World Resources Institute (1996) 328–29.

16. United Nation's Environment Programme (1993). Chlorofluorocarbons (CFCs) refer to the Group I compounds: CFC-11, CFC-12, CFC-113, CFC-114, and CFC-115. Halons refer to the Group II compounds: Halon-1301, Halon-1211, and Halon-2402.

Data on consumption of CFCs (Group I) and halons (Group II) are based on official reports submitted to the Ozone Secretariat, UNEP, under the terms of the Montreal Protocol (40–42).

17. United Nation's Environment Programme (1993). Emissions of nonmethane volatile organic compounds presented in the above table generally represent official country emissions estimates as reported in "state of the environment"-type reports or as reported to the European Monitoring and Evaluation Program. As methods of estimation may vary between countries, intercountry comparisons should be made with caution (43).

TABLE 1.10

Demographic and Environmental Statistics of Slovakia

Total population 1995[1]	5,353,000
Urban population 1992[2]	57.1%
Average annual population increase 1990–1995[1]	0.4%

Average annual growth in labor force 1991–2000[1]	1.1%
Total area in square kilometers 1994[3]	49,012
Density per square kilometer[3]	109
GNP per capita[4]	$1,950
Life expectancy in years[5]	
male	69
female	77
Literacy rate[6]	NA
Access to safe drinking water (for Czechoslovakia) [7]	
for rural population	100%
for urban population	100%
Land use[8]	
cropland	34%
permanent pastures	17%
forest and woodland	41%
other land	8%
Protected areas (for Czechoslovakia)[9]	
in square miles	7,582
of total land area	15.4%
Deforestation in square miles per year (for Czechoslovakia)[10]	0
Number of cars in 1991[11]	NA
Carbon dioxide emissions (000 metric tons)[12]	36,999
Sulfur dioxide emissions (for Czechoslovakia) (000 metric tons)[13]	
in 1980	3,100
in 1989	2,564
change between 1980–89	-17%
Nitrous oxide emissions (for Czechoslovakia) (000 metric tons)[14]	
1980	1,204
1989	1,122
change between 1980–1989	-7%
Greenhouse gases	
Methane (000 metric tons)[15]	320
Chlorofluorocarbons 1990 (for Czechoslovakia) (metric tons)[16]	5,870
Halons 1990 (for Czechoslovakia) (metric tons)[16]	160
Nonmethane volatile organic compounds (for Czechoslovakia)[17]	295

1. World Resources Institute (1996) 190–91.

2. United Nations (1996) 171.

3. United Nations (1996) 126–33.

4. World Resources Institute (1996) 166–67.

5. Reddy (1994) 828.

6. United Nation's Educational, Scientific, and Cultural Organization (1995) 1–8 to 1–17.

7. World Resources Institute (1994). Figures dating generally from 1988 are supplied to the World Health Organization (WHO) by national governments and may represent optimistic assessments. *Urban population's* access to safe drinking water is defined as access to piped water or to a public standpipe within 650 feet of a dwelling or housing unit. *Rural population's* access to safe drinking water is defined as treated surface water or untreated water from protected springs, boreholes, and sanitary wells located such that a family member need not spend a disproportionate amount of the day fetching water (WHO, 553, 684).

8. World Resources Institute (1996). Land use data is provided to the Food and Agriculture Organization of the United Nations (FAO) by national governments in response to annual questionnaires. FAO compiles data from national agricultural censuses. Because land use changes can reflect changes in data reporting, procedures along with actual land use changes, apparent trends should be interpreted with caution.

Cropland includes land under temporary and permanent crops, temporary meadows, market and kitchen gardens, and temporary fallow. Permanent crops are those that do not need to be replanted after each harvest, such as cocoa, coffee, fruit, rubber, and vines. It excludes land used to grow trees for wood or timber. *Permanent pasture* is land used for five or more years for forage, including natural crops and cultivated crops. This category is difficult for countries to assess because it includes wild land used for pasture. Grassland not used for forage is included in *other land*. *Forest and woodland* includes land under natural or planted stands of trees, as well as logged-over areas that will be reforested in the near future. *Other land* includes uncultivated land, grassland not used for pasture, built-on areas, wetlands, wastelands, and roads (216, 222).

9. World Resources Institute (1994). 1990 total protected areas (over 2,471 acres) under national protection in one of five World Conservation Union categories and where access is at least partially restricted: scientific reserves; national and provincial parks; natural monuments and natural landmarks; managed nature reserves and wildlife sanctuaries; and protected landscapes and seascapes. *Percent of total* is calculated on the basis of total land area (553, 683).

10. World Resources Institute (1992). *Deforestation* is defined as the permanent conversion of forest land to other uses. Areas that are logged are not counted as deforested if natural or artificial reforestation is planned (479, 591).

11. Seager, et al. (1995) 92–99.

12. World Resources Institute (1996) 326–27.

13. United Nation's Environment Programme (1993). Per capita emissions of SO_2 in 1990 are based on UN population statistics for 1990 unless otherwise indicated. The calculation of emissions of SO_2 per unit GDP is based on World Bank estimates of GDP in 1990 in U.S. currency as reported in the World Development Report 1992. Emissions of SO_2 per unit GDP are given in kg a^{-1} per 10^3.

Note that emissions are given in units of 10^3 t a^{-1} as sulfur dioxide (SO_2); to convert to emissions in 10^3 t a^{-1} as sulfur (S) divide by 2.0.

Data presented in the above table generally represent official country emissions estimates as reported in "state of the environment"-type reports or as reported to the European Monitoring and Evaluation Program. As methods of estimation may vary between countries, intercountry comparisons should be made with caution. Trends observed within each country are more reliable than comparisons between countries (44–46).

14. United Nation's Environment Programme (1993). Per capita emissions of NO_x in 1990 are based on UN population statistics for 1990 unless otherwise indicated. The calculation of emissions of NO_x per unit GDP is based on World Bank estimates of GDP in 1990 in U.S. currency as reported in the World Development Report 1992. Emissions of NO_x per unit GDP are given in kg a^{-1} per 10^3 (47–48).

15. World Resources Institute (1996) 328–29.

16. United Nation's Environment Programme (1993). Chlorofluorocarbons (CFCs) refer to the Group I compounds: CFC-11, CFC-12, CFC-113, CFC-114, and CFC-115. Halons refer to the Group II compounds: Halon-1301, Halon-1211, and Halon-2402. Data on consumption of CFCs (Group I) and halons (Group II) are based on official reports submitted to the Ozone Secretariat, UNEP, under the terms of the Montreal Protocol (40–42).

17. United Nation's Environment Programme (1993). Emissions of nonmethane volatile organic compounds presented in the above table generally represent official country emissions estimates as reported in "state of the environment"-type reports or as reported to the European Monitoring and Evaluation Program. As methods of estimation may vary between countries, intercountry comparisons should be made with caution (43).

References

Albrecht, C. 1987. "Environmental Policies and Politics in Contemporary Czecho-slovakia." *Studies in Comparative Communism* 20, 291–302.

Alcamo, J. M. 1992. *Coping with Crisis in Eastern Europe's Environment*. Pearl River, N.Y.: Parthenon.

Andersen, Mikael Skou. 1994. *Governance by Green Taxes: Making Pollution Prevention Pay*. Manchester, U.K.: Manchester University Press.

Andersen, Terry Lee, and Donald Leal. 1991. *Free Market Environmentalism*. Boulder: Westview Press.

Baptist, Johannes. 1994. *Managing the environment: the role of economic instruments*. Paris: Organisation for Economic Co-operation and Development, OE Publications and Information Centre.

Barde, Jean-Philippe. 1994. E*conomic instruments in environmental policy*. Paris: Organisation for Economic Co-operation and Development, OE Publications and Information Centre.

Beckerman, Wilfred. 1974. *Two Cheers for the Affluent Society: A Spirited Defense of Economic Growth*. New York: St. Martin's Press.

Bennett, Jane, and William Chaloupka, eds. 1993. *In the Nature of Things: Language, Politics and the Environment*. Minneapolis: University of Minnesota Press.

Bolan, R. S. 1992. "Organizing for Sustainable Growth in Poland." *Journal of the American Planning Association* 58, 301–311.

Brenton, Tony. 1994. *The Greening of Machiavelli: The Evolution of International Environmental Politics*. London: Earthscan Publications.

Brown, Lester R. 1995. *Who Will Feed China: Wake-Up Call for a Small Planet*. New York: W.W. Norton and Co.

Bryant, Pat. 1989. "Toxics and Racial Justice." *Social Policy* 20 (Summer): 48–52.

Bullard, Robert D. 1990. *Dumping in Dixie: Race, Class and Environmental Quality*. Boulder: Westview Press.

Bullard, Robert D. ed. 1993. *Confronting Environmental Racism: Voices from the Crossroads*. Boston: South End Press.

Cairncross, Frances. 1994. *Green Inc.: A Guide to Business and the Environment*. Washington, D.C.: Island Press.

Caldwell, Lynton K. 1990. *International Environmental Policy: Emergence and Dimensions*. Second Edition. Durham: Duke University Press.

Carson, Rachel. 1962. *Silent Spring*. New York: Fawcett Crest Books.

Cleary, David. 1991. "The 'Greening' of the Amazon." In *Environment and Development in Latin America: The Politics of Sustainability*, ed. David Goodman and Michael Redclift, 116–140. Manchester, U.K.: Manchester University Press.

Debardeleben, J. ed. 1991. *To Breathe Free: Eastern Europe's Environmental Crisis*. Washington, D.C.: Woodrow Wilson International Center for Scholars.

Desai, U., and K. Snavely. 1998. "Emergence and Development of Bulgaria's Environmental Movement." *Nonprofit and Voluntary Sector Quarterly*, Forthcoming

Diamond, Larry. 1992. "Economic Development and Democracy Reconsidered." *American Behavioral Scientist* 35, 4/5 (March/June): 450–99.

Drengson, Alan R. 1989. *Beyond Environmental Crisis: From Technocratic to Planetary Person*. New York: Peter Lang.

Evernden, Neil. 1985. *The Natural Alien*. Toronto: University of Toronto Press.

Feffer, J. 1992. *Shock Waves: Eastern Europe After the Revolution*. Boston: South End Press.

Fox, Warwick. 1990; 1995. *Toward a Transpersonal Ecology: Developing New Foundations for Environmentalism*. Boston: Shambhala Publications; Albany, New York: SUNY Press.

Frankland, E. Gene, and Donald Schoonmaker. 1992. *Between Protest and Power: The Green Party in Germany*. Boulder: Westview Press.

Fuller, Kathryn S. 1994. "President's Note." *Conservation Issues* 1 (2) (August).

Gamman, John K. 1994. *Overcoming Obstacles in Environmental Policy Making: Creating Partnership Through Mediation*. Albany, N.Y.: State University of New York Press.

Goodman, David and Michael Redclift, eds. 1991. *Environment and Development in Latin America: The Politics of Sustainability*. Manchester, U.K.: Manchester University Press.

Grand, Julian. 1991. *The theory of government failure*. Bristol, England: School for Advanced Urban Studies, University of Bristol.

Grubb, Michael, Matthias Koch, Abby Munson, Francis Sullivan, and Koy Thompson. 1993. *The Earth Summit Agreements: A Guide and Assessment*. London: Earthscan Publications.

Hardin, Garrett. 1968. "The Tragedy of the Commons." *Science* 162 (3859): 1243–48.

Hecht, Susanna and Alexander Cockburn. 1989. *The Fate of the Forest*. London: Verso.

Hidefumi, Imura. 1990. "Economic Incentives as a Means of Environmental Policy: Interactive Effects of Standards and Economic Incentives in Air Pollution Control in Japan." In *Environmental Charges*, ed. H. C. Binswanger and M. Jänicke, 57–91. Berlin: Forschungsst elle für umweltpolitik.

Hodge, Ian. 1995. *Environmental Economics*. New York: St. Martin's Press.

Hudson, James F., E. Lake, and D. Grossman. 1981. *Pollution-Pricing. Industrial Responses to Wastewater Charges*. Lexington: Lexington Books.

Inglehart, Ronald. 1990. *Culture Shift in Advanced Industrial Society*. Princeton: Princeton University Press.

International Union for Conservation of Nature and Natural Resources (IUCN). 1991. *Caring for the Earth: A Strategy for Sustainable Living*. Gland, Switzerland: IUCN.

Jancar-Webster, B., ed. 1993. *Environmental Action in Eastern Europe: Response to Crisis*. Armonk, N.Y.: M. E. Sharpe.

Jänicke, Martin. 1990. *State Failure: The Importance of Politics in Industrial Society*. Cambridge: Polity Press.

Leiss, William. 1994. *The Domination of Nature*. Boston: Beacon Press.

Lipset, S. M. 1960. *Political Man: The Social Bases of Politics*. Garden City, N.Y.: Doubleday.

Lowi, Theodore J. 1986. "The Welfare State, the New Regulation and the Rule of Law." In *Distributional Conflicts in Environmental-Resource Policy*, ed. Allan Schnaiberg, Nicholas Watts, and Klaus Zimmerman, 109–49. New York: St. Martin's Press.

Majone, Giandomenico. 1989. *Evidence, Argument and Persuasion in the Policy Process. Changing Institutional Constraints.* New Haven: Yale University Press.

Marcus, Alfred A. 1982. "Converting Thought to Action: The Use of Economic Incentives to Reduce Pollution." In *Environmental Policy Implementation*, ed. Dean E. Mann, 173–184. Lexington: D.C. Heath.

McNeely, Jeffrey A. 1988. *Economics and Biological Diversity: Developing and Using Economic Incentives to Conserve Biological Resources.* Gland, Switzerland: International Union for Conservation of Nature and Natural Resources (IUCN).

Merchant, Carolyn. 1980. *The Death of Nature: Women, Ecology and the Scientific Revolution.* San Francisco: Harper and Row.

Milbrath, Lester W. 1984. *Environmentalists: Vanguard for a New Society.* Albany, N.Y.: SUNY Press.

Mitnick, Barry M. 1980. *The Political Economy of Regulation: Creating, Designing, and Removing Regulatory Forms.* New York: Columbia University Press.

Newhouse, John. 1992. "The Diplomatic Round: Earth Summit." *New Yorker*, June 1.

Niskanen, William A. 1971. *Bureaucracy and Representative Government.* Chicago: Aldine.

Organization for Economic Cooperation and Development (OECD). 1989. *Economic Instruments for Environmental Protection.* Paris: Organization for Economic Cooperation and Development.

Ostrom, Elinor. 1990. *Governing the Commons: The Evolution of Institutions for Collective Action.* Cambridge: Cambridge University Press.

Ostrom, Elinor, Larry D. Schroeder, Susan G. Wynne. 1993. *Analyzing the Performance of Alternative Institutional Arrangements for Sustaining Rural Infrastructure in Developing Countries.* Bloomington: Workshop in Political Theory and Policy Analysis, Indiana University.

Paehlke, Robert C. 1989. *Environmentalism and the Future of Progressive Politics.* New Haven: Yale University Press.

Pearce, David. 1986. "Efficiency and Distribution in Corrective Mechanisms for Environmental Externality." In *Distributional Conflicts in Environmental-Resource Policy*, ed. Allan Schnaiberg, Nicholas Watts, and Klaus Zimmerman, 15–37. New York: St. Martin's Press.

Pearce, David, A. Markandya, and E. Barbier. 1989. *Blueprint for a Green Economy.* London: Earthscan Publications.

Porter, Gareth, and Janet W. Brown. 1991. *Global Environmental Politics.* Boulder: Westview Press.

Redclift, Michael R. 1987. *Sustainable Development: Exploring the Contradictions.* London: Methuen.

Redclift, Michael R. 1989. "The Environmental Consequences of Latin America's Agricultural Development: Some Thoughts on the Brundtland Commission Report." *World Development* 17, 3 (March): 365–377.

Redclift, Michael, and David Goodman. 1991. "Introduction." In *Environment and Development in Latin America*, ed. David Goodman and Michael Redclift, 1–23. Manchester, U.K.: Manchester University Press.

Reddy, Marlita A., ed. 1994. *Statistical Abstract of the World.* New York: Gale Research Inc., An International Thompson Publishing Company.

Reilly, Charles A. 1993. "NGO Policy Makers and the Social Ecology of Development." *Grassroots Development* 17, 1: 25–35.

Robinson, John. 1994. "Conservation and Development." *Conservation Issues* 1 (2) (August).

Rogers, Raymond A. 1994. *Nature and the Crisis of Modernity: A Critique of Contemporary Discourse on Managing the Earth.* Montreal, Canada: Black Rose Books.

Sachs, Wolfgang. 1992. *The development dictionary: a guide to knowledge as power.* London: Zed Books.

Samuelson, Paul A. 1983. *Foundations of Economic Analysis.* Cambridge: Harvard University Press.

Schnaiberg, Allan, and Kenneth A. Gould. 1994. *Environment and Society: The Enduring Conflict.* New York: St. Martin's Press.

Schnaiberg, Allan, Nicholas Watts, and Klaus Zimmerman, eds. 1986. *Distributional Conflicts in Environmental-Resource Policy.* New York: St. Martin's Press.

Seager, Joni, Clark Reed, and Peter Stott. 1995. *The New State of the Earth Atlas.* New York: Simon & Schuster Inc.

Shiva, Vandana. 1989. *Staying Alive: Women, Ecology and Survival in India.* London: Zed.

Sikorski, Wade. 1993. *Modernity and Technology: Harnessing the Earth to the Slavery of Man.* Tuscaloosa: University of Alabama Press.

Simon, Julian L. 1980. "Resources, Population, Environment: An Oversupply of False Bad News." *Science* 208 (27 June): 1431–37.

———. 1981. *The Ultimate Resource.* Princeton: Princeton University Press.

Singleton, F., ed. 1987. *Environmental Problems in the Soviet Union and Eastern Europe.* Boulder: Lynne Rienner.

Tietenberg, T. H. 1992. *Environmental and Natural Resource Economics*. Third Edition. New York: Harper Collins.

Tokar, Brian. 1987. *The Green Alternative: Creating an Ecological Future*. San Pedro, California: R. & E. Miles.

Tucker, William. 1982. *Progress and Privilege: America in the Age of Environmentalism*. Garden City, N.Y.: Doubleday.

United Nations. 1996. *1994 Demographic Yearbook*. New York: United Nations.

United Nations Educational, Scientific, and Cultural Organization. 1995. *'95 Statistical Yearbook: Facts on Education, Technology, Culture, and the Media Worldwide*. Lanham, MD: UNESCO Publishing and Bernam Press.

United Nations Environment Programme. 1993. *Environmental Data Report 1993–94*. Cambridge: Blackwell Publishers.

Watts, Nicholas. 1986. "Introduction: From Consensus to Dissensus: The Role of Distributional Conflicts in Environmental-Resource Policy." In *Distributional Conflicts in Environmental-Resource Policy*, ed. Allan Schnaiberg, Nicholas Watts, and Klaus Zimmerman, 1–14. New York: St. Martin's Press.

Wells, Michael, and Katrina Brandon with Lee Hannah. 1992. *People and Parks: Linking Protected Area Management with Local Communities*. Washington, D.C.: The World Bank.

White, Lynn, Jr. 1973. "The Historical Roots of Our Ecological Crisis," and "Continuing the Conversation." In *Western Man and Environmental Ethics: Attitudes Toward Nature and Technology*, ed. Ian G. Barbour, 18–30, 55–64. Reading, Mass.: Addison-Wesley.

Wilson, James Q. 1980. *The Politics of Regulation*. New York: Basic Books.

World Commission on Environment and Development. 1987. *Our Common Future*. Oxford: Oxford University Press. [Brundtland Commission Report, Gro Harlem Brundtland, Chairman].

World Resources Institute. 1992. *The 1992 Information Please Environmental Almanac*. Boston: Houghton Mifflin Company.

———. 1994. *The 1994 Information Please Environmental Almanac*. Boston: Houghton Mifflin Company.

World Resources Institute, in collaboration with United Nations Environment Programme, United Nations Development Programme, and the World Bank. 1996. *World Resources 1996–97*. New York: Oxford University Press.

Wright, John W., ed. 1995. *The Universal Almanac*. Kansas City: Andrews and McMeel, a Universal Press Syndicate.

Wright, Michael. 1994. "Conservation and Development." *Conservation Issues* 1 (2) (August).

Ziegler, C. E. 1987. *Environmental Policy in the USSR*. Amherst: University of Massachusetts Press.

Zimmerman, Klaus. 1986. "Discussion: Distributional Considerations and the Environmental Policy Process." In *Distributional Conflicts in Environmental-Resource Policy*, ed. Allan Schnaiberg, Nicholas Watts, and Klaus Zimmerman, 95–108. New York: St. Martin's Press.

2

THE POLITICS OF ENVIRONMENTAL POLICY IN THE PEOPLE'S REPUBLIC OF CHINA

LESTER ROSS

Introduction

The People's Republic of China (PRC) has made substantial progress in developing environmental legislation and a complementary regulatory structure. These gains are related directly to economic reforms and to the opening to the outside world that began in the 1970s and brought both greater emphasis on efficiency and greater awareness of the costs associated with pollution and environmental degradation. However, the economic growth and devolution of power unleashed by the reforms also have created new environmental stresses and taxed the regulatory capacity of governmental authorities. As a result, some environmental stresses are increasing even as progress is made on other fronts. Restrictions on political participation limit discussion on environmental issues, which only occasionally acquire political salience. Over time, however, there is a trend toward greater environmental awareness. International pressure on the PRC to conform its conduct to international environmental norms further influences domestic policy making in support of environmental regulation.

The Early Years: Production before Protection

The People's Republic of China was slow to direct attention to environmental protection in comparison to the industrialized democracies (although not in comparison to Eastern European and many third world countries), but it has made significant strides in law and policy in recent years. The first semblance of an environmental policy did not emerge until the 1970s, before which (and to some extent even afterward) the regime's economic development strategy lurched between the extremes of a centrally planned, largely single-minded pursuit of economic growth and a more decentralized insistence on communal egalitarianism. Under central planning, particularly at its height during the early to mid-1950s, the State Planning Commission (SPC) was dominated by the heavy industrial ministries and, to a lesser extent, other production-oriented ministries that emphasized expanding output rather than raising efficiency or pursuing social goals. Under the communal mode, as exemplified by the abortive great leap forward of 1958 through 1960, production targets were increased on virtually every front without regard to resource constraints.

In both instances, by bringing new lands into cultivation and raising yields through multiple cropping and the intensive application of fertilizers and pesticides, economic policy rested on resource-intensive growth strategies oriented toward Stalinist-style heavy industry, the national defense industry, or expanding agricultural production. Those resource-intensive growth strategies were not counterbalanced by noticeable concern for the environment in a policy process that was dominated alternately in leftist phases by Maoist ideologues and at other times by output-oriented state planners and production ministries. This was true even for ecologically related policy sectors such as forestry and water resources management, which otherwise enjoyed considerable elite support. Thus, tree planting programs faltered for years because of a misallocation of resources in favor of timber production and tree planting as opposed to forest management, unrealistically low prices for wood products, and the immense rural demand for energy from biomass (Li, et al. 1988:205–21; Richardson 1990:170–86; Richardson 1966:55–60). Similarly, dam construction and agricultural reclamation promoted hydroelectric power, flood control, and agricultural output at the expense of fishery, inland shipping, and other interests, resulting in a loss of natural habitat, a contraction of the inland navigation network, and the silting of waterways, while much of the populace was left without access to a safe and reliable water supply (Smil 1984:62–68).

Nor was there much opportunity in the PRC for officials, intellectuals, ordinary citizens, or even scientists, who have been founts of environmentalism in more pluralistic societies, to express countervailing views. Critics of official policy, such as the noted economist Ma Yinchu who, as president of Beijing (Peking) University in 1957, had the temerity to endorse population planning to ease the pressure of population on limited resources, were disgraced and removed from positions of influence (Bernstein 1982:50–51; Hou 1990:155–56). Ordinary citizens who sought redress for environmental harms risked detention and other sanctions (Ross and Silk 1986).

The Reform Era

This situation changed beginning in the late 1970s when economic and, to a lesser extent, political reforms were introduced amid rising awareness of the social costs of pollution and ecological destruction. This should not be taken to mean that reform was synonymous with environmentalism in the Communist party or that conservatives were implacably opposed to environmental protection. In fact, the first pollution control programs, directed at air pollution in Shenyang (the capital of Liaoning) and water pollution in the Guanting Reservoir north of Beijing, commenced while Mao Zedong was alive and the prospects for reform were still dim. Rather, the reform process directly and indirectly set in motion changes that have enhanced environmental regulation while they also imposed new stress on the environment.

Specifically, reform-minded officials gradually recognized that over-emphasis on centrally planned heavy industry and disregard for market prices had distorted the PRC's economic structure and incentives. Moreover, they realized that resource scarcity, aggravated by population growth, necessitated somewhat greater attention to conservation. They therefore resolved in varying degrees to deemphasize heavy industry in favor of light industry and the service or tertiary sector, expand foreign trade and investment, and increase the role of market forces and producer incentives, first in agriculture and subsequently in other sectors of the economy. These reforms unleashed a sustained economic expansion, particularly in the southeast and other areas of coastal China where central planning was relaxed to the greatest extent.

Environmental protection benefited indirectly from the decline in heavy industry, in favor of the less energy- and resource-intensive light industry and service sectors and a rise in efficiency as the government promoted conservation and enterprises began to focus more on profits than on output. The reforms also greatly expanded China's linkages with the outside world, including scientific and intellectual discourse, which increased awareness of environmental protection. The reforms also weakened the capacity of the Communist party and the state to control society, allowing greater latitude for the expression of unorthodox values, including environmentalism. Environmental protection also benefited directly from increased funding, although the expanding economy itself often overwhelmed the growth in regulatory capacity and the rise in popular awareness of environmental values.

Naturally, the economic reforms encountered considerable opposition from more conservative officials, state-owned heavy industry, and inland areas. Some officials remained committed to the development of heavy industry relative to the economy as a whole, and most insisted on retaining tight control over society, which necessarily limited the emergence of such societal forces as environmentalism. Nevertheless, awareness of environmental protection has become more widely diffused among officials. Debate often concerns whether and to what extent economic development will be shaped by environmental needs and the extent to which particular projects are environmentally beneficial. It is now much less common to see issues framed without regard to environmental conditions, and such phenomena are likely to diminish further as the country becomes wealthier and younger, and as better-educated officials assume positions of responsibility.

Administration and Legislation

The PRC has created a nationwide administrative structure centered in the National Environmental Protection Agency (NEPA),[1] which supervises local bureaus down to the county level throughout the country. Although lacking ministerial status comparable to that of most other departments of government, especially production-oriented ministries such as the Ministry of Chemical Industry and the Ministry of Metallurgical Industry, NEPA's position within the government has improved with the expansion of its responsibilities and stronger backing from the powerful State Science and Technology Commission (SSTC), the SPC and, indeed, the Communist party. The SPC in particular has established a section with responsibility for environmental protection, including the environmental protection chapters of the Five-Year State Plans for Economic and Social Development and the fifteen-year long-term development program (1996–2010). NEPA sets long-term policies in accordance with China's Environmental Protection Work Program (1993–1998), in addition to the above-mentioned state plans. NEPA also provides the secretariat for the State Committee on Environmental Protection (SCEP), an interagency body under the State Council that helps coordinate policy and resolve relatively cumbersome interagency disputes.[2]

China's legislative bodies also have begun to acquire more meaningful lawmaking and oversight roles, in contrast to their customary images as rubber stamps. The National People's Congress (NPC) in 1992 debated the Three Gorges Project, and many deputies declined to support the project, as discussed below. Institutionally, the NPC has established a specialized committee structure to enhance its lawmaking and oversight capacity, led by the Environment and Resource Protection Committee (ERPC) chaired by former NEPA Administrator Qu Geping (Ross 1994). Citizens frequently voice their concerns on issues such as pollution to their deputies in the local people's congresses, who are beginning to be chosen in competitive elections. Thus, although the NPC in terms of policy formulation remains subordinate both to the Communist party and to the administration, it has become a more significant player in the decision-making process.

The NPC's role has expanded in part because formal legislation has become an increasingly important factor in the policy process in the post-Mao era. Formal legislation is recognized as necessary in virtually all fields of public policy now that the Communist party no longer is capable of moving the country by stringent political controls and ideological orthodoxy, although enforcement typically is sporadic and generally remains subject to influence by local and other economic and political interests. Several major statutes have been enacted, including the revised Environmental Protection Law (1989) (EPL), the Air Pollution Prevention and Control Law (1987, as amended 1995) (APPCL), the Water Pollution Prevention and Control Law (1984, as amended 1996), the Solid Waste Law (1995) and the Water and Soil Conservation Law (1991).[3] Further revisions of the EPL and the Marine Environmental Protection Law (1992) are in the drafting stage, along with other legislation, particularly a hazardous waste law and a noise pollution law. Many sets of regulations to implement environmental law as well as emissions and technology standards also have been issued on a variety of subjects.[4]

These statutes and regulations proscribe certain behaviors and mandate various procedures for reducing the incidence and magnitude of future environmental problems, including such modern regulatory instruments as environmental impact assessments, discharge permits, and effluent charges.[5]

Growing recognition of the importance of environmental protection now also affects elite circulation and career advancement to a modest extent. The Communist party and the state have revised their criteria for evaluating the performance and promotion of officials. Provincial and municipal officials in particular are now evaluated in part on the basis of their individual performance and that of their jurisdiction on environmental norms. Moreover, a vice-governor, a vice-mayor, or a vice-magistrate in each jurisdiction is assigned responsibility for environmental protection. Officials in general also now devote more attention to environmental matters, in part because the political reforms have accorded citizens greater latitude to express their opinions, particularly on lifestyle and social issues such as noise and air pollution. For example, citizens who resorted to direct action to halt particularly egregious pollution harms were treated leniently and even exonerated in a number of instances because protesting against pollution was deemed a justification for behavior that previously could have been deemed illegal or counterrevolutionary (Ross and Silk 1986). Nongovernmental organizations are being established, although their autonomy remains circumscribed (Cook et al. 1994). When environmental problems become salient, careers and policies can be affected suddenly. The governor of Gansu was removed from office in 1993, in part because of his ineffective response to chronic pollution from a local factory that had aroused popular protest (Brauchli 1993). Long-standing pollution problems in the Huai River valley of central and eastern China went largely unattended for years despite popular discontent and NEPA's proposals for remediation. But after epidemics and crop failures occurred in 1994 when industrial discharges went unchecked during a drought, the state council was galvanized into approving a crackdown on pollution and increasing spending on pollution control (Lin 1995; Zhu 1994). The reverse also arises. When an official's support base erodes, environmental issues may be dredged up by his or her critics. For example, when President Jiang Zemin orchestrated an attack on Beijing municipal officials in 1995, one issue was the approval by local authorities of a commercial development in downtown Beijing, in disregard of applicable regulations on building height (Wang 1995).

The new policy infrastructure and somewhat heightened environmental consciousness have coincided with the deemphasis on heavy industry and greater attention to efficiency resulting from the ongoing economic reforms. As a result, the rate of increase in reported pollution loadings has slowed substantially, despite rapid increases in economic growth and industrial output. However, the validity of such data on pollution trends is limited by rudimentary monitoring and an inadequate data base (Zhang 1992). Moreover, such statistical series do not report pollution by township and village enterprises (TVEs) that have flourished under the economic reforms (NEPA 1991). Such enterprises officially accounted for only 5.70 percent of the gross value of industrial output in 1991 (State Statistical Bureau 1992:403). However, this figure is almost certainly an underestimate. Moreover, the TVEs have been increasing production by more than 20 percent a year. Therefore, the failure to report pollution by TVEs is significant and suggests some of the apparent improvement in pollution control actually constitutes a shift of pollution from urban to rural areas, where such enterprises are found in large numbers, rather than an absolute reduction in pollution. The national government belatedly recognized the problem and has begun to assemble data on resource consumption, pollution loadings, pollution incidents, and regulatory compliance by TVEs (NEPA 1991).

Problems and Politics

Although there has been considerable progress in terms of policy development, and even some measurable accomplishments, many problems have yet to be addressed fully, and new ones continue to emerge. The following are among the more important such problems.

Economic Inefficiency and Pricing Irrationality

For many years the PRC operated under a somewhat limited but nevertheless rigid state planning system with stringent price controls for key commodities. The system produced great waste and discouraged efficiency because it diminished incentives for innovation and economical use of materials. Moreover, those industries that suffered from artificially depressed fixed prices for their products, such as coal and water supply, could not afford to make investments that would benefit the environment, such as coal washing, treatment of mine wastes, water purification, and wastewater collection and treatment systems.

Since the Third Plenum of the Eleventh Central Committee of the Communist party in 1978, the PRC has made enormous progress in economic development by relaxing the dead hand of command planning in favor of somewhat more flexible guidance planning, market measures, and expanded foreign trade and investment. Prices in most instances are allowed to find their own levels, and in many others they are permitted to float within defined price ranges. The result has been modestly to discourage production of unwanted goods and overconsumption of underpriced goods, with attendant benefit for the environment in terms of reduced consumption of energy and other materials and reduced discharges of waste materials per unit output in certain industries and at certain plants.

However, the PRC still has far to go in terms of economic rationalization and price reform, especially with regard to the price of energy and raw materials such as coal and water. Progress in this regard slowed in late 1994 because of concern over the potential for popular protest occasioned by rampant inflation. Nevertheless, the trend is apparent, and even conservative officials have come to support reform in general. Coal prices in particular began to be decontrolled in 1994 (Wu 1994). As price reform advances in this regard, there should be substantial environmental benefits.

Transboundary Pollution

The PRC is a unitary rather than a federal polity in which the central government alone enjoys sovereign power. The central government also frequently exercises its power to realign domestic administrative boundaries. Nevertheless, the provincial-level administrative entities (provinces, self-governing municipalities, and the heavily non-Han Chinese autonomous regions) and, to a lesser extent, the subprovincial units in practice enjoy extensive autonomy. On the one hand, this limits the potential for repressive rule by the central government and fosters administrative laboratories for policy innovation. The central government often tests policies in particular localities before imposing them on a nationwide basis, and environmental statutes typically permit localities to adopt regulations and standards that are more stringent or more detailed than the national norms. On the other hand, it hampers the ability of the central government to raise revenues or implement laws and regulations on a uniform basis. Enforcement of environmental and safety regulations in many localities remains sporadic. An additional deficiency is the difficulty that arises in addressing transboundary pollution problems (e.g., effluent from upstream sources contaminating downstream areas). Such problems are widespread throughout the country. Their resolution requires the intervention of higher level officials, but the situation might also benefit from the establishment of special administrative entities such as air pollution control districts and sewerage authorities to address transboundary pollution. The Huoi River Valley water pollution control effort noted above is jointly led by NEPA and the Ministry of Water Resources, and may constitute a model in this regard.

The Urban-Rural Dimension

Environmental protection has focused on the PRC's urban areas where industry and residents are densely concentrated.[6] For example, central or district heating systems, based in part on town gas, have been introduced in a growing number of cities, particularly in northern China. Environmental regulations have been tightened on major polluters, and small industrial pollution sources located in urban centers and the Huoi River Valley have been forced to close, merge, or relocate outside the cities (Kahn 1996). In addition, as noted earlier, mayors and their cities are now evaluated in part on the basis of their performance on various environmental norms, which has raised their knowledge and awareness of environmental issues. These changes have had a beneficial impact on the urban environment, although much more remains to be done.

However, the PRC's rural environment has come under new stresses that have not yet been addressed effectively. Specifically, rural economic reforms that included the dismantling of many elements of the collective economy unleashed a surge of economic entrepreneurship, including rural industrialization. This phenomenon is particularly pronounced in the coastal areas of southern and eastern China where growth is fueled by the export market, but it also can be found on the periphery of large cities throughout the country. Such factories typically lack pollution controls and often have outmoded equipment, the higher operating costs which are offset by lower labor costs and more abundant land and other resources.

Rural industrialization also has been spurred by the forced exodus from city centers of small, heavily polluting factories such as dyeing and electroplating works. These factories have relocated to rural areas where land and water are more plentiful and the population density is lower. Although such rural areas are better equipped to buffer industrial pollution, they also have less extensive environmental regulation. As a result, even a few small factories sometimes exert a deleterious impact on the local environment.

Environmental regulation in rural areas merits much higher priority than it has received so far. However, strengthening regulation is a difficult proposition because of the great bias in favor of economic growth, opposition from the rural areas to any constraints on their economic development, and the scattering of pollution sources across wide areas. Many enterprises are subject to little or no regulation of any kind, not just in terms of environmental protection, and it is unlikely that regulation can be strengthened quickly in the context of diminished state and Communist party power, particularly given strong biases in favor of economic development. Indeed, not only is economic development the source of local prosperity, but it also creates some of the wherewithal both for the official compensation and for irregular enrichment of local officeholders.

The reforms also have aggravated some stresses in agriculture. Higher farm prices and expanded management and property rights for farmers and herdsmen generally have boosted output, but not without environmental problems. Grasslands in some areas have been degraded by allowing herdsmen to increase the sizes of their herds without regulating their exercise of grazing rights. Irrigation management has been weakened in some instances. Agriculture also makes extensive use of irrigation and fertilizers and other agricultural chemicals in large quantities without appropriate controls. The result is widespread salinization and surface and groundwater contamination.

Population Pressure and Resource Scarcity

Despite extensive population controls, the PRC's population continues to increase at a rate of approximately 1.4 percent per year, for a net natural increase of 17 million people per year (National Report 1992:47). The population rose to 1.2 billion in 1995 and is expected to rise to 1.3 billion by the end of the century and to 1.6 billion by 2030. Such a vast population exists in a country with a geographical area about as large as that of the United States, but with little more than half the arable land and only about 80 percent of the water resource.

There is great concern in China over the environmental and nutritional effects of such a large population (National Conditions Investigation Group 1992:14–20). Although such population pressure can be managed, it puts great stress on the natural resource endowment, particularly as consumption increases. Beijing and other cities in dry northern China have suffered from insufficient water supplies for many years, resulting in groundwater depletion and surface subsidence. This problem is likely to get worse in the course of economic development because consumption is positively correlated with income. A rationalization of the pricing system to reflect the scarcity values of water, energy, and other commodities has made only halting progress because of opposition from industrial users and ordinary consumers.

Among the measures imposed to address these problems is mandatory urban planning in all of China's cities. In addition, relocation of industry and population away from urban centers is encouraged but is dependent on further improvements in transportation, the further development of a market in land-use rights, and a narrowing of the disparities between the quality of life in urban and in rural areas.

Major Development Projects

The PRC has built many large public works projects, including dams, industrial plants, and new industrial cities. Historically, such projects were decided on the basis of the state plan, with some latitude for local bargaining. Environmental impacts, resettlement costs, and safety considerations all were given insufficient attention. The results included widespread problems such as the drying up of lakes (e.g., Baiyangdian in Hebei), the silting of reservoirs, and the siting of such major pollution sources as chemical plants and steel mills upwind and upstream of population centers such as Beijing.

This situation has improved, at least for medium- and large-size projects. Regulations that require environmental impact assessments were introduced beginning in the 1980s, and greater attention to resettlement costs also was mandated. Although the environmental impact statement process initially was confined to the postapproval stage and usually had little if any influence on political decision makers, article 13 of the EPL now mandates that the process take place during the feasibility study, before the project is approved.[7] Moreover, there is somewhat greater latitude to express opposition now than in the past, albeit not as much as in the period immediately before the June 1989 Tiananmen massacre. In addition, multilateral and foreign donor countries and organizations, such as the World Bank, insist upon much more elaborate and thoroughgoing analyses of environmental and human impacts before they will agree to finance all or part of a project (Whitcomb 1992:32–33).[8]

As a result, projects undergo closer scrutiny and potentially encounter more dissent. The most controversial project now under consideration, the $17.3 billion Three Gorges dam and reservoir, to be built in a scenic area of the upper Changjiang (Yangtze) River, is planned to generate 84 billion kilowatts of electricity annually from 17.68 million kilowatts of installed hydroelectric generating capacity. The proponents of the project include many officials in the SPC and other macroeconomic agencies as well as most officials in the Ministry of Water Resources and the Ministry of Communications, downstream interests in Hebei and other provinces vulnerable to flooding, navigation interests, and industries and communities to be served by the project's navigational access and hydroelectric power production (Lieberthal and Oksenberg 1990:269–338; Yao Jianguo 1992).

Conversely, opponents of the project focus on the high up-front capital investment requirements and the high financial costs of relocating 700,000 or more people. There also are fundamental objections to the strategy of building a massive dam on the main stem in contrast to a series of smaller projects on tributaries as well as the main stem of the Yangtze. The opponents also object to the cultural impact of raising the water level in one of China's most beautiful and historically significant natural features, the environmental impacts, and the risk of catastrophic failure, as well as the economic and human costs of the project, including resettlement costs (Fearnside 1993; Barber and Ryder 1993).

The proponents, led by the State Council's Office for Economic Development of the Three Gorges Area, moved the project through the National People's Congress in the spring of 1992. Nevertheless, opposition was so widespread that, in an extraordinary expression of dissent, 177 of the 2,608 deputies voted no and another 664 abstained (McGregor 1992). Construction has commenced, and the project is likely to proceed. However, finances continue to present difficulties. The international capital markets and the multilateral development banks have not been responsive, in part because of the project's environmental and resettlement controversies. Therefore, the government has been forced to cobble together a domestic financing package consisting of subsidized State Development Bank loans, a nationwide electricity surcharge, dedication of all electricity revenues from the existing Gezhouba facility on the Yangtze River, and other sources. Such financing remains fragile (Smith 1995). In addition, new environmental controversies have emerged. The upstream city of Chongqing, long a proponent of the project for its navigation and urban renewal benefits, has had some second thoughts because of concern that the impoundment will disturb toxic and hazardous sediments from the river bottom.

Global Warming and Other International Concerns

The PRC's expanded commitment to environmental protection originally rested on the presumption that economic development and environmental protection would proceed in tandem rather than follow the historic pattern under which economic policy showed little or no heed for the environment.[9] By implication, environmental protection might slow the pace of economic development but need not foreclose the potential for growth in the economy as a whole. Consequently, the impact on particular industries would be modest, and the PRC could continue to anticipate catching up to the world's most advanced countries. Opposition to environmental protection from the SPC, the Ministry of Finance, and the production ministries was overcome by the Communist party leadership with the promise that the burden of environmental protection would be introduced only gradually in accordance with the PRC's financial capacity. Indeed, regulatory enforcement was adjusted according to the fortunes of each industry (e.g., the more prosperous chemical industry was subjected to more rigorous demands than the less prosperous coal industry), and plants were renovated, relocated, or merged rather than closed for environmental or other reasons.

However, recent concern over ozone depletion and global warming has created international regimes predicated on stabilization and/or reduction of the consumption of particular commodities, such as chlorofluorocarbons (i.e., the Montreal Protocol), and greenhouse gas emissions, such as carbon dioxide emissions (i.e., the Framework Convention on Climate Change), to each of which China is a party. The PRC as well as many other developing countries fear that the international regimes will be dominated by the advanced industrialized countries to protect their own interests at the expense of the developing countries. The PRC in particular produces 1.2 billion tons of coal a year and relies on coal for 73 percent of its commercial energy production, including 75 percent of industrial fuel, 65 percent of chemical feedstocks, and 85 percent of urban residential fuel. Thus, the PRC's sulfur dioxide and carbon dioxide emissions from coal combustion are huge, although per capita energy consumption is still less than one-third of the global average (National Report 1992, part 2). Therefore, international controls on such emissions would pose a major problem for the PRC's economy, although coal washing, more efficient combustion, and flue gas controls can greatly reduce pollution emissions (WuDunn 1992).

Such concerns led the PRC to convene the Ministerial Conference on Environment and Development in Beijing in June 1991. Ministers from forty-one developing countries attended. The resulting Beijing Ministerial Declaration on Environment and Development (Ministerial Conference 1991) expressed serious concern regarding the need for international cooperation to promote environmental protection and sustained development (article 2), but it also insisted on the right of the developing countries to develop (article 3), the need for the developed countries to transfer resources to and finance environmental protection in the developing countries (articles 4, 8–9, 12–14, 21–24), and opposition to interference in the internal affairs of developing countries and the attachment of conditions to aid or to development financing (article 6). The declaration thus expressed clearly the determination of the developing countries, particularly the PRC, to drive a hard bargain for concessionary financing and technology transfer at the United Nations Conference on Environment and Development (UNCED) in Rio de Janeiro in June 1992, in exchange for their cooperation on global environmental issues.

This same theme was reiterated in greater detail by the PRC in its first National Report of the People's Republic of China on Environment and Development. The national report was coordinated by the SPC under the supervision of a leading group, consisting of officials from the SPC, SSTC, Ministry of Foreign Affairs, and NEPA. The national report expressly stated:

There should be a clear recognition of the main responsibility for global environmental degradation to date and the main obligation for its resolution. . . . International cooperation for environmental protection must be based on the principle of "common but differentiated responsibilities," and the developed countries are duty-bound to make more and practical contribution [sic] to international cooperation in this regard, while taking the lead in adopting environmental protection measures. This should include the following two aspects:

First, to provide the developing countries with new and additional financial resources to enable them to participate more effectively in the international cooperation for environmental protection, or to compensate them for the economic losses incurred in implementing obligations under international legal instruments. The "adequacy" of these financial resources must be emphasized. Symbolic or limited funds provided mainly for publicity purposes will not contribute to solving practical problems. . . . Such financial resources . . . should not merely be a reallocation of the present flow of development assistance. . . .

Second, to provide the developing countries with requisite advanced technologies for pollution control and environmentally sound technologies on preferential and non-commercial terms. These technologies should not be regarded as commodities in the general sense of the word, and as such, be left to the market mechanism for their transfer. From the point of view of responsibility to the common interests of humanity, these technologies should be considered as a common wealth of all mankind, and their transfer as due contribution to the common cause of humanity (National Report 1991:109–10).

The PRC has continued to express these themes at meetings to implement the United Nations Framework Convention on Climate Change and other forums. Fundamentally, China demands that the developed countries assume a large share of the costs of such programs, but also is increasingly aware that preventive measures are in China's interest (World Bank et al. 1995). Joint implementation and other measures to ease China's compliance costs are under consideration.

Conclusion

Environmental policy has developed quite rapidly since the late 1970s, largely as the result of greater elite awareness of the importance of environmental protection. Such awareness has been fostered by the PRC's expanded involvement in international affairs, notably science, politics, and economics. Expanded participation in international affairs is a direct result of the post-Mao reforms, which also have contributed to environmental protection by reorienting the economy away from heavy industry and by encouraging greater attention to raising efficiency. However, the reforms also have resulted in increased economic activity and rising consumption (e.g., motor vehicle usage), which is placing increased stress on the environment, including rural areas that are undergoing rapid industrialization.

With regard to environmental policy as such, many problems remain even though the PRC has enacted an impressive series of laws and regulations. Legislation in certain areas such as hazardous waste control has yet to be enacted, although this is now recognized as a priority need. Rural environmental regulation is largely nonexistent. Some programs that have been instituted, such as the creation of more than six hundred nature preserves (with still others planned), look more impressive on paper than they do in the field. Funding for environmental protection is increasing but is barely half the amount needed, according to PRC officials (Chandra 1994). Regulators often are prevented from taking vigorous enforcement action against polluters by political leaders and other agencies more concerned with economic growth than with environmental protection. Moreover, limits on the freedoms of organization and expression inhibit the growth of an indigenous environmental movement that could counterbalance the emphasis on economic growth (Hou 1990:157–58).

Despite these limitations, however, the PRC has made substantial strides in developing environmental policy, including sophisticated policy instruments and a monitoring network, and one no longer encounters the public hostility or indifference to environmental protection among officials that used to be found in the PRC. Moreover, PRC officials have begun to acknowledge the harm posed to their country by global warming and other environmental catastrophes. Therefore, environmental protection can be expected to advance further through expanded access to advanced science, technology, law, and management, as well as pressure from the international community.

Notes

An earlier version of this chapter was presented at the International Conference on "China's Environment: Meeting Local and Global Challenges," Portland State University International Studies Program and Northwest Regional China Council, Portland, Oregon, May 7–8, 1992.

1. NEPA is the lead agency in most areas of environmental policy. There are exceptions, however. In particular, the State Oceanographic Administration is the lead agency for marine environmental protection, the National Nuclear Safety Administration has principal responsibility for the regulation of radiation, the Ministry of Forestry

manages most nature preserves and is responsible principally for forest management, the Ministry of Agriculture has principal responsibility for fisheries management, and the Ministry of Water Resources is the lead agency for water resources management.

2. Premier Li Peng, while still a vice-premier, became the first chairman of the SCEP. Following Li's elevation to premier, State Councilor Song Jian, chairman of the SSTC, concurrently became chairman of the SCEP.

3. These and other statutes are translated in Ross and Silk (1987), *China Laws for Foreign Business*, and/or Lu (1995).

4. For translations of some of the more important regulations, see the sources cited in Ross and Silk (1987).

5. Effluent charges are discussed in Ross et al. (1990). For further treatment, see World Bank (1992).

6. Residential and industrial areas are in particularly close proximity because each unit (*danwei*) generally has been responsible for providing housing and other services for its members. This feature of social organization, coupled with an absence of zoning laws that allowed factories to locate upstream and/or upwind of population centers, resulted in large numbers of people living very close to major pollution sources. The social welfare role of *danwei* is diminishing as economic goods and services become more widely available on the market and as profit-oriented economic entities seek to shed such burdens.

7. See also article 26 of the EPL; *Environmental Impact Statement Management Methods* (1989).

8. The PRC actively solicits foreign aid for environmental protection. In 1992, the China Council for International Cooperation on Environment and Development (CCICED) was established for this purpose. See *Seeking Foreign Aid for Environment Issue, 1992*.

9. See then Vice-Premier Li Peng's statement at the Second National Environmental Protection Work Conference in 1984, "Protecting the Environment Is a Major Task Facing China," translated in Ross and Silk (1987), 35–43.

References

Barber, M., and G. Ryder, eds. 1993. *Damming the Three Gorges: What Dam-Builders Don't Want You to Know*. 2nd ed. Toronto: Probe International.

Bernstein, R. 1982. *From the Center of the Earth*. Boston: Little, Brown and Company.

Brauchli, M. P. 1993. "China's Hinterland Seeks Coast's Progress." *Wall Street Journal*, 3 November, A8.

"The Bulletin of Main Pollution Source Condition Investigation of the National Small Town Industry 1991." 1992. *Environmental Protection* 2: 5 (in Chinese).

Chandra, R. 1994. "China Environment: Getting Rich Without Messing Up Planet." *Inter Press Service*, 24 March.

China Environmental Yearbook Editorial Committee, ed. 1992. *China Environmental Yearbook 1992* (in Chinese). Beijing: China Environmental Science Publishing House.

China Laws for Foreign Business. 1985. North Ryde, N.S.W.: CCH Australia, Ltd.

"China urges harsh penalties for polluters." 1994. *Reuters*, 6 April.

Cook, J. W., D. M. Lampton, K. F. F. Quigley, P. Riggs, W. J. Van Ness, Jr., M. J. Vondracek, and P. D. Wright. 1994. *The Rise of Nongovernmental Organizations in China: Implications for Americans.* New York: National Committee on U.S.-China Relations, Inc., Policy Series No. 8.

"Economists Want to See More Bankruptcies." *Beijing Review* 34 (34): 9.

Fearnside, P. M. 1993. The Canadian Feasibility Study of the Three Gorges Dam Proposed for China's Yangzi River: The Impact Assessment Profession's Dirtiest Laundry. Presented at the 13th Annual Meeting of the International Association for Impact Assessment, Shanghai, China, 11–13 June.

Gazette of the State Council of the People's Republic of China. 1991.

He, B. 1991. *China on the Edge: The Crisis of Ecology and Development.* San Francisco: China Books and Periodicals, Inc.

Hou, W. 1990. "The Environmental Crisis in China and the Case for Environmental History Studies." *Environmental History Review* 14: 151–58.

Jin, Ni, and Wang Guoning. 1994. "Relaunch for Committee on Environment." *China Environment News*, April, 2.

Kahn, J. 1996. "China's 'Greens' Win Rare Battle on River." *Wall Street Journal*, 2 August, A8.

Li, Jinchang, F. Kong, N. He, and L. Ross. 1988. "Price and Policy: The Keys to Revamping China's Forestry Resources." In *Public Policies and the Misuse of Forest Resources*, ed. R. Repetto, and M. Gillis, 205–45. Cambridge: Cambridge University Press.

Lieberthal, K., and M. Oksenberg. 1990. *Policy Making in China: Leaders, Structures and Processes.* Princeton: Princeton University Press.

Liu, Y. 1995. "Plants to Clean Up or Close on Huaihe." *China Daily*, 18 April, 2.

Lu, R. 1995. *Handbook of Regulations on Environmental Protection in China.* Washington: Resources for the Future.

McGregor, J. 1992. "Dam Vote, Rebuke of Li Reveal Defiant Legislature." *Asian Wall Street Journal Weekly*, 13 April, 2.

Ministerial Conference of Developing Countries on Environment and Development. 1991. *Beijing Ministerial Declaration on Environment and Development.* Beijing: State Science and Technology Commission.

National Conditions Investigation Group Under the Chinese Academy of Sciences. 1992. *Survival and Development: A Study of China's Long-Term Development.* Beijing: Science Press.

National Report of the People's Republic of China on Environment and Development. 1992. Beijing: China Environmental Science Press.

Richardson, S. D. 1966. *Forestry in Communist China.* Baltimore: Johns Hopkins Press.

———. 1990. *Forests and Forestry in China: Changing Patterns of Resource Development.* Washington, D.C.: Island Press.

Ross, L. 1990. "The Changing Profile of Dispute Resolution in Rural China: The Case of Zouping County, Shandong." *Stanford Journal of International Law* 26(1): 15–66.

———. 1994. "The Next Wave of Environmental Legislation." *China Business Review* 21(4): 30–33.

Ross, L., and M. A. Silk. 1986. "Post-Mao China and Environmental Protection: The Effects of Legal and Politico-Economic Reform." *UCLA Pacific Basin Law Review* 4: 63–89.

———. 1987. *Environmental Law and Policy in the People's Republic of China.* Westport, Conn.: Greenwood Press.

Ross, L., W. Cheng, M. A. Silk, and Y. Wang. 1990. "Recent Developments in Environmental Law and Policy." *China Business Review* 17(4): 38–43.

"Seeking Foreign Aid for Environment Issue." 1992. *Beijing Review* 35(18):10–12.

Shen, L., and C. Zhou. 1992. *Overview of Economic Development, Present Situation and Prospects for Environmental Protection and Energy Conservation in China.* Paper presented at the U.S.-China Conference on Energy, Environment, and Market Mechanisms. Cited in William U. Chandler, "An energy profile of China." In *Energy Needs of the People's Republic of China*, Sen. Comm. on Energy and Natural Resources, S. Hrg. 103–38, 11 March 1993.

Smil, V. 1984. *The Bad Earth: Environmental Degradation in China.* Armonk, N.Y.: M. E. Sharpe, Inc.

———. 1993. *China's Environmental Crisis: An Inquiry into the Limits of National Development.* Armonk, N.Y.: M. E. Sharpe, Inc.

Smith, C. S. 1995. "China Dam Project Is Hard Sell Abroad." *Wall Street Journal*, 3 May, A10.

State Statistical Bureau, ed. 1989. *China Statistics Yearbook 1989* (Chinese language ed.). Beijing: China Statistics Publishing House.

———. 1992. *China Statistics Yearbook 1992* (Chinese language ed.). Beijing: China Statistics Publishing House.

Tyler, P. 1994a. "Nature and Economic Boom Devouring China's Farmland." *New York Times*, 27 March, 1, 8.

———. 1994b. "China Migrants: Economic Engine, Social Burden." *New York Times*, 28 June, A3.

Walker, T. 1994a. "China Development Bank Focuses on Infrastructure." *Financial Times*, 24 June, 20.

———. 1994b. "China Plans to Build Up Large-Scale Car Industry by 2010." *Financial Times*, 5 July, 1.

Wang, K. 1995. "Projects in Beijing Should Toe the Line." *China Daily*, 21 January, 4.

World Bank. 1992. *China Environmental Strategy Paper*. Washington, D.C.: World Bank, Report No. 9669-CHA.

World Bank, United Nations Development Programme, National Environmental Protection Agency, and State Planning Commission. 1995. *Issues and Options in China's Greenhouse Gas Emissions Control*.

Wu, Y. 1994. "Coal Prices to Be Set by Market." *China Daily*, 28 November, 8.

WuDunn, S. 1992. "Difficult Algebra for China: Coal = Growth = Pollution." *New York Times*, 25 May, 1.

Zhang, K. 1992. "Intensify Statistical Reforms, Enhance the Functions of the Entire System." In *China Environmental Yearbook 1992*, 99–103.

Zhu, B. 1994. "State Plans to Clean Up Big River in Three Years." *China Daily* 10 November, 1.

3

Environmental Policy and Politics in Indonesia

Robert Cribb

Introduction

Indonesia is a tropical archipelago of over seventeen thousand islands stretched between the Asian and Australian mainlands. With a population of about 190 million, it is the fourth most populous country in the world and the largest in Southeast Asia. During the three and a half centuries following 1600, the Dutch colonized the region, spreading their control gradually from isolated forts and enclaves to create a sprawling colonial empire. Just as the Indonesian national identity developed within the Dutch colonial framework, so did the economic and social character of the country. The Dutch generally discouraged industrial development, and their rule drained the country of capital, so that Indonesia declared independence in 1945 with no more than a rudimentary industrial sector. The country's economy was heavily dependent instead on agriculture and on the export of raw materials, notably the products of plantations and mining. Colonial policies—from health and education to taxation—tended, though not altogether intentionally, to encourage rapid population growth. The environmental issues that faced Indonesia during the first decades after independence, therefore, were primarily a consequence of population pressures.

From the late 1960s, after the overthrow of President Sukarno's left-leaning government and the installation of the so-called New Order, a military-dominated government under President Suharto, Indonesia embarked on a program of rapid, Western-style economic development, involving heavy investment in infrastructure, stimulation of industrial development, extensive reforms in agriculture (generally known as the "Green Revolution"), and an opening of the economy to foreign trade and investment. Indonesia's rate of population increase now has slowed dramatically, and the direct pressure of human habitation on the environment has perhaps lessened; but indus-trialization, agricultural development, and the need for foreign exchange to finance these programs have led to the emergence of major new environmental issues. As Indonesia approaches the twenty-first century, one of the most pressing questions is whether continued economic growth can be reconciled with environmental protection.

Environmental Issues

Environmental issues are seldom quarantined, either from each other or from broader social and political issues, but for Indonesia it can be said that these issues have been clustered in three fairly distinct areas: protection of forests, management of agriculture, and control of pollution. In the last decade, fisheries and nuclear power have emerged as new important issues.

Indonesia (see map 3.1) is located in the moist tropics, and, with the exception of the drier islands of Nusatenggara (the Lesser Sundas) that lie in Australia's rain shadow, much of the country was covered with rich tropical rainforest before human settlement. The clearing of forests was an inevitable part of the spread of human habitation in the archipelago. In Java (see map 3.2) and other regions where recent volcanic activity had produced deep, rich top soils, human settlement tended to take the form of permanent hamlets and villages; in Kalimantan (Borneo) and other regions where the rainforest grew on a much thinner layer of humus above leached and impoverished subsoils, the characteristic form of agriculture was swidden, or slash-and-burn, under which areas of forest were cleared, cultivated for a few years, and then abandoned to allow regeneration of the forest and rejuvenation of the soil. The clearing of forests other than for agriculture is a much more recent phenomenon. After the spread of Islam across Java from the fourteenth century, there is some evidence of deliberate clearing of forest to provide grassland for wild deer, hunted by Javanese lords in place of wild pig, that were now prohibited by Islam. Because records are sparse, it is virtually impossible to chart the course of deforestation on Java and Sumatra, but indirect evidence exists in the record of siltation along the coast; with the removal of forest cover, loose volcanic soils easily eroded and washed seaward. The Sumatran city of Palembang, capital of the empire of Srivijaya from the seventh to the eleventh centuries and located then on or close to the coast, is now sixty kilometers from the sea; the Javanese trading city of Demak, coastal in the sixteenth century, is now several kilometers inland. Nonetheless, until the late eighteenth century, uncleared forest land was sufficiently abundant that the contest over land was not a significant element in indigenous politics.

However, forests were also a resource in their own right. Since Indonesia first entered the world economy as an exporter of spices and forest products soon after the beginning of the Christian era, competition over scarce and

MAP 3.1

National Parks and Nature Reserves in Indonesia

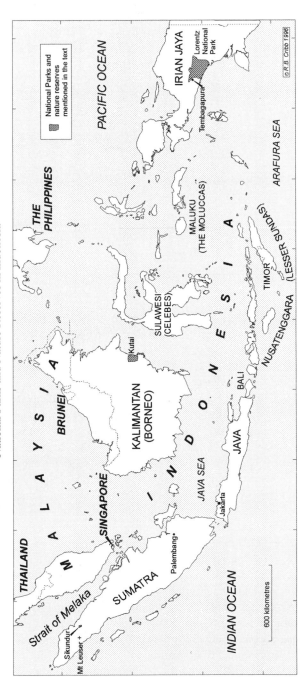

Source: Robert Cribb, 1996.

MAP 3.2

Java, Indonesia

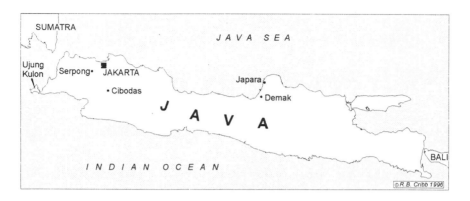

Source: Robert Cribb, 1996.

valuable natural resources has been a feature of politics in the region. The camphor gatherers of northern Sumatra developed a secret language to keep their discussions confidential in the presence of outsiders; collectors of poison from the *upas* tree (*Antiaris toxicaria*) produced fantastic legends about the tree's fatal effect on all who approached it. Sandalwood from Timor was an important trade item from early times, and control of production forests was an important source of wealth. From about the fifteenth century comes the first evidence of Javanese rulers managing the island's teak forests for timber production. During the seventeenth century, the Dutch raided communities throughout Maluku (the Moluccas) to uproot clove and nutmeg trees growing outside their areas of control. The Dutch also exercised a tight control over the teak forests of Java, whose production was an important source of colonial income. However, that control did not extend to managing the forests for sustainable production, and even in the seventeenth century there were signs of serious forest degradation in areas such as Japara.

By early in the nineteenth century, therefore, when population growth on Java had made land—including forest land—a scarce resource, it was inevitable that hesitant Dutch initiatives to protect the remaining forests on broader environmental grounds were widely seen by Indonesians as continuing the old tradition of restricting access to natural resources by some groups in order to enable access by others. The Dutch were concerned initially with the hydrological consequences of deforestation. With much of the population and many of the largest cities located on flood plains, the risk of human and material loss from flooding during the wet season increased as the upland forest cover was diminished. By early in the twentieth century, the colonial authorities also were concerned that the rapid siltation of irrigation canals would hinder their efforts to increase food production. In addition, the Dutch began to be concerned about more specific conservation issues. The extensive hunting of birds of paradise and crowned pigeons in West New Guinea for the European fashion industry raised the prospect that part of the archipelago's distinctive wildlife might be lost to extinction. Similar fears emerged over rhinoceros, over *Rafflesia* (a parasitic plant producing the largest of all flowers), and over the giant monitors or "dragons" of the island of Komodo. These fears prompted the Dutch both to restrict trade in wild animals and wild animal products and to set aside areas of the colony as nature reserves. In the early twentieth century, too, a growing awareness of the biogeographical importance of Indonesia led to the creation of scientific reservations intended to preserve whole ecosystems, rather than just selected species. The Dutch created a patchwork of mostly small reserves across the archipelago, although they put few resources into actually managing these reserves (Cribb 1988; Peluso 1992; Boomgaard 1993).

This limited protection for forests was largely abandoned during Japanese occupation from 1942 to 1945, when large areas of forest on Java and other islands were cleared for new agricultural projects and to provide fuel. After the struggle for independence ended in 1950, too, little protection was given to forests. The country had been impoverished by nearly a decade of occupation and war, and protection of forests seemed to most policy makers to be an expensive luxury. The inclination to allow land clearance was strengthened by a widespread belief that the end of colonialism should mean the end of colonial restrictions, especially restrictions that seemed to bar Indonesians from improving their welfare by extending agriculture. A growing international trade in endangered species added a further threat to the survival of some wildlife. The pressure on forests in the islands outside Java also grew with the revival of a colonial-era program to resettle people from densely populated Java and Bali to the sparsely populated regions of Sumatra, Kalimantan, and Sulawesi (Celebes). Known as "transmigration," this program has resulted in the transfer of nearly 2 million people to the outer islands. Settlers were provided with land, accommodation, tools, and other basic facilities and were expected to turn jungle into agricultural settlements. Although some of the transmigrant settlements were highly successful, many suffered from poor planning and administration. Not only were the facilities and support provided to the settlers often inadequate, but the land chosen for settlement was sometimes unsuitable. The shallow rainforest topsoil often was exhausted within a few years, leaving barren, leached subsoil in which little could be grown. The transmigration program also put pressure on forests surrounding the settlement areas, because struggling settlers often turned to hunting and collection of forest products to eke out an existence (Otten 1986; *Ecologist* 1986).

From 1967, the pressure on forests on the islands outside Java intensified. In order to finance the military government's massive program of economic reconstruction, vast areas of lowland tropical rainforest, especially in Sumatra and Kalimantan, were allocated to logging concessions. These were then harvested by foreign firms, initially American and Japanese, later South Korean, through joint ventures with Indonesians. These joint ventures formed the basis for dozens of fortunes amongst members of the military and bureaucratic elite. During the early 1970s, timber came second only to oil as a source of foreign exchange for Indonesia. The logging was conducted under regulations that protected upland forests (areas above five hundred miles) and that provided for selective logging, replanting, and harvest on a thirty-five-year cycle, but in practice the loggers moved in with virtually no supervision, clear-felling their concessions and often straying beyond them—consciously or otherwise—into protected areas. During these years, the Indonesian navy ran a private logging operation in the heart of the South Sumatra reserve, while at the behest of loggers, the government removed some of the richest timber areas from the Kutai reserve in Kalimantan, allowed them to be logged, and then restored them to the reserve. Although the government paid lip service to the need for forest preservation, the immediate demand for foreign exchange was so great that practical measures to limit clearing were ignored.

At about this time, a second environmental issue began to emerge as an unexpected consequence of one of the New Order's more successful policies. Since independence, Indonesia's food production gradually had been slipping behind its rate of population growth. By the mid-1960s, Indonesia had become the world's largest importer of rice and faced severe famines in a number of regions. Determined to end this drain on foreign exchange and to raise the standard of living for the Indonesian people, the New Order embarked on an ambitious program of agricultural development. This program of intensification, under the Indonesian rubric of Bimbingan Massal (BIMAS, "Mass Guidance"), involved the introduction of new high-yielding varieties of rice, the application of chemical pesticides and fertilizers, and the adoption of new agricultural techniques, especially those involving mechanization (Booth 1988, ch. 5). Although the results of the program were spectacular, eventually even allowing Indonesia to begin exporting rice on a modest scale, a number of serious environmental consequences appeared. Pesticides killed the fish that once had been grown in the flooded rice fields, so that peasants' access to animal protein diminished. They also severely reduced by poisoning the population of wild birds, spiders, and benevolent insects that previously had helped to keep insect pests at bay. Because adequate instruction in the use of insecticides was not always given, too, cases of human poisoning began to appear. Fertilizers, particularly the heavy use of triple superphosphate (TSP) in rice-growing areas of Java and Bali, led to the clogging of streams and irrigation channels with algae and other water plants. The growth pattern of the new fast-ripening varieties of rice, moreover, meant that the life cycle of insect predators was no longer broken by the annual harvest and fallow period. Planthoppers called *"wereng"* swarmed in huge numbers, especially on Java, consuming the leaves of rice plants and transmitting a viral disease that blighted the crop. Moreover, the BIMAS program's dependence on new, specially developed rice varieties led to the neglect and in some cases the disappearance of much older local varieties that sometimes were especially suited to local conditions and sometimes preferred by consumers for their superior taste. In recent years, this loss of varieties has been slowed by the development of a market for traditional rices as a gourmet food item, but the overall genetic diversity of Indonesia's rice stock has been diminished.

To add to these difficulties, during the 1970s the early phases of industrialization began to present Indonesia with a significant pollution problem. Indonesia's industrial development was based initially on cheap labor and on short-cuts in safety and pollution regulation. Industrial firms from dyeing works to cement factories were able to pour effluent into the rivers, the groundwater, the seas, and the air with no effective legal restriction. The consequences of unrestricted pollution have included an outbreak of minamata disease (mercury poisoning) in a fishing community in Jakarta Bay, extensive damage to estuarine fisheries in Kalimantan as a result of effluent from plymills and gold mines, and widespread respiratory disease in the area south of Jakarta caused by emissions from local cement factories. As in the case of logging, environmental protection appeared to be a luxury that Indonesia could not afford if it were to modernize rapidly (Cribb 1990).

Politics of Environmental Issues

Indonesia is a unitary state under a constitution that concentrates power in the hands of the president. The president appoints the cabinet, as well as the provincial governors, and is empowered to issue a wide range of presidential instructions and government regulations that do not need the legislative authority of the parliament. In Indonesian political practice, laws passed by Parliament are usually rather general statements of principles and requirements and seldom contain regulatory machinery; this is left to the president and to the government departments. The president's powers of patronage give him enormous informal influence alongside his extensive official authority. Parliamentary elections are held every five years, but the role of the People's Representative Assembly is largely confined to reviewing and passing legislation presented by the executive government. The dominant party in parliament, Golkar, is very much the party of the government, acting as an electoral vehicle and as a framework for recruiting political support for the government, but largely lacking an independent identity or ideology. For the most part, therefore, government policy on the environment, and on other matters, is formulated within the executive branch of government.

The process of policy formulation within the Indonesian government is still poorly understood, for few observers have been able to show in detail the process by which policy is created (for a rare detailed study of the policy process, see MacIntyre 1991). Although President Suharto takes a close interest in the detail of government policy and strongly influences many policy decisions, specific elements of government policy evidently are often hammered out in negotiation and competition between different sections of the bureaucracy with differing views on the national interest, the various interests of the ruling elite, and the broad political acceptability of rival policies. The large government departments—industry, agriculture, forestry, finance, and so on—exercise a major role, but their power is tempered by other government institutions, including the security services, nondepartmental planning bodies such as the State Planning Authority BAPPENAS, semi-independent think tanks, and nondepartmental ministries. The latter are ministries of state that have no executive authority in any field of government but that have the task of seeing that a particular issue is properly taken account of in all government decision making.

One of the most important bureaucratic battlegrounds has been the Ministry of Forestry, where the profile of the national parks and conservation division has risen gradually over the years. Forestry was once a part of the Agriculture Ministry, and forest management was seen purely in terms of harvesting a national resource. Nature conservation was the responsibility of the director of the botanical gardens at Bogor, near Jakarta, and effective protection of the reserves inherited from the Dutch was limited to the nearby montane jungle of Cibodas and outstanding areas of Ujung Kulon on Java's southwestern tip and Mount Leuser in north Sumatra, where funds for patrol and protection came largely from outside bodies such as the World Wildlife Fund. When forestry became a separate ministry and took over responsibility for conservation, the section remained peripheral to the department's interests; the 1974 through 1979 Five-Year Plan budgeted Rp120 million (then about U.S. $300,000) a year for conservation staff and nothing at all for expenses. During the 1980s, however, the political decision to create a major system of national parks, together with the emergence of younger foresters with overseas training that had included a conservation element, dramatically raised the profile of conservation, and Perlindungan Hutan dan Pelestarian Alam (Forest Protection and Nature Preservation) is now a full directorate general within the department, presiding over a large and adequately, though not generously, funded bureacuracy, including its own seconded conservation police who patrol the perimeter of national parks against poaching and illegal clearing.

The most important nondepartmental ministry is that of the environment. For two decades, the environment was paired with population affairs in a ministry headed by Emil Salim, an American-trained economist and one of the group of policy makers, often referred to as the "Technocrats," who largely guided the Indonesian economy during its extraordinary recovery in the 1970s and 1980s. Separated from population affairs in 1993, the Environment Ministry is now headed by Sarwono Kusumaatmadja, a former secretary general of the government party Golkar. The link with population affairs reflected the belief that rapidly growing population was the greatest threat to the Indonesian environment, and the ministry achieved its greatest success in the sustained implemetation of a nationwide family planning program that has lowered birth rates in many regions dramatically. Despite the impressive political credentials of both ministers, the ministry has been rather less successful in achieving a central role in environmental policy making. Although Emil Salim registered a number of important victories, such as saving the unique lowland rainforest at Sikundur in north Sumatra from logging and protecting a rare species of bat in Java whose habitat was threatened by limestone mining, he never was able to win for the ministry a routine powerful role in Indonesia's complex planning process. In consequence, the ministry has put its greatest efforts into shaping the way in which environmental issues are discussed. In particular, it has endeavored to influence the next generation of Indonesian policy makers by persuading the educational authorities to insert an environmental element in much of the national curriculum.

Each of these institutions brings to policy making its own ideological and technical assumptions, but these considerations also are shaped by broader policy disagreements within the cabinet. The Technocrats, who have dominated policy making since 1967, favored a development model which includes import substitution, relative openness to Western and Japanese investment and an emphasis on exploiting Indonesia's areas of comparative advantage in international trade. This approach has been challenged, however, especially in recent years, by advocates of greater economic nationalism. Although neither approach was more concerned with environmental issues in principle, in the present context the economic nationalists, sometimes called the "Technologists" or "Engineers" because many of their leading figures have engineering degrees, have been more inclined than the Technocrats to advocate development at all costs, including environmental damage if necessary. This group, for instance, strongly advocates developing substantial nuclear power capacity in Java. In the past, President Suharto has been adept at balancing the demands and interests of different factions within his cabinets, but the 1993 cabinet lineup was seen widely as increasing the power of the Engineers, led by Technology Minister B. J. Habibie, at the expense of the Technocrats, and this may diminish the influence of environmentalist advocates in government, at least in the short term.

Also important in government policy are the personal interests of regime members. Since the establishment of the New Order, individuals in and close to the government have used their positions for personal advantage. In some cases this has taken the form of outright corruption, but more often official positions have been used to obtain inside information and to acquire permits, government contracts, and the like. The profits available in a rapidly reconstructing economy were thus channeled into the families of those who made the key economic decisions. This state of affairs has given the Indonesian administrative elite a strong personal stake in the country's continuing economic growth, and this has implications when it comes to proposing measures for environmental protection.

The influence of nongovernmental forces on decision making is also difficult to chart. On a few issues, especially those related to the role of Islam in the state, members of Parliament have been able to influence government policy by sheer force of conviction, despite their generally subordinate role. On no occasion so far have members of Parliament felt strongly enough moved to tackle the government on an environmental issue. The press, too, can play a significant role in bringing issues before the public, though it is subject to varying degrees of political censorship. In general, the press has the freedom to pursue stories potentially damaging to sections of the government only when it has the tacit backing of other sections of the government that wish to see an alternative policy pursued.

The most direct attempts to influence government policy have come from independent social organizations or NGOs, among which environmentalist groups are prominent. During Emil Salim's term in office, the Indonesian Environmental Forum (WALHI) played a particularly significant role in identifying specific cases where action was needed and mobilizing publicity and support through its extensive network of associated environmental organizations and action groups and through its international connections. WALHI enjoyed excellent relations with Emil Salim and often coordinated its strategies with him to ensure that campaigns focused on achievable targets. On the whole, the Indonesian government views these groups with deep suspicion. During the 1950s and early 1960s, Indonesian political parties, including the Communist party (PKI), mobilized support thoughout society using similar groups. The community became deeply divided, and the resulting social conflict contributed to the massacres of 1965 and 1966 in which perhaps half a million Indonesians on the Left perished.

The present government is both strongly anti-Communist and strongly committed to political calm and stability, and it therefore distrusts popular attempts to influence government policy. Nonetheless, Suharto's long hold on power has been made possible partly by his ability to play the Populist ruler, to anticipate and meet the strongest aspirations and demands of his people. NGOs provide the government with an important means of listening to the public.

This range of influences can be seen in the process by which each of the environmental issues outlined above came onto the political agenda in Indonesia.

In the early 1970s, the Indonesian government did not see commercial logging as an environmental threat. The authorities had inherited from the Dutch an awareness of the hydrological need to preserve upland forests, but believed that the harvesting of lowland forests could be carried out without serious long-term effects and that the forests there would regenerate without the need for close management as long as they were left undisturbed. The government therefore was diligent in driving squatters from forest land in Java and began a long-term program to encourage shifting cultivators in the interior of Kalimantan to move from the uplands to the coastal regions to reduce the potential erosive effects of their swidden (slash-and-burn) agriculture. At the same time, however, the authorities gave virtually no attention to monitoring the consequences of logging operations or to seeing that the loggers obeyed even the meagre regulations that were in force. In retrospect, we can see that these priorities were misconceived. Properly managed, the damage that swidden agriculture causes to rainforest appears to resemble that caused by minor local disturbances such as landslides, fires, and storms. Swidden agriculture is unlikely to cause long-term forest destruction. Extensive logging of lowland forest on the other hand has now been shown to lead to irreparable ecological damage. In the 1970s, however, not only were these conclusions less transparently obvious than today (see, e.g., Manning 1971), but the government had another agenda in pursuing the swiddeners: mobile tribespeople in the interior of a large island close to the border with Malaysia were seen as a security risk, while their apparently simple way of life was seen as primitive and undesirable. The fact that elite interests were served by unrestricted logging, of course, inhibited the government's willingness to look closely at the ecological effects of the industry.

During the 1970s, however, the government moved toward greater forest protection in three ways. First, the Indonesian government began a serious conservation program, involving the setting aside of large areas of relatively untouched country as national parks. In collaboration with the World Wildlife Fund (now the Worldwide Fund for Nature), Indonesian scientists identified areas of major biological significance across the archipelago. By the early 1980s, a total of nineteen national parks had been declared, covering an impressive 11.9 million hectares, just over 6 percent of the country's land area. These measures were accompanied by attention to the conservation division within the Forestry Department as mentioned above. The division's status was upgraded; it received funding more commensurate with its tasks; its personnel were given proper training both within Indonesia and abroad; and older personnel involved in corrupt practices, such as dealing in endangered species or cutting timber from reserves, were gradually eased out of service. The new national parks were planned using the latest techniques, especially the inclusion of maritime zones and provision for buffer zones in which local people were permitted to continue collecting forest products without damaging the integrity of the parks themselves.

This change in policy took place partly because Indonesia's rulers were receptive to the technocratic arguments in favor of the conservation of genetic material and the preservation of unique ecosystems. The long-term destructive effects of clear-felling were now far better known and recognized than they had been a decade earlier. The hope—still largely unfulfilled—of a significant ecotourism market in Indonesia also gave encouragement. Even more important, Salim's environment ministry was able to cast the issue in such a way that conservation and nationalism coincided. Rather than arguing, as some countries have done, that the forests are a national resource to be exploited without reference to the rest of the world, Salim's ministry argued that the global economic order committed a crime against Indonesia by forcing it to destroy its natural heritage. The destruction of forest and wildlife was thus made unpatriotic. The government also responded to a growing environmental awareness amongst the country's new middle class. Larger and more affluent than at any stage in Indonesian history, these middle classes were developing an increasing interest in conservation and were prepared to suggest that Indonesia's level of prosperity now made conservation more than a luxury.

The second major initiative to protect forests came during the 1980s when a ban was gradually placed on the export of untreated logs from Indonesia. This measure was conceived primarily on economic grounds. The economy had diversified to a point where timber exports were no longer crucially important to the regime's survival. Moreover, Indonesia was increasingly aware that tropical forests were a diminishing resource in the region—the forests of the Philippines were largely exhausted, while Thailand had placed a total ban on export of timber to conserve its jungles—and that there was no especial advantage in rapid exploitation. Indonesia's planners also were determined that the country should add value to its exports in order to promote local industrial development. Although the measure was introduced over a number of years, it slowed the rate of forest clearance significantly because of the time and investment needed to install factories and to reshape markets. In mid-1992, the ban was rescinded as part of Indonesia's contribution to global trade liberalization, but heavy export taxes—considered slightly less objectionable under the Uruguay Round—were imposed in its place. No significant increase in the export of untreated logs has taken place.

The third initiative came in the late 1980s during the term of Hasjrul Harahap as forestry minister. For the first time, Indonesian authorities began to give closer attention to the logging practices of timber firms and to cancel the permits of firms that had failed to meet conditions of selective logging or replanting within earlier concessions. Here, too, a combination of nationalism and economic interest was at work. There was a growing feeling that the foreign timber firms that had logged so extensively in the late 1960s and early 1970s had taken advantage of Indonesia in a time of economic weakness and should not be allowed to continue doing so. Awareness of the growing scarcity of tropical timber, however, also played a crucial role.

The environmental problems of the Green Revolution had fewer political ramifications. The question was simply how the damaging effects of pesticide and fertilizer use could be diminished, while at the same time the crop could be protected from the *wereng*. In this case, policy was channeled through the president himself, who in 1986 issued a presidential decree banning the use of fifty-seven varieties of pesticide, phasing out the previous official subsidy on pesticides, and announcing the introduction of a national policy of integrated pest management (IPM). By reducing the use of pesticides, the government hoped to encourage the return of benign predators on the enemies of rice. At the same time, the government promoted measures to break the insect's life cycle by planting other crops after at least the second rice harvest of the year. The program, devised with the assistance of the FAO (United Nations Food and Agriculture Organization), involved extensive consultation with and training of farmers, which ensured that it was comprehensively followed. The policy was strikingly successful. After suffering severe disruption to rice production between 1974 and 1979, and after receiving scientific warnings of the likelihood of similar massive disruption following new *wereng* outbreaks in Java and Sumatra in the mid-1980s, Indonesia has achieved a steady increase in rice production with no major insect problems and with significantly reduced problems of pesticide poisoning. The IPM policy was a case of effective authoritarian government. With President Suharto convinced of the need for swift action and with a straightforward, if demanding, technical solution available, Indonesia was able to implement policy change with striking rapidity (Fox 1991:74–81).

The environmental problems of industrial pollution, by contrast, do not have such a straightforward solution. Industrial pollution was barely recognized as a problem until the late 1970s; there was no significant heritage of colonial concern as there had been over watershed protection. Whereas logging, moreover, is an area of the economy whose overall importance is diminishing, industrial production is Indonesia's hope for the future. Although not necessarily wanting to follow exactly in the footsteps of South Korea, Taiwan, and the other newly industrializing countries of the region, Indonesia's economic ambitions lie clearly in the direction of industrialization.

The first hesitant measures to limit industrial pollution came in 1978 with a directive from the industry minister that industry should "avoid and overcome" pollution. This intention was given legislative force only gradually. In 1982, Parliament passed a basic law on the environment that set out with surprising explicitness that businesses that polluted the environment were responsible to their victims for compensation and to the state for the rehabilitation of the environment. Only in 1986 were the first operating regulations issued to give force to the environment law, and the government then gave firms a long period of grace in which to familiarize themselves with the regulations and to prepare to meet their requirements. For hazardous and toxic wastes, the regulations finally came into force in 1990; for other industries it was 1992. The regulations provide for a complex machinery of procedures. Industrial developers must first conduct a general environmental survey to determine whether the proposed project needs environmental clearance; this decision is made by an expert committee. If the project raises environmental concerns, then the developer must conduct a full environmental impact analysis and must draft an environmental management plan to overcome the predicted hazards. This plan may include the payment of compensation to farming or fishing groups whose livelihood may be affected. The regulations also provide for fines of up to Rp 100 million (U.S. $50,000) or ten years' imprisonment for illegal pollution.

The forces behind pollution control are complex. To begin with, the Indonesian government has become strongly aware of the long-term costs of permitting unrestricted pollution. The scale of the clean-up now begun in Eastern Europe has only reinforced the conviction, at least in some circles, that pollution could hamper the long-term development prospects of the country. In addition, the nationalist view, which objects to the developed world, especially Japan, cleaning up its own environment by placing dirty industries in the third world, has been influential. Indonesia's first significant pollution crisis came with the grounding of a Japanese tanker just south of Singapore in 1975, making it especially alert to the international dimensions of pollution. Pollution also has become a Populist issue. Scattered across the country are dozens of cases of poor farmers or fishermen deprived of their livelihood by the careless location of polluting industries, and Indonesia's NGOs have been active in rebuking the government over its failure to look after the interests of the weak.

Even more important, powerful bureaucratic forces favor tighter environmental regulation as a means of limiting the power of Indonesia's growing private sector. When the New Order took power in 1966, the Indonesian economy was a wasteland, but the combination of foreign aid, developmentalist policies and favors for people in and close to the elite have produced a large and prosperous private sector. The businessman Liem Sioe Liong, for instance, who is close to the president, controls a vast and diverse empire with interests thoughout the region. The New Order, however, inherited a large state sector—banks, insurance firms, plantations, factories—from the Sukarno era, and the bureaucracy retains something of a broadly Socialist distrust for private enterprise, preferring to see economic as well as political initiative reserved to the state. Since the second half of the 1980s, the state sector has been under considerable pressure to deregulate the economy and even to embark on privatization. In the face of these demands, elements of the otherwise conservative bureaucracy have found merit in environmental protection as a means of maintaining state regulation of the economy.

Effectiveness of Environmental Policies

Indonesia's bottle of environmental achievements is half full and half empty. Measured against the mid-1970s, Indonesia has made remarkable and dramatic progress in placing environmental issues on the political agenda and in seeking and adopting solutions to the more pressing environmental problems. Measured against what remains to be solved, Indonesia's performance is less impressive.

The clearing of forest in Indonesia continues at a dramatic rate. Although the number of hectares cleared per year seems to have retreated from the peak of the early 1970s, the proportion of Indonesia's surviving forest that disappears each year does not seem to have changed. In Kalimantan and Sumatra, the clearing of forest has led to severe problems of flooding in the lower reaches of the larger rivers. A large proportion of the once-abundant forests of Java had been cleared before 1970, but pressure has continued on the small forested areas that then survived. There are now almost no substantial stands of primary forest in central Java, and few such areas survive outside national parks in west and east Java. The coastal mangroves on which fisheries depend are being lost to firewood and residential developments, and the Java tiger, which survived until the late 1980s, is now almost certainly extinct. Nor have the authorities established an entirely satisfactory relationship with people living in and around forest areas. Swidden farmers are seldom recognized as having any title to the land they cultivate, and the establishment of buffer zones and attempts at social forestry have not greatly diminished the state's tendency to see itself as the sole proprietor of the forests.

The picture is most promising in the national parks. The existing national park estate covers large, ecologically sustainable areas of great significance.

The Lorentz National Park in Irian Jaya (West New Guinea), for instance, running from mangroves at the coast up to the snow-capped Puncak Jaya has been designated as internationally important under the 1995 World Heritage Convention. In recent years, moreover, parks have taken precedence over other government projects, with logging concessions in Sumatra and transmigration projects in Irian Jaya being canceled in favor of conservation. The National Parks Service is now a relatively well-funded, professional body, with good international connections and a fairly clear set of management plans that should enable the survival of existing parks into the foreseeable future. Even in the parks, though, there are problems. In the more remote regions of the archipelago, parks are not as well protected as they should be. Poaching, both for food and for the international trade in endangered species, remains a problem, as does illegal farming and the collection of valuable forest products such as rattan. The Lorentz National Park contains within its boundaries the massive Freeport copper mine at Tembagapura. On Java and in the more closely settled areas of Sumatra, the pressure from visitors on a small number of popular sites is already causing problems, and these are likely to grow as environmental interest spreads.

The integrated pest management program, by contrast, has been a major success. Rice production has continued to grow, space has been found for other crops, thus adding to nutritional diversity, and the ecosystem of the rice-producing regions has started to return to its original balance. Important problems remain: the program requires continuing careful management of the agricultural cycle, and maintaining the initial style of consultation and coordination between farmers, scientists, and bureaucrats has not been easy. There is evidence, moreover, that the use of pesticides on crops other than rice has grown substantially since the introduction of the IPM program. Significant social concerns are still raised by the intensification of agriculture—the Green Revolution is alleged to have led to the pauperization of women and to the growth of a rural proletariat—but these are beyond the realm of environmental policy, and the IPM program remains a remarkable example of a well-conceived program to achieve ecological balance in agriculture.

The Indonesian government's achievements in pollution control are perhaps hardest to judge, because so little time has elapsed since control measures were implemented. Even before the pollution control regulations came into force, some government officials began a vigorous campaign to enforce compliance within their regions, and it appears that some important reductions in effluent production have been achieved. Officials seem to have been spurred not only by a desire to assert their authority over private enterprise but also by a characteristically bureaucratic drive for impressive results that could be included in annual reports. In many cases, however, the authorities seem to have concentrated on the easy targets, on firms without sponsors among the elite and on industries where pollution control measures can be implemented easily and cheaply. The more difficult cases, such as Liem Sioe Liong's cement factory south of Jakarta, have not yet been tackled. There is evidence, moreover, that business owners close to the government are using the rigid enforcement of environmental regulations as a weapon against less well-connected competitors. In a number of instances, independent firms have been forced out of business by the application of environmental controls, only to find elite-linked firms taking over their licenses and markets and being permitted to operate without regard for the regulations.

Perhaps the most serious environmental threat to Indonesia, however, is one that has so far received little attention. Indonesia's offshore fisheries provide a livelihood to hundreds of thousands of the poorest people in the country; together with inland fisheries and coastal aquaculture, they also are responsible for producing a major part (around 60 percent) of the animal protein intake of the Indonesian population. Dried, salted fish are traded far inland to provide the necessary nutritional complement to agricultural produce (Rice 1991). Indonesia's fisheries, however, face a treble threat from pollution, habitat destruction, and over-fishing. An outbreak of minamata disease caused by mercury poisoning of fish and the destruction of estuarine fisheries in parts of Kalimantan, mentioned above, as well as occasional oil spills in the Strait of Melaka (Malacca), which carries vast quantities of oil from the Middle East to Japan, have received some public attention, but the long-term effects of pollutants washed into the sea from rivers simply has not been investigated properly. The destruction of the mangrove breeding grounds for prawns and fish also has been mentioned, but coral reefs also have been seriously damaged both by mining for limestone and by smothering as a result of sedimentation from runoff. Evidence of over-fishing comes from the disappearance of species from their former habitats and from the fact that Indonesian fishermen appear to be ranging more widely than ever before in the search for catches; Indonesian fishing boats are increasingly common along the northern coast of Australia, and the Balinese sea turtle fishermen, who once supplied the market with catches from the seas close to Bali, now travel over a thousand kilometers to find a harvest.

Because the population dynamics of marine organisms are still imperfectly understood, the consequences of these ecological changes have been difficult to follow. The scientific uncertainty that made it possible to ignore warnings about the consequences of clear-felling lowland rainforest in the late 1960s now hampers acceptance of the need for action on fisheries. For instance, observers often have been content to measure stable overall catches as a sign of sustainability in marine fisheries and not to take account of changes in the composition of catches or the fact that fishermen are ranging more widely in search of catches, although both phenomena strongly indicate overfishing. Careful examination of colonial records, in fact, shows changes in the abundance of fish species as a result of overfishing in the Strait of Melaka during the early twentieth century (Butcher n.d.), and it has been shown that, even earlier, fishing for *trepang* (also known as *bêche-de-mer* or sea cucumber) for the Chinese market led to the virtual disappearance of edible species from Indonesian waters between the fifteenth and the eighteenth centuries (Macknight 1976). Evidence from elsewhere suggests that the pattern of transferring fishing operations to new species and new fishing grounds may precede a catastrophic collapse of fish stocks as a consequence of removing not one but many species from the ecosystem.

Until now, the Indonesian government has treated fishing primarily as a political issue of regulating access to a resource. In 1980, the government banned trawling in western Indonesia, and in 1983 the ban was extended to other regions, except the Arafura Sea, mainly because of clashes between large mechanized trawlers and small-scale traditional or artisanal fishermen. In doing so, Indonesia chose to preserve, at least for the time being, the livelihood of fishing communities that otherwise would have no source of income, though reports suggest that the regulations are insufficiently policed (Evicted 1990); immediately to the south, Australia has followed a similar policy, allowing some access to traditional Indonesian fishermen within the Australian Fishing Zone, which runs two hundred miles off the coast (Campbell and Wilson 1992). In both countries, however, this policy faces serious problems in its insistence that fishermen preserve traditional and often unsafe fishing practices and in the difficulty of identifying both "traditional" fishermen and the regions they have traditionally fished (Campbell and Wilson 1992; Pannell 1993). Neither technocratic arguments nor nationalist considerations nor the political and economic interests of the ruling elite have yet been able to generate a coherent environmental policy for Indonesian fisheries.

The issue of nuclear power, too, has entered the political agenda. Indonesia began preparing for a nuclear power capability in the 1970s, and in 1987 a thirty-megawatt nuclear reactor began generating power at Serpong, west of Jakarta. The government now plans to have twelve reactors supplying power to the electricity grid by the year 2015. The nuclear program is driven by a number of considerations. Advocates of nuclear power argue that Indonesia's substantial reserves of coal, oil, and gas represent a resource that will be increasingly valuable for purposes other than power generation. In order to be able to conserve that resource while still supplying the growing electricity needs of a modernizing society, Indonesia needs, they say, to begin now the long process of developing its nuclear energy capacity, and those advocates promise that nuclear power stations eventually will become a safe and reliable source of cheap and abundant energy. The adoption of nuclear energy is strongly supported in the upper levels of government by the so-called

Engineers, who believe Indonesia should independently develop a capacity in high technology. Opponents of nuclear energy have argued in response that the development and recurring costs of nuclear power do not make it economically attractive and that it brings unacceptable hazards, especially in a volcanic region such as Java. This debate, of course, is a familiar one in the Western world, and both sides have made extensive use of data derived from abroad in making their respective cases. As this book goes to press, the political ascendancy of the Engineers seems to be working in favor of accelerating the nuclear program, but the long development and construction periods involved mean that the program will be chronically vulnerable to delay (Belcher 1988; Serpong 1988; Anung and Karyadi 1992).

Conclusion

As a newly industrializing country, Indonesia shares in the environmental problems of both the first and the third worlds. To the long-standing problems associated with rapid population growth have been added a range of technologically complex and economically difficult issues arising out of accelerated modernization. The protection of forests and other natural ecosystems from population pressure, the management of new agricultural techniques, and the control of pollution have presented Indonesia with the need to make politically contentious and economically complicated decisions. In making these decisions, however, Indonesia has been relatively fortunate in a number of respects. First, the processes of industrialization and agricultural intensification that have created enormous problems elsewhere in the world had barely begun in Indonesia before the late 1960s. By this time, of course, much had been lost in Indonesia as a result of population growth, but the fact that careless development and modernization could lead to irreversible environmental damage had been widely accepted, even if the extent of the damage and the implications of attempting to prevent it had not been fully recognized. In developing a range of policies, from conservation and forest management to pollution control, Indonesia had the advantage of being able to adapt knowledge and techniques from elsewhere to its own circumstances. By contrast, in areas where the international and scientific consensus is unclear, as in fisheries, Indonesia's policy performance has been unimpressive.

Second, Indonesia has been cushioned from the need to develop at all costs by its abundant oil revenues, which have been obtained at relatively little environmental cost. In its exploitation of the forests during the 1970s and 1980s, the government often was predatory and reckless; in its handling of pollution, the government has been dilatory and careless; but oil revenues brought Indonesia to a level of economic development where the environmental costs of ill-conceived policy could at least receive a hearing. Even though it appears that Indonesia will go ahead with its program to develop nuclear power, the maturity of the debate over the issue is an encouraging sign of Indonesia's capacity to evaluate the costs and benefits of policies that may damage the environment.

And third, Indonesia's political system has been relatively conducive to long-term environmental planning. Because the government does not expect to be removed at election time or by civil unrest, it can prepare for the long haul. Current planning takes place within the broad framework of a twenty-five-year development program. The long-term consequences of environmental degradation can be considered readily within such a framework. At the same time, although the Suharto government has been ruthless and brutal in suppressing dissent, it claims to aspire to a culture of negotiation and compromise, and within the bureaucracy procedures generally ensure that most points of view are heard. Environmentalist arguments have faced great resistance from time to time, but never the implacable ideological hostility they sometimes meet in the West. The result has been perhaps fewer environmentalist victories but a broader willingness to consider environmental issues.

Environmental policy is a relatively new element on the political agenda in Indonesia. Policy formulation does not follow clear and recognizable paths but rather is negotiated between different sections of the elite, with an eye on technical necessity and feasibility, the economic interests of the elite, and the political needs of the regime. Because little had been achieved by way of environmental protection before the early 1970s, Indonesia has made dramatic progress in environmental protection during the past two decades. With the easiest and most obvious decisions taken, however, the coming decades are likely to see environmental politics becoming a good deal more contentious.

References

Anung, M., and D. B. Karyadi. 1992. "Dependency in the Nuclear Era." *Environesia* 6(4/5):18–20.

Belcher, Martha. 1988. "Nuclear Power: The Indonesian Debate." *Environesia* 2(2):1, 4.

Boomgaard, Peter. 1993. "Protection de la nature en Indonésie pendant la fin de la période coloniale (1889–1949)." *Revue Française d'histoire d'outre-mer* 53(299): 307–44.

Booth, Anne. 1988. *Agricultural Development in Indonesia.* Sydney: Allen & Unwin.

Butcher, John. n.d. "The Salt Farm and the Fishing Industry of Bagan Si Api Api." Unpublished paper.

Campbell, Bruce, and Bu Wilson. 1992. *The Politics of Exclusion: Indonesian Fishing in the Australian Fishing Zone.* Perth: Indian Ocean Centre for Peace Studies.

Cribb, Robert. 1988. *The Politics of Environmental Protection in Indonesia.* Clayton, Vic.: Monash University Centre of Southeast Asian Studies.

————. 1990. "The Politics of Pollution Control in Indonesia." *Asian Survey* 30(12):1123–35.

The Ecologist. 1986. 16(2/3). Special issue on transmigration.

"Evicted from the sea." 1990. *Environesia* 4(1):13–15.

Fox, James J. 1991. "Managing the Ecology of Rice Production in Indonesia." In *Indonesia: Resources, Ecology, and Environment*, ed. Joan Hardjono, 74–81. Singapore: Oxford University Press.

MacIntyre, Andrew. 1991. *Business and Politics in Indonesia.* Sydney: Allen & Unwin.

Macknight, C. C. 1976. *Voyage to Marege.* Melbourne: Melbourne University Press.

Manning, Chris. 1971. "The Timber Boom (with special reference to East Kalimantan)." *Bulletin of Indonesian Economic Studies* 7(3):30–60.

Otten, Mariël. 1986. *Transmigrasi, Myths and Realities: Indonesian Resettlement Policy, 1965–1986.* Copenhagen: International Workshop for Indigenous Affairs.

Pannell, Sandra. 1993. "Mabo and Indonesian Fishing off Australia." *Inside Indonesia* (December):16–18.

Peluso, Nancy L. 1992. *Rich Forests, Poor People: Resource Control and Resistance in Java.* Berkeley: University of California Press.

Rice, Robert C. 1991. "Environmental Degradation, Pollution, and the Exploitation of Indonesia's Fishery Resources." In *Indonesia: Resources, Ecology, and Environment*, ed. Joan Hardjono, 154–76. Singapore: Oxford University Press.

"The Serpong Nuclear Reactor." 1988. *Environesia* 2(2):3, 8.

4

FOREST TALES: POLITICS, POLICY MAKING, AND THE ENVIRONMENT IN THAILAND

JONATHAN RIGG AND PHILIP STOTT

The world does not consist of jewels alone,
Sand and other elements play their part,
All substance, high, middle, low, holds balance,
Its destruction is not caused by one single element.

—Angkhan Kanlayanaphon
(Trans. Manas Chitakasem)

The Rise of Environmentalism in Thailand

A sense of the environment and principles of environmental management have a long history in Thailand and predate by many centuries the modern rise of "environmentalism,"[1] which has its roots in the early part of the twentieth century. In many ways, this modern environmentalism has, until recently, largely ignored more ancient T(h)ai[2] political ecologies, being largely an import from the West or North, adopted primarily by those who went abroad for their education, namely royalty, wealthy middle-class Thais, and formal masters and research students attending overseas universities in North America, Australia, and Europe. Particularly over the last decade, however, attempts have been made to find an intrinsically Thai philosophical and ethical basis for "environmentalism," founded on animism, Buddhism, "myth-making" about the T(h)ai past,[3] traditional human-land relationships, and local (often village-level) environmental issues and concepts. This has not been a concerted movement, and it has involved many different, and often conflicting, political interest groups, from the radical to the mainstream. These range from key figures in the former hunting community to students, short-story writers and novelists, intellectuals, Buddhist thinkers, newspapers such as *The Nation* (see figure 4.1), members of the wider royal family, local villagers, and foreigners living and working in Thailand or visiting and acting from outside the country. In many ways, these have all performed as unwelcome pressure groups on governments and government departments, some of which, such as the Thai Royal Forest Department, have been unable to act effectively in an environmental framework because of patron-client barriers, corruption, lack of political power, and the dearth of properly trained staff.

Thus, although it is true to say that, like many other governments both in the developed and in the developing worlds, the Thai government has recently "discovered" the environment, it has been largely responding to pressure groups and concerns mainly highlighted and articulated by "outsiders." Because of this, it has been rare for army leaders, politicians, and government officials to have played a proactive role in the process, and when they have done so, as with The Green Isarn (Isan Khiaw) project initiated under General Chaovalit Yongchaiyut in August 1987, it has been for obvious and often fairly crass political objectives. Some official documents, most notably the Seventh Five-Year National Economic and Social Development Plan (1992–1996), it is true, now pay clear lip service to concepts such as sustainable development,

FIGURE 4.1

Student Cartoon of the "Biased" Thienchai Committee. Created to deliberate on the Nam Choan proposal, the committee is shown packed with individual groups who would benefit from construction: electricity appliance, cement and machinery salesmen, and logging interests. The animals look in horror.

Source: *The Nation*, "Nam Choan Inquiry: The Environmental Dilemma of the Decade" (Bangkok: The nation, 1988).

the maintenance of the Kingdom's natural resource base, forest protection, soil erosion, and land degradation. However, the main discourse remains outside government, in the publications, music, films, videos, and actions of a set of varied actors, including nongovernmental organizations and seminongovernmental organizations (such as the Thailand Development Research Institute [TDRI]), Buddhist monks, some politicians (such as Chamlong Srimuang, who became a minister but has since resigned [McCargo 1993]), certain elements of the media, students, and groups that evince both left-wing and right-wing tendencies, as well as anarchic, socialist, and Fascist traits. Because extensification and land appropriation remain at the heart of Thai development, the political ecology of access to environmental resources is also everybody's concern.

As indicated previously, however, the new, extragovernmental discourse is seeking to find an expression of environmentalism more rooted in traditional T(h)ai values, although the debate is unfocused both in time and space and frequently is conducted at a somewhat simplistic level (see for example, Supaphan Na Bangchang 1990:286; Stott 1991a). Nevertheless, sustainable human-land and human-water relationships have a long and integral role in T(h)ai history, as with the ancient Tai canal-weir (mu'ang fai) irrigation systems of the northern intermontane basins, and philosophical expositions concerning the relationship between the king and the environment. The latter is perhaps best exemplified in the Traibhumikatha, (the three worlds), one of the fullest treatises on Buddhist cosmology, traditionally thought to have been written by Phya Lithai in Sri Satchanalai around A.D. 1345, but possibly a much later compilation (late eighteenth/nineteenth century) (trans. Reynolds and Reynolds 1982). Similarly, nature has long played an important role in Thai literature, especially in the poetic form known as nirat (travel poems) (e.g., the nirat of Suntho'n Phu from the first reign of the Bangkok period), and it continues as a key discourse in modern forms of Thai literature (cf., Angkhan's 1976 poem that opens this chapter; Manas Chitakasem 1991). All these sources, and many others, are being plundered by environmental elites to find a truly Thai environmental discourse. Similarly, the essentially antistate community culture school of thought (wattanatham chumchon) espoused by intellectuals, such as Prawet Wasi (1931–), Apichart Thongyu (1954–), Bamrung Bunpanya (1945–), and Niphot Thianwihan (1947–) (Chatthip Nartsupha 1991) aims to link Thai characteristics with international concerns and circumstances (both Buddhist and Christian, particularly Roman Catholic). This disparate movement seeks to organize villagers and village communities to resist the power of the state, to bargain with capitalism, to raise village consciousness, and to develop sustainability through concepts such as Buddhist agriculture and agro-forestry societies. Indeed, the wider use of Buddhism to generate environmental discourses is now commonplace in Thailand, if not always entirely convincing (e.g., Chatsumarn Kabilsingh 1987; Seri Phongphit 1988; Shari 1988; Stott 1991a; Taylor 1991). Pedersen (1992:156), for example, writes of Asian religions and environmentalism in general: "They substitute a modern crisis-ridden knowledge about nature for whatever knowledge about nature that was contained in the scriptures. They make up a thing that never was before." This view contrasts markedly with those who argue that Buddhism espouses a "moral ecology" that can offer an alternative middle way to environmentally friendly development (or antidevelopment).

With the reigns of Rama IV and V, however, there was a move to "modernize" the state, which turned attention away from intrinsic T(h)ai values to Western science and bureaucracy, thus laying the foundations for early environmental concerns based on non-Thai discourses and values. This is exemplified by the establishment of the colonial-style Forest Department as part of the Ministry of the Interior in 1896 under H. A. Slade, its first director and a British forester trained at the French Forestry School in Nancy, with later experience in the Imperial Forestry Service in Burma (Myanmar), and by the introduction of Western development advisers, such as J. Homan Van der Heide and Sir Thomas Ward, in the early twentieth century (Brown 1988). These represent the first in a long line of foreign advisers who, by the 1960s, with the American involvement in mainland Southeast Asia, became legion, and from whom grew the first real modern and scientific environmentalist discourse in Thailand. But much of this discourse was temporary, ill-informed, readily ignored, or neglected by government and officials, and little was directed to the realities of Thai political ecology.

Today, within Thai society, the environment is seen in broad terms and is deemed to include all natural and physical environments, including the land, the sea, fresh water, the air, fauna, and flora, but also the cultural and social environments.[4] In many cases, from a Western viewpoint, there appears to be a tendency for a great muddle in this respect (e.g., Pasuk Phongpaichit 1989), but the elite Thai word for nature, *thammachat*, actually embraces all natural phenomena, such as rain, wind, and sun, and even human behavior. It is not surprising, therefore, that the terms *environment* and *environmentalism* mean very different things in different states and cultures, and we must be careful not to impose a purely Western interpretation on the Thai discourse, or more correctly, on the many different T(h)ai discourses. Critiques of environmentalism in Thailand, this one included, often suffer from a need to pigeonhole the Thai experience within a Western framework. Such attempts are always open to the accusation that they have "failed to appreciate" or "take account of" those issues—semantic and otherwise—that are uniquely Thai and that do not easily make the transition to a Western intellectual setting. Nonetheless, this retreat into what might be termed the "tyranny of the unique" can become a catchall for serious shortcomings both at the applied and at the academic levels. For example, it can be argued reasonably that the wide definition of *thammachat* has been accompanied by a willingness to resort to unsubstantiated cause and effect relationships and a failure to offer concrete and realistic policy suggestions.

Because of this wide range of concerns that in the Thai context come under the term *environment*, the following discussion will focus on one key facet of the overall debate, namely forest degradation and management. As will be made clear, Thailand's forests represent a stage on which most of the current dramas in Thailand's so-called environmental crisis are being acted out.[5] Moreover, to the outside world, the destruction of the Thai forests, coupled with the noise and pollution of Bangkok, comprise the essential environmental images of the country. For many, forest decline represents the most tangible evidence of environmental deterioration, and it has become a metaphor for the wider issues. Moreover, tropical forests are high on the agendas of the countries of the North in their concerns about the developing world; their position on the agenda within Thailand, however, varies greatly from discourse to discourse, from political actor to political actor, and from place to place.

Thailand's Forests: A Case Study in Environmental Policy

Forests: From Abundance to Dearth

In common with much of the rest of Southeast Asia, Thailand was, until relatively recently, a land of forests (Stott 1991b). In 1687, French explorer Simon de La Loubère estimated Siam's population to be only 1.9 million; in 1822, the British emissary, John Crawfurd, gave a figure of 2.79 million (Reid 1988:13). By the middle of the nineteenth century, the population had risen to some 5 million, but the land still remained more than 75 percent forested and the civilized world of the T(h)ai *mu'ang* (the state) remained literally encircled by the *pa thuan*, the wild, uncivilized, barbarous forests, full of energy, but not really part of the T(h)ai civilized state (Haas 1964; Stott 1991a; Taylor 1991). In 1688, Nicolas Gervaise (1928) wrote *The Natural and Political History of the Kingdom of Siam*, in which he relates how the king of Golconda, a powerful Shi'a kingdom in the Deccan in south India from 1518 through 1687, boasted to a Siamese visiting his kingdom that "the King of Golconda is a king of men, while your King is only king of the forests and mosquitoes!" (Stott 1978). Thailand's image as a forested realm has a long history. And even as late as 1961, according to official statistics, 53 percent of the country remained under some sort of forest cover, and Thailand continued to be one of the world's largest exporters of tropical timber.

However, over the twenty-five years since 1961, Thailand's forests have been denuded at an unprecedented rate.[6] By 1986, the Royal Forest Department estimated that the kingdom's forest resource had declined by almost half, to 29 percent of land area. Over the same period, the country had shifted from a position of wood surplus to wood deficit and had become a net importer of tropical timber.[7] But even this figure of 29 percent is a significant overestimate. It includes land under plantation crops such as rubber and oil palm and, in some cases, land on which there is not a single tree standing. It is a de jure classification, bearing little relation, in many cases, to whether the land is de facto forested. Most commentators put the actual land area under *relatively* undisturbed forest today as no more than 20 percent, and probably closer to 15 percent, or even less (see for example Stott 1991a:151; Gray, Piprell, and Graham 1991; Hirsch 1987:132). Moreover, the process of forest denudation continues apace (Stott 1990).

Deforestation has occurred across the kingdom (see Table 4.1). But the forces driving the process have taken slightly different forms in each of the regions. In the north and west, where the most valuable trees, including the largest areas of teak, were concentrated, deforestation has been driven by commercial logging. Hill peoples practicing swidden agriculture also constitute a "background" factor in forest loss (but see below), while security concerns on the part of the state also have played a role. In the central region, clearance of land for agriculture, and especially for rice cultivation, has been paramount. This opening up of the central plains occurred largely before World War II (see Sharp and Hanks 1978). Since then, there has been a secondary expansion into dryland crops, especially maize, at the margins of the central plains. In the northeast, it has been the spread of dryland crops such as cassava,

TABLE 4.1

Forest Loss and Agriculture, by Region (1961–1988)*

Region	% land area under forest				% land area under farmholdings			
	1961	1973	1976	1988	1962	1971	1976	1988
Central Plains	53	36	33	24	30	35	43	52
North	69	67	60	47	12	17	22	32
Northeast	42	30	25	14	25	40	46	58
South	42	26	28	21	25	27	30	43
Whole Kingdom	53	43	39	28	22	30	35	46

* The dates for regional forest loss and area under farmholdings do not coincide for the 1960s and 1970s. Variations in how data were collected means that the figures should be used only to indicate general trends. The figures for the western and eastern regions are subsumed within the central plains.

Sources: MOAC (various) and 1962 Agricultural Census.

kenaf (an inferior jute substitute), and maize on to upland unsuited to rice cultivation since the 1960s that has been instrumental in forest loss. The same is true in areas of the eastern region, a center of cassava cultivation. Also in the northeast, the need to deny guerrillas of the Communist party of Thailand (CPT) safe refuge was an important factor during the 1960s and 1970s. Finally, in the southern region, the spread of plantation agriculture and, again, the need to deal with CPT insurgents has been important. The former has, of course, replaced natural forest with an artificial forest ecosystem.

Forest-Associated Legislation

Laws governing some aspects of the exploitation of forests and wildlife can be traced back to the Sukhothai period (1238–1350) and to the inscriptions of King Ramkhamhaeng, possibly dating from 1292.[8] Modern forest legislation dates from the creation of the Forest Department in 1896 under King Chulalongkorn. The first three directors general of the Forest Department were all British; the first Thai was not appointed to the post until 1924, and he was trained in Burma and India. However, it is important to stress that it was not until after World War II that conservation and protection of forests became an issue in Thailand (see Kamon Pragtong and Thomas 1990; Hafner 1990). Before that time, forest legislation was aimed at rationalizing the productive use of forests, drawing initially upon the British experience in Burma (Myanmar) and India.[9] It is also true that like many actions of the Siamese government at the time, forest policy was designed to secure the kingdom and centralize state control over both people and resources.[10] Legislation during this early period included, for example, the Teak Trees Protection Act of 1897 and various laws to control the marking of trees (for felling) and the paying of royalties and other duties on valuable species (Table 4.2). There was no sense of environmental crisis during these early years, whether actual or beckoning. Local customs and national laws were founded on the assumption that the forest resource was sufficiently extensive and population pressure sufficiently low to make legislation aimed at protection/conservation unnecessary. Lohmann (1992:87) has written that "the philosophy of the RFD [was] . . . that the 'tropical forest is a cash crop' under its jurisdiction."; similar sentiments were shared by farmers, hill peoples, and others. The forest was treated largely as a resource to be exploited, not protected, and notions of conservation were largely absent.

This generalized characterization of the past can be disputed on two grounds. First, on the basis that villages *did* have rules of access to, and use of, the forest resource. And second, that—as outlined above—there *did* exist a sense of the environment that predated modern environmentalism. However, as we note, the environment as it was traditionally perceived and managed in

TABLE 4.2

Thailand: Selected Forest-Related Legislation, 1896–1991

Legislation focused upon the rational exploitation of the forest resource

1896:	Royal Forest Department created
1897:	Forest Protection Act
1897:	Teak Trees Protection Act
1913:	Forest Care Act (revised 1936) widens RFD remit to include species in addition to teak in its categorization of "reserved" and "unreserved" trees
1938:	Protection and Reservation of Forests Act (revised 1953 and 1954; repealed 1964)
1941:	Forest Act (revised in 1948, 1951, and 1960)
1947:	Forest Industry Organization (FIO) established by RFD to manage and harvest timber
1956:	FIO reorganized and set up as agency separate from the RFD

Legislation with a growing degree of protection measures

1960:	Forest Act revised to include protection measures
1960:	Wildlife Protection and Reservation Act
1961:	National Parks Act; Khao Yai becomes Thailand's first National Park
1961:	Forest Police and Forest Protection Units formed
1964:	National Forest Reserves Act gazettes certain areas as forest reserves
1965:	First Wildlife Sanctuary gazetted

Environmental protection becomes the dominant theme

1975:	National Environment Board (NEB) becomes first Thai agency with a specific environmental remit
1985:	Development of the National Forest Policy involving all concerned agencies
1988:	Nam Choan Dam project shelved
1989:	Total logging ban introduced following fatal floods in South Thailand
1990:	Thailand signs the Convention on International Trade in Endangered Species (CITES) of flora and fauna
1992:	Enhancement and Conservation of National Environmental Quality Act drafted
1992:	Comprehensive National Environment Act comes into force

Thailand cannot be equated with modern notions of conservation and protection. The forest (*pa*) was a wild and dangerous place to be tamed in the interests of humans. It was not something to be protected and preserved in itself. The same notions are visible in many other cultures: in the Lake District of England before William Wordsworth (1770–1850), who "positively exuded a reverence for nature" (Simmons 1993:102), for example, and in Indonesia where the words for national park—*taman nasional*—imply management and manipulation, not protection.

It is also argued here, and this is likely to be of greater dispute, that in Thailand, communal strategies of resource use had little to do with conservation, or often even with ownership. This is illustrated in contemporary analysis of the Grandstaff and others (1986) of the use of trees in paddy fields in the northeastern region.[11] The study looked at rules of access and use of trees on private land under varying conditions of resource scarcity. In areas where land and forest were abundant, the authors found that "paddy fields not under cropping are open to grazing and other forms of communal use," and "in areas like the Roiet site anyone may cut off or even saw off dead branches from a privately owned tree at any time without permission, including branches three or four inches in diameter" (286). Communal ownership of such resources— even though they occurred on privately owned land—was the norm. However, in areas of land scarcity trees are "preserved for the children" (280), and "even the leaves are private property" (286). In these sites, trees are actively planted and "no communal rights exist for anything on a person's land, including anything from trees and even rice stubble in the fields" (281).[12] This study shows the dynamics and interrelationships between ownership, pressure on resources, and use. It also hints at a past when there were few constraints on use. This is not to imply that village woodlands and forest were an entirely open-access resource. But to equate current rules of ownership and use with the past is to miss the point that there was little *need* for such a tightly defined set of rules. The *mu'ang fai* irrigation systems, perhaps the most famous traditional communal management system in Thailand, were based on a clear requirement for an overarching village control system. They were exceptional, and their presence should not be used to argue that similar management systems were in use in other arenas.

Whether the forest was treated, in practice, as an open-access resource, it is clear that from the 1960s, under the dual effects of rapid population growth and commercialization (see Santhat Sermsri 1989; Hafner 1990; Rigg 1992), allied with a growing environmental awareness among certain groups, legislation began to shift in focus toward the protection of forests and their fauna (see table 4.2). Even so, it was still true that the dominant theme remained the use of forests as an economic resource. It was during these two decades that the latent conflicts between economic development, population growth, and agricultural extensification on the one hand, and environmental protection on the other, began to rise to the surface. While beforehand, Thailand's resource base seemed large enough to absorb such ambiguities and conflicts, the 1960s, 1970s, and 1980s saw land conflicts, landlessness, land degradation, erosion, forest loss, overhunting, and pollution becoming increasingly common and stark realities (see Lohmann 1992; Hirsch 1990c).

By the early 1980s, such ambiguities could no longer be tolerated. Protection, preservation, and conservation have thus come to dominate the political and legislative debate. The Seventh National Five-Year Economic and Social Development Plan (1992–1996) for example made considerable play of environmental issues and endorsed the "polluter pays principle" (NESDB n.d.[b]). This was underscored by the drafting of an environmental "master law" in February 1992, the Enhancement and Conservation of National Environmental Quality Act BE 2535, which was designed to introduce an integrated and powerful set of environmental laws to control all aspects of environmental deterioration, including aspects pertaining to forest management (Jolly 1992:48). In June 1992, the legislation came onto the statute books as part of a wider National Environment Act, a piece of legislation that, at least on paper, is both powerful and progressive (Handley 1992b:40).

The act is groundbreaking in a number of respects. First, it embraces an integrative and interdisciplinary approach to environmental issues. Second, it decentralizes control over the environment to the provincial level, taking some power away from ministries in Bangkok. Third, the act enables funds to be allocated through an environmental fund, thereby allowing it to act independently of other government agencies. And finally, it endorses the role of NGOs in environmental management. Former Prime Minister Chuan Leekpai also created a new Ministry for Science, Technology, and Environment, once again demonstrating his environmental credentials.

Yet, although the National Environmental Quality Act is progressive, the degree to which ministers and ministries can, and do, ignore plans remains an important constraining issue limiting the effectiveness of environmental management. A number of reasons have been put forward to account for this. First, ministries are highly centralized and tend to operate as "kingdoms," answerable only to themselves.[13] Second, corruption and cronyism make the overriding of objectives set out in planning documents relatively common. Third, there is not a commitment to the concept of development planning in many sections of government. And, finally, the speed of change, the necessity to achieve economic progress above all else (and until recently at all costs), and difficulties of planning in a relatively anarchic market economy, make planning documents almost redundant before they leave the printers. As Hardjono (1991:2) has written with respect to the environment in Indonesia: "The pace that the government has been forced to adopt in development undertakings in an effort to keep up with the demands that have arisen . . . has not infrequently resulted in policies whose long-term implications have been overlooked, sometimes unwittingly but too often quite consciously." Nonetheless, barring a return to authoritarian military government, environmental awareness has become a *sine qua non* for politicians and government officials alike.

Forest Policy: Contradiction and Response

This, then, is the broad thrust of forest legislation as it has evolved with the changing resource base over the last century. However, it tells us little about the way in which legislation has been converted into policy and policy into action. In Thailand, the rhetoric and the reality of forest policy throughout the postwar period often have been sharply at odds.

Measures to protect Thailand's forests and/or harness them more effectively in the interests of the state date, essentially, from the 1960s with the 1960 Forest Act, the 1961 National Parks Act, and the 1964 National Forest Reserve Act. The latter allowed land to be classified more easily as forest reserve, and large areas of cultivated land—some under legal tenure—were *de jure* converted. It was at this time that a target of reserving 50 percent of Thailand's land area under forest cover was first declared (Feder et al. 1988). This figure was later reduced to 40 percent and remains enshrined in national development plans despite the diminishing forest resource (e.g., NESDB n.d.[a]: 138). But at the same time as the need to protect forests was becoming more urgent (both for conservation and for exploitation), so farmers' need for land also was becoming more acute. Population growth between 1960 and 1990 averaged 2.5 percent per year, while commercialization was spreading and becoming more pronounced. There was a rapid expansion of cropping—particularly of such upland cash crops as cassava, maize, kenaf, and sugarcane—under a process of agricultural extensification (see Lohmann 1992; Rigg 1987; Hirsch 1990a) (figure 4.2).

By 1985, land classified as forest reserve covered 21.8 million hectares, 42 percent of Thailand's land area (TDRI 1987:81). In 1991, national parks and wildlife sanctuaries accounted for 11 percent or 5.7 million hectares (Gray, Piprell, and Graham 1991).[14] Land under cultivation meanwhile more than doubled from 10.1 million hectares in 1960 to 20.6 million hectares in 1985, the latter figure representing 40 percent of the country's land area (figure 4.2).[15] The latent contradiction between a fast-expanding farmland frontier and the classification of large areas of land as forest reserve quickly became apparent. By the middle 1980s, 20 percent of forest reserve land (nearly 5 million hectares) was under cultivation by about 1 million squatter households (Feder et al. 1988:17), and encroachment from 1961 through 1985 averaged 520,000 hectares per year (TDRI 1987:81). A rather later survey estimates that 12 million people—about one-fifth of Thailand's population—live and farm on protected land (Pravit Rojanaphruk 1992). As a result, a large portion of officially designated forest reserve land has not a single tree standing on it. But despite these trends and the blatant undermining of the RFDs policies, little was done either to reformulate the policies and their targets or to police forest reserve land more assiduously.

FIGURE 4.2

Forest, Farmland, and Population in Thailand

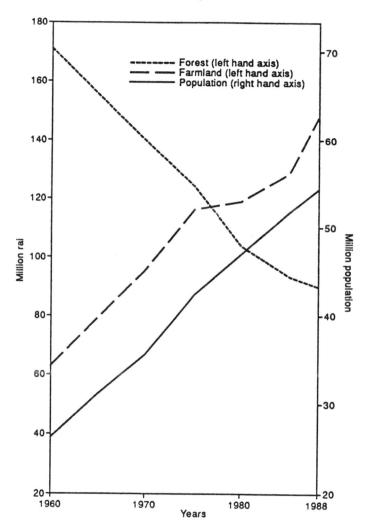

Sources: NSO, *Statistical Handbook of Thailand 1993*, (Bangkok: National Statistical Office, 1993). MOAC, *Agricultural Statistics of Thailand Crop Year 1992/93*, (Bangkok: Center for Agricultural Statistics, ministry for Agriculture and Cooperative). Alpha Research, *Pocket Thailand in Figures in 1994*. (Bangkok: Alpha Research Co., Ltd).

Part of the reason for this apparent lack of concern lay in the need to defeat the Communist party of Thailand (CPT).[16] Loyal farmers were actively encouraged to settle on designated forest reserve land to displace the CPT or deny them safe refuge. *Ban* (village) Teppattana in Buriram province in the northeast region is just such a community (map 4.1). It was established by the army as a "defence volunteer village" on forest reserve land. Sanitsuda Ekachai (1990a:53) quotes *Mae* (mother) Kongsri, a fifty-year-old resident of the village: "We were encouraged to burn down trees, so that the guerrillas could not make use of the forests. . . . [We] were given plots of land to till as well." At the same time as they were encouraging the settlement of forest reserve land, the authorities were reluctant to evict farmers already living on such land, fearing that they would then become willing recruits into the CPT (Lohmann 1992:92). This policy was formalized in 1974 when an amnesty was declared for all squatters on forest reserve land. In 1975, the Forest Village Program was established, along with the National Forest Land Management Division to allot land to farmers living in forest reserves on the basis of 15 *rai* (2.4 hectares) per household. The program had the dual objective of protecting forest land from further encroachment by giving existing squatters legal status, while at the same time countering the threat of communism (Lert Chuntanaparb and Wood 1986 19–40). It is worth noting that the phrase "to go to the forest" became synonymous with becoming a member of the CPT.

By the early 1980s, the CPT was moribund while environmental awareness was on the rise. With this, a de facto shift in policy occurred as the government began to activate legislation that had been on the books for years, but which had been effectively ignored with the greater need to defeat the CPT. Farmers—now no longer bulwarks against communism—became instead threats to the kingdom's environmental integrity. The inhabitants of Ban Tepattana, mentioned above, for example, have been evicted from their farms on forest reserve land in a watershed area (Sanitsuda Ekachai 1990a).

The National Forest Land Allotment program (better known as STK or Sor Tor Kor) was designed by the RFD to prevent further forest encroachment by giving squatter farmers "right-to-farm" (usufruct) certificates, thus partially recognizing their claims. Introduced in 1982, by 1985 over 1 million hectares had been classified under the program covering 624,000 farm families[17] (TDRI 1987:83,87). The intention of the STK scheme, like the Forest Village Program before it, was to halt encroachment of forest reserve land by giving farmers legal ownership to their land. It was hoped that this would encourage them to settle and invest in their land (rather than abandoning it when fertility declined) and to work with the RFD to replant degraded forest and protect standing forest. Both the STK and the Forest Village programs implicitly accept the absurdity of treeless "forest," and by doing so place the manage-ment of the kingdom's remaining forests on a more realistic footing. The

MAP 4.1

National Parks and Wildlife Sanctuaries in Thailand.

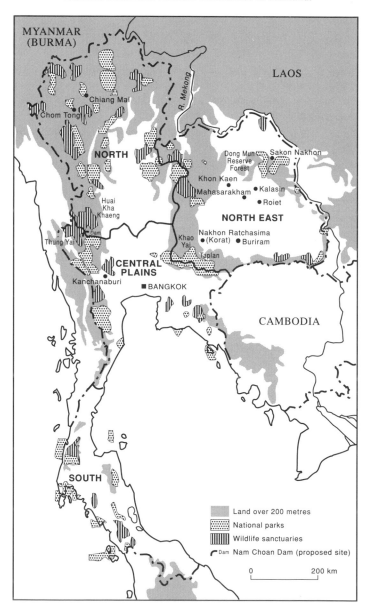

Source: Jonathan Rigg and Philip Stott

problem is that the STK usufruct certificate cannot be used as collateral to borrow money from institutional lenders, nor can it, in theory, be sold. The STK needs to be upgraded to NS-3 or *chanot* (full title deed) status before farmers can derive the benefits of full ownership. In light of this, it is unlikely that investment in the land has occurred to the extent envisaged.

A more recent, and yet more controversial, scheme has been the Land Redistribution Program for the Poor Living in Forest Reserves, known as Khor Jor Kor. Proposed by General Suchinda Kraprayoon in 1990 and managed by the army,[18] the intention was to move 250,000 families living on 2.25 million hectares of forest reserve land to degraded forest land covering 800,000 hectares.[19] Nearly 1.5 million hectares of the abandoned forest reserve would then be turned over to private plantation companies for replanting to fast-growing trees, such as *Eucalyptus camaldulensis*. The facts that the land earmarked for resettlement was already occupied, that not all households were to be offered land (because of a lack of formal house registration), and that farmers were expected to meet their livelihoods on landholdings nearly a third smaller—and often of poorer quality—than those from which they were being evicted seemed not to concern the implementing agency. However, this lack of concern becomes understandable when the hidden agenda behind the scheme is revealed: Most commentators believe that the Khor Jor Kor program was an attempt by the army to make money by cooperating with private tree plantation companies, while at the same time garnering political kudos by disguising it under the banner of environmentalism (e.g., Handley 1992a:48). It is also true that not all this land was devoid of forest. Local communities have been instrumental in protecting some areas of community forest on forest reserve land. Now, it seemed, plantation companies intended to clear this land, derive profit in the process by selling the valuable timber, and then replant the land with eucalyptus. The irony of the army and its business associates protecting the forest by taking it out of the hands of those who were protecting it in the first place was palpable.

Fortunately, however, following demonstrations in Bangkok and Nakhon Ratchasima (Korat), the interim government of Prime Minister Anand Panyarachun abandoned the program in July 1992, pending a reappraisal, and this allowed villagers to return home.[20] What the confrontation over the Khor Jor Kor program also illuminated starkly was the contrasting systems of logic employed by officials and farmers to mobilize their arguments and explain their actions. The deputy governor of the province of Nakhon Ratchasima, Poj Chaimaan, following a series of demonstrations in late 1992 was quoted as saying: "I don't know if the people are really going to help preserve the forest or destroy it. We don't have any way out and the society at large is confused. But if proper zoning is not done soon, more people will move into the forest, which could mean the end of the forest. And villagers don't understand the importance of the forest like academics do." On the other side of the political and mental ravine stood the village head of Ban Daan Lakor, one of the communities classified as lying within the boundaries of a national park. Eschewing the arguments of science, Tinnakorn Arjharn responded: "It's time to decide which side is right and what rights people have" (Pravit Rojanaphruk 1992).

A second thrust of the RFD's policy in the 1980s was a reforestation program carried out by various RFD agencies, including the Silviculture Division, the National Forest Land Management Division, and the Watershed Management Division.[21] In 1983, new legislation also allowed private companies to invest in forest plantations on state forest reserve land (NTUSFP 1987:41). The various schemes drew upon a number of management strands, including agroforestry, social forestry, the establishment of village woodlots, and commercial plantations. Much of the focus has been upon the rehabilitation of degraded forest lands. The program is intended to raise incomes and reduce poverty in rural communities, generate revenue, reduce/stabilize erosion, and protect wildlife. However, progress has been slow: the Fourth Five-Year National Economic and Social Development Plan (1977–1981) set a reforestation target of eighty thousand hectares per year; the actual rate was forty-four thousand hectares per year; for the Fifth Five-Year Plan (1982–1986), the figures were forty-eight thousand hectares per year and thirty-six thousand hectares per year,[22] respectively (TDRI 1987:82; Lert Chuntanaparb and Wood 1986:16–17). Lert Chuntanaparb and Wood (1986) list numerous problems that have contributed to this record of underachievement (which is mirrored in other plans), concluding that the "main problem is the undirected policy in degraded forest land management" (13). Other problems associated with the implementation of Thailand's forestry policies *in general* include a lack of coordination between concerned departments, insufficient and poorly trained personnel, an inadequate budget, and a lack of realism in forest policy given the conflicts that exist between conservation, population growth, and commercialization.

In addition to RFD-managed programs, the Forest Industry Organization (FIO) also has played a significant role in reforestation. Devolved from the RFD in 1956, the FIO was established to promote forest industries (as opposed to the RFD's more protection-oriented role). It was not until 1967 that the FIO began to replant logged land and establish commercial wood plantations.[23] Lert Chuntanaparb and Wood (1986) state that the general objectives of the FIO plantation program were to "protect its image and reputation" (by then, rather sullied), to "help [the] RFD improve the condition of the country's forests" and to "prepare the raw material for its own use in the future" (51). New villages were established on degraded land, households given 0.5–1 *rai* (0.08–0.16 hectares) of land to build a house and establish a home garden, and 10 *rai* (1.6

hectares) to farm. They were then employed in the planting program for the plantation. Between 1968 and 1982, an average of 3,300 hectares of plantation were planted annually, and the FIO established forty-two forest villages (TDRI 1987:84; Lert Chuntanaparb and Wood 1986:49–60). In some cases, the lack of enthusiasm among villagers for such schemes was linked to the feeling that they were being used as short-term, cheap labor to satisfy the needs of outsiders. As Opart Panya (1992:153), who worked on such a project for two years, states: "The fact of the matter is, as farmers well know, the hidden agenda of this strategy is to eventually drive them out of these plantations" when the canopy has closed and crop cultivation is no longer possible. To circumvent such an outcome, he notes, farmers sabotaged trees (for example by cutting tap roots) and tried to mold the management of the plantation so that it would serve their best interests. What is telling about Opart Panya's summary is that, despite "a relatively soft and friendly approach" by "new" foresters "living in the community and working closely with local people," the project was still a failure (158). This indicates that the critical difficulty lay not with poor implementation by heavy-handed officials, but in a fundamental conflict between the needs of the farmers and those of the managing organization.

It is also true that the logic of the FIO's approach to reforestation has created a management environment where natural forest is removed to make way for plantations. Compensatory planting means that the FIO is in theory obliged to replant one *rai* of land for every *rai* that it logs—which creates an inertia that encourages the logging of natural forest in favor of plantations. Fortunately, perhaps, the replanting targets set by the FIO have never been met.

A criticism leveled at almost all of the reforestation projects outlined above is that they have tended to use exotic—primarily *eucalyptus*—rather than indigenous species. For example, between 1966 and 1985, *Eucalyptus camaldulensis* was planted on 57 percent of all plantation land devoted to fast-growing species (TDRI 1987:86).[24] Among the problems associated with such species are potential soil exhaustion and degradation, increased system sterility, and market saturation. The emphasis on such exotics also has detracted from research into the economic and ecological value of indigenous tree and shrub species.

King Bhumibol Adulyadej was one of those calling for indigenous species to be planted in place of eucalyptus. But his voice—unlike those of most environmental groups—cannot easily be ignored. An example of this was the announcement in 1994 of a project to replant 5 million *rai* (800,000 hectares) of degraded forest land across the kingdom with indigenous species over a period of only three years (see Tasker 1994:19).[25] If this target is achieved, it will mean an annual rate of reforestation more than seven times greater than that achieved during the Fifth Five-Year Plan (1982–1986). The program is being explicitly linked to the fiftieth anniversary of the king's accession to the throne, which fell in 1996. It is hoped that private companies will undertake replanting to show their respect for the king and their concern for the environment. The companies will buy saplings from the RFD and then agree to replant areas already identified and surveyed in fifty-nine of the country's seventy-six provinces. Given this two-pronged link with the king and the environment, there is a significant chance that the targets will be met—few companies can afford not to be involved in such a program. But once again, there appears to have been little attention paid to the farmers who might occupy and cultivate such degraded former forest. Reports stress the environmental desirability of replanting Thailand's forests, without any concomitant concern for the human costs that such a massive program might engender.

Although the RFD's approach to forest management has altered dramatically, it is still poorly placed to deal with some of the issues and problems that it faces. The three conservation-oriented divisions of the department—the National Parks, Wildlife Conservation, and Watershed Management divisions—are poorly funded and generally unable to fully carry out their environmental mandate. It is partly for this reason that many Thai NGOs with an environmental remit—such as the Project for Ecological Recovery (PER)—rather than working *with* the state in the interests of conservation, have tried to protect forests *from* the state (see below).

The furore in 1993 over who should manage Thailand's national parks illustrates how the environmental debate in Thailand is developing. The suggestion by the Tourist Authority of Thailand that it should take over ownership of some parks from the National Parks Division of the Royal Forestry Department was sharply criticized by pressure groups such as the Project for Ecological Recovery (PER). In their view, this was Thailand once again selling out to the highest bidder at the expense of the environment—in the guise of that much-abused word *ecotourism* (see Handley 1994). The fact that the kingdom's national parks have been abused, mismanaged, and degraded for decades while under the control of the National Parks Division was lost amidst the verbiage. The fact too that many parks—such as Khao Yai, Koh Phi Phi, Koh Chang, and Koh Samet—already are overrun with illegal bungalow developments also has been obscured. Finally, the role that tourism *might* play in protecting parks from hunting and logging—prevalent in, for example, the Thaplan National Park—scarcely has been addressed.

Other Actors in Forest Protection

The Royal Forest Department is clearly the most important official actor when it comes to forest management and protection. However, many of the most innovative approaches have come from individuals, groups, and agencies with no direct connection with the RFD. They include NGOs, semi-NGOs, local groups, students, academics, members of the royal elites, Buddhist monks, and the army. It is at this rather fragmented, unofficial level that the debate is richest and where the origins of much policy—as illustrated in the following discussion—often lie. The ideals and methods of alternative development, long promoted by NGOs, have become the "new orthodoxy." The Seventh Five-Year Development Plan (1992–1996) for example, embraces concepts such as people's participation, self-reliance, and decentralization (NESDB n.d.[b]:133–40). The value of community forests, indigenous multipurpose trees, and village woodlots are now part and parcel of RFD-speak. Many of the formally marginalized voices and views have become, or are becoming, part of the mainstream.

Forest Monks. Forest monks and forest *wats* (monasteries) have come to the attention of many Thais as concern for the kingdom's wild areas has increased. Situated at the boundaries of civilized space, the monasteries were established to ensure an "unambiguous separation and distance from mundaneness, with its defilements and untamed sensuality" (Taylor 1991:109). Originally, the small clearings in the forest represented tiny areas of order in an otherwise untamed world; today, the forest monasteries often guard the only remaining areas of forest in an entirely tamed and cultivated world. Given this reversal, it is not surprising that monks should have been at the forefront of conservation efforts. They have protected their forests from encroachment by farmers and illegal loggers by effectively sanctifying the ground, and they have encouraged villagers to plant trees while promoting environmental consciousness. As Taylor concludes in his case study of Wat Dong Sii Chomphuu (Pink Forest Monastery) in Sakon Nakhon province: "With an awareness of the ecosystem and the importance of sustainable cultural practices, forest monks like Ajaan Thui have in recent times become a vital means of protecting the remaining peripheral forests" (Taylor 1991:121) (see map 4.1).

In the case of Phra Acarn Pongsak Tejadhamma, the abbot of Wat Palat in Tambon Mae Soi (Amphoe Chom Tong)—about 70 km to the south of Chiang Mai (see map 4.1)—this concern for the environment led to the establishment of the now nationally famous Dhammanat Foundation. Its aims "are to reconcile not only Hmong [hill people] and *khon mu'ang* [rice cultivating lowlanders], but also officials and people, and people and Nature, above all through the [Buddhist] teaching of *sinlatham*, that is the maintenance of balance within the individual, society, the environment, and the *mu'ang*" (Stott 1991a:148–49). The links between these monk conservationists and official agencies are becoming clearer. The RFD lent assistance in the form of labor and equipment to the Dhammanat Foundation, while prominent businessmen, politicians, and members of the military support many of these forest monasteries. However, other vested interests often oppose such monks, calling them Communists and seeking to undermine their reputation, frequently through scurrilous and contrived propaganda. The most renowned recent confrontation between a monk and officialdom came when the conservationist monk Phra Prachak Khuttajitto led demonstrations against national park boundary changes in Nakhon Ratchasima in 1990. In late 1992, he received a one-year sentence for damaging government property. The interest in Forest Buddhism also has led to an outpouring of religious literature of a conservationist bent (e.g., Seri Phongphit 1988; Shari 1988; Chatsumarn Kabilsingh 1987). It may be true that this literature is oriented primarily to Thailand's educated elite and growing middle class, but it represents an important trend, namely an "indigenization" of environmental thought (Stott 1991a:150–52).

Pressure Groups. Perhaps the greatest success of Thailand's environmental movement to date has been the shelving of the Nam Choan Dam. This project, in Kanchanaburi Province near the frontier with Myanmar (Burma), represented the final part of a three-dam project begun in 1966[26] (see map 4.1). The first two dams were completed in 1978 and 1981, and the Nam Choan Dam received the official go-ahead in 1982. Opposition to the dam and associated reservoir focused on the impact they would have on the contiguous Huai Kha Khaeng and Thung Yai wildlife sanctuaries. These sanctuaries contain one of the few remaining stands of deciduous riverine forest in Thailand, and conservationists view the area as incomparable in size (5,775 square kilometres) and quality. Opposition to the project was mobilized at all levels: marches and demonstrations were held in the town of Kanchanaburi, a petition handed to the then prime minister Prem Tinsulanond, rallies organized in Bangkok, editorials written in national newspapers (see figure 4.2), politicians pressured into taking a stance, and international environmental groups encouraged to add their support to the campaign. Such was the degree of opposition that it led the "biased" Thienchai committee (Hildyard 1987:211)— set up to deliberate on the project—to recommend that the dam be shelved. This decision was taken for political expedience, prompted by fears of political crisis, and did not indicate any acceptance on the part of the authorities that the environmental costs might outweigh the economic benefits of the project. Nonetheless, it represents the most important change of policy brought about by public pressure and focusing on an environmental issue.

This success also has given heart to environmentalists fighting on other fronts. A total logging ban was introduced in January 1989, prompted by a human crisis that was presumed to have environmental roots. In November 1988, severe rains in southern Thailand led to disastrous floods leaving at least 350 dead. The severity of the floods and the high death toll both were blamed on the clearance of forest in the surrounding area. The ensuing public outcry, orchestrated by Thailand's fledgling but increasingly influential environmental lobby, forced the government to impose a logging ban, in spite of opposition from powerful logging interests and their associates in Parliament and the army (Paisal Sricharatchanya 1989; Hirsch and Lohmann 1989). The growing power of grassroots groups to influence government policy also is reflected in the shelving of the Khor Jor Kor program (see above) and in villagers' campaigns against the expansion of eucalyptus plantations.

In many cases, NGOs see the state as the enemy and certainly as part of the problem. The difficulty with this in terms of forest management, however, is that it is not possible to sideline the state in such matters, however attractive that might be. Indeed, the state is both the root of the problem and the route to its alleviation. As Friedmann (1992:7) writes in his book on alternative development:

> Although an alternative development must begin locally, it cannot end there. Like it or not, the state continues to be a major player. It may need to be made more accountable to poor people and more responsive to their claims. But without the state's collaboration, the lot of the poor cannot be significantly improved. Local empowering action requires a strong state.

The Army. Efforts at reforestation and protection are not just the preserve of NGOs. Recognizing the importance of the environment in the public's perception, even the army has undergone a process—superficial perhaps—of "greening." In 1986, the then army commander-in-chief General Chavaolit Yongchaiyut announced his Green Isan or Isan Khiaw project. This project's central aim was to re-green the northeastern region of the country (also known as the Isan Region). Cynics stated that the only greening likely to be in evidence was an increased number of army fatigues. For the army, however, it represented an attempt at self-justification at a time when the military's role was coming under scrutiny with the reduced threat of attack from Vietnam. A project aimed at the dual problems of rural poverty in the northeast (Thailand's poorest region) and environmental deterioration was deemed to be suitably appropriate. For a time, the project seemed always to be in the news—both on army-run TV channels and in the independent media.[27]

Hill Peoples. Of all the groups in Thailand blamed for deforestation, none has been so maligned as those of the northern and western hill peoples (see map 4.1). Numbering more than 550,000, and divided (officially) into nine subgroups, they live at the margins of the T(h)ai state in an overlapping sense: geographically as they occupy the highland borderlands with Myanmar and Laos; religiously in their animist or Christian, rather than Buddhist, beliefs; culturally in their distinct ways of life; and economically in their partial separation from the mainstream of T(h)ai economic life. The twin facts that hill peoples are concentrated in the northern and western forested areas and that they practice "environmentally destructive" systems of shifting cultivation have meant that most government officials and many independent analysts see them as a principal cause of deforestation. General Prapas Charusathira, former minister of the interior, for example, stated quite explicitly in 1967:

> Because of their inefficient method of cultivation the tribes have been steadily despoiling the land of the [northern] region. Parts of it have been permanently ruined for agriculture. The removal of the forest cover [by the hill tribes] has not only depleted timber resources but has interfered with the watersheds of the rivers which irrigate the rice plains on which the economy of the nation depends. (quoted in Wanat Bhruksasri 1989:13)

But this perception of the links between the hill peoples, deforestation, and land degradation has proved remarkably persistent. The independent—and influential—Thai Development Research Institute (TDRI), for example, recently argued: "For the Royal Thai government, the hill tribes pose a series of profound political, social and ecological problems. Much highland deforestation . . . can be laid directly at their door" (TDRI 1987:80). There is not space here to recite the arguments over the ecological impacts of shifting cultivation,[28] but suffice it to say that the Thai government has not been reluctant to use its supposedly environmentally destructive system of agriculture as a reason to settle the hill tribes in *nikhom* (resettlement villages) and actively evict them from forest reserve land. The whole process also has received, to some degree, a royal imprimatur with the king's projects to resettle hill peoples and direct them away from opium production. The fact that the hill peoples are a politically and economically powerless minority group, living at the margins of the T(h)ai state, makes them a useful scapegoat, deflecting criticism away from such explanations as corrupt officials, incompetent management, and ineffective policy making and implementation.

Land scarcity also has brought the hill tribes into conflict with lowland rice farmers and environmental groups. As the land frontier has closed, so *khon mu'ang* (lowlanders) and *chaaw khao* (hill people)—previously separated by their occupation of different ecological zones—have begun to compete for the same land. At Mae Sai, for example, lowland farmers have resorted to fencing off watershed areas to prevent the Hmong hill people from clearing the forest and planting cabbages (a favorite cash crop).

Although the hill peoples often have found themselves unfairly blamed for forest encroachment and destruction, there is a sense in which their traditional, extensive systems of agriculture are untenable in a Thai context where land is becoming an increasingly scarce resource and where other actors are competing for that resource.[29] Although shifting cultivation can be viewed as an environmentally sustainable system of agriculture, given abundant land, this is not the case in a context of resource scarcity. Across the northern and western regions, fallow periods are declining and hill farmers are being forced to intensify cultivation to maintain yields. Schmidt-Vogt (1995), for example, in his study of the Akha, hints at such pressure-induced changes when he reports a switch from swidden farming to wet rice cultivation: "These latest developments indicate a fundamental change in attitude: instead of abandoning the site—the usual strategy of the Akha in such a predicament [of land scarcity]—the villagers have intensified land use and changed their cropping system" (58–59).

Rhetoric and Reality, Conflicts and Contradictions in Forest Policy

It is thus not unusual for policies of environmental protection to be contradictory, ineffective, ignored, and undermined. But in Thailand, such factors mitigating against implementation are more pronounced than is usual. Successive Thai governments have been slow to respond to the spectre of environmental deterioration and rapid forest loss. It is broadly accepted by almost all commentators that the elites with power in Thailand—businessmen, politicians, and the army particularly (there is a considerable degree of overlap among the three)—have found it in their interests to limit the drafting of legislation and to ignore that legislation that has made its way onto the statute books. Many members of the elite have valuable timber concessions of their own or are in a position to gain through the expeditious allocation of concessions. Tales of army officers hunting in national parks or of businessmen logging protected forests with the cognizance of local officials are all too common, while officials who try to carry out their duties properly are simply moved or, even worse, murdered. It should not be forgotten that the 14 October 1973 uprising was triggered partly by a forestry hunting scandal when an army helicopter crashed and the bodies of high-ranking officers were found in the wreckage, along with the carcasses of animals shot in the newly created Thung Yai Naresuan Wildlife Sanctuary. However, not only did these elites stand to benefit personally, they also believed, along with most policy makers, that Thailand's economic growth was—and is—predicated on relatively loose environmental controls. To coin a phrase, politicians and bureaucrats felt that environmental awareness was a luxury that the kingdom could ill afford. The tragedy of the contradictions between forest policy and practice were highlighted in September 1990 when Seub Nakhasathien, chief of the Huai Kha Khaeng Wildlife Sanctuary, shot himself, depressed at his inability to stop the forces of environmental destruction, in particular corruption and hunting and logging at Huai Kha Khaeng.

The Royal Forest Department, as the principal government agency engaged in forest management, often has come under scrutiny. More often than not, the assessments have been critical of the RFDs operations, philosophy, and approach. However, the department is relatively powerless to determine the essence of policy. As Kamon Pragtong and Thomas (1990:167) note:

> The forestry profession seeks to apply ecological principles in managing forest resources to meet societal goals. But as an agency of the government, a forest department is both empowered and restricted by policies of higher governmental authority, which themselves are influenced by events, movements, interests, and personalities in the larger society.

This is not to say that the RFD could not have done more to promote forest conservation, but ultimately the responsibility must lie with higher agencies of government.

The contradictions between aims and actions can be seen in the way the Khor Jor Kor project, noted above, was implemented in Nong Yai, a village in Nakhon Ratchasima Province. Farmers squatting on forest reserve land were moved in 1991 and 1992 to a new area, five kilometers away. To allot fifteen *rai* (2.4 hectares) to each family as promised, land had to be taken from farmers already on site; they, in turn, were promised new land. To furnish this new land, the army persuaded the RFD to redraw the borders of the nearby Taplan National Park. That land—sixteen hundred hectares—was cleared of valuable stands of timber (the implication in some reports being that the proceeds from this timber were accruing to members of the army), making nonsense of the 1989 logging ban and of the broad thrust of government policy (see Sanitsuda Ekachai, 1992) (map 4.1).

But it is not just the powerful who have managed to circumvent the principle of forest policy. The 1960 Forest Act allows farmers to harvest legally 0.2 m^3 (sometimes more) of timber from forest reserve for domestic use. Houses built using this timber can be sold after two years, and farmers exploit the provision by constructing rough house frames (sometime of teak). As Hafner (1990:80–81) writes: "In Ban Non Amnuay, a new village in the Dong Mun National Reserved Forest in Kalasin province, sixty of these 'houses built for sale' were constructed between 1983 and 1985 with timber cut from the reserved forest" (see also Taylor 1991:112) (map 4.1).

Conflicts between groups competing for the same resource also have accentuated the problems that, arguably, always have been inherent in Thailand's forest policy. Some of these problems have been touched on already: conflicts between shifting-cultivating hill peoples and rice-growing lowlanders, between conservationists and farmers, between monks and villagers, and between commercial farmers and subsistence cultivators. The government's policy of encouraging crop substitution programs to wean hill peoples off opium poppy cultivation has led to a surge in land clearance in the north as farmers plant low-value cabbages instead. This, in turn, has brought widespread condemnation from lowland villagers who see a link between their rivers running dry and the clearance of watershed forests (see Stott 1991a:148; Sanitsuda Ekachai 1990b).

International Dimensions to Thailand's Forest Policies

There is sometimes a tendency to view a country's environmental policies only in their national context. However, in Thailand's case, the effects of forest policy also have had marked international dimensions in recent years. Most notably, the imposition of the total logging ban in January 1989, coupled with the increasing lack of valuable forest in Thailand,[30] encouraged logging firms to turn to neighboring countries for wood, notably Myanmar, but also Laos. In the case of Myanmar, the foreign-exchange-starved government leased twenty concessions on its eastern border with Thailand to Thai army-backed companies (see Hirsch 1993). The problem of deforestation in Thailand has, in effect, been displaced to Myanmar, a country with the region's largest reserves of teak and other valuable hardwoods. The failure of the Thai government to respond to gross human rights abuses in Myanmar has been linked to the Thai army's lucrative association with the *junta* in Rangoon, thus bringing together in a single equation two highly contentious issues—human and environmental exploitation. More recently still, Thailand was the object of international condemnation in 1992 and 1993, when it refused to introduce UN sanctions against the Khmers Rouges and seal the Thai-Cambodian border during implementation of the 1991 peace agreement. Many commentators put the intransigence of Thai authorities down to the lucrative timber deals that had been struck between the army and/or army-backed Thai firms and the Khmers Rouges.

The need to see Thailand's forest policies in regional, rather than just national, perspective is linked intimately to the exhaustion of the kingdom's own natural resources. It has become essential, if Thailand is to maintain its fast-track, resource-intensive route to development, to exploit the reserves of neighboring countries. This applies not just to timber: fisheries, energy (dams), and minerals are also part and parcel of this internationalization of the environment in the region (see Hirsch 1993, 1995). Although a discussion of the international dimensions of Thailand's development strategy on the environments of neighboring countries is beyond the scope of this discussion, it is important to note that just as the former colonial powers exploited the environments of those countries they colonized, so with greater differentiation in the developing world, a similar process of neocolonial environmental exploitation is emerging among the countries of the South. Some people may object to the use of the term neocolonial in this context, due to its pejorative historical associations. However, the effects of the move by Thai logging firms into neighboring countries is similar to the role played by foreign companies in Thailand and elsewhere during the colonial period. Indeed, the Lao government, for one, appears to see it in these terms, as do some Thai academics. In July 1989, the state-run Radio Vientiane broadcast a commentary, presumably with official sanction, that stated: "Having failed to destroy our country through their military might [referring to a border conflict between the Thai and Lao armies at Ban Rom Klao in 1987 and 1988], the enemy has now employed a new strategy in attacking us through the so-called attempt to turn the Indochinese battlefield into a marketplace" (quoted in Tasker 1989:25–26).

Environmental Policy in Thailand:
Reflections on History and Culture

This discussion of forest policy in Thailand has tried to place the topic squarely within the arenas of culture and history and not to look at environmental dilemmas only in terms of contemporary economic and political processes. An understanding of why Thailand today is a forest-poor country, when as little as forty years ago it was more *pa* (forest) than *mu'ang* (civilized), must be rooted in an appreciation of what has gone before; in other words, in history. At the same time, the T(h)ai view of the forest needs to be appreciated if the processes of forest destruction, and the wider issue of environmentalism, are to be placed within a local context. The internationalization of the environment noted above means more than just the transfer of impacts across national boundaries. It also means that there has begun to emerge a single world view vis à vis the environment. This view, and the academic and political agendas which inform it, are very much part and parcel of the North's milieu. The South's—in this instance Thailand's—voice also needs to be heard; and this is not important just to satisfy the desire among many academics to hear different voices. It also has a significant applied role, for ultimately solutions to Thailand's environmental crisis also must incorporate an understanding of those factors that are uniquely Thai.

In this regard, it must be remembered that, until recently, for most T(h)ai people, the forest remained largely outside the T(h)ai civilized world, a land to be cleared for rice production and a realm to be tamed and rightly brought under the merit of the king. The forest was essentially a non-T(h)ai landscape feature. Thus, it is not surprising that the earliest modern "environmentalism" came from a certain stratum of the urban elite, who continue to give the forest and wild places of Thailand a new set of values as "wilderness," as "recreational land," and as an "international image maker." There is the need to turn *pa* (wild forest) into *thammachat* (nature safely tamed) for the urban heart of the state; a new cosmology is being born, but the environment will be changed in the very act of being saved. In the meantime, the complex battle for access and control of Thailand's environmental resources, Thailand's essential political ecology, will continue, often violently, on the pioneer margins of the state.

Notes

1. The term *environmentalism* here is used to refer to the discourse as it has emerged in the countries of the North. However, it is accepted that there are multiple environmentalisms, not one neatly defined and demarcated variety. In a sense, then, we are referring more to a state of mind and an ideology of environmentalism than to a discrete and easily identifiable set of ideas.

2. *T(h)ai* here is used to emphasize that while Thailand is primarily populated by people belonging to the Tai linguistic and cultural group, there are also significant numbers of non-Tais who are nationals of Thailand (most notably some of the hill peoples), while at the same time there are also many Tais who live in, and are citizens of, neighboring countries.

3. For example, the *wattanatham chumchon* (community culture, also known as the Cultural Development Perspective (CDP) movement); see Chatthip Nartsupha (1991) for general background, and Rigg (1991b, 1993) and Hewison (1993) for contrasting views of the perspective.

4. See, for example, the range of papers presented at the symposium held under the auspices of the Siam Society in 1987 and entitled *Culture and Environment in Thailand* (Siam Society, 1989).

5. Not everyone in Thailand perceives that a crisis exists. Nor is this crisis perceived in the same way. For farmers, the crisis may be manifested in a lack of fuel wood or wild forest products; for logging companies in the logging ban and the tightened policing on illegal logging; for conservationists in the loss of biodiversity. It is also true that the crisis has changed complexion through time.

6. Between 1980 and 1990 the annual rate of deforestation was thought to be 2.5 percent, the highest in Southeast Asia (UNDP 1992:172).

7. Much of the tropical hardwoods exported from Thailand today are logs transshipped through Thailand from the neighboring countries of Myanmar (Burma), Laos, and Cambodia.

8. King Ramkhamhaeng—or Rama the Brave—is perhaps Thailand's most illustrious monarch. In recent years, however, historians and archaeologists have begun to question the veracity of the famous inscription no. 1 of 1292, arguing that it might be a forgery (see Chamberlain 1991).

9. The first director general of the Forest Department was H. A. Slade, and the department was initially located in Chiang Mai in the north, an indication of the overriding significance of teak (*Tectona grandis* L.f) at this stage (see Brown 1988:114–19).

10. That said, Terwiel (1989) and Bowie (1992) both show the remarkable extent to which "central" powers in Siam controlled the lives of villagers in the nineteenth century and earlier. Terwiel (1989:251) concludes that "one of the rather unexpected findings [of his study] has been the discovery of the size and efficacy of the nineteenth-century government apparatus. . . . It would seem that the population registered for corvée did indeed have to perform duties, or pay to be exempted, and that living at some distance from Bangkok did not place a person beyond the reach of government officials."

11. Although the paper does not examine wild lands/forest per se, it is pertinent and represents one of the few studies that takes a dynamic look at changing patterns of resource use and ownership.

12. It is interesting that as trees and forest become increasingly scarce in an area, so traditional taboos on the use of certain species alters. *Mai bok* (*Irvingia malayana*) is a traditionally forbidden wood because it is associated with bad luck; *mai waa* (*Eugenia cumini*) is said to cause epidemics; *mai pho* (*Ficus religiosa*) is left unharmed because it is a holy tree, the tree under which the historic Buddha attained enlightenment. However, in villages where trees are scarce, all these traditional taboos, bar the last, are ignored under the demand for fuel wood (Sukaesinee Subhadhira et al. 1988:49).

13. A point noted in the Seventh Five-Year Plan (1992–1996), where over-centralization is seen as one reason why the "bureaucratic system is unable to adjust to changes and cannot adequately respond to national economic and social transformation" (NESDB n.d.[b]:4).

14. There is some overlap between forest reserve land and land gazetted as national parks and wildlife sanctuaries.

15. The area of farmland in 1988 was 23.6 million hectares, 46 percent of Thailand's total land area.

16. The CPT reached the height of its influence in the late 1970s when it was able to mobilize around 14,000 guerrillas. At the time, there was a widespread perception that Thailand could go the same way as its Indochinese neighbors to the east, and "fall" to communism.

17. There is some discrepancy over the figures for the STK program. NTUSFP (1987) and Lert Chuntanaparb and Wood (1986) claim 416,000 hectares were registered under the scheme, accounting for 257,000 families.

18. Through the Internal Security Operations Command (ISOC), an agency initially created to coordinate the fight against the Communist party of Thailand.

19. The army has always seen itself as having an important role to play in development. So far as the conservation of forests is concerned, the most notable program has been the army's Isan Khiaw (Green the northeast) scheme (see below and also the introduction to this chapter).

20. For a collection of newspaper pieces on the Khor Jor Kor program see TDSC (1992).

21. Reforestation dates back to 1906 when the Burmese *taungya* system was used to plant teak (*Tectona grandis*) (Lert Chuntanaparb and Wood 1986:9–10).

22. This final figure covers years 1982 through 1985.

23. Until then, the FIO usually acted only as a coordinating body supervising logging concessions managed by private firms. The changes in national forest policy, noted above, to a more conservation/protection-oriented strategy led, in turn, to changes in the FIO approach to its work.

24. See also Apichai Puntasen, Somboon Siriprachai, and Chaiyuth Punyasavatsut (1992) for a discussion of the corruption and rent-seeking that underlie the development of many eucalyptus plantations.

25. Reforestation will proceed under the plan at a rate of 1.3 million *rai* in 1994, 1.6 million *rai* in 1995, and 2.0 million *rai* in 1996, the fiftieth anniversary of the king's reign.

26. For more detailed discussions, see Hirsch (1988), Stewart Cox (1987), Rigg (1991a).

27. The brutal suppression of the May 1992 demonstrations in Bangkok was a public relations disaster for the army, nullifying any effect such projects as Isan Khiaw might have been having. Significantly, however, Chavalit Yongchaiyut, now retired from the army and leader of the New Aspirations party, has used the Isan Khiaw scheme to promote his career as a civilian politician.

28. For an excellent "defense" of the Hmong, perhaps the most vilified of the hill tribes, see Tapp's excellent case study (1989). He writes that the Hmong demonstrate a "fundamental harmony of man and nature . . . shifting cultivation encourages a diversified economy, [and] preserves and maintains the existing ecosystem far better than a mono-culture such as one based on rice. Nor is shifting cultivation the main cause of deforestation in Northern Thailand" (64).

29. For example, environmental groups, the state, and lowland farmers.

30. It is arguable that the main impetus behind the search by logging firms for alternative sources of wood in neighboring countries was the simple fact that there was little easily accessible forest left in Thailand to exploit. The logging ban merely reinforced this trend, which has its basis in a simple scarcity of resources.

References

Apichai Puntasen, Somboon Siriprachai, and Chaiyuth Punyasavatsut. 1992. "Political Economy of Eucalyptus: Business, Bureaucracy and the Thai Government." *Journal of Contemporary Asia* 22 (2):187–206.

Bowie, Katherine A. 1992. "Unraveling the Myth of the Subsistence Economy: Textile Production in Nineteenth Century Northern Thailand." *Journal of Asian Studies* 51(4):797–823.

Brown, Ian. 1988. *The Elite and the Economy in Siam c. 1890–1921.* East Asian Historical Monographs. Singapore: Oxford University Press.

Chamberlain, James R., ed. 1991. *The Ram Khamhaeng Controversy: Collected Papers.* Bangkok: The Siam Society.

Chatsumarn Kabilsingh. 1987. "How Buddhism Can Help Protect Nature." In *Tree of Life: Buddhism and Protection of Nature.* Geneva.

Chatthip Nartsupha. 1991. "The Community Culture School of Thought." In *Thai Constructions of Knowledge*, ed. Manas Chitakasem and Andrew Turton, 118–41. London: SOAS.

Feder, Gershon, Tongroj Onchan, Yongyuth Chalamwong, and Chira Hongladarom. 1988. *Land Policies and Farm Productivity in Thailand.* Baltimore: Johns Hopkins University Press.

Friedmann, John. 1992. *Empowerment: The Politics of Alternative Development.* Oxford: Basil Blackwell.

Gervaise, N. 1928. *The Natural and Political History of the Kingdom of Siam.* Trans. H. S. O'Neill. Bangkok: Siam Observer Press.

Grandstaff, Somluckrat, Terry Grandstaff, Pagarat Rathakette, David Thomas, and Jureerat Thomas. 1986. "Trees in Paddy Fields in Northeast Thailand." In *Traditional Agriculture in Southeast Asia: A Human Ecology Perspective*, ed. Gerald G. Marten, 273–92. Boulder: Westview Press.

Gray, Denis, Collin Piprell, and Mark Graham. 1991. *National Parks of Thailand.* Bangkok: Communications Resources Thailand.

Haas, Mary. 1964. *Thai-English Student's Dictionary.* Stanford: Stanford University Press.

Hafner, James A. 1990. "Forces and Policy Issues Affecting Forest Use in Northeast Thailand, 1900–1985." In *Keepers of the Forest: Land Management Alternatives in Southeast Asia*, ed. Mark Poffenberger, 69–94. West Hartford: Kumarian Press.

Handley, Paul. 1992a. "Rich Thais, Poor Thais." *Far Eastern Economic Review*, 20 August, 48.

———. 1992b. "New Rules, but Old Attitudes." *Far Eastern Economic Review*, 29 October, 40.

———. 1994. "Parks Under Seige." *Far Eastern Economic Review*, 20 January, 36–37.

Hardjono, Joan. 1991. "The Dimensions of Indonesia's Environmental Problems." In *Indonesia: Resources, Ecology, and Environment*, ed. Joan Hardjono, 1–16. Singapore: OUP.

Hewison, Kevin. 1993. "Non Governmental Organizations, Rural Development and Populism: A Partial Defence of the Cultural Development Perspective in Thailand." *World Development* 21(10):1699–1708.

Hildyard, N. 1987. "Stop the Nam Choan!" *The Ecologist* 17(6):210–11.

Hirsch, Philip. 1987. "Deforestation and Development in Thailand." *Singapore Journal of Tropical Geography* 8(2)129–38.

———. 1988. "Dammed or Damned? Hydropower Versus People's Power." *Bulletin of Concerned Asian Scholars* 20(1):2–10.

———. 1990a. *Thai Agriculture: Restructuring in the 1980s and 1990s*. Occasional Paper No. 12. Sydney, Australia: Research Institute for Asia and the Pacific, University of Sydney.

———. 1990b. "Forests, Forest Reserve and Forest Land in Thailand." *The Geographical Journal* 156(2):166–74.

———. 1990c. *Development Dilemmas in Rural Thailand*. Singapore: Oxford University Press.

———. 1993. *Political Economy of Environment in Thailand*. Manila: Journal of Contemporary Asia Publishers.

———. 1995. "Thailand and the New Geopolitics of Southeast Asia: Resource and Environmental Issues." In *Counting the Costs: Economic Growth and Environmental Change in Thailand,* ed. Jonathan Rigg, 235–259. Singapore: Institute of Southeast Asian Studies.

Hirsch, Philip, and Larry Lohmann. 1989. "Contemporary Politics of Environment in Thailand." *Asian Survey* 29(4):439–51.

Jolly, David. 1992. "Cleaning up Their Act." *Far Eastern Economic Review*, 20 August, 46–48.

Kamon Pragtong and David E. Thomas. 1990. "Evolving Management Systems in Thailand." In *Keepers of the Forest: Land Management Alternatives in Southeast Asia,* ed. Mark Poffenberger, 167–86. West Hartford: Kumarian Press.

Lert Chuntanaparb and Henry Wood. 1986. *Management of Degraded Forest Land in Thailand.* Bangkok: Northeast Thailand Upland Social Forestry Project, Kasetsart University.

Lohmann, Larry. 1992. "Land, Power and Forest Colonisation in Thailand." In *Agrarian Reform and Environment in the Philippines and Southeast Asia*, 85–99. London: Catholic Institute for International Relations.

Manas Chitakasem. 1991. "Poetic Conventions and Modern Thai Poetry." In *Thai Constructions of Knowledge*, ed. Manas Chitakasem and Andrew Turton, 37–62. London: SOAS.

McCargo, Duncan. 1993. "The Three Paths of Major-General Chamlong Srimuang." *South East Asia Research* 1(1): 27–67.

NESDB. n.d.(a). *The Sixth National Economic and Social Development Plan 1987–1991*. Bangkok: National Economic and Social Development Board.

————. n.d.(b). *The Seventh National Economic and Social Development Plan 1992–1996*. Bangkok: National Economic and Social Development Board.

NTUSFP. 1987. *Summary Report: Human-Forest Interactions in Northeast Thailand*. Bangkok: Northeast Thailand Upland Social Forestry Project.

Opart Panya. 1992. "Farmer Response to a Grass-Roots Approach to Forest Management." *Pacific Viewpoint* 33(2):151–58.

Paisal Sricharatchanya. 1989. "Too Little, Too Late." *Far Eastern Economic Review*, 12 January, 40.

Pasuk Phongpaichit. 1989. "The Economic Development Culture and the Environment." In *Culture and Environment in Thailand*, 337–43. Bangkok: The Siam Society.

Pedersen, P. 1992. "The Study of Perception of Nature: Towards a Sociology of Knowledge About Nature." In *Asian Perceptions of Nature*, ed. Ole Bruun and Arne Kalland, 148–58. Nordic Proceedings in Asian Studies no. 3. Copenhagen: NIAS.

Pravit Rojanaphruk. 1992. "Villagers Vow to Hold Their Ground." *The Nation*, 4 December, C1.

Reid, Anthony. 1988. *Southeast Asia in the Age of Commerce 1450–1680: The Lands Below the Winds*. New Haven: Yale University Press.

Reynolds, F. E., and M. B. Reynolds. 1982. *Three Worlds According to King Ruang: A Thai Buddhist Cosmology*. Berkeley Buddhist Studies Series No. 4. Berkeley: University of California (Asian Humanities Press/Motilal Banarsidass).

Rigg, Jonathan. 1987. "Forces and Influences Behind the Development of Upland Cash Cropping in Northeast Thailand." *The Geographical Journal* 153(3):370–82.

————. 1991a. "Thailand's Nam Choan Dam Project: A Case Study in the 'Greening' of South-East Asia." *Global Ecology and Biogeography Letters* 1:42–54.

―――. 1991b. "Grass-Roots Development in a Hierarchical Society: A Lost Cause?" *World Development* 19(2–3):199–211.

―――. 1992. "Forests and Farmers, Land and Livelihoods: Changing Resource Realities in Thailand." Paper presented at a workshop on the political ecology of Southeast Asia's forests, School of Oriental and African Studies, London.

―――. 1993. "A Reply to Kevin Hewison." *World Development* 21(10):1709–13.

Sanitsuda Ekachai. 1990a. "Trees of Our Choice." *Behind the Smile: Voices of Thailand*, 53–55. Bangkok: Post Publishing.

―――. 1990b. "Cabbages Worse Than Opium Poppies." *Behind the Smile: Voices of Thailand*, 164–67. Bangkok: Post Publishing.

―――. 1992. "This Land Is Our Land." *Bangkok Post*, 17 June.

Santhat Sermsri. 1989. "Population Growth and Environmental Change in Thailand." In *Culture and Environment in Thailand*, 71–91. Bangkok: The Siam Society.

Schmidt-Vogt, Dietrich. 1995. "Swidden Farming and Secondary Vegetation: Two Case Studies from Northern Thailand." In *Counting the Costs: Economic Growth and Environmental Change in Thailand*, ed. Jonathan Rigg, 47–64. Singapore: Institute of Southeast Asian Studies.

Seri Phongphit. 1988. *Religion in a Changing Society: Buddhism, Reform and the Role of Monks in Community Development in Thailand*. Hong Kong: Arena Press.

Shari, M. H. 1988. *Culture and Environment in Thailand: Dynamics of a Complex Relationship*. Bangkok: The Siam Society.

Sharp, Lauriston, and L. M. Hanks. 1978. *Bang Chan: Social History of a Rural Community in Thailand*. Ithaca: Cornell University Press.

Siam Society. 1989. *Culture and Environment in Thailand*. Bangkok: The Siam Society.

Simmons, Ian G. 1993. *Interpreting Nature: Cultural Constructions of the Environment*. London: Routledge.

Stewart Cox, Belinda. 1987. "Thailand's Nam Choan Dam: A Disaster in the Making." *The Ecologist* 17(6):212–19.

Stott, Philip. 1990. "Stability and Stress in the Savanna Forests of Mainland South-East Asia." *Journal of Biogeography* 17(4/5):373–83.

―――. 1991a. "*Mu'ang* and *pa*: Elite Views of Nature in a Changing Thailand." In *Thai Constructions of Knowledge*, ed. Manas Chitakasem and Andrew Turton, 142–54. London: School of Oriental and African Studies.

―――. 1991b. "Asian and Pacific Ecology." In *Handbooks to the Modern World: Asia and the Pacific*, ed. R. H. Taylor, 1555–1576. New York: Facts on File.

Stott, Philip, ed. 1978. *Nature and Man in South East Asia*. London: School of Oriental and African Studies.

Sukaesinee Subhadhira, Noangluk Suphanchaimat, Suriya Smutkupt, Suchint Simaraks, Weera Pakuthai, Kanlaya Subarnbhesai, and Panada Petchsingha. 1988. "Fuelwood Situation and Farmers' Adjustments in Northeastern Thai villages." In *Rapid Rural Appraisal in Northeast Thailand: Case Studies*, ed. George Lovelace, Sukaesinee Subhadhira, and Suchint Simaraks, 29–45. Khon Kaen: Khon Kaen University.

Supaphan Na Bangchang. 1990. "The Role of Buddhism in Conservation and Development in Thai Society: The Case of Mae Soi Valley." Paper presented to the 4th International Conference on Thai Studies, Kunming, May, 1990.

Tapp, Nicholas. 1989. *Sovereignty and Rebellion: The White Hmong of Northern Thailand*. Singapore: Oxford University.

Tasker, Rodney. 1989. "New War of Words." *Far Eastern Economic Review*, 27 July, 25–26.

———. 1994. "Trees and Jobs." *Far Eastern Economic Review*, 3 March, 19.

Taylor, J. L. 1991. "Living on the Rim: Ecology and Forest Monks in Northeast Thailand." *Sojourn* 6(1): 106–25.

Terwiel, B. J. 1989. *Through Travellers' Eyes: An Approach to Early Nineteenth-Century Thai History*. Bangkok: Duang Kamol.

TDRI. 1987. *Thailand: Natural Resources Profile*. Bangkok: Thailand Development Research Institute.

TDSC. 1992. "No Democracy, No Land Rights for the Landless." *TDSC Information Sheets, no. 5*. Bangkok: Thai Development Support Committee.

UNDP. 1992. *Human Development Report 1992*. New York: Oxford University Press.

Wanat Bhruksasri. 1989. "Government Policy: Highland Ethnic Minorities." In *Hill Tribes Today: Problems in Change*, ed. John McKinnon and Bernard Vienne, 5–31. Bangkok: White Lotus.

5

ECONOMIC GROWTH WITH POLLUTION: TAIWAN'S ENVIRONMENTAL EXPERIENCE

JUJU CHIN-SHOU WANG

Introduction

As Taiwan emerges as one of the newly industrialized countries, increased pollution goes hand in hand with an increase in the Gross National Product (GNP). The last two decades have demonstrated the flaws in a development policy whose goal is to maximize monetary income; those years have underscored the need for holistic and comprehensive perspectives. Events repeatedly have shown the need to evaluate economic success by criteria that reflect all components of human welfare, including long-term sustainability of natural resources and ecological systems, rather than by those that measure progress solely in terms of the flow of money (Hsiao et al. 1989). Environmental pollution is considered one of the most serious social problems in industrialized Taiwan and is perceived as a negative aspect of the "Taiwan experience."

Taiwan is creating a new political culture. Martial law, which had been in effect since the government moved from mainland China and which had lasted thirty-eight years, was lifted on 14 July 1987. Since then, the government has tolerated opposition political activities and citizen organizations. Thus, the interplay of environmental policy and politics in Taiwan is complicated.

Overview of Environmental Problems

Taiwan's industrialization has been synonymous with the country's economic development. During the 1960s, in the initial stage of industrialization, Taiwan consumed large quantities of resources and inflicted great harm on its environment while it pursued development (Boulding 1966).

Researchers have discovered that economic development without concern for the environment often results in a fall into the "poverty of affluence" (Wachtel 1983; Galbraith 1984), and social development without environmental protection similarly can result in a fall into the "barbarity of civilization" (Wang 1995).

Taiwain's environmental problems did not develop over a brief span of time; they result from a special kind of interaction among people, space, and activity through time. When this interaction reached a certain threshold or critical mass, increasingly serious problems developed.

According to the "ecological triangle"—people, space, and activities (Tilly 1974)—environmental problems in Taiwan could be elaborated in terms of three newly developed concepts. 'Environmentally aggressive people,' 'environmentally aggressive space,' and 'environmentally aggressive activities,' all part of the paradigm shift in Taiwan from another set of concepts: 'environmentally defensible people, space, and activities' (Wang 1994).

Environmentally Aggressive People

Habermas (1970) suggested three important relationships in human life—human and human, human and nature, and life and death. The deterioration of the human and nature relationship is the most crucial cause of environmental problems.

Even three thousand years ago, the Chinese people saw the relationship of human and nature as two sides of one coin. The theory that humankind is an integral part of nature actually is an inherited Chinese ecosophy—wisdom or knowledge about the ecosystem. For example, a new law promulgated in California regulates the size of fishnet holes so that only the larger fish are caught. This custom is part of the Chinese heritage that dates back three thousand years (Yuan 1989). The traditional view that knowledge and action are not one is, paradoxically, one of the factors that contributes to environmental dilemmas.

The Chinese people have low social control for two reasons. First is the Chinese national characteristic to "sweep the snow only in front of one's own house." And second is the lack of public regard, long denounced, which also intensifies the seriousness of pollution. The word *public* in the phrase *public regard* implies "public goods." It means that such things as air, water, and land are shared by all. Because they do not belong to the private sphere, public goods fall into "no-man's land"—they belong to all of us and, consequently, to none of us. Environmental quality, as a result, suffers.

Taiwan's population density, which ranks second in the world, also is a necessary condition for pollution. Although extensive research normally indicates a positive correlation between population density and social pathology, these two variables are negatively related in Chinese society (Porteous 1977). In China, environmental pollution that results from high density does not cause social problems. However, from the perspective of environmental sociology, that view implies that the "human bubble" of the Chinese people is smaller. The Chinese often consider crowdedness or high density as a way of life and thus are more willing to tolerate pollution.

Environmentally Aggressive Space

Long deemed a basic unit of carrying capacity, "space" in an environmental sense can be used to absorb, diffuse, segregate, and dilute environmental pollution. In Taiwan, not using available space has produced counteractions that accumulate and duplicate pollution. Concentration in space or high density in land use reduces the carrying capacity of space and engenders many kinds of environmental problems.

The first factor is population density. Taiwan's average population density of 587 persons per square kilometer would not produce environmental stress if the population were distributed equally over the whole country. However, differences in population density across different districts is comparatively great in Taiwan. The population density in Taipei's downtown areas, for example, is as high as nine thousand persons per square kilometer. In such a situation, tremendous environmental stress is inevitable. Sixty-seven percent of Taiwan's population live in the three metropolises of northern, central, and southern Taiwan, which cover only 18 percent of Taiwan's total area. The carrying capacity of these spaces has long been exceeded. Consequently, environmental quality has deteriorated, not surprisingly, at an amazing rate.

The second factor is the distribution density of factories in industrialized Taiwan. Currently, Taiwan has 2.68 factories per square kilometer, which is 6.5 times greater than the United States and 2.3 times greater than Japan. If those areas that cannot be used for human settlement are subtracted, Taiwan has 5.3 factories per square kilometer. This average value can create a false impression. In Kaohsiung municipality, for instance, 2,183 factories are listed as causing pollution (EPA 1995b). However, official figures seriously underreport the problem. The above-mentioned factories are the only registered pollution-causing factories. Four times as many unregistered "underground factories" are also operating. Pressure from environmental protection groups and from the production cycle, especially the pollution-causing factories, gives rise to the phenomenon of "filtering-down." Pollution problems that accompany industrialization spread from urban to rural areas and on to foreign countries.

The final factor is the number of motor vehicles. Up to December 1994, 16.5 million motor vehicles were registered in Taiwan, averaging 459 per square kilometer; two-thirds of those were motorcycles. That is fifteen times the number of vehicles registered ten years ago. In Taipei, in 1994, the space available for each vehicle was reduced from 92.55 to 30.60 per square kilometer (Bureau of Statistics 1994).

Not only does density in space cause friction in space, but it creates other environmental problems as well. Space theoretically can be classified into "space of production" and "space of living," or "open space" and "closed space." Generally speaking, residuals produced by factories in the process of production (e.g., air pollution, water pollution, and noise) possibly might exert some influence on a neighboring community. A factory cannot fully practice self-purification of air and water when it is situated close to a residential community, and accordingly, production costs are increased. However, the community is directly exposed to the circle of pollution, and social costs thus are increased. Approximately 24 percent of registered factories are situated in or near residential districts. No matter which existed first, factories or residential districts, planning and zoning of space have been problematic from the beginning.

The incompatibility of city space also engenders ever-increasing pollution. Some people still are accustomed to a life style of running a store downstairs and living upstairs. Traditionally, some households even use their living rooms as factories. Space incompatibility is increased enormously as people create unlimited functions in limited space. For example, opening private shrines and *KARAOK* (singing with a big TV screen either in an apartment or in a public hall) in residential areas produces serious noise pollution, among other problems. Administrative boundaries create a blind spot in environmental protection since "borderless" environmental problems cannot be solved efficiently (Wang 1994). Examples include the burning of scrap metals along the border between Tainan and Kaohsiung in southern Taiwan and the widespread garbage dumps along the urban-rural borders of towns and cities all around Taiwan.

Topography (see map 5.1) often becomes the limiting or promoting factor in carrying capacity. The geography of the Taipei basin, for example, generally is called a "geography for storing pollution." Taipei often has serious air pollution problems as a consequence of being basinlike and windless. Even though Taiwan's rainfall amounts to 2,105 millimeters per year, six times the world average, this does little to dilute water pollution. During the dry season, from May to September, pollutants cannot be washed away; they remain in the riverbeds. Then, during the rainy season, deposited pollutants are washed downstream, and this leads to serious water pollution in the lower reaches of the rivers.

MAP 5.1

Topography of Taiwan

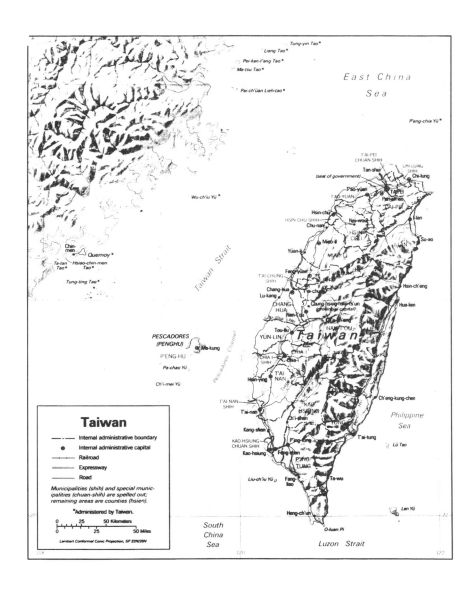

Source: Central Intelligence Agency, 1992.

Environmentally Aggressive Activities

Environmental pollution is considered to be the residue and entropy accumulated from various human activities, both economic and social.

As an export-oriented island economy, especially one centered on products with smaller value-added production in the early production cycle, Taiwan utilizes many resources to produce its GNP. Today Taiwan consumes 66 million tons of primary resources, an average of 1,833 tons per square kilometer, every year to support various activities of production and daily life. To remain competitive, both private and state enterprises in Taiwan have long adopted the strategies of appropriating funds for pollution penalty budgets and illegally discharging pollutants to avoid investing in pollution control.

Consumption patterns in commercialism and industrialization promote the social circulation of materials, which increases pollution. Industry aims at replacing products, not in providing durable products. The enormous waste that results from high consumption also is regarded as an index of life quality, and high consumption is valued. The social circulation of life-style materials, compared with the biological circulation of materials (the circulation of the materials necessary for survival), is intended to enable people to live better or even more luxuriously. Such an increase in consumption constitutes the "fast-food culture," which accelerates various production activities; it also speeds up consumption activities. Greater environmental pressures are generated across the whole process. The garbage problem is perhaps one of the most conspicuous examples. From 1975 to 1985, and 1985 to 1990, average garbage generation per person rose from 0.5 to 0.74 to 1.0 kilograms per day. Currently, Taiwan dumps 8.5 million tons of garbage yearly, 1.12 kilograms per person per day (EPA 1995).

Pork production in Taiwan is second only to that of the Netherlands. To supply the consumers of Taiwan and Japan with pork, hundreds of ranches are raising 1 million pigs, an average of 280 pigs per square kilometer. Because some ranches are located beside rivers and reservoirs, they cause severe water pollution.

Traffic activities reinforce vitality and accelerate mutual interaction, and a rapid mass transportation system currently is under construction in Taiwan. Meanwhile, however, in Taiwan, almost everyone has a car. During rush hours, Taipei is known as the world's largest parking lot. The result is an obvious waste of resources, and because of the resulting air pollution, everyone pays a higher social cost in time, energy, and respiratory disease. Air pollution costs U.S. $0.32 billion each year (Wang 1995).

Environmental Loads

Urbanization and industrialization obviously have intensified the interaction among people, space, and activities in Taiwan. Taiwan has serious problems with pollutants, separately and in combination, that affect air, water, soil, living organisms, and the amenities we take from our environment. The following figures summarize the total environmental loads in Taiwan. First, the Pollutant Standard Index (PSI) is greater than 100 approximately thirty days out of a year. Forty percent of the SOx monitoring stations fail to meet the environmental standard. Second, in 17 percent of the residential areas, the average noise level exceeds 65 db, which is not good for living (Environmental Quality Foundation 1996). Third, 26 percent of the twenty-one major and twenty-four minor rivers are severely polluted. Forty-four townships dump their garbage beside the banks of the twenty-one major rivers. Lack of proper sewage treatment intensifies the water pollution problem. Twelve of twenty-one dams cannot supply tap water due to eutrophication. Fourth, 30 percent of the garbage produced in cities and 70 percent of industrial wastes are not disposed of properly. Two thirds of garbage disposal sites in 292 townships island-wide are either full or will be full within one year. Fifth, 83 percent of the rain is acid rain, with some measuring an acidity level of 4.3 pH. Sixth, 3.2 percent of Taiwan's land area (1,167 square kilometers) is suffering land subsidence ranging from 1.5 cm to 2.88 meters. The coastal line has declined from 10 meters to 100 meters in various sites. Moreover, fifty-three out of sixty beaches are polluted by a variety of medical wastes (Environmental Quality Foundation 1996).

These environmental loads permeate the island, as shown in the island-wide pollution map conceived by environmental groups in Taiwan (see map 5.2). In general, rural areas suffer from industrial pollution, while urban areas experience pollution problems from daily activities.

Environmental Policy

The formulation of environmental policies in Taiwan can be divided into six stages in terms of institutional changes and policy shifts.

Sanitation-Oriented Period (1955–1970)

The history of government-sponsored environmental affairs can be traced back to 1955 when the Laboratory of Environmental Sanitation under the Bureau of Health, Ministry of Interior, was established. When Taipei switched from a municipal to a metropolitan governmental entity in 1967, the city established its Bureau of Environmental Sanitation. In addition, the Taiwan Provincial Government launched a five-year project of island-wide environmental sanitation. In this period, environmental problems were viewed narrowly as sanitation problems and largely were ignored by the government and the general public.

At the same time, industrialization—particularly at the initial stage of the production cycle—was underway in Taiwan. Pollution resulting from the

MAP 5.2

Pollution Map of Taiwan

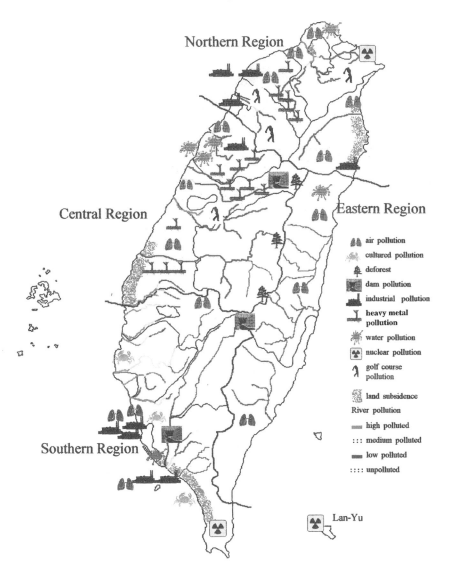

filtering-down process from other developed countries was conspicuous. For instance, Taiwan has absorbed many relocated factories from Japan. To meet Japanese needs Taiwan must export great quantities of pork and shrimp. As activities were carried out to meet these quotas, seashore land subsided and water became polluted (Miyamoto 1992). On 26 August 1970, the government, through the Ministry of Interior, sponsored a meeting on pollution abatement and proposed to enact environmental legislation and set up a responsible institution.

Initiation Period (1970–1975)

In 1971, the Department of Health (DOH) was restructured and expanded from the Bureau of Health, Ministry of Interior. The Bureau of Environmental Sanitation (BES), under the DOH took charge of environmental affairs. BES, however, was responsible only for air pollution control and garbage disposal. Other environmental affairs were distributed among different agencies. For example, Police Administration managed noise and hawker problems and the Ministry of Economy (MOE) controlled water pollution. Along with the institutional development, several major pollution control laws were enacted during this period. In July 1974, the Water Pollution Control Act and the Waste Disposal Act were promulgated to mark the first step of environmental initiatives. One year later, the Air Pollution Control Act was passed.

At the same time the pollution control legislations were enacted, grassroots social and academic organizations were active in raising public awareness. For example, the Rotary Club and the Junior Chamber International sponsored environmental campaigns against pollution—the street clean-up movement and the dirt-free movement. Moreover, major academic associations, such as the Environmental Sanitation Association of the Republic of China (ROC), the SCOPE China Committee, and the Environmental Protection Association of the ROC, were established during this period as well.

Environmental Awareness Period (1975–1979)

A pollution boom brought on by the rapid economic advance was the major issue of this period. To control environmental problems, an ad hoc task force was organized that integrated the DOH, MOE, the Taiwan Provincial Government, and the Kaohsiung municipal and prefecture governments. The task force was charged with carrying out a pollution control pilot project in Taiwan. The pilot project, conducted from 1975 through 1977, focused on the Kaohsiung area, which suffered from heavy-industry pollution. In 1977, as a result of comparative research on environmental issues among institutions in the United States, Japan, and Singapore, the Commission of Research and Evaluation in Taiwan proposed to set up a national authority to take charge of environmental affairs.

Transitional Period (1979–1982)

In March 1979, a comprehensive ten-year Environmental Protection Program, covering five categories and including ninety-two items, was launched. Among the five categories, institutionalization and legislation had top priority. Consensus on promoting environmental affairs was reached, but concrete governmental actions did not follow. Public participation in the antipollution movement was popular and made possible the first successful lawsuit in 1981. One hundred sixteen farmers sued a brick manufacturer in central Taiwan charging that air pollution had damaged their cultured products. They won the case and received compensation of New Taiwanese $26 million (U.S. $1 million). Pollution-caused factory relocation brought powerful social pressure, mainly from local citizens. For example, eight steel mills in Taipei were relocated or forced to stop operations during this period. The Environmental Impact Assessment (EIA) system also was introduced into Taiwan during this period. Two pilot EIA projects, the Northern Industrialized Zone and the Feu-Tui Dam in the Taipei area, were undertaken by the BES and National Taiwan University, respectively.

Adjustment Period (1982–1987)

On 29 January 1982, the Bureau of Environmental Protection (BEP), expanded from the BES, was established to handle pollution control affairs. Its major goal was to establish a healthy and comfortable environment. In July of the same year, the Taipei and Kaohsiung municipalities also set up their Bureaus of Environmental Protection. At the same time, the Bureau of Health both at the city and at the county levels rearranged their laws on environmental protection.

In 1983, the Provincial Environmental Authority, Department of Environmental Protection (DEP), was set up to take care of other environmental problems. The Kaohsiung Regional Environmental Monitoring Center which was set up then is still in operation. During this period institutionalization was underway to set up an environmental network. Trial and error characterized this period in terms of ambitious environmental projects such as the Natural Conservation Project in the Taiwan Area (1984), the Garbage Treatment Project of the City (1984), and the EIA Promotion Project (1985). Evaluations of these projects were marked as policy statements because of the involvement of various agencies. To better manage large-scale environmental projects, the Ad Hoc Environmental Team of the Executive Yuan cabinet comprised of leaders of related agencies was established in May 1986.

Developing Period (1987–)

On 22 August 1987, the Executive Yuan united the environmental protection authorities by upgrading the former Bureau of Environmental Protection, under the Department of Health, to form the Environmental Protection Administration (EPA). The Executive Yuan also passed the "Guideline for Environmental Protection Policy for the Present Stage" in late 1987. It was stated clearly, early in the guideline, that environmental protection was to be a national priority higher than economic development. Later, the policy was restated so that environmental protection was emphasized equally with economic development.

Although the most important legislation, the Draft of Environmental Basic Law, was submitted by the Executive Yuan in May 1988, the so-called environmental constitution was opposed in the congress (Wang 1993). From then on, under interesting names, various measures on pollution control rather than on environmental management have been taken to combat rapidly growing pollution. For example, the Nobel Project was to check the pollution from university laboratories; the Rambo Project was to fight industrial pollution; and the ET Project was responsible for recycling activities. To better educate the public, a Center of Environmental Education was established jointly in 1988 by the EPA and the National Normal University. In order to manage pollution cases reported by the public the EPA launched its pollution hotline in August 1991. Other farsighted steps have been initiated. For example, the environmental labeling system and (Green Mark) the Environmental Green Plan were started in 1991. A long-term National Environmental Protection Plan was launched in 1994. Further, the Environmental Impact Assessment Act was promulgated at the end of 1994.

Basically, the government is aware of public discontent, but because it has not yet reached consensus on how to respond, it has not been in a position to take effective action. Various planning documents and environmental policies and regulations have been formulated and, in some cases, passed. However, much of the law has not been effectively implemented (Hsiao et al. 1989). Environmental movement thus reflects the public's discontent.

In the environmental movement as well as in the consumer rights movement advocates from the community have begun to affect governmental policy and practices in Taiwan. The Consumers Foundation, a nonprofit organization, has been guarding people's environmental rights in terms of testing, investigation, follow-up with legal action, and lobbying. The Homemakers' Union, comprised of housewives with higher education, has recruited and trained "environmental mothers" for local action in the community. Moreover, the Taiwan Environmental Protection Union, an activist group, is famed for its antinuclear activities. A newly established environmental group, the Green Consumer Foundation, joined with the Environmental Beautification Foundation, has devoted itself to wildlife conservation and has been involved in a worldwide Clean-up the World campaign since 1993. Integration among various environmental groups has been initiated in regard to large-scale national issues, such as the antinuclear movement against the fourth nuclear power plant. Thirty thousand people staged an antinuclear protest in May 1994. Moreover, on World Environment Day, 5 June 1994, a grass-roots earth summit was held to organize the Grass-Roots Sustainable Development Commission (SDC) to cope with the decisions made in the Rio Earth Summit of 1992.

Hsiao (1988) analyzed 112 environmental protest actions that occurred in the 1980s. He discovered that most of the actions were post-facto protests to mitigate against or seek compensation for existing injuries or loss to individuals. It seemed that all actions were focused on a single environmental issue, and thus, few actions spawned permanent organizations. Moreover, antipollution actions were initiated primarily by local residents and supported by concerned scholars and intellectuals. Some antipollution actions even became coercive or violent.

For years, the island-wide environmental protest actions directed to environmental improvements dominated the arena of environmental politics in Taiwan. People in Taiwan learned that protest was the only method that brought results. Polluting factories were forced either to improve the condition immediately or to pay compensation to the victims. Some factories were even forced to shut down or to move to other locations. A few preventive actions have succeeded in forcing prospective plants to withdraw from their planned construction, for example the DuPont titanium dioxide plant. To ease upcoming environmental conflicts, environmental units at the central and local levels have launched their hotlines.

However, Yeh (1989) identified the other side of the coin, the side that reflects institutional deficiencies. For example, in the DuPont and Lin-Yuan cases he discovered that protesters did not seek court relief and that not a single public hearing regarding the issues was held by the responsible authorities during the whole process. In addition, not a single legal provision or precedent was cited by either party, either in the confrontations or in the negotiations. Similar observations can be made in most of the environmental protest cases. Following the growing pains that occurred through the environmental conflicts, the Pollution Conflict Treatment Act was passed in January 1992.

The mass media also plays a key role in shaping environmental policy in Taiwan. The three main functions of mass media are surveillance, interpretation, and linkage (Dominick 1987). From the national media, this concern has diffused into the local newspapers. Over time coverage has shifted primarily from bringing knowledge and awareness to the public to covering policies, programs, government activities, crises, citizen's groups, and more recently, local problems and issues (Stone 1989). Some newspapers in Taiwan, such as the *Independent Daily Post*, present a more critical view toward environmental issues. Occasionally, three major television stations are asked to refrain from reporting too much on sensitive environmental issues. To balance this "information monopoly," more and more private cable television and radio broadcasting stations are being operated. In particular, some private broadcasting stations, such as the Voice of Taiwan, provide on-air forums where listeners can call in to discuss environmental issues.

The stages of change in environmental policy reflect the interaction over time between the development and environmental sectors. The state's major strategy in dealing with environmental issues has been "push and go." Basically, the state continues to remind the public that pollution is a necessary evil. Environmental affairs are thus a favor to the people. After martial law was lifted in 1987, environmental groups associated with several antipollution movements began to challenge the myth of growth. Political groups, especially the opposition party, have put pressure on the ruling party and the state through various environmental issues and have declared that the ruling party (KMT) is the major source of pollution. In addition to global pressures, both environmental and political groups have triggered significant social forces to help push the formulation of environmental policy in Taiwan.

Assessment of Policy Effectiveness

Two conventional ways exist to evaluate policy effectiveness—cause-effect and cost-benefit. In addition, two other criteria are available—policy legitimacy and institutional implementation (Vig and Kraft 1994). Public satisfaction with environmental quality may, in part, reflect cause and effect.

Public opinion surveys reveal that environmental quality ranks high among social concerns of the Taiwanese people, that environmental consciousness has increased rapidly since the mid-1980s, and that people are extremely pessimistic about Taiwan's environmental future (Hsiao et al. 1989).

Hsiao (1986) conducted sample surveys of the public's opinion about social problems. For each of eighteen items, respondents were asked to rate how serious the problem was at present and then to estimate how serious it would be five years later. In 1983, environmental pollution ranked sixth most serious of the eighteen social problems; in 1986 it ranked second, exceeded only slightly by juvenile delinquency. In 1983, 70 percent of the public rated pollution as serious or very serious, but in 1986 that figure increased to 88 percent. In 1983, 51 percent of the public believed pollution would get worse over the coming five years, while this percentage increased to 70 percent in 1986. Academia Sinica (1992) conducted an island-wide social survey and discovered that 51.9 percent of the respondents rated pollution as a serious social problem in 1985, and 82.3 percent did so in 1992. When asked whether they were satisfied with their living environment, in 1990, 19.7 percent were satisfied (Academia Sinica 1992), but in 1995, only 16.9 percent were satisfied (Executive Yuan of Taiwan 1995). A recent survey conducted by the Executive Yuan indicated that traffic congestion, pollution, and inflation are the three most serious social problems in Taiwan (Executive Yuan of Taiwan 1995). In a decade, pollution has moved to the top of the list of the public's major concerns.

The Hsiao survey revealed, moreover, that in 1983, 59 percent believed that governmental actions had not been adequate to deal with environmental problems; by 1986, this percentage had increased to 64. In a 1986 survey of the general public's satisfaction with government policies, the overall rating of environmental policies was poor (30.7 percent) as compared with a high rating for the living standard (78.7 percent). The EPA in Taiwan (1992, 1993) conducted two surveys to check green marketing and environmental effectiveness. Ninety percent of the respondents realized the seriousness of environmental problems, and 69.5 percent were willing to buy green products. Another survey revealed that 94.5 percent of the respondents cared about the environment in 1993, an increase from 92.7 percent in 1992. However, respondents earned an average score of only 34.5 in environmental knowledge. A Gallup poll indicated that 78.8 percent of the respondents believed the government cared about the environment in June 1992, while this figure declined to 71.4 percent in March 1993 and to 67.9 percent in June 1993.

Among various channels utilized to register complaints about pollution, hotlines received the most complaints; 22,769 or 19.9 percent of all complaints in 1989 and more than 25 percent of complaints in 1992. This was followed by writing letters and making requests from the cabinet (Executive Yuan) and other agencies (EPA 1993b). This figure coincides with those from Japan, where the pollution complaint hotline was popular (Environmental Agency, Japan 1993).

At present there are twenty eight hotlines for pollution reports and complaints in Taiwan. These hotlines, all in the public sector, are spread over twenty-one prefectures and cities and two municipalities (Taipei and Kaohsiung). In addition, the central EPA and the Taiwan Provincial Government operate one main hotline and three regional hotlines. The EPA hotline, established in July 1991, has become the national line for reporting pollution complaints. A hotline operated by the New Environment Foundation from February to April of 1989 was the only private pollution complaint hotline. Research conducted by Wang (1992b) on pollution hotlines revealed that (1) a high degree of anonymity for hotline cases indicates that more and more people are making the first move in dealing with pollution in their daily life in a self-protective fashion. The implication is that callers are attempting to protect both their living environment and their privacy; and (2) pollution and public nuisances exist everywhere and occur at any time. Environmental protection evidently has not been integrated into city and regional planning.

According to figures presented by the EPA, utilizing various channels including hotlines, the public reported a total of eighty-six thousand pollution cases in 1994. The Taipei municipality and the prefecture together accounted for more than half the pollution cases reported. At the local level most cases reported were associated with garbage problems, while the Taipei municipality received more complaints about noise problems. Since 1988, when martial law was lifted, 259 serious pollution disputes or conflicts, mostly from the pollution complaint cases mentioned, have occurred. Industrial regions such as Kaohsiung city and prefecture accounted for one third of the cases. Among these cases, chemical factories, garbage dumping sites, and power plants were the three major targets of environmental complaints (EPA 1995).

Local residents, frustrated by the inaction and ineffectiveness of public authorities in managing environmental problems and hazards, have increasingly turned to direct action. Public protests about pollution and natural resource protection have become increasingly common, better organized, and, in some cases, more aggressive (Hsiao 1989).

In terms of the cost-benefit relationship, without pollution abatement, the growth rate of the GNP would be 0.23 percentage points higher than the actual GNP growth rate, which registered 6.75 percent per annum from 1987 through 1991. The social cost of air pollution accounted for 5.1 percent of the GNP in 1991 (Liang et al. 1993).

The cost-benefit relationship also shows that for Taiwan's rice sector, during the first production period of 1990, a one-unit (0.01 ppm) increase in the concentration level of sulfur dioxide (SO_2) increased the cost of social welfare at least $92 million NT. Similarly, social welfare costs increased about $110 million NT dollars for the Taiwan rice sector for each one-unit (0.01 ppm) reduction in the ozone concentration level. The figures indicate a need to improve air quality in Taiwan (Liang et al. 1993).

Willingness to pay for clear air is positively related to the level of pollution and household income for owner-occupied homes. The mean value of the marginal willingness to pay for clean air is $130 NT ($5.00 U.S.) per household in Taipei municipality and $17,800 NT ($685 U.S.) per household in Taipei prefecture (Liang et al. 1993).

Among environmental policies in Taiwan up to 1995, the environmental impact assessment (EIA) system introduced in the 1970s played an important role. Later, in 1985 a five-year promotion program was launched, and in 1990 it was extended to 1993 when a new EIA Act was initiated. During the nine-year period, 393 EIA cases were reviewed and 261 cases were passed. Entering the new EIA era, Taiwan's EPA reviewed another 145 cases and passed 107 cases in 1994 and 1995 (EPA of Taiwan 1996) (see table 5.1). Among these cases, urban development projects, nineteen in 1994 and twenty-nine in 1995, were very conspicuous.

In a high-density society such as Taiwan, social impact is a gray area in environmental impact assessment. After evaluating fifty-two EISs released

Table 5.1

EIA Cases after Enactment of EIA Act

Categories / Years	Industrial Development	Transportation Development	Mining Project	Reservoir Dam Development	Agriculture Forestry & Fishery Development	Recreational Resort, Golf Course Development	Educational & Medical Development	New Town High-Rise Building & Urban Renewal	Environmental Engineering Project	Nuclear Power or Other Energy Development	Others	Total
1994	11	11	0	5	0	3	7	19	7	2	2	67
	(11)	(8)	(0)	(4)	(0)	(1)	(11)[1]	(9)	(4)	(3)[1]	(0)	(51)
1995	12	5	0	3	0	3	9	29	12	3	2	78
	(8)	(6)[1]	(0)	(2)	(0)	(2)	(9)	(14)	(11)	(4)	(0)	(56)

( ) indicates cases approved
1. Some cases carry over from previous year.

Source: EPA of Taiwan, 1996.

between 1982 and 1989, Wang and Hsiao (1989) presented a general picture of the social impact assessment (SIA) practice in Taiwan. Major goals of EIA or SIA are to streamline the policy-making process and to promote public involvement. SIA, to the extent it is seen as presuming a Western style of public participation and involvement, is unacceptable in many developing countries (Burdge and Roberston 1990). At the current stage, SIA in Taiwan has a managerial-technocratic orientation, in a formal but quasi-statutory setting, according to Gagnon's (1993) community empowerment framework. Theoretically, SIA, a limiting factor of EIA, will play a more significant role in dealing with intangible social elements in developing countries particularly in new industrialized nations such as Taiwan. In the long run, the benefits of SIA and suggestions for its implementation proposed by Burdge (1990) are intended to promote more sound "Third-World Edition" SIAs to cope with cultural differences.

Both quantitatively and qualitatively, social impact assessment in Taiwan largely has been neglected and unsuccessful because it lacks a sound data base, an appropriate social impact assessor, guidelines and methodologies, capable conflict prediction, concrete mitigation measures, and long-term environmental policy. One of the common shortcomings of SIA in Taiwan is the GIGO effect (garbage in, garbage out). It is essential to set up a national data bank that integrates the bio-region concept (McDonald 1990; Wang 1992). In regard to impacts on society, it is urgent to promote policy impact assessment, regulatory impact assessment, and total impact assessment. The newly enacted EIA Act of 1994 eventually included policy impact assessment, total impact assessment and the retroactivity principle, which make it a powerful legislation.

In addition, in 1988 the EPA established a checking system for EIA projects in order to oversee their follow-up steps for environmental management. Chen (1992) reviewed sixteen cases and discovered that (1) the planning unit did not release EIS to the execution or construction counterparts so that strategies for environmental monitoring and management became simply paperwork; (2) the construction unit did not hire environmental staff and thus could not carry out the promised strategies; (3) planners provided little or no budget to conduct environmental management measures mentioned in the EIS, including an environmental monitoring plan and mitigation; and (4) respective authorities did not take the responsibility to check post-EIA steps. It seems that the EIA system in Taiwan is only a "reference" for other responsible agencies. However, as a preventive means to promote a sound environment, the EIA system still plays an important role in easing the problems of rapid development in Taiwan.

Another environmental policy worth noting is the Green Mark system, which began in early 1992. Compared with other environmental policies conducted by the EPA in Taiwan, the Green Mark system is a relatively far-sighted step toward the worldwide trend of a green consumer movement. Up to June 1996, the Green Mark committee initiated thirty-three categories and approved 370 items to earn a Green Mark (figure 5.1). According to a survey relating to Green Mark, 72 percent of the potential applicants indicated that the government has not promoted Green Mark, and as a result, most consumers are unaware of products which carry the Green Mark (ITRI 1994).

FIGURE 5.1

Green Mark of Taiwan

環保標章我最愛　力行環保最實在

請愛用環保標章產品，追求舒適之環境品質！

Source: EPA of Taiwan 1994.

It is said that budget is the reflection of policy (Vig and Kraft 1994; Wang 1988), and Taiwan's environmental budget accounts for 0.86 percent of the total national budget. The environmental budget in 1992 was about $1.2 billion U.S., a 100 percent increase from the budget in 1989. Sixty-seven percent of the budget was for garbage disposal, 38 percent of which went toward incinerator construction, 29 percent for garbage collection. If the expenditures for garbage collection and disposal are subtracted from the budget, Taiwan's environment budget was only 0.27 percent of the total national budget, compared with the United States' 0.46 percent, Japan's 0.66 percent, and Germany's 0.48 percent (Liang et al. 1993).

Applying the concept of 'socialization' in terms of maturation and internalization, through the focus group method, Wang (1994) evaluated twenty-one policy-oriented environmental affairs following a framework of people, space, and activities (see table 5.2). The term *maturation* refers to

TABLE 5.2

Degree of Socialization of Environmental Issues

Items	Degree of Socialization	
	Maturation*	Internalization*
Environmental consciousness	M	L
Environmental employment	M	L
Environmental politics	H	L
Environmental impact pollution	M	M
Environmental institution	M	L
Enterprises (public/private sector)	L	L
NGO environmental groups	M	H
Environmental protests	M	L
Pollution distribution	L	L
Industrialized zone	L	L
Land use	L	L
Pollution appeal	M	L
Environmental enforcement	M	L
Environmental budget	M	M
Environmental policy/regulation	M	L
EIA system	M	L
Green business	L	M
Environmental R and D	M	M
Environmental education	M	L
EPA image	M	M

*L = Low (0 points); M = Medium (3 points); H = High (5 points).

Source: Juju Wang, 1995.

degrees of all-dimensional consideration through the policy's life cycle. *Internalization* refers to degrees of uniqueness and integration of the policy into Taiwan's special socioeconomic and political environment.

Among twenty-one items evaluated, some specific examples are presented here in order to elaborate their content and context. First, the major environmental strategies of most private enterprises are to appropriate monies for penalty and to discharge pollutants illegally through underground pipes rather than to install pollution-control equipment. Second, among one hundred state-run enterprises, eleven have had encounters with the antipollution movement through their neighboring community residents. Third, Taiwan has eighty-three industrial parks. Although most of them are equipped with discharge treatment facilities, they cannot operate effectively due to a high turnover rate of factories and heterogeneity of factories. For example, in eighteen of twenty-eight major industrial parks monitored by the EPA, the discharges failed to meet environmental standards. Industrial zones in Taiwan are ironically referred to as "pollution protection zones." Nevertheless, in the name of the industrial great wall, more industrial zones are being planned in the area around the east coast where they will compete with five of the sixteen wetlands in Taiwan.

The EPA's image could be an appropriate indicator by which to judge the effectiveness of its environmental policies. In 1986, when the central Bureau of Environmental Protection (BEP) reached its fourth year, the *United Daily News* conducted a survey asking readers to score the BEP in terms of its overall performance. The average score collected from the respondents of Taipei was only fifty-eight, which is a "failing" score. The next year, in 1987, the *China Time Weekly* conducted an island-wide telephone survey: 69.8 percent of the 2,800 respondents in the survey were not satisfied with the job done by the environmental agencies, both at the central and the local levels. Among the respondents, 34.9 percent proposed setting up an environmental court to handle pollution-related disputes. In 1988, the EPA's first anniversary, ten environmental groups awarded fifty-one out of one hundred points for the EPA's capability in controlling pollution, enforcing legislation, and handling pollution disputes.

In addition to the domestic evaluations of environmental policies in Taiwan, a Gallup poll requested by Taiwan's Bureau of Information surveyed the people of G7 nations. Taiwan's performance on environment protection and conservation was ranked only three on a ten-point scale, indicating a negative image of Taiwan's performance.

In evaluating the degree of environmental policy implementation ranging from lowest 1 to highest 5, Taiwan's overall score was 32 out of 105 points, in terms of three categories that covered twenty-one indicators (see table 5.3). Among the categories, space-related environmental affairs earned no score at all, indicating the severity of "friction of space."

TABLE 5.3

Overall Score of Environmental Policy Implementation

Category	Socialization	Maturation (50%)	Internalization (50%)
People	20	8	14
Space	0	0	0
Activities	24	12	18
Total	44	20	32

Source: Juju Wang, 1995.

To promote better environmental enforcement, the EPA established an enforcement and inspection team in June 1992. According to its two-year performance report, the team has inspected seventy-five thousand factories, shut down twenty-four, and issued tickets to seven thousand that failed to comply with environmental regulations (EPA 1995).

Environmental Policy and Politics

Recognizing that nothing is apolitical in Taiwan, environmental policy making there has been politicized since it is considered antigrowth or even antigovernment. As in other countries, three major actors—the state, business groups, and environmental groups—are involved in the interplay of environmental policy making and politics in Taiwan.

With a strong progrowth ideology, the state of Taiwan tends to apply GNP as the only measure of the overall national welfare. Through its policy-making process the state constantly emphasizes the maxim that the higher the GNP, the higher the quality of life. The state often conducts major actions without considering either environmental or social impacts. For example, the Six-Year National Construction Project, the Hsinchu Science City Project, the Economy Promotion Project, and the Southward (Southeast Asia) Expansion Policy were decided on only because of political and economic considerations. In particular, the Economy Promotion Project intends to release 160 thousand acres of farmland which will have a tremendous negative impact on the environment as a whole. The Southward Expansion Policy has been criticized as "environmental colonialism" aimed at relocating pollution-causing industries outside of Taiwan. Following such large-scale projects, increases in the GNP have brought about another increase in gross national pollution, and again, development or growth is obtained at the expense of the environment.

In one unique case, the Lan-Yu Radwaste Storage Site (LYRSS), which ruined the environment of the Yami tribe can better identify the interplay of environmental policy and politics (Wang 1992). Located in the southeastern part of Taiwan, Lan-Yu (Orchid Island), an island forty-five square kilometers in size with two thousand Yami inhabitants, had the reputation of being "a biological and ecological paradise." It was the only oceanic culture in China and the last paradise of cultural preservation due to its unique cultural aspects. Low-level waste management was initiated in 1972, and LYRSS has been operating since 1982. During that period, Taiwan was governed by martial law, and environmental justice was ignored. Despite their cultural and ecological uniqueness, the Yami people have suffered various negative impacts, ranging from biased stereotyping, to identity crisis, to human zoo effect through tourism. In an environmental sense, Lan-Yu has been treated as a "back yard" for Taiwan. LYRSS was pushed from Taiwan to Lan-Yu through a top-down and one-way decision-making process without any public participation. Even the Yami people were not informed. Since 1982, the anti-LYRSS movement has been closely associated with cultural conservation and environmental justice, and recently the Yami people have promoted an alternative political movement, the Yami Autonomy movement.

Institutionally speaking, the EPA is designated as responsible for pollution prevention and control, as well as for waste management. Other environmental concerns ranging from national parks and wildlife protection to nuclear energy are under the jurisdiction of other government agencies. Policy implementation thus is segmented and fails to be integrated effectively. Although the EPA plays a supervisory role in the twenty-three cities and prefectures, much of the agenda of the departments of Environmental Protection at the local level is set by their individual directors who are appointed by city mayors or prefecture commissioners. Thus, the integration between central and local levels is segmented. The island-wide garbage war partially reflects the environmental anarchism in terms of growth ideology and tensions among local governments.

As mentioned earlier, wildlife conservation, water resources conservation, national parks, and forestry are cared for by other agencies. Thus, environmental authority is distributed in many different sectors. Its low position at the agency level and its ineffective integration among various agencies have put the EPA in the position of "curing" rather than "preventing" environmental pollution. Due to its lower level and weaker role, the EPA has been criticized as a subordinated department under the Ministry of Economy. In addition, personnel of local environmental units are hired by local government, and those positions have become, more or less, political rewards of the election process. Taiwan's EPA thus can not effectively supervise the local environmental units because of political interference.

Basically, the commitments made by the state are mostly caught by the issue attention cycle, derived either by global pressure, the recent CITES sanction case, environmental disasters, or political pressures from the opposition party (DPP) or environmental groups. Despite the newly enacted EIA act in 1994, the prime minister promised to build Taichung International Airport and Southern Cross Highway for the 1995 national election. The latter project goes through a mountainous natural reservation area (NRA), which is regulated by article 52 of the Cultural Resource Conservation Act. Any NRA is not subject to change and destruction. Again, it is obvious that environmental legislation is ineffective when it meets politics.

However, the industrial and manufacturing sectors, strongly supported by the state, always claim that pollution control investments or environmental regulations affect their business interests and further economic investment. The industrial leaders, some of whom are congressmen themselves, also play a key role in the ruling party and more or less place pressure on the government. In other words, the state is "captured" (Bernstein 1955) by the dominant classes, industrial and business people, who are the spokespersons for development in Taiwan. As a result, first, a lower percentage of the GNP, 0.06 percent, is devoted to pollution control. Second, some fundamental laws, such as the Environmental Basic Law, have been ignored in Congress for more than ten years due to the opposition of business interests. Third, because of pressures from the industrial and business sectors, President Lee, in a public speech, asked to ease the environmental standard. However, research conducted by Chung (1992) indicated that the investments of only four of seventeen manufacturers declined because of environmental reasons. Moreover, investments in pollution control actually promoted the economic output by \$62.4 billion NT in 1991. During the national election in 1992, the ruling party (KMT) told the BEP of Taipei to ease environmental enforcement on motorcycles.

Through the democratic system with its election process, the people's voice on the environment has been released. In the 1986 national election 80 percent of 306 congressional and senatorial candidates listed environmental issues as their campaign topics. Environmental issues had become the most popular of the top ten campaign topics, followed by social welfare. In 1989, 64 percent of the sixty-nine city mayoral and prefecture commissioner candidates presented environmental issues as their campaign topics. In the 1991 national election more candidates, 90 percent, chose environmental issues for their election campaign.

In addition, some "green congressmen" are questioning environmental issues in Congress. For example, a 1990 survey by the EPA (1991) indicated that eighty-nine congressmen had raised questions 578 times on environmental issues. Congressman Chao, with twenty questions, gained a reputation as the most green. Later, Chao became the second administrator of the EPA in Taiwan.

Moreover, a group of congressmen, mostly medical doctors, organized an "Amenity Forum" to promote environmental legislation in Congress. Another group of congressmen, from different political parties, established an "Environmental Legislation Promotion Union" in 1996 to join the trend. Under the prodevelopment atmosphere in Taiwan, a Gallup poll asking about the EPA (1991) showed that 62.5 percent of the respondents favored the environment when it conflicted with development.

In the 1992 and 1994 local elections, the major opposition party, the Democratic Progress party (DPP), won more than ten seats at the provincial, municipal, and prefectural levels by placing emphasis on environmental issues. The Taipei prefecture, the largest one in Taiwan with a population of 3 million and two nuclear power plants, refuses to issue a construction permit to an additional nuclear power plant, which is part of the national energy development policy. Ilan prefecture in western Taiwan has successfully made the biggest oil refinery plant withdraw, primarily through setting strict environmental standards. Ilan prefecture thus maintains a better environmental quality compared with others in Taiwan. In these cases, the opposition party often united with environmental groups to place more pressure on the state. It is worth noting that the Green party, the seventy-ninth registered political party in Taiwan, was established in January 1996 and won one seat in the subsequent national senatorial election. However, environmentalists, through the channel of the opposition party, participated in elections and became green representatives at various levels. At this stage, environmental politics has became a powerful means to promote better policy-making in Taiwan.

The case of golf courses represents well the complicated interplay among the three key actors in Taiwan. There are eighty-four golf courses in Taiwan. Twenty of these are located in Hsinchu prefecture alone, making it a golf prefecture as well as an environmental sink area. Kuan-si township, an agriculture-oriented rural settlement of Hsinchu prefecture, accommodates eight golf courses, possibly making that prefecture number one in the world in terms of density of number of golf courses. However, only four of the eighty-four golf courses are operated legally. Thus, high-ranking governmental officials, including the president, play on the illegal golf courses. They have been criticized strongly for this by environmental groups. For example, the president, the premier, and the head of Congress each keep three or four membership cards for the illegal golf courses. Among others, a KMT congressman holds ten membership cards for the illegal golf courses. Some membership cards are presented to these politicians by the golf course owners who are known as "red-top" businessmen and who have close relationships with governmental leaders. The term *golf politics* implies that political and business interests are exchanged between businessmen and politicians on the golf courses. The relationship developed on the golf courses is certainly the major part of the politician-businessman complicity structure.

To deconstruct that complicity structure, environmental groups in Taiwan have been struggling with the state and golf course owners. Recently, two environmental groups accused forty-three golf courses of occupying about eighty-two acres of public land. This has attracted public attention to the matter of how golf courses have impact on the environment as a whole and what the relationship is between the state and golf course owners. Again, environmental anarchism is presented to question the state's role and its capability to deal with the environmental issues surrounding the golf course case. The opposition party and environmental groups have called several public hearings on the issue and have gained considerable exposure in the mass media. At the end of 1994, environmental groups sent a group of representatives to ask the president not to play golf on the illegal courses and to return his membership cards. On 12 March 1995, a national holiday devoted to tree planting, environmental groups went to an illegal golf course in Taoyuan prefecture, where the president owns a house and has a membership card, to plant trees in order to protest the golf politics. A 1995 Gallup poll indicated that 34 percent of the respondents wanted to "ask the government to ban her officials to play golf," while 43 percent agreed that the president should give up his golf membership cards.

Environmental groups and one hundred or more congressmen are initiating a battle to promote the EPA to a higher status—the Ministry of Environment (MOE). The state is against the proposal. The proposed MOE will integrate natural conservation and land use planning into its duties. This new development would have an impact on the interplay of politics and policy in Taiwan. First, the new MOE could be involved in each stage of environment-related affairs, ranging from land use planning to natural conservation to environmental management. Second, within the administrative hierarchy, upgrading the EPA from the agency level to the ministry level could result in increased budgetary and other resources for the environmental sectors. Third, it is expected that the MOE would play a more positive role in promoting better environmental policy, rather than being a rubber stamp unit. Radical environmentalists, however, are likely to reject the above idea and continuously stress the political reform associated with opposition political parties. Fourth, based on some common goals, environmental groups, in addition to their existing role as pressure groups, would form a partnership with environmental agencies to conduct some community-based environmental programs.

Despite her global economic activities, Taiwan faces an unusual situation known as "one China policy," due to her long-time political conflict with mainland China. After withdrawing from the United Nations, it is difficult for the Taiwan government to take part in international environmental affairs, such as global conventions and treaties. The Industrial Technology Research Institute (ITRI), a nationally supported NGO research unit, thus has been representing the government in international environmental activities. In most cases, governmental officials acting as consultants of the ITRI are able to attend international conferences or meetings on environmental issues. Basically, few opportunities exist in which Taiwan can take an initiative. The NGO approach is the only way to deal with the "one China politics." For instance Taiwan, with nine other countries, was involved in establishing a Global Ecolabeling Network (GEN) in 1994. In this sense, Taiwan with her economic power and unique political situation could well be the most powerful NGO in the world.

Conclusion

Taiwan, one of the four Asian dragons, has earned a bad reputation in its social and environmental performances. For instance, the acronym ROC (Republic of China) also stands for "Republic of Casino," the money and garbage flood of the underground economy and the island-wide garbage war. The term *pigsty*, a name given to Taiwan by Germany's *Mirror Post*, paints another negative image for Taiwan, one that symbolizes her unsound living environment. This term correlated with 1995 and 1996 public polls that measured the country's "environmental pain index," which ranged from 1 (no pain at all) to 5 (extremely painful). The total score from the twenty items polled was 73.66 and 72.92 out of 100, reflecting a high degree of public discontent with the living environment (see table 5.4).

Realizing the seriousness of environmental problems in Taiwan, the state initiated an ambitious National Environmental Protection Plan to seek a better environment by the year 2010. Concrete objectives have been set according to current environmental conditions. For example, unhealthy Pollution Standard Index (PSI) days will be reduced to 5 percent annually, as compared with 8.2 percent today; residential noise levels over 65 decibels will be reduced from the current 17 percent to 10 percent; the length of rivers with very serious pollution will be reduced from 11 percent to 7 percent; unqualified drinking water will decrease from 5 percent to 3 percent; and the garbage growth rate will decline from 10 percent to 5 percent. Although the objectives of the plan sound reasonable, because of some structural constraints it may be optimistic to expect the Taiwanese society to reach them. First, the EPA has little authority to make decisions on development or growth input, such as importing or producing cars or establishing factories, and it handles only "end of pipe" pollution problems. Second, among various central agencies, the EPA is weak. It can make plans, but it cannot be sure that other agencies will cooperate or follow its lead. In addition, pressures through the politician-businessman

TABLE 5.4

Environmental Pain Index (1996)

Items	Index (above 60)
River pollution	79.6
Water source pollution	79.2
Auto air pollution	72.6
Industrial water pollution	71.6
Plastic waste	70.6
Industrial air pollution	67.6
Abandoned cars/bikes	67.4
Garbage	66.3
Noise	65.4
Ocean pollution	64.6
Wandering dogs	63.3
Soil erosion	60.1

Source: Environmental Quality Foundation, Taiwan, 1996.

complicity structure inevitably will interfere in formulating and implementing environmental policy.

Businessmen and interest groups have tended to control the state by using moving-out and no-vote strategies. Despite the slogan Leave Your Root in Taiwan proposed by the government, more and more businesses and factories are moving to mainland China. To deal with this trend, the government must provide concrete incentives, including the deregulation of environmental standards. Golf politics is a specific case that displays how business groups capture the state. Following suit, business groups have utilized the no-vote strategy to put pressure on the government. The no-vote approach also applies to those factories whose pollution fines are too high to pay. In most cases, congressmen who represent the business groups carry the message in Congress or directly to the EPA.

However, environmental groups in Taiwan are very unhappy about the EPA's overall performance, although the EPA was established in part as a result of the antipollution movement promoted by environmental groups in the 1970s. Even though the cabinet has begun the structural adjustment necessary to upgrade the EPA to the Ministry of Environment, environmental groups have questioned the organization's credibility, primarily on three grounds: the golf course case already mentioned, release of 160 thousand acres of farmland, and the action of the EIA regarding the fourth nuclear power plant. While serving as a responsible agency in regard to the EIA and realizing the ecological function of the farmland, the EPA has taken no action to intervene. In a sense, the distance between environmental groups and the state has grown greater. Environmental groups need new direction, such as a national trust movement, the green consumer movement, and international networking, so that other dimensions can be pursued.

Economic activities generally are expected to maximize profits within a short time. Environmental protection, however, attempts to minimize long-term risks and disasters. Environmental philosophy is that minimum harm to the environment is the maximum profit for sustainable development. The government has begun to recognize that environmental protection is good economics, partially due to the worldwide trend and the pressure of possible sanctions on Taiwan because of ineffective wildlife conservation and measures of the GATT green trade. However, the public in Taiwan suffering from lower environmental quality has begun to pay more attention to the environment and to take action to defend it in various ways. Grass-roots activities are an essential part of the paradigm shift from the dominant social paradigm to the new ecological paradigm (Humphrey and Buttel 1986; Milbrath 1989).

Peasant folklore of old China told a classic story. Through good luck and hard work, a family becomes rich over several decades. Then, they turn their backs on the land, stop minding the irrigation systems, become contemptuous of the difficulty and dirty work required to maintain soil fertility, begin spending wildly, and fall into debt. The land declines, debts come due, and the family returns to poverty. This folktale actually further elaborates the negative side of the "Taiwan experience" and implies that effective environmental policy is the best strategy for sustainable development.

References

Academia Sinica. 1992. *Social Survey in the Taiwan Area.* Taipei: Academia Sinica.

Bernstein, M. 1955. *Regulating Business by Independent Commission.* Princeton: Princeton University Press.

Boulding, K. E. 1966. "The Economics of the Coming Spaceship Earth." In *Towards a Steady-State Economy*, ed. H. E. Daly. New York: W. H. Freeman.

Burdge, R. J. 1990. "The Benefits of Social Impact Assessment in Third World Development." *Environmental Impact Assessment Review* 10:123–34.

Burdge, R. J., and R. A. Robertson. 1990. "Social Impact Assessment and Public Involvement Process." *Environmental Impact Assessment Review* 10: 81–90.

Bureau of Statistics. 1994. *National Statistics of the R.O.C.* Taipei: Executive Yuan.

Chen, Y. R. 1992. "The Function of EIA Follow-up and Supervision in Environmental Management System." *Proceedings of Fifth Environmental Planning and*

Management Conference, 29–36. Taipei: Chinese Institute of Environmental Engineering.

Cheng, L. R. Lilly. 1989. "The Promotion of Environmental Protection through Media and Community Movement." *Proceedings of the Sino-US Bi-National Conference on Environmental Protection and Social Development*, 17–33. Taipei: EPA of Taiwan.

Chung, C. R. 1992. *Environmental Protection and Social Development*. Taipei: EPA.

Dominick, J. R. 1987. *The Dynamics of Mass Communication*. New York: Newberry Award Records.

Environmental Agency, Japan. 1993. *Environmental Report of Japan*. Tokyo: EA.

Environmental Protection Administration, Taiwan, ROC. 1991. *Working Report of the Congress*. Taipei: EPA.

EPA of Taiwan. 1992. *Survey on Green Marketing*. Taipei: Gallup Co.

———. 1993. *Environmental Effectiveness of the Government*. Taipei: Gallup Co.

———. 1993b. *Annual Report of Pollution Hot Line*. Taipei: EPA.

———. 1994. *Greenmark Handbook of Taiwan*. Taipei: EPA.

———. 1995. *Yearbook of Environmental Statistics*. Taipei: EPA.

———. 1995b. *Local Environmental Information in Taiwan*. Taipei: EPA.

———. 1996. *Environmental Monthly Statistics*. Taipei: EPA.

Environmental Quality Foundation, Taiwan. 1996. *A Public Survey on Environmental Pain Index*. Taipei: EQF.

Executive Yuan of Taiwan. 1995. *National Survey of Life Satisfaction of the Public*. Taipei: Executive Yuan.

Gagnon, C., P. Hirch, and R. Howitt. 1993. "Can SIA Empower Community?" *Environmental Impact Assessment Review* 13:229–53.

Galbraith, J. K. 1984. *The Affluent Society*. Boston: Houghton Mifflin.

Habermas, J. 1970. *Toward a Rational Society*. Boston: Beacon Press.

Hsiao, H. H. Michael. 1988. *Anti-pollution Movements of Taiwan in the 1980s*. Taipei: EPA.

———. 1986. "Up and Down: Ranking of Social Problems in Taiwan." *All-Round Magazine* 45:150–62.

Hsiao, H. H. Michael, Pen-Chi Chiang, Lucia Liu Severing Laus, and Yun-Peng Chu. 1989. *Taiwan 2000: Balancing Economic Growth and Environmental Protection.* Taipei: Institute of Ethnology, Academia Sinica.

Hsiao, H. H., and C. S. Wang. 1990. "Social Impact Assessment in Environmental Impact Assessment: The Case of Taiwan in the 1980s." *NTU Journal of Sociology* 20:1–40.

Humphrey, C., and F. H. Buttel. 1986. *Environment, Energy and Society.* Malabour, Florida: Krieger Co.

Industrial Technology Research Institute. 1994. *Eco-mark Execution Report.* Taipei: EPA.

Liang, C. Y., Y. Lu, T. C. Hsiao, T. H. Yang, C. T. Lu, and Z. T. Fu. 1993. *The Macro Effect and Cost-Benefit Analysis of the Environmental Protection Policy in Taiwan.* Taipei: Institute of Economics, Academia Sinica.

McDonald, G. 1990. "Regional Economic and Social Impact Assessment." *Environmental Impact Assessment Review* 10:25–36.

Milbrath, L. W. 1989. *Envisioning a Sustainable Society: Learning Our Way Out.* New York: State University of New York Press.

Miyamoto, C., ed. 1992. *Asian Environmental Problems and Japan's Responsibility.* Tokyo: Kamokawa Press.

Porteous, J. D. 1977. *Environment and Behavior.* Reading, MA.: Addison-Wesley.

Stone, R. A. 1989. "The Environmental in American Print Media: Growth and Trends in Coverage of Issues." In *Proceedings of the Sino-US Bi-National Conference on Environmental Protection and Social Development,* 35–51. Taipei: EPA of Taiwan.

Tilly, C. 1974. *An Urban World.* Boston: Brown & Co.

Vig, N. J., and M. E. Kraft. 1994. *Environmental Policy in the 1990s.* Washington, D.C.: Congressional Quarterly Press.

Wachtel, P. C. 1983. *The Poverty of Affluence.* New York: The Free Press.

Wang, C. S., and H. H. Hsiao. 1989. "EIA's Social Scope: Theory and Practice." *EIA Conference Proceedings,* 53–70.

Wang, Juju. 1988. "Budgetary Impact and Executive Budgetary Decision Making of the U.S. EPA Under Reagan's Administration." *Environmental Protection Quarterly* 11 (2):77–93.

———. 1991. "Environmental Problems in Taiwan." In *Social Problems in Taiwan,* ed. Yang and Yeh, 187–220. Taipei: Mega Press.

————. 1993. *Environment and Society.* Taipei: Youth Lion Press.

————. 1992. "Cultural Gap and Public Involvement: The Case of Lan-Yu Radwaste Storage Site Case, Taiwan." *International Journal of Mass Emergencies and Disasters* 10 (3):465–76.

————. 1992b. "The Poverty of Affluence: An Analysis of a Pollution Hot Line in Industrialized Taiwan." *NCCU Sociology Journal* 26:82–106.

————. 1994. *Environmental Sociology in Taiwan.* Taipei: Laurate Press.

————. 1995. "Socialization of Environmental Protection Affairs in Taiwan." In *Social Observation on Environmental Protection*, 78–112. Taipei: Youth Lion Press.

Wang, R. T. 1992. "The Trend of Environmental Policies in Taiwan." *Proceedings of Fifth Environmental Planning and Management Conference,* 1–14. Taipei: Chinese Institute of Environmental Engineering.

Yeh, J. R. 1989. "Citizen Participation in Environmental Regulation in Taiwan: Regulatory Reform Toward a Meaningful Participatory Democracy." In *Proceedings of the Sino-US Bi-National Conference on Environmental Protection and Social Development*, 77–93. Taipei: EPA of Taiwan.

Yuan, C. L. 1989. *Environmental History of China.* Peking: Chinese Environmental Press.

6

ENVIRONMENTAL POLICY AND POLITICS IN INDIA

R. K. SAPRU

Introduction

India achieved independence in 1947 after about two hundred years of British rule. Soon thereafter, in 1951, the country initiated the process of planned development to raise the living standard of its people and to open to them new opportunities for a richer and more varied life. As a result of sustained efforts, considerable progress has been made in many sectors of its economy. A largely agrarian feudal economy at the time of independence has been transformed into one based on a well-developed and highly diversified infrastructure that has immense potential for industrialization. The country now has a resilient agricultural economy and is nearly self-sufficient in food production. Average life expectancy has risen from 33 years in 1951 to 60.8 years in 1994, and the death rate has decreased from 27.4 per thousand in 1951 to 9.2 in 1994. The birth rate has decreased from 40 per thousand in 1951 to 28.5, and the infant mortality rate has declined from 140 per thousand live births in 1975 to 74 in 1994. The literacy rate has improved from 18.3 percent in 1951 to 54 percent in 1994, and the educational base has widened. The country has made much progress in the economic sector as a result of the new wave of liberalization set in motion in June 1991. Further, the government has made significant changes in environmental policy in the past two decades. Consequently, the quality of life has improved. However, in spite of impressive progress in certain areas, the country still faces problems.

Environmental Issues

Demographic Pressures

India has had to combat demographic pressures as well as pressures resulting from the livestock population. In a region desperately striving to overcome the centuries-old burden of social and economic backwardness, both these factors have had an enormous impact on the quality of life and on the environment. Although the 1991 census recorded a marginal decline in the annual population growth rate, from 2.2 percent from 1971 through 1981 to 2.11 percent from 1981 through 1991, the country now holds more than 920 million people, a number that likely will increase to 1 billion before the twentieth century ends.[1]

Pressure on Land and Erosion of Topsoil

In India, high population density coexists with a high level of poverty. India has a land mass of about 329 million hectares (nearly 2.4 percent of the total land area of the world); of this, 166 million hectares are arable and 141 million hectares currently are under cultivation. Because of topographical (see map 6.1) and ecological constraints and increased demand for nonagricultural uses, there is little scope to increase the area under cultivation.[2] The per capita availability of land in India has declined from 0.89 hectares in 1950 to less than 0.40 hectares in 1991, and with the assumed rate of population growth, that figure will decline further to 0.30 hectares by the year 2007. Modern agricultural techniques threaten to intensify inequalities in landholding as small and marginal farmers can no longer afford the costly technology and chemical fertilizers required for food production.

More than 60 percent of the country's arable land suffers from environmental degradation. Vast tracts are in danger of becoming wastelands from the pressure of twin forces: on the one hand, misappropriation of natural resources by the rich for luxury consumption; on the other, the struggle for survival that leads poor farmers to extend outward to marginal farmlands, destroying forests and encroaching on already limited grazing lands (Gadgil 1993). Massive shifts in land use, generated both by a rapidly growing population seeking subsistence and by commercial interests responding to growing demand, had equally deleterious results.

Industrialization and urbanization have added to the agricultural scramble. The urban population of India, according to the 1991 population census, has increased from 159.46 million in 1981 to 217.18 million. Urban areas are advancing on adjoining agricultural land, and roads and concrete structures that consume precious topsoil are being built. The accumulated backlog in urban housing, along with the housing needs for the additional urban population, has aggravated the problem further, resulting in proliferation of slums and squatter settlements and decay of the city environment. The poor, whose access to basic services such as drinking water, sanitation, education, and basic health services is shrinking, suffer the most. An estimated 6,000 million tons of top soil with essential nutrients are flowing into the sea every year. As this soil washes downstream, it creates havoc by silting rivers and

MAP 6.1

Topography of India

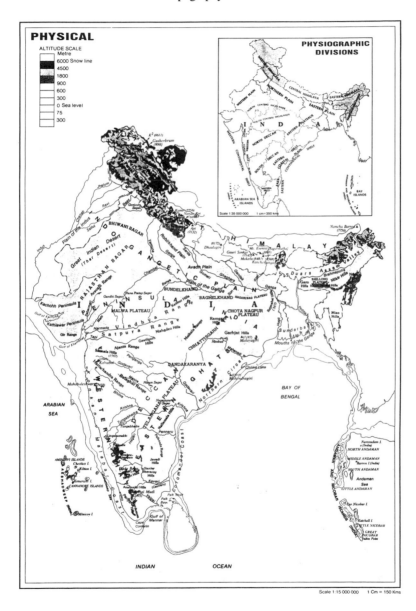

Source: S. Muthia, et al., eds. *An Atlas of India* (New Delhi: Oxford University Press, 1990), 2.

dams, raising riverbeds, and unleashing floods. The ravines and gullies of
India bear stark witness to the effects of erosion. Between 1953 and 1987,
floods claimed 50,374 human lives and destroyed crops in an average area of
more than 3.51 million hectares, affected 31.84 million people, damaged 1.2
million houses, killed 0.1 million cattle, and damaged public property worth
Rs.768 crore (a crore = US $10 million) per year.[3]

Deforestation

Throughout India, the area of the environment most depleted in the
present century has been forest land. The paucity of India's forest cover is
apparent from the fact that of the 75 million hectares classed as forest, 64
million hectares sustain actual forest cover; and out of this, only 35 million
hectares have adequate cover, which accounts for only about 9 percent of the
geographical area of the country at present.[4] The major cause of deforestation
is excessive felling of trees for commercial timber and, to a lesser extent, for
firewood, which still constitutes the major source of cooking energy.

Deforestation has created crushing workloads for nearly all villagers,
particularly women and children who bear the brunt of the fuel, water, and
food collecting burden. In addition, deforestation has caused immense loss to
the living natural resources. An estimated 15,000 plant species out of a world
total of 250,000, and 75,000 animal species out of a world total of 1.5 million
are threatened by human activity on land and forests.

Pollution

Of the various kinds of environmental pollution (air, water, land, noise,
radiation, and odor) that impinge upon the living and natural resources, water
pollution is by far the most serious in its implications for the health and well-
being of people. A staggering 70 percent of the available water in India is
polluted; almost 73 million workdays are lost due to water-borne diseases, and
an estimated 2 million deaths are caused by water pollution. Estimates also
show that 60 to 70 percent of water pollution is caused by municipal sewage,
and yet only 7 percent of the population is served by drainage systems. The
fourteen major rivers in India carry 85 percent of the surface run-off and cover
83 percent of the country within their drainage basins. One-fourth of the
Ganges River is dangerously polluted by human and industrial wastes.
According to the Central Ganga Authority (created in 1985), an estimated sixty
thousand animal carcasses are dumped in the river annually.

Air and noise pollution have become increasingly important aspects of
environmental pollution in the wake of rapid industrialization and urbanization. According to studies conducted in selected cities by the National
Environmental Engineering Research Institute (NEERI), the quantity of SO_2
has tripled in fifteen years. A major contributor to air pollution is the

automobile. A vehicular pollution survey conducted in 1993 in Delhi revealed that while ambient lead concentration values were in the range of 0.098 $\mu g/NM^3$ to 0.862 $\mu m/NM^3$, the values of suspended particulate matter (SPM) ranged between 388 $\mu m/NM^3$ and 613 $\mu g/NM^3$.

NEERI studies also reveal that the level of lead from automobile exhausts and from industry ranges from 1.0 to 16 ppm in Calcutta, 0.2 to 14 ppm in Bombay, and 0.2 to 18 ppm in Delhi, whereas the criteria of air quality as recommended by the World Health Organization (WHO) is 0.5 ppm. In the city of Ludhiana (Punjab), the availability of oxygen in the ambient air is 19 percent rather than 21 percent, which is the normal concentration. In some localities of Bombay and Delhi, the concentration of monoxide is as high as 35 ppm, which far exceeds the safe permissible limit of 9 ppm. Delhi leads the country in incidence of lung diseases, with 30 percent of its population suffering from respiratory diseases caused by pollution from poisonous gases.

Similarly, noise pollution surveys conducted in 1993 in Delhi, Lucknow, and Indore reveal that the noise levels (60 to 70 decibels) in these cities in residential, commercial, and silence zones have exceeded the prescribed standards as recommended by WHO. Continued exposure to high levels of noise results in interference, fatigue, and a temporary shift of hearing that may cause permanent loss of hearing.

Environmental Policies

India is among the few countries of the world that refer specifically in their constitutions to the need for environmental protection. Chapters on directive principles of state policy and fundamental duties explicitly enunciate the national commitment to protect and enhance the quality of the environment.[5] Articles 48A and 51A(g) to the forty-second Amendment laid the foundation for sustainable development: The "state shall endeavour to protect and improve the environment and safeguard the forests and wildlife of the country" (The Constitution of India 1994:79). It is the duty of the citizen "to protect and improve the natural environment including forests, lakes, rivers and wildlife and to have compassion for the living creatures" (The Constitution of India 1994:81). The judicial interpretation of article 21 of the Indian Constitution has widened the scope of the right to life and personal liberty to include the protection of the environment as the duty of the state.[6] The forty-second Amendment also expanded the list of concurrent subjects (matters over which both the central and state governments have jurisdiction) by incorporating "Population Control and Family Planning" and bringing "Forests" and "Protection of Wild Animals and Birds" from the state list to the concurrent list. The country also has a clearly articulated National Conservation Strategy and Policy Statement on Environment and Development

(1992), Policy Statement for Abatement of Pollution (1992), National Forest Policy (1988), and National Water Policy (1987) that are blueprints for state action to complement legal and other measures already taken.

Besides constitutional provisions, more than two hundred central and state laws have been enacted from time to time that relate, directly or indirectly, to environmental protection and management. To provide an overview of environmental regulation in India, this section digests the main national environmental statutes.

The Water (Prevention and Control of Pollution) Act (1974), pursuant to the enabling resolution of twelve states under article 252(1), and the Air (Prevention and Control of Pollution) Act (1981) under article 253 of the Indian Constitution, were passed by the Union Parliament to prevent and control water and air pollution. These acts created the apparatus for implementation through central and state pollution control boards. Parliament also enacted the Water (Prevention and Control of Pollution) Cess Act (1977) to create incentives for pollution control. The act requires local authorities and certain designated industries to pay a cess (fee) for water consumption.

Keeping in view the inadequacies of the existing environmental laws as well as the demand to improve the quality of the environment, the government of India enacted the Environment (Protection) Act (1986), under article 253 of the Indian Constitution. This general legislation promotes laws for managing and controlling hazardous substances, conserving ecologically fragile areas, and guiding central and state pollution control boards in fixing standards for industrial pollution as well as water, air, and noise pollution.

The Public Liability Insurance Act (1991) provides immediate relief to victims of accidents that arise from handling hazardous substances. This act is in addition to such legislative measures as the Factories Act (1948), the Mines Act (1952), the Motor Vehicles Act (1939), and the Hazardous Wastes (Management and Handling) Rules (1989) that prescribe measures to control such factors as environmental safety in factories and vehicular pollution. Individual states also have matching legislation in many cases.

In the field of conservation of natural resources, including forestry and wildlife, a few statutes have been enacted. The Indian Forest Act (1927), enacted during the British period, is being amended to bring it into conformity with the new National Forest Policy (1988). Alarmed at India's rapid deforestation, the central government enacted the Forest (Conservation) Act in 1980, which requires approval of the central government before a state de-reserves a reserved forest, uses forest land for nonforest purposes, or clears forest land for reforestation. The Wild Life (Protection) Act (1972), enacted pursuant to the enabling resolutions of eleven states under article 252(1) of the Indian Constitution, provides for establishing state wildlife advisory boards; promulgating regulations for hunting and trading wild animals and birds; and establishing a Zoo Authority, sanctuaries, and national parks. Mention may also be made of the Insecticides Act (1968), which regulates all aspects of use of insecticides and pesticides.

In addition to legislative measures that provide for a system of regulation, there are judicial remedies under the Indian Penal Code (1860), the Code of Civil Procedure (1908), the Code of Criminal Procedure (1973), and Public Interest Litigation. Sections 133 to 144 of the Criminal Procedure Code provide effective and speedy remedies to prevent and control public nuisance and air, water, and noise pollution. Similarly, sections 268, 269, 277, 278, 284 to 286, and 290 of the Indian Penal Code stipulate as offenses various acts that affect the environment.

Apart from existing central and state enactments that deal with pollution control, several major institutions have been established. The Department of Environment (1980) and later the integrated Ministry of Environment and Forests (1985) were set up to recognize explicitly the pivotal role that environmental conservation must play in sustainable development. The Union Ministry also appoints expert committees to undertake environmental impact assessments of projects that require approval of agencies such as the Central Water Commission, Central Electricity Authority, Planning Commission, and Public Investment Board. Laws are implemented through the ministries and agencies of the central and state governments. Besides the state departments of environment and the central and state pollution control boards, institutions such as the National Wastelands Development Board (1985), National Afforestation and Eco-Development Board (1992), Central Ganga Authority (1985), Central Zoo Authority (1991), and Animal Welfare Board of India (1962) all play a significant role in implementing environmental policies and laws. In such fields as solid wastes, water treatment, health, and sanitation— which pertain to common amenities—the state governments, municipalities, and panchayats (village/local governments) play a significant role in protecting the environment.

Environmental Politics

Center-State Conflict

Central and state government politics exert a significant impact on efforts to ensure environmental protection. The important issue is whether the Union Parliament or the state legislatures are better suited to enact measures to protect the environment.

The framers of the Indian Constitution did not consider specifically whether the Union Parliament or the state legislatures should regulate laws on environmental subjects. Instead, the distribution of environmental subjects within the three lists (one list of matters under central government jurisdiction, a second list of matters under concurrent or joint jurisdiction and a third list of matters under state government jurisdiction) was influenced by the Government of India Act of 1935. At the meeting of the Drafting Committee of the Constituent Assembly in July 1949, proposals from the Ministry of Agriculture to transfer the subjects of "Forests" and "Fisheries" from the state list to the concurrent list were opposed by representatives of the provinces.[7] Proposals of the ministry were rejected, and the subject of forests remained on the state list. It was only in 1976 that the item "forests" was brought to the concurrent list by the 42nd amendment of the Indian Constitution. Similarly, another proposal jointly moved by the ministries of Health and Home Affairs regarding removal of the items "public health and sanitation" from the state list to the concurrent list was not accepted at the meeting.[8]

When the central government enacted the Water Act in 1974, since Parliament has no power to make such a law for the states, it had to resort to article 252 of the Indian Constitution which allows Parliament to act only at the request of the states.

The central government can legislate regarding subjects under state jurisdiction only with the consent of the state governments. This limitation on central government had led to a tendency among the states to delay formulation and implementation of environmental policies.

The environmental policy was explicitly incorporated into the Indian Constitution in 1976 by adding articles 48A and 51A(g). There was considerable debate in the Lok Sabha[9] (lower house of Parliament) over these articles, but the late Prime Minister Indira Gandhi used her enhanced political power to push environmental measures through Parliament.

In addition, article 253 of the Indian Constitution gives the Parliament power to make any law to implement India's international obligations as well as any decision made at an international conference. Apparently, that article empowers the central government to enact laws on any entry contained in the state list. The central government has used its power under article 253 to enact the Air Act of 1981 and the Environment Act of 1986 to carry out the decisions made at the United Nations Conference on the Human Environment in 1972. Further, expansion of the concurrent list by transferring the entries "forests" and "protection of wild animals and birds" from the state list gave the central government power to make laws regarding those subjects. Moreover, the central government may enact laws on state subjects for states whose legislatures have consented to central legislation. Thus, the Water Act (1974) was enacted by Parliament pursuant to enabling resolutions by twelve states.

Under India's federal structure, the central government exercises much more power to legislate measures for environmental matters than the description of powers contained in the Indian Constitution for the state governments suggests. However, implementation of these policies faces a variety of difficulties at the state level.

The central government has had most of the resources, while the states, deprived of resources, have had to represent regional interests and stake claims for resources from the central government. In addition, in the course of articulation of political power, there had been growing centralization and bureaucratization of political power in the central government.

The controversy between the central government and the Himachal Pradesh (H.P.) state government over the commissioning of Rs4,500 crore for the 1,500 megawatt Nathpa-Jhakri Project (NJP) in the Sutlej Basin in Himachal Pradesh is one example. The Himachal Pradesh government (headed by Chief Minister Virbhadra Singh), which has a 25 percent share in the Nathpa Jhakri Power Corporation (NJPC), has asked that the headquarters of the corporation be shifted from New Delhi to the state capital of Shimla (*The Tribune* 1994b). The state government also has insisted on the NJPC taking on more employees of the Himachal Pradesh Electricity Board, a state government agency. The Union energy minister, did not agree to these pleas (*The Tribune* 1994a). Apparently, this ongoing tussle between the central government and the H.P. government has cast a shadow on the 1,500 megawatt Nathpa-Jhakri Project. This project, for which a memorandum of understanding was signed between the Himachal Pradesh and Haryana state governments in 1977 and 1978, has had many problems and is progressing slowly.

Centralization also is reflected in the implementation of the Forest Conservation Act (FCA) of 1980. Under this act, the states in India are required to seek permission of the central government before destroying forests or using forest land for nonforest purposes. Thus the act froze the ownership and management of forest lands by the states. This shifted the locus of political articulation from the states to the central government. The decision about whether a part or the whole of the forests should be preserved or put to an alternative use came to be guided by national importance and articulation of interest at the national level as opposed to regional and state interests.

The act necessarily raised the issue of how to resolve the two claims: (1) to use forest land for the purpose of development, such as to construct dams on rivers, locate industries, convert forests to plantations for such crops as tea, coffee, or rubber; and (2) to conserve forests for sustainable development. The guidelines did not indicate that permission should not be given at all. However, permission should be given after the environmental status of the forests was appraised and compensatory afforestation was taken care of.

The guidelines permitted such things as river valley projects and transmission cables, while projects in the interest of the forest dwellers, such as permitting cultivation on forest lands and shifting cultivation, were prohibited. Thus, if the central government favored development projects at the national level, the welfare activities in the forest areas, such as constructing roads, setting up schools, and carrying out minor irrigation work, suffered. After all, the decision to construct Narmada Dam and submerge forests and to give forest land for rehabilitation of affected persons is a part of the political-economic imperative of the state. Similarly, despite the FCA, encroachments in many states were regularized with the permission of the central government.[10] The conflict between the central government and the states illustrates the centralization and bureaucratization of political power.

Industry, Agriculture and Environmental Politics

Economic growth and environmental conservation are two important components of sustainable development. Each has its own contribution to make to sustainability. The corporate sector affects the environment and is affected in return by it. Two factors intensify the environmental politics associated with rapid industrialization. First, as emissions from industries increase, government tends to regulate emission standards through environmental legislation. Second, as industrial towns expand, more people are exposed to pollution. Unchecked, the pollutants discharged by heavy industries, such as petrochemical, paper and pulp, cement, metallurgy, and iron, damage the health of local people, reduce agricultural output, and create political problems.

Public-sector enterprises in India own the most polluting industries and control important natural resources. Based on environmental criteria, state-owned enterprises tend to be less efficient than private enterprises.[11] Both central and state governments face many pressures in making and enforcing environment-related policy and laws. Industry influences the environmental policy-making process through the business lobby and representatives of business interests. Stringent environmental policy proposals receive grudging response from the industry. At the same time, business representatives try to manipulate policies to cater to their interests through administrative agencies that have strong political alliances with private polluting industrial interests.

With the introduction of liberalized policies in the industry sector at the central government level, states such as Punjab, Haryana, and Himachal Pradesh also amended their industrial policies recently by introducing better incentives. These include sales tax deferments, an uninterrupted power supply, and time-bound environmental clearance of projects. For example, the Punjab Pollution Control Board (PPCB) can give consent within fifteen days to operate an industry in the "Green Category of Industries" (except one that is highly polluting).[12] These industrial policies introduced by the state governments have contributed to the rapid industrial development that often is opposed to the environmental policies.

Most industrialists in India are politically powerful. They have links with the ruling parties both in central and in state governments. Often politics intervenes, and pollution from industry continues. For instance, in Punjab, the power supply to the Shreyan Paper Mills in Ahmedgarh,[13] which was disconnected on 11 November 1994 at the direction on the Punjab Pollution Control Board (PPCB) for causing water-borne diseases in Bathinda, was restored on 19 November 1994 on the verbal order of the political secretary to the Punjab chief minister. The PPCB, in its report, stated that the paper mill was discharging about eight thousand kilolitres per day of effluents into the Sirhind Canal which supplied water to many rural and urban water supply systems. After local residents threatened the paper mill and the president of the Punjab Beopar Mandal demanded action against the mill management, the state government ordered that the mill be closed. The president of the Bathinda Municipal Committee said, however, that "closure of [the] factory is a political gimmick of the ruling party." He believed the state government feared the water pollution issue would affect the Gidderbaha Vidhan Sabha (state assembly) election in Punjab in May 1995 because many villagers of the constituency got drinking water from the Sirhind Canal. He was afraid the mill would be allowed to function after the election was over.

In another case, on 31 January 1995 the PPCB ordered that electricity be disconnected to a paper mill because it was not in compliance with environmental regulations. The Punjab State Electricity Board (PSEB) did so on 10 February 1995, but the power was restored on 11 February. Meanwhile, the PPCB has devised an alternative to closing offending industries by obtaining bank guarantees to grant extensions to defaulting units. The PPCB had granted extensions to about 182 units against the bank guarantees, keeping in view the interests of labor.

The central and state governments have developed various administrative arrangements to implement environmental laws. However, these arrangements have increasingly been politicized, and the environmental policy process continues to be influenced by vested interests.

The process of economic development, which began in the 1950s, has intensified subsidized flows of resources to the industrial and intensive agricultural sectors. This policy, which India's first prime minister, Jawaharlal Nehru, followed with a view to industrializing India and emulating the West, deviated from the ideas of Mahatma Gandhi who believed that independent India must focus on empowering the local people and enhancing their quality of life. The policy initiated by Nehru was to industrialize at all costs, and that meant subsidized input prices for the industrial and agricultural sectors.

Present government policy promotes maximum use of chemical fertilizers and pesticides that are made available at subsidized rates. The organized industrial sector and the intensive agricultural sector obtain resources at high levels of subsidies. Agricultural produce is undervalued because of a lower wage rate for labor on the farm and because forest resources have been made available at a lower cost. For example, paper mills received bamboo at prices as low as Rs.1.50 per ton when market prices were higher by a factor of two thousand (Gadgil, Prasad, and Ali 1983).

Industry's commercial use of subsidized forest resources exhausts the resources and causes increasing numbers of "ecosystem people [to become] ecological refugees." The problem is summarized beautifully by M. Gadgil in the following paragraph:

> Ecosystem people deprived of access to the resources they need to survive have spawned the second segment of India's population: ecological refugees. Many of these people were uprooted when their lands were submerged under river valley projects or acquired for industry. Others, such as river fishermen, are suffering because polluted rivers yield few fish. Most such people flock to urban centers, although few succeed in entering the organized industry and service sector. They then swell the urban slums. These urban poor, with access neither to electricity or natural gas nor to wood that can be freely gathered, constitute a significant demand for commercial fuelwood. Both ecosystem people and ecological refugees may together be said to constitute the subsistence sector (Gadgil 1991:12–13).

The extensive development of state-sponsored (i.e., heavily subsidized) irrigation farming too has become a major cause of loss of forest land. This is apparent in some of the perennially irrigated farms that grow sugarcane in Maharashtra, Karnataka, Uttar Pradesh, and other states of India. These are latent but unintended consequences of the "Green Revolution" strategy of rural development (Dhanagare 1993).

Underpriced natural resources and subsidized resource flows benefit members of the industrial-agricultural owning class who use them, the bureaucrats who administer them, and the politicians who decide who is to receive them. Underpricing creates wide opportunities for corruption and gain and makes the agencies vulnerable to influence from the economically and politically powerful. Forestry agencies come under heavy pressure to provide low-cost natural resources to industry and water authorities come under pressure to build irrigation infrastructures that will serve politically important areas.

Politics of Floods

India lacks a comprehensive policy on flood control and flood protection programs. The First Five-Year Plan (1951–56) put more faith in large dams than in embankments to store flood waters. The plan document stated that "the construction of large dams to store these flood waters is the most effective way of preventing flood damage" (Government of India 1952:339). While dams were constructed on the rivers Damodar and Mahanadi, the idea of a dam on the Kosi River in Nepal had to be shelved. In the face of severe floods in 1954, attention shifted once again to embankments. To quote from Rashtriya Barh Ayog (1980): "Although embankments do not provide absolute immunity from the floods, they will ensure a very large measure of protection, which given good maintenance, should prove to be of a lasting character" (India, National Commission on Floods 1980b:144). In 1957, a high-level committee on floods outlined numerous dangers of constructing embankments. Again in 1978, the Working Group on Flood Control warned against new embankment schemes. The group felt that dams should be built quickly in flood-prone basins. And finally, the Rashtriya Barh Ayog (1980) carried out a comprehensive evaluation of available flood control measures but failed to break any new ground. Instead of recommending any one physical measure such as a dam or an embankment, it stressed the implementation of an integrated set of measures. "In the absence of any viable measure, one may have to live with floods," (India, National Commission on Floods 1980:228).

Similarly a model bill was drawn in July 1975 that recommended preparation of flood control schemes, land use regulations, prohibition of obstructions to rivers and drains, and disaster preparedness and evacuation (Verghese 1990).[14] When the central government circulated the bill to the states, only Manipur could adopt the bill as the Manipur Flood Plain Zoning Act, 1985. Obviously the political leaders are not seriously looking for changes they themselves can bring about in the management of flood plains.

In the wake of continuing floods, flood relief and flood control programs have assumed political dimensions in India. Politicians both at the state and at the central levels often discuss short-term rather than long-term measures for flood control. The focus often is on ad hoc measures such as flood relief. The ad hoc approach toward droughts evolved because drought management has been treated as a problem of relief expenditures to be taken care of by the Finance Commission, rather than as a problem of development to be taken care of by the Planning Commission (Dubhashi 1992). The amount provided by the central government for flood relief often has been a politically contentious issue, especially when the party ruling a flood-affected state opposed the central government.

On the politics of flood control and flood relief, the Centre for Science and Environment observed:

This entwining of political interests with flood control and relief measures is a telling commentary on the extent to which the politics of power can degenerate, where political capital is sought to be made out of even human misery. Little wonder then that the state government has displayed clear evidence of the lack of a political will to proceed alternatively with flood control measures." (Center for Science and Environment 1991:124).

Flood relief operations provide ample scope for politicians, public officials, and contractors to indulge in blackmarketeering, distribution of substandard materials, and diversion of funds. For example in 1988, after the fourth wave of floods in Assam, the prime minister of India accused the Mahanta state government of misusing relief funds and channeling them into areas of lower priority ("State Diverting Funds" 1988). When the chief minister of Mahanta regretted that the central government was delaying the release of funds, the prime minister replied that the state government had not submitted its official memorandum on time ("State Diverting Funds" 1988). In answer, Mahanta charged that the central government forms required vast amounts of data that could be collected only after the floods receded ("PM Plays Dirty" 1988).

Within the state, Abdul Hameed, a member of Parliament who belonged to the United Minority Front, accused the ruling Assam Gana Parishad of discrimination in distributing relief, of rampant corruption in the Flood Control Department of the state government, and of a nexus between contractors and officials. He also complained that the flood-affected people who began coming into towns in search of jobs were being harassed by officials as illegal Bangladeshi immigrants ("Assam MPS Demand" 1988).

The erosion of river banks and the recurring incidence of their repair also generate a potential for income for politicians, engineers, and contractors. Newspapers continue to hint at political big wigs in Bihar who stand to benefit from flood control operations. Arvind Narayan Das writes on flood politics in Bihar:

Public works engineering became another flourishing trade. With the construction of roads, dams, embankments and canals after independence, the industry's turnover increased tremendously and all manner of entrepreneurs jumped into it. As much of the construction was of earthen structures in flood prone areas, it was a virtual cornucopia, ever filling up with every monsoon. Where the natural flow of water reduced chances of damage and renewal of public works, strenuous efforts were put in by the public works agencies and contractors to impede it and create waterlogging and flooding. Among such people was the late lamented Lalit Narayan Mishra who, starting as a petty contractor organizing shramdan (voluntary gift of labor) during the construction of the

Kosi embankment, turned making money to play politics and playing politics to make money into a fine art. (Das 1987:11)

At the center of the environmental crisis that has gripped the entire spectrum of politics is the question of whether it is desirable to have large dams on river valleys in India. Many dam-building projects have been severely criticized for a variety of reasons—size, viability, displacement, safety, impacts, and cost-benefit sharing. The Narmada Valley projects, the Tehri Dam and the Indira Gandhi Nahar, have been gearing up for a confrontation between the people affected by these projects and the state and central governments. Here the reference is directly to the execution of the Sardar Sarovar Project (SSP), which involves constructing a 1,210-meter concrete gravity dam across the Narmada River in Gujarat, a 460-kilometer main canal that leads to the Gujarat-Rajasthan border, and two hydro-electric powerhouses with an aggregate capacity of 1,450 megawatts, as well as other works incidental or ancillary to the project.

The main controversy arises because the Narmada Water Disputes Tribunal agreed in 1979 with Gujarat and decreed that the Sardar Sarovar Dam must be 455 feet high (approximately 139 meters). However, the Madhya Pradesh government and environmentalists and activists under Narmada Bachao Andolan (NBA) who have been working under the leadership of Medha Patkar are demanding that the height of the dam be reduced. Even the report of the independent review commissioned by the World Bank under the former UNDP director, Bradford Morse, found inadequacies in the design of the SSP. The committee summed up by saying that

problems of human and environmental impact encompass all aspects of the Projects, including the uncertainties of hydrology, the upstream questions, the impact downstream, the command issue areas, the health risks, the deficiencies in resettlement policy and implementation in each of the three states as well as the canal. None of these issues can be ignored. (Report of the Independent Review 1992:355–356)

While the Gujarat government took an inflexible stand on the entire controversy, Medha Patkar's determined fight centered on the fate of thousands of *adivasis* (tribals) who would be ousted by the project and on damage to the environment that the project would entail. In view of the stand of Narmada Bachao Andolan (NBA) (Save Narmada movement), the Union government was forced to set up a five-member committee in August 1993 to review all aspects of the project.[15]

The committee's report was not made public because of a series of wrangles in the Gujarat High Court. It was released to the public finally in

December 1994 on the directive of the Supreme Court. One would have expected the Union government, now armed with this unanimous report, to intervene and bring about a settlement between the contending governments of Gujarat and Madhya Pradesh, as well as between the authorities in charge of the project and the NBA. However, so far there has been no such effort on the part of the central government, and the Gujarat government has persisted in its recalcitrant mood.

The role of the central government's Ministry of Environment and Forests has been ambiguous throughout, with members paying lip service to avoid discontent. A three-member bench of the Supreme Court observed that the government's response is "beautifully vague and non-committal" (Sangvai 1995:543). The Court continues to say that it is deeply disturbed by the Union government's refusal to consider even the most basic issues discussed in the review report.

Meanwhile, the five-member committee says in its report that it had to work under several constraints, including ambiguity of scope. Subsequent clarifications meant only that the benefits of the dam had to be appraised and suggestions made to improve its implementation.

Despite these constraints, the committee has questioned the viability of the project by saying that the quantum of water available could be much less than had been assumed. "We recommend that if the dependable quantum of flows is of a lower order than what had been assumed earlier, the implications of this for the planned benefits and the consequent steps that need to be taken should also be examined quickly" (Expert Committee on Narmada 1994).

The report also calls upon the government to prepare within six months a master plan for rehabilitation, pointing out that the government had been lagging behind in this area. In addition, a scheme for drinking water needed to be prepared as early as possible.

The basis of the NBA's stand against the Sardar Sarovar Project is that it firmly believes in the undesirability of having dams in India. As the Expert Committee noted, "The N.B.A. expressed fundamental doubts regarding the soundness of the [Sardar Sarovar] Project" (Expert Committee on Narmada 1994).

Politics of Forest Exploitation

The continuing exploitation of forests in many parts of India reflects the lack of political will in enforcing the provisions of the Forest Conservation Act of 1980. Commercial exploitation through private contractors, hobnobbing between forest departmental officials and the so-called forest mafia, and activities of the politicians have led to the fast depletion of forests (Gupta 1990).

Unrestricted and illegal felling of pine and Khair trees in the Kunihar forest division in Solan district of Himachal Pradesh, is a case in point.

Situated on the border with Haryana, the range has become a heaven for smugglers, poachers, and pirates operating from across the border (Kashyap 1995). As an eye-wash, forest officials have fined some of the law breakers, but people of the area have termed these actions "theatrical" as no criminal prosecution has been launched in any of these cases. However, the forest officials fear that if the cases are handed over to police, then their involvement may come to light. The issues of timber smuggling, illicit felling of trees, and unchecked soil erosion in ecologically fragile mountain areas of Himachal Pradesh were subjects of discussion in the State Assembly recently, but the discussion concluded with an assurance from the forest minister that an "ecological task force" would be set up.[16]

The Forest Conservation Act undoubtedly is an important central law as it prohibits the state governments from allotting any forest land for any nonforest purpose. This restriction on the state governments, however, applies only to the reserved forests and is not applicable to village forests or protected forests. Thus, some state governments can declare protected forest lands as nonforest areas and, later on, can allocate them to industries or other agencies (Menom 1987). Further, the amendment to the FCA, passed in 1989, goes against the provision in the policy resolution that, wherever possible, degraded lands should be made available for tree farming either on lease or on the basis of a "tree patt" scheme. This provision in the amendment specifically disallows lease to any nongovernment agency except with the prior approval of the central government.[17] This nullifies all hope of giving degraded lands to tribal cooperatives or organizations for purposes of watershed development, including plantation and cultivation. On the whole, the afforestation programs under the forest policy have been most popular with already successful farmers who switch from crop farming to more lucrative tree farming. In addition, states have leased large portions of degraded state forest land to industrial firms for fast-growing trees, such as eucalyptus and pine, which have value as timber in commercial markets. These changes in crop production and land use have negative effects on the poor and landless. Mass eucalyptus planting is particularly controversial. In many parts of India, people protest against planting eucalyptus on farmers' fields.

Environmental activists working in the tribal areas complain that megaprojects, such as the Tehri Dam or the Sardar Sarovar Project which involve large-scale destruction of natural forests, are cleared by the central government, while small projects that directly benefit adivasis and forest dwellers are not cleared on the ground that some of them involve the use of degraded forest lands. They further assert that this is because the spillover from large projects goes to politicians and bureaucrats who therefore take a direct interest in getting clearances for such projects (Andolan 1992). In addition, as the political control of the central government has weakened (the ruling congressional party at the center does not enjoy an absolute majority in the Lok Sabha), states have been staking claims to regularize encroachment on forest lands. For example, the central government has given permission to Madhya Pradesh to settle 89,526 persons over an area of 103,873 hectares of encroached forest land ("No Let Up" 1991). Similarly, the Punjab government, under Chief Minister Beant Singh, has been calling on the Union Ministry of Environment and Forests for the denotification of eight thousand acres of land that fall in fifteen villages, to set up a new township in the vicinity of Chandigarh.

Problems in Policy Implementation

Even when simple and straightforward ways of coping with environmental problems exist, the central and state governments both have found it difficult to translate them into effective policy. Policy making in the environmental protection area has frequently outpaced administrative capacity to analyze and implement policies. Laws and regulations governing environment policies are multiplying, and often the result is a large number of contradictory regulations that are beyond the capacity of governments to enforce. The reasons for the gap between environment policy intentions and enforcement include lack of institutional capacity, and poor functioning of state pollution control boards; lack of coordination and cooperation; inadequate public involvement, and centralized policy process.

Lack of Institutional Capacity

The present institutional structure and administrative capabilities for implementation of environmental laws and policies are by no means adequate in the face of the complexities of environmental, political, social, and economic problems. Here the institutional structure refers to the whole system of rules and regulations by which administrative capabilities, tasks, and responsibilities are clearly defined among the administrators.

Section 5 of the Environment Act of 1986 empowers the central government to require any person, officer, or authority to comply with directions that include "the power to direct (a) the closure, prohibition or regulation of any industry, operation or process; (b) stoppage or regulation of the supply of electricity or water or any other service" ("The Environment (Protection) Act and Rules, 1986" 1990:260). When such wide powers have been vested with the state, it is surprising that on 7 February 1995 the Indian Supreme Court had to order the thirty industrial units, including multinational companies in West Bengal, to install pollution control devices within three consecutive months or face closure and fines up to Rs.5,000 for every day they failed to comply, after conviction for the first offense (*The Times of India* 1995).

The apex court was forced to play the role of the executive because the West Bengal Pollution Control Board failed to act against these industrial units. At the end of the hearing, a two-judge bench of the Supreme Court expressed its displeasure by adding: "These multinational concerns have huge resources, yet they are not bothered about protecting the environment" (*The Times of India* 1995). The functioning of the state boards for the prevention and control of water pollution is not free from political constraints. The Water Act does not prescribe any qualification for membership on the boards, except for the chairman and secretary. A board may be packed with members who have certain political objectives. Further, a board does not have any coercive or punitive power and acts only as a prosecuting agency against violators. In the case of the Shreyans Paper Mills, referred to earlier in the chapter[18] which were discharging about eight thousand kiloliters of effluents per day into the Sirhind Canal, the PPCB moved the court of the subdivisional magistrate, Bathinda, against the industry under section 133 of the Criminal Procedure Code. The case has been hanging fire for more than six months. There have been allegations that the PPCB has been dragging its feet ever since the political secretary to the chief minister evinced interest and that they had deliberately not been sending the results of samples collected.

Most industries in the states have not come out strongly to comply with provisions of the act. Industry management hesitates to apply for consent of the board because of the extra financial and technological burden. The board, on its part, imposes conditions on industry such as treating the effluents and discharging them in an appropriate manner (Sapru 1989). Industry hesitates to comply with those conditions on various grounds, such as absence of technology for treatment, nonavailability of land, lack of funds, and absence of proper disposal points. Further, even when an industry installs a treatment plant, management may evade its operation in order to save the unproductive expenses of running the plant. Industry, therefore, often uses various means to circumvent the provisions of law. The board does not have adequate power to force the industry to comply with conditions, except by prosecuting the erring business. President of the Punjab Chamber of Commerce and Industry succinctly regretted that the Pollution Control Board was interested only in the prosecution of industrialists and not in helping the industrial sector install pollution control devices.[19]

The technological means for improving environmental performance of industrial activities are slowly developing in India. Under existing laws, all pollution-generating industries are required to install pollution abatement measures, either individually or collectively. In return, the central and state governments will provide attractive fiscal incentives. The Tamil Nadu government, for example, with assistance from the World Bank, has taken on the task of setting up roughly thirty common effluent treatment plants throughout the state, to treat effluents from facilities such as dyeing units and leather tanneries. Similarly, the Punjab Pollution Control Board has installed "model demonstration plants" to treat effluents from heat treatment, electroplating units, cupola furnaces, and fluidized bed furnaces.[20] A survey of 2,700 industrial units by the Central Pollution Control Board in 1993, for example, indicated that only 28 percent had efficient waste treatment plants. But the existence of better technologies does not guarantee that these technologies will be adopted, especially by small-scale industries for which the costs of control in relation to output may be large. While many smaller industrial units might find it difficult to install individual effluent treatment plants (ETP), the bigger units either have faulty ETP or fail to maintain the prescribed limits with respect to effluent discharge.

Analysis of the functioning of the central/state pollution control boards, established in Union Territories and in all major states, reveals several gaps. The Water and Air Acts lay down specifications to limit the concentration of pollutants in the effluent and emissions. But once an industrial unit starts functioning, it is difficult for the board to regulate the standards or enforce any punitive measures in case of violation, unless the situation becomes grave. Boards seem to have adopted a soft line vis-à-vis the industry and prefer to be persuasive rather than punitive.

The member secretary of the PPCB observes: "Whenever the industry is granted consent subject to some conditions it does not care to comply with those conditions and Board does not posses ways and means to force the industry to comply with conditions except launching prosecution against erring industry" (Garg and Tiwana 1987:111). Further, the powers given to water boards are advisory and consultative in nature. Boards have the right to monitor existing polluting sources, but they are unable to order the closure of an offending industry. Moreover, because litigation procedure is dilatory, expensive, and technical, boards have largely failed to prosecute offending industries. The annual reports of the central/state boards are full of cases that could not be prosecuted successfully on account of those factors. Given the complexity of pollution control laws, an industrial unit may find that the cost of compliance is heavier than the cost of defiance. Political pressures also play a significant role in all antipollution control measures (Ranga, Sastry and Prakash 1989).

The practice of large-scale corruption and other forms of bribery among officials has stalled the implementation of pollution control laws to a significant extent. Industry owners commonly perceive that public servants can be bought by monetary incentives. Therefore, industrial polluters reason that they have recourse to cheaper ways than to comply with regulations that may entail significant cost.

Citing an experience of Punjab, the member secretary of the PPCB observes:

Whenever the Board officers and officials visit the industry to inspect and collect samples of treated and untreated effluents, they are quite often made to wait at the gate of the industry till the industry makes arrangement either to close the process causing pollution or to commission the treatment plant. In extreme cases the industry does go to the extent of shutting down the industry itself. Sometimes the connivance of the officers and officials collecting or testing the sample cannot also be ruled out. (Garg and Tiwana 1987:111)

Given this image, public servants are not likely to feel enthusiastic about enforcing environmental laws. Even in cases where public officials are inclined to implement the environmental laws, their authority and position are undermined by the alliance of industrial magnets and local politicians. They fall to the captivity of economic interests and monetary incentives and find their escape in formalistic enforcement.

Lack of Coordination and Cooperation

Poor coordination and missing links among the administrative institutions have stood in the way of implementing environmental policy actions. At the administrative level, different departments are concerned with environmental safety and protection. The Department of Environment and Controller of Explosives and Mines are responsible for safety standards. The Pollution Control Board is connected with the factories only to the extent they affect the environment; the Factories Inspectorate is connected with occupational safety of workers; and the controller of explosives is responsible for checking on the contravention of the rules regarding storage of most hazardous gases under pressure. This artificial division of responsibility for controlling health hazards that emanate from the same source invariably leads to lack of coordination.

Similarly, while the reclamation of wastelands is the responsibility of the National Wasteland Development Board (NWDB) in the Union Ministry of Rural Development and of a similarly constituted National Afforestation and Eco-Development Board (NAEB) in the Union Ministry of Environment and Forests, the treatment of eroding agricultural lands continues to be the charge of a forgotten division in the Union Department of Agriculture. Agricultural lands threatened by waterlogging and salinization are nobody's responsibility, and they are rarely mentioned in any official documents.

A large number of poverty alleviation schemes operate under the aegis of the Union Ministry of Rural Development. These also are intended to improve the productivity of the land through soil and water conservation measures. Some important schemes are the Jawahar Rozgar Yojana, the Employment Guarantee Scheme, and the Integrated Rural Development Programme (IRDP). These programs, of course, are apart from the Drought Prone Areas Programme

(DPAP) and the Desert Development Programme (DDP) that have been under implementation since 1970 and 1977, respectively. They are supposed to ameliorate exactly the same kind of lands as the National Wasteland Development Board lands which have become badly degraded because of denudation, drought, and desertification. For want of effective coordination, each of these schemes, as well as those taken up by the National Wasteland Development Board, the National Afforestation and Eco-Development Board, and the soil conservation division of the Union Agriculture Department, wastes large sums of money by taking up works on a sectoral basis and in isolated patches, without following the integrated watershed approach.

Present administrative and planning structures have evolved over a long time. Environmental policy is the most recent development in this respect. A general characteristic of present environmental policy is its emphasis on prohibitions and regulations. Obviously a development policy in which environmental policy will be a key factor for improving the quality of the environment is impossible without a simulataneous design of coordinating channels among the various functional areas of policy concern. Lack of proper coordination and cooperation among the administrative institutions is an important loophole in the whole institutional set-up.

Lack of Public Involvement

Public involvement in environmental management programs such as afforestation, flood control, wildlife protection, and control of pollution puts tremendous pressure on bureaucracy to produce results. By staging demonstrations, protests, and mass movements, the public has largely offset the power base of vested-interest groups and built a power structure of its own to enforce environmental actions. The Chipko movement in the Uttar Pradesh hills and the Appiko movement in Western Ghats of Karnatka were launched against tree-felling for commercial purposes. In protest against the decision of the Bharat Aluminum Company (a central government public sector undertaking) to mine bauxite, the tribals offered satyagraha (they lay down on the road, obstructing the entry of vehicles), and later their demand was justified by a committee of the Department of Environment. Direct action by small farmers against a eucalyptus plantation of Karnataka and a campaign against a plantation of Australian acacia in Wyanadu (through Prakriti Samrakshan Samiti—a grassroots activist organization) in the state of Himachal Pradesh in February 1988 were resorted to. Environmental conservation movements have been launched against construction of dams over Bhagirathi (the Tehri dam in the state of Uttar Pradesh), Subernarekha in Bihar, and Narmada in Madhya Pradesh. The administrators, who are in touch with the people, can play a vital role in making the voice of the people effective. Sunderial Bahuguna (leader of the Chipko movement and an environmental activist) relates his own experience: "I have personal experience of such administrators who instead of blindly implementing the orders from the state government to crush the chipko movement, visited the areas, met the people and the activists and allowed the movements to continue" (Bahuguna 1989:379).

The government, through its enforcement agencies, has done little so far to prove that it is capable of controlling the environmental problems. The government must recognize the stabilizing influence of the Himalayan farmer on the local ecology and support the development of local agro-forestry systems and the participation of the people (Center for Science and Environment 1991).

However, the public in India has not provided a necessary clientele to the environmental protection bureaucracy. Local movements against deforestation, construction of dams, and pollution activities are sporadic in nature. In the context of a limited resource base and unlimited development aspirations, the environmental movements largely have failed to put pressure on implementors to produce results.[21]

Centralized Policy Process

Frictions between central and state government relations also have affected the enforcement process adversely. In the area of environmental protection, the policy process is heavily centralized. Policy decisions taken at the central level, including setting goals and procedures, ignore the local policy culture. Khator contends that the policy slippage in Indian environmental regulation is due more to the inherent faults of either the design of the policy or the implementation network (Khator 1989).

The Central Ministry of Environment is responsible for carrying out environmental impact assessment of development projects. The environmental impact assessment of development projects so far has been done by "executive order," issuing the provisions of the Environment Protection Act (1986) to ensure implementation of the suggested guidelines. This procedure, however, does not cover private sector projects. But a meaningful assessment of impacts is possible only when a reliable set of measurements exists for the environmental parameters. In the absence of standards, it is difficult to determine correctly, in quantitative terms, either the beneficial or the harmful impacts of the projects.

India was more than willing to adopt environmental policies and programs, but when the time came for implementation, it lacked political will to proceed. It is still questionable whether the environmental quality has improved at all, in terms of safe water, clean air, and healthy living conditions. Environmentalists and policy makers increasingly realize that wide enforcement gaps exist in Indian environmental policy.

Conclusion

India faces environmental problems of great magnitude that threaten efforts to raise living standards, that worsen health conditions, and that reduce income from agriculture and other sources. In metropolitan areas, increased congestion, industrial expansion, and lack of emission controls result in unhealthy levels of air and water pollution. In rural areas, pressure to grow both more food and cash crops has led to massive losses of forest, topsoil, plants, and animals.

A wide range of programs that require urgent environmental actions includes preserving arable land, forest, and water resources; reducing pollution from electrical power generation (fossil fuel and coal consumption), transport, and heavy pollution-intensive industries; promoting better sanitation; introducing cleaner technologies; removing subsidies that encourage use of fossil fuels, irrigation water, pesticides, chemical fertilizers, and excessive logging; and assisting local areas vulnerable to damage.[22]

Although these environmental problems undermine the goals of development, the desirability of development is universally recognized. A basic question today, therefore, is not whether to choose development or environment. It is how to select patterns of development that improve the quality of environment (Sapru 1986).

The causes of environmental degradation are many. The prevailing conditions of poverty, centuries of developmental stagnation, rapid population growth, growing pressure on land, commercialization of natural resources, inadequate control of polluting industries, and inappropriate agricultural practices are major sources of environmental impoverishment in India.

However, inadequate attention has been given to the environmental problems that damage the health and productivity of the large number of people, especially the poor who constitute nearly 50 percent of India's population. Addressing the environmental problems faced by the people will require sustained development—meeting the needs of the present generation without compromising the needs of future generations (World Commission on Environment and Development 1987). It is imperative that new policies be designed to promote income growth, alleviate poverty, and improve the environment. First, we should attempt to remove impediments that stand in the way of environmental action.

An important question that must be asked is whether the pollution control measures imposed by the state and central governments are keeping pace with industrial development. Anyone familiar with India would say that effective pollution control measures are yet to be implemented. Among the more important pollution control measures suggested are (1) implementing common effluent treatment plants and common solid incineration plants, for which World Bank loans and fiscal incentives from the central and state governments are easily accessible; (2) encouraging cooperative and private enterprises to set up waste disposal systems that would convert municipal garbage and industrial wastes into electric power/bio-gas; (3) setting up a state-level council, supported by executive agencies and advisory bodies, to guide in the formulation and correct implementation of various pollution control measures and regulations relating to such areas as health, transportation of hazardous goods, and pollution monitoring; and (4) setting up environmental laboratories and institutes to carry out research and disseminate information relating to environmental pollution.

The Policy Statement for Abatement of Pollution in India stresses that "the emphasis will be on clean technologies and not clean-up technologies" (Asian Recorder 1992:22246). The focus therefore must be on source reduction and substitution of chemicals with safe alternatives. To achieve this objective, a mix of instruments, including laws, fiscal incentives, educational programs, information campaigns and public participation, is needed. In India, the environment policy is still in its developmental stage and is based on penal procedures and curative pollution control methods. What it probably does not contain is the close link between poverty and environmental problems that makes a compelling case for greater support of programs that alleviate poverty, slow population growth, and address ecological degradation that hurts the poor.

A set of "market friendly policies"[23] is needed to attack the underlying causes of environmental degradation. These policies include developing human resources through education, health, nutrition, and family planning; creating a healthy environment for work; fostering integration with the global economy; and promoting sound management of natural resources. These policies need to be placed at the top of the political agenda. Policy makers need to ensure that the necessary laws, regulations, finances, and personnel are in place to address environmental problems. Effective implementation requires efficient administrative machinery and strong political commitment.

Powerful industrialists, rich farmers, and fishermen, all of whom fiercely defend their rights to exploit resources, bring political pressures to bear on government to modify proposed environmental policies and actions. Other influences may persuade government to set the wrong priorities. Therefore, it is important that countervailing political pressures be built through the ecology movements to prevent those powerful interests from taking initiatives and decisions that lead to environmental impoverishment.

A review of existing environmental laws that relate to water and air identifies institutional failure as the most frequent and persistent cause of poor performance. Central and state governments both must recognize the necessity to strengthen their institutional arrangements for environmental management.

These include building necessary technical skills, providing adequate finances, and clarifying environmental regulations. In addition to these clear needs, experience suggests two priorities. First, the implementing agencies need to be held accountable for the effects of their environmental actions and need to be kept separate from regulatory and monitoring bodies. Second, to ensure consistency and cost effectiveness in the management of pollution and wastes and the protection of the forests, coordination and cooperation among participating organizations are required.

Development projects that have not sought out detailed local knowledge often have failed. Local participation yields high economic and social benefits and environmental returns when implementing programs of afforestation, soil and water management, wildlife protection, and flood control. At the local level, community groups can do much to preserve their environment and improve living standards. Without their backing it is difficult for political leaders to support long-term strategies that may entail high expenditure and change patterns of development. In addition, central and state governments both need to forge partnerships with industry and farmers' associations, business groups, women's groups, and other nongovernmental organizations (NGOs). These organizations, which have been at the forefront of the environmental movement, must be involved in environmental planning and implementation. Their expertise and dynamism are needed to preserve the environment and achieve the goal of sustainable development.

Notes

1. According to a report of the Standing Committee of Experts on Population Projections (1989), the Indian population will grow from 844 million in 1991 to 1,006 million in the year 2001 and 1,102 million in 2007.

2. In some of the states, such as Punjab, the situation is serious where more than 83 percent of the area is under cultivation.

3. See also Central Water Commission, *Water and Related Statistics* (New Delhi: CWC, 1989).

4. The National Forest Policy, announced in December 1988, stipulates that the country as a whole should aim at keeping about 33 percent of its geographical area under forest cover.

5. Refer especially to articles 47, 48A, and 51A(g) of the Indian Constitution.

6. *T. Damodar Rao vs. The Special Officer, Municipal Corporation of Hyderabad*, AIR 1987, A.P. 171, 181.

7. See B. Shiva Rao, ed., *The Framing of India's Constitution: A Study* (Bombay: N. M. Tripathy, 1968), 5:635.

8. *Ibid.*, 634–35.

9. See Lok Sabha Debates, eighteenth session, fifth series, vol. 65, no. 5, 29 October 1976.

10. For example, the center has given permission to Madhya Pradesh to settle 89,526 persons over 103,873 hectares of encroached forest land. See "No Let Up in Tree Felling," *The Times of India*, 5 April 1991.

11. For example, the Supreme Court of India on 3 December 1994 threatened the closure of the Rs5000 crore Mathura Refinery for its failure to install requisite pollution control devices, thus causing damage to the Taj Mahal.

12. For example, in 1993 and 1994 more than 4,500 units in the green category industries were approved by the PPCB. Information to this effect was obtained from the PPCB.

13. Information regarding pollution by the paper mills was collected from the PPCB.

14. B.G. Verghese, *Waters of Hope* (New Delhi: Oxford and IBH, 1990).

15. The five-member committee consisted of L. C. Jain, former member of the planning commission; Dr. Vasant Gowarikar, scientific adviser to the prime minister; Ramaswamy Iyer, former secretary to the Union Ministry of Water Resources; Dr. Kulandaiswamy, vice-chancellor of Indira Gandhi Open University; and Dr. Jayant Patil, member of the planning commission.

16. Proceedings of the Vidhan Sabha of Himachal Pradesh, held in Shimla the first week of April 1995.

17. Significantly, the Union government's new draft Forest Bill, poised to replace the Indian Forests Act of 1927, proposes to restrict people's right to state-owned reserved forests. It also sharply limits the area or extent of village forests over which dwellers can exercise independent control.

18. Information in respect to the paper mill has been collected from the PPCB.

19. For a detailed discussion, see K. K. Puri, "Environment Pollution Management: A Case Study of Ludhiana City," in *The New Environmental Age*, ed. R. K. Sapru and S. Bharadwaj (New Delhi: Ashish Publishing House, 1990), 376–77.

20. This information was obtained from the Department of Science, Technology, and Environment, Punjab Government, Chandigarh.

21. See also Jayanta Bandyopadhyay and Vandana Shiva, "Political Economy of Ecology Movements," *Economic and Political Weekly* 23(24):1223–32.

22. For more extensive reviews of policy and program options, see *World Development Report* 1992.

23. See *World Development Report* 1991, which describes a set of "market-friendly" policies for development.

References

Andolan, Narmada Bachao. 1992. *Towards Sustainable and Just Development*. Baroda: NBA.

Asian Recorder (New Delhi). 1992 April 15–21. XXXVIII, 16:22246–47.

"Assam MPs Demand Flood Control Steps." 1988. *The Sentinel* (Guwahati). August 11.

Bahuguna, Sunderlal. 1989. "Environment Conservation for Survival." *The Indian Journal of Public Administration* 35 (3):374–379.

Center for Science and Environment. 1991. *State of India's Environment: A Citizen's Report*. New Delhi: CSE, 124.

"The Constitution of India 26 January 1950." 1994. In *Constitutions of the Countries of the World*, vol. VIII, eds. Albert Blaustein, and Gisbert H. Flanz, 1–353. Dobbs Ferry, New York: Oceana Publications.

Das, Arvind N. 1987. "Bihar Society in Perspective." In *Bihar Stagnation or Growth*, ed. A.N. Sharma and S. Gupta. Patna: Spectrum Publishing House.

Dhanagare, D. N. 1993. "Sustainable Development, Environment, and Social Science Research in India." *The Indian Journal of Public Administration* 39 (3):551–563.

Dubhashi, P. R. 1992. "Drought and Development." *Economic and Political Weekly* 27 (13):A-29.

"The Environment (Protection) Act and Rules, 1986." 1990. In *Commentaries on Water & Air Pollution Laws*, Third Edition, 255–309. Allahabad, India: Law Publishers India (P) Ltd.

Expert Committee on Narmada. 1994. *Review Report of the Sardar Sarovar Project*. New Delhi: Government of India.

Gadgil, Madhav. 1991. "Restoring India's Forest Wealth." *Nature and Resources* 27 (2):12–13.

———. 1993. "Restoring India's Forest Land." *The Indian Journal of Public Administration* 39 (3):586–602.

Gadgil, Madhav, S. N. Prasad, and R. Ali. 1983. "Forest Management in India: A Critical Review." *Social Action* 33, 127–55.

Garg, M. R., and N. S. Tiwana. 1987. "Enforcement of Environmental Law and Management of Pollution Control." In *Environment Management in India*, ed. R. K. Sapru, 103–122. New Delhi: Ashish Publishing House.

Government of India, Planning Commission. 1952. *The First Five Year Plan, 1952–57*. New Delhi: Controller of Publications.

Government of India, Planning Commission. 1992. *Eighth Five Year Plan, 1992–97*, vol. 2. New Delhi: Controller of Publications.

Gupta, S. K. 1990. "Impact of Socio-economic Change on the Ecology of Himachal Pradesh." In *Himalyan Environment and Culture*, ed. N. K. Rustomji, and Charles Ramble, 27–47. Shimla: Indian Institute of Advanced Study.

India, National Commission on Floods. 1980. *Report* (vol. I). New Delhi: Ministry of Energy and Irrigation.

India, National Commission on Floods. 1980b. *Report* (vol. II). New Delhi: Ministry of Energy and Irrigation.

Kashyap, Arvind. 1995. "No Check on Illegal Felling of Khair Trees." *Chandighar Newsline*, 5 April.

Khator, Renu. 1989. "The Enforcement Gap: A Comparative Study of Indian, British, and American Pollution Regulations." *The Indian Journal of Public Administration* 35 (3):593–606.

Menon, Ramesh. 1987. "Forest Land Fiddle." *India Today*, 1–15 July, 49–55.

"No Let Up in Tree Felling." 1991. *The Times of India*, 5 April.

"PM plays dirty, says Mahanta." 1988. *The Telegraph* (Calcutta), 20 September.

Ranga, S. P., and Prakash M. S. Sastry. 1989. "Control of Water Pollution in Andhra Pradesh." *The Indian Journal of Public Administration* 35 (3):548–560.

Report of the Independent Review. 1992. *Sardar Sarovar*. Ottawa: Resource Futures International.

Sangvai, Sanjay. 1995. "Re-opening Sardar Sarovar Issue." *Economic and Political Weekly*. XXX, II:524–544.

Sapru, R. K. 1986. "Relevance of International Economic Issues to the Human Environment." *The Indian Economic Journal* 33 (3):81–84.

———. 1989. "Water Pollution Management in Chandigarh." *The Indian Journal of Public Administration* 35 (3):578–81.

"State Diverting Funds: PM Sanctions Rs.40 Crore for Flood Relief." 1988. *The Sentinel* (Guwahati), 15 September.

The Times of India. 1995. 8 February.

The Tribune. 1994a. 16 May.

————. 1994b. 17 May.

Verghese, B. G. 1990. *Waters of Hope.* New Delhi: Oxford and IBH.

World Commission on Environment and Development. 1987. *Our Common Future.* Oxford: Oxford University Press. [Brundtland Commission Report, Gro Harlem Brundtland, Chairman].

World Development Report. 1991. Published for the World Bank. New York: Oxford University Press.

World Development Report. 1992. Published for the World Bank. New York: Oxford University Press.

7

ENVIRONMENTAL POLICY AND POLITICS IN MEXICO

STEPHEN P. MUMME

Since the mid-1980s, Mexico's environmental predicament has captured global attention as a leading example of the perils of rapid industrialization as well as the possibilities for policy reform. Debate on the North American Free Trade Agreement (NAFTA) also has drawn attention to Mexico as a test case for linking environmental regulation to trade policy. Serious questions have been raised concerning Mexico's regulatory capacity and its ability to cope with rapid economic growth.

This chapter examines in four parts Mexico's environmental policy with an eye toward understanding better its contemporary predicament. The first section briefly describes Mexico's environmental dilemma. The second section provides background on the development of Mexico's environmental policy and describes basic patterns and problems of policy formulation and implementation. The third section looks at policy implementation and program performance under the administration of Carlos Salinas de Gortari. The chapter concludes with a summary assessment of the impact of politics on recent policy reforms as Mexico enters a new environmental policy era.

Environment and Development in Mexico

If, in the 1980s, *crisis* was the most common adjective used to describe the Mexican economy, much the same could be said of its environmental predicament. Forty years of rapid industrialization that thrust Mexico into a leading economic position among the Latin American economies had taken a devastating toll on its natural resources and the health of its citizens. Its ecological crisis was evident in the net reduction of forest at an annual loss rate exceeding 1 million acres annually, second only to Brazil in Latin America, and in the disappearance of thousands of species of fauna and flora in a nation with one of the world's highest levels of biodiversity. Its celebrated natural lakes, Lake Chapala and Lake Patzcuaro, are severely degraded. More than 60 percent of its rivers are contaminated, oil development on the Mexican Gulf coast has severely damaged national fisheries and aquatic life, and more than half of Mexico's municipalities suffer from insufficient sanitation and sewage facilities. Mexico City is an international synonym for venomous air pollution, and the nation as a whole sustains one of the highest rates of pulmonary disease on the globe. It is hardly an exaggeration to say that the deterioration of Mexico's environment has been comprehensive and on a magnitude with few rivals in Latin America and the industrializing world (*Excelsior* 1990c; *La Jornada* 1992a; Monge 1991; *World Resources* 1990–91; Wright 1990).

Mexico's environmental predicament, similar to that of other advanced industrializing countries, is rooted in an economic development strategy that favors rapid industrialization over rural development (Vernon 1963). That policy has imposed a high price on Mexican society. Neglect of rural areas has displaced rural populations and fed the stream of migration to Mexico's urban centers (see maps 7.1 and 7.2). That same neglect contributed to the erosion of soils and the depletion of forests, generally associated with the decline in productivity and wealth in the rural subsistence economy. Nor has Mexico's development policy spared the urban masses presumed to benefit from those policies. Mexico's urban underclass, already burdened with inadequate employment, poor working conditions, inadequate health and welfare services, and other problems, is even more vulnerable to the health risks associated with pollution (Barkin 1990:41–56).

Over the past two decades, such conditions gradually have been recognized as a policy problem by successive Mexican administrations. While still reluctant to acknowledge the environmental costs of its economic development strategy, Mexico's political leaders have become sensitive to international concern with environmental preservation as well as to the domestic political costs associated with incipient popular mobilization on environmental issues. It is useful, then, to review the development of Mexico's environmental policy to better assess recent reforms in this issue area.

Mexico's Environmental Policy Framework: Policy Formulation and Implementation

It is important to situate Mexico's experience with environmental policy in the context of its unique one-party-dominant, presidential political system. By any standard, Mexico's political system is one of the world's most enduring single-party-dominant political systems (Camp 1993). The Institutional Revolutionary Party (PRI) has monopolized the electoral and policy arenas for over sixty years, conferring enormous policy authority on Mexican executives during their six-year, nonrenewable term of office and structuring interest representation heirarchically, along corporatist lines. Mexico's policy-making

MAP 7.1

Total Population of Mexico

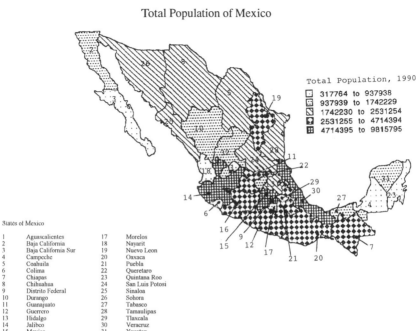

Total Population, 1990

- ☐ 317764 to 937938
- ☒ 937939 to 1742229
- ☒ 1742230 to 2531254
- ▣ 2531255 to 4714394
- ▦ 4714395 to 9815795

States of Mexico

1	Aguascalientes	17	Morelos
2	Baja California	18	Nayarit
3	Baja California Sur	19	Nuevo Leon
4	Campeche	20	Oaxaca
5	Coahuila	21	Puebla
6	Colima	22	Queretaro
7	Chiapas	23	Quintana Roo
8	Chihuahua	24	San Luis Potosi
9	Distrito Federal	25	Sinaloa
10	Durango	26	Sohora
11	Guanajuato	27	Tabasco
12	Guerrero	28	Tamaulipas
13	Hidalgo	29	Tlaxcala
14	Jalibco	30	Veracruz
15	Mexico	31	Yucatan
16	Michoacan	32	Zacatecas

Source: James B. Pick, and Edgar W. Butler, *The Mexico Handbook: Economic and Demographic Maps and Statistics.* (Boulder: Westview Press, 1994), 31.

system thus has concentrated policy initiative in the presidential sash and sharply restricted its public availability. While policy factions in and out of government are frequently consulted, and some—entrepreneurs, for instance— exert considerable influence, most policy development resembles the "inside access" pattern of elite-dominated policy formation described by comparative policy theorists (Mumme, Bath, and Assetto 1988:9–11).

Mexican environmental policy has been forged in this context. As a distinct body of law, it originated with the UN Stockholm Conference on the Human Environment in 1972. Mexico, under the leadership of President Luis Echeverria (1970–1976) who sought to project Mexico's international influ- ence, hosted a regional preparatory meeting in 1971 and in 1972 produced both a formative national environmental law and accompanying regulatory ordinances for air and water pollution. These laws were generated almost entirely in-house at the upper levels of Mexico's Ministry of Health and the foreign policy bureaucracy. Legislation on air and water pollution remained

Map 7.2

Proportion of Population Urban

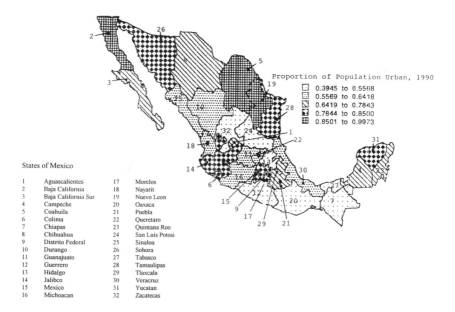

States of Mexico

1	Aguascalientes	17	Morelos
2	Baja California	18	Nayarit
3	Baja California Sur	19	Nuevo Leon
4	Campeche	20	Oaxaca
5	Coahuila	21	Puebla
6	Colima	22	Queretaro
7	Chiapas	23	Quintana Roo
8	Chihuahua	24	San Luis Potosi
9	Distrito Federal	25	Sinaloa
10	Durango	26	Sohora
11	Guanajuato	27	Tabasco
12	Guerrero	28	Tamaulipas
13	Hidalgo	29	Tlaxcala
14	Jalibco	30	Veracruz
15	Mexico	31	Yucatan
16	Michoacan	32	Zacatecas

Source: James B. Pick, and Edgar W. Butler, *The Mexico Handbook: Economic and Demographic Maps and Statistics.* (Boulder: Westview Press, 1994), 59.

largely unenforced throughout Echeverria's presidency, and conservation programs were scattered and uncoordinated.

Echeverria's successor, Jose Lopez-Portillo, did little to change this state of affairs. Toward the end of the Lopez-Portillo *sexenio* (six-year term), rising public concern with air quality in Mexico City, voiced by professional organizations and the media, provoked a modest investment in an air quality monitoring network and resulted in the first study of vehicular emissions in the Federal District. These measures led to a rewriting of the national environmental law in 1981 that extended its scope to include hazardous and nuclear wastes and generally broadened its formal reach. Some measure of the relative unimportance of environmental concerns, however, is seen in the utter ommission of any reference to environmental preservation in the national planning documents and presidential speeches throughout the Lopez-Portillo years, particularly the much-touted Global Development Plan of 1980, which set out the energy-based development strategy of the Lopez-Portillo government (Secretaria de Programacion y Presupuesto 1980).

The administration of Miguel de la Madrid was the first to put environmental reform on the presidential agenda. Amending the 1981 environmental law, de la Madrid created a new cabinet-level ministry, the Secretariat of Urban Development and Ecology (SEDUE). He simultaneously undertook a year-long campaign to promote environmental concern, encouraged the formation of environmental interest groups, and elevated public and official attention to environmental values, incorporating "ecology" as a policy category in government planning documents. Unfortunately, the climate of severe economic austerity precipitated by the 1982 economic crisis effectively restricted environmental policy to symbolic and educational activities. The emergence of a number of small but very vocal environmental advocacy groups during the de la Madrid years did, however, significantly increase media attention devoted to environmental concerns and resulted in criticism of the government's unresponsiveness to environmental matters. De la Madrid's policy performance was further sullied by an embarrassing gas explosion in Mexico City in 1984, the severe earthquake of 1985, a serious oil spill on the Mexican Gulf Coast, worsening air pollution in Mexico City, and an embarrassing fight with environmental organizations over the initiation of Mexico's first nuclear power plant at Laguna Verde, Veracruz (Stevis and Mumme 1991:55–81).

Criticism of SEDUE's regulatory ineffectiveness led to yet another reform of the environmental law in March 1988, associated with the electoral campaign of Carlos Salinas de Gortari (*Diario Oficial* 1988:23–57). The 1988 environmental law improved on the past in several respects. At the administrative level, it enhanced SEDUE's authority, investing it with greater coordinating power in environmental administration, strengthening its hand in enforcement of environmental regulations, and clarifying the competencies and authority of related agencies with environmental mandates. It specified, for example, a division of labor between SEDUE and the federal district government (DDF) in enforcing environmental regulations within the federal district. The law further required environmental impact assessments for all federal public works, potentially polluting industries, mining, tourist development, sanitary facilities, and other types of private sector construction. To facilitate compliance, it mandated the elaboration of specific technical standards (*normas tecnicas*). It further provided for the development of state and local environmental laws, and it amplified opportunities for civic participation in environmental enforcement.

In May 1992, the Salinas administration took the further step of abolishing SEDUE, folding its functions into a new superministry, the Secretariat of Social Development (SEDESOL). Ecology and environmental functions are now allocated to two new semiautonomous agencies, the National Institute for Ecology (INE) and the Federal Attorney General for Environmental Protection (PFMA). Subsequent sections of this chapter examine these reforms.

Policy Formulation

Policy formulation in modern Mexican politics tends to center on the "output" side of the political process, which is another way of saying that legislatures and representative assemblies play a diminished role in formulating and deciding public policy. Mexico has a "state corporatist" system, one that limits and directs interest articulation and aggregation in ways that shore up state authority and that penalizes interests that remain outside the system (Spalding 1981:139–61). In this context, interest groups and private citizens frequently must resort to what has been described as a petitionary, or bargaining, approach with government officials in order to place issues on the government agenda. Much policy is initiated inside the government, relegating interest groups to a reactive and supportive role in promoting policy initiatives.

Environmental policy certainly fits this pattern. Environmental organizations have few effective channels through which to pursue their policy goals. Formal representation is dominated by the government party, of which many citizens remain suspicious and cynical. While some activists elect to work within the party, most eschew formal association with the PRI. Opposition parties at best play a symbolic role in interest articulation, through party forums, platforms, and occasional speeches in legislative committees and plenary sessions of the Mexican Congress. Mexico's ecology party (PEM), which first emerged in the 1988 presidential elections, has suffered from factionalism and limited resources and has yet to attract a following outside Mexico City. In its first appearance on the national ballot in 1991 congressional elections, PEM failed to get the 1.5 percent of the national vote that would qualify it for legal recognition as a national party (Chavez 1991:22). On the administrative side, environmentalists often are consulted, but government officials enjoy considerable discretion in deciding who they invite to participate. Knowing this, leaders of environmental organizations have been cautious in participating in government-dominated consultative forums.[1]

The justice system fails to offer an alternative avenue for interest group influence at present. Environmental organizations have virtually ignored the Mexican courts. Not a single case has been successfully brought by an environmental advocacy organization against the government or the private sector. This is due to several factors. First, Mexico's system of judge-made law lends itself to considerable delay, amplifying the costs of legal action to plaintiffs. Injunctive relief can be obtained readily by defendents in the form of the *amparo*, a broad-based stay of action against government enforcement that may be granted by the courts at the request of the regulatee (Tucker 1956). Second, the lack of technical norms and regulatory standards, till recently, made it impossible to sustain a claim in the courts. Indeed, the law was far more serviceable to defend the interests of polluters than to punish them. This is particularly true in cases where the government was the defendant, given broad judicial discretion and the absence of precise standards. Third, Mexican environmental groups lack the monetary resources to pursue legal action.

Such structural barriers to policy influence are evident in the pattern of policy initiative over the past two decades. Since 1971, Mexican environmental initiatives have come mainly from the government bureaus, with modest support from a limited number of professional organizations and educators. In 1980, few environmental organizations existed in Mexico, and those that did were elite-dominated conservationist groups such as Ducks Unlimited, the Nature Conservancy, and PRONATURA with limited functional interests (habitat preservation). Such groups were content to work behind the scenes to influence government officials. De la Madrid, in 1982 and 1983, broke from this trend by encouraging the formation of broad-based, pollution-oriented advocacy groups and providing them a measure of voice in government policy making. The 1983 environmental reforms legitimized and ceded new institutional channels for petition and protest at SEDUE and DDF. Groups such as the new Mexican Ecology movement, the Grupo de Cien, the Alianza Ecologista, the Pacto de Ecologistas, and the Partido Verde (green party) were invited to participate in government policy forums on ecological and urban planning themes, given access to the government-dominated press, and provided with formal channels for expressing environmental concern.

The result was a significant increase in news coverage of environmental issues and an embarrassing tide of public criticism directed at the government. Environmental sensitivity in Mexico City was reflected in opinion polls that identified urban pollution as either the second or third highest priority of the city's public, surpassed only by economic recovery and personal security concerns (*Excelsior* 1988a; *Uno Mas Uno* 1992a). In sum, by the time of the 1988 presidential elections, environmental issues were a significant political preoccupation in urban areas, contributing to the government's tarnished political image.

The Salinas administration thus assumed office at a time of unprecedented environmental concern. Instead of offering environmental groups greater institutional voice in policy making, however, it opted to restrict interest group influence. Shortly after taking office, the Salinas administration made overtures to leaders of several fledgling environmental groups, several of whom joined the government in administrative positions. This could be seen as a classic cooptative device.[2] Various environmental organizations also complained of intimidation and selective exclusion from government policy forums, and there is some circumstantial evidence that this indeed occurred (Puig 1992).

Advocacy groups also are concerned about government responsiveness to citizen complaints under the 1988 Environmental Law. The 1988 law provides that ordinary citizens may file a formal protest with SEDUE (now PFMA within the new Secretariat of Environment, Natural Resources and Fisheries), which then has fifteen days to inform the violator and thirty days to investigate and produce a formal response that indicates the action to be taken. Advocacy groups have been reluctant to employ the procedure, complaining of delays and failure to apply all but symbolic sanctions to violators.[3]

Under these circumstances, the preferred action-generating strategy of environmental advocacy groups is to dramatize problems in the media or other public settings, hoping to embarrass the government to such an extent that it takes administrative action. Foreign media are preferred to domestic media, since foreign media, particularly U.S. media, due to binational economic linkages, shape elite opinion. Such media-oriented strategies have been evident particularly in the NAFTA debate.[4]

In sum, the Salinas administration's contributions to policy formulation at the national level were minimal, limited to developing regulatory norms and standards that enhance the potential use of the courts to enforce environmental standards and the assigning SEDESOL the responsiblity to implement the law. These changes had little impact during the Salinas *sexenio*. Indeed, the bulk of the evidence points to further politicization of environmental interests and a greater government effort to manage them within the policy system.

Policy Implementation

Policy implementation in Mexico's presidential system is highly centralized, dominated by the federal bureaus that control the lion's share of the national budget. In addition, Mexican policy implemention exhibits certain essential features that prevail across substantive policy areas. First, much Mexican policy is liable to the charge of "formalism," in which statutory gestures substitute for material commitments in policy implementation. Second, Mexican policy implementation is disjunctive and discontinuous, if only due to the disruptive effects of the sexenial cycle and the extraordinary shuffling of personnel from one presidential administration to the next. Third, Mexican policy implementation, until recently, has been dominated by *politicos* rather than *tecnicos*. In the 1970s the balance of influence shifted toward technical expertise. Even so, many *tecnicos* remain encumbered by the demands of a patronage-ridden political system, and certain agencies are still dominated by patronage concerns. Fourth, Mexican policy implementation tends to be ad hoc and nonprogrammatic, despite the use of quasi-indicative planning instruments, owing to economic scarcity, lack of budgetary accountability, and the relative ease of shifting funds across institutional accounts, and the quasi-autonomous character of many cabinet-level agencies in the absence of direct presidential intervention and oversight (Camp 1993; Grindle 1977; Story 1986).

Each of these policy characteristics is evident in the development of environmental policy, one of the most recent entries on the Mexican policy agenda. Until quite recently, Mexican environmental policy was highly formalistic in nature, with little presidential commitment to the policy area. As seen above, this changed under de la Madrid. Even so, macroeconomic conditions precluded serious investment in this policy area (Belausteguigoitia 1992).

On the second point, it is certainly true that environmental policy has been plagued by sexenialism. In the 1982 sexenial transition to de la Madrid, for example, almost none of the technically qualified specialists in the old Subsecretariat of Environmental Improvement were invited into the newly formed Ecology division of SEDUE, squandering precious talent and institutional experience in the process.

On the third point concerning politicization, environmental policy is such a young policy area that politicization has been virtually unavoidable because of the lack of technically trained environmental engineers, biologists, and policy specialists. Even when specialists were available, the evidence suggests that political goals routinely overroad technical expertise in implementation decisions.

Finally, the ad hoc, nonprogrammatic nature of Mexican environmental policy implementation is evident in the fractionalization of agency mandates, the failure to set environmental priorities, the limited authority of central coordinating institutions, the lack of follow-through in environmental projects, the reliance on short-term public campaigns, the paucity of fiscal resources allocated to environmental enforcement, and fiscal uncertainty concerning government commitments (Mumme, Bath, and Assetto 1988).

In addition to these general attributes, Mexican environmental policy is characterized by a voluntarist, less punitive approach to regulatory compliance. Government officials reject punitive enforcement of environmental regulations, preferring a strategy of *concertacion* that is, in practice, a blend of exhortation and negotiation with actual or potential polluters (*Excelsior* 1988b). Until late in the de la Madrid administration, few polluters were seriously penalized for violating environmental standards. The government preferred to sign *convenios*, written pledges of compliance, with parastate and private sector enterprises to achieve regulatory aims.[5] These were and continue to be honored frequently in the breach.

Policy Implementation and Program Performance Under Salinas

Policy Implementation

During its tenure in office the Salinas administration improved on the past in several respects. Among the most significant contributions is specifying standards that give force to the 1988 environmental law—the battery of *reglamentos* and *normas tecnicas* mentioned earlier. While by no means guaranteeing better enforcement, such standards are necessary, if not sufficient, to that purpose. Salinas thus laid the foundation for a less formalistic environmental policy.

Muddying the waters, however, Salinas also has pursued vigorously the development of state and municipal environmental codes. Twenty-nine Mexican states now have a state ecology law (Newman 1994). These measures, part of a general initiative toward administrative decentralization and devolution of powers to Mexican states (Newman 1994; Ranger 1991), are nevertheless highly problematical in the Mexican context. While state powers are to be consistent with the 1988 environmental law, state ecology laws create ambiguities and potential conflicts with federal legislation that may hamper rather than improve enforcement. The more fundamental problem here, however, is that states have little real autonomy from central authorities and relatively little independent budgetary authority. Thus far, it is clear that the decentralization of Mexican environmental policy to the states has not been accompanied by similarly enhanced fiscal authority (General Accounting Office 1992:21). Under these circumstances, state laws may impede the enforcement of federal law by blurring lines of regulatory responsibility and underfunding state environmental agencies.[6]

Salinas also took a swipe at the sexenialism of the past, retaining, as seen earlier, several senior environmental administrators from the de la Madrid administration and placing greater emphasis on the development of a skilled corps of *tecnicos* in the environmental ministry. He also retained most of SEDUE's environmental staff in merging its functions into the new super-ministry, SEDESOL. As part of his NAFTA initiative, he committed his administration to increasing the number of technically qualified personnel in environmental administration.[7] Here, however, the results remain to be seen. The buildup of environmental staff since 1991 thus far has been accomplished in haphazard fashion, and it is by no means clear that these new personnel have been trained adequately for their new assignments. Advanced education of new personnel takes considerable lead time, and these efforts have yet to mature fully.[8]

It is certainly true that Salinas brought a more programmatic approach to environmental policy, though much policy remains ad hoc and responsive to immediate political pressures. The Salinas administration focused public investment on a few high-priority programs. Here, Mexico City air quality, the Integrated Border Environmental Plan (IBEP), forest preservation, and river basin cleanup stand out (*Excelsior* 1991b, 1992). Salinas also energetically pursued foreign assistance and credits to fund key programs and solicited technical assistance from the United States and a number of European countries.

Many of Salinas' environmental actions, however, resemble the ad hoc environmental remediation of the past. The numbers of plant inspections and sanctions, for example, increased dramatically in 1991—from 1,380 in 1989 to 3,119 in 1991—in response to the considerable international scrutiny directed at Mexico in the context of the NAFTA debate (General Accounting Office 1992:19) but these subsided after 1992 (Newman 1994:38–39). Few permanent closures resulted from this heightened enforcement; the celebrated case of the demobilization of the March 18 refinery remains an anomaly.[9]

Salinas likewise maintained and intensified the voluntarist approach to regulatory compliance. During his administration, numerous *convenios* continued to be signed with commercial and industrial establishments. These compliance agreements commit the signees to meet government pollution standards, specifying timetables for installation of antipollution equipment and other implementation objectives. Salinas' senior environmental officials repeatedly championed a nonpunitive, negotiated approach to compliance and prefered to assert the need for *concertacion* rather than sanctions. To a considerable extent, economic austerity and the threat of unemployment associated with fines, partial closures, and closures account for this. Budgetary resources allocated to SEDUE increased after 1989 with Salinas pledging 1 percent of the national budget to environmental protection (General Accounting Office 1992:20). Even so, in 1992, national environmental protection received only 66.8 million USD (General Accounting Office 1992:20).

Along these same lines, the Salinas administration pursued privatization and market-based instruments for environmental protection. As a result, user fees, pollution permits, licenses, and other mechanisms of privatizing the costs of environmental preservation are now actively under consideration. New laws on agrarian reform, fisheries, forests, and water management already have been adopted (*Comercio Exterior* 1992a, 1992b; Szekely, Sanchez, and Abardia 1992). Proposed sanitation policy reforms in the Federal District would also privatize functions such as municipal garbage collection, assessing fees for service (*Uno Mas Uno* 1992d).

The creation of SEDESOL in 1992 certainly was intended to strengthen the programmatic character of environmental policy. Much remains to be seen, however. In principle, consolidating SEDUE's powers in two functionally distinct semiautonomous agencies had merit, but the administrative change in itself was not sufficient to overcome the structural deficiencies in Mexican environmental policy.

Two problems were immediately apparent. First, environmental functions were folded into a new, very powerful agency, while the formal visibility associated with these functions was reduced. Ecology was no longer a cabinet-level function. This diminished its political visibility. Within SEDESOL, ecology functions received greater fiscal support, but still accounted for only

1.8 percent of the agency's programmed expenditures in 1993 (*El Mercado de Valores* 1993). If budgets are at least a partial indicator of the influence and priority attached to subsidiary parts of an organization, ecology remained a minor function within the total structure of SEDESOL's commitments.

Second, while the reform was intended to rationalize the regulatory arena and strengthen enforcement, lines of authority among agencies remain blurred. The institutional reforms did not articulate clearly with the 1988 environmental law. For example, DDF retained its former jurisdiction over ecology programs in the Federal District, authority established in the 1988 law, but this was left unspecified in the constitutive authority for the new environmental agencies. Implementation of agency functions was contingent on shared authority with various other cabinet departments, yet the division of labor was vague. In the case of enforcement, coordination between the attorney general for environmental protection and the Mexican Justice Department remained undetermined.[10] The allocation of functions also appeared contradictory and confusing. The Ecology Institute, for instance, had the mandate to administer certain protected areas, yet the PFMA was assigned responsibility for investigating potential infractions of the environmental law. Or, in yet another example, the Ecology Institute was given the authority for developing laws, norms, and standards regulating environmental protection, yet PFMA was responsible for channeling citizen participation in environmental policy formulation and implementation (*Diario Oficial* 1992; Newman 1994:27–28). Such ambiguities must be reconciled if the two agencies are to synchronize their functions and exercise meaningful policy authority in this sphere.

Program Performance under Salinas

Thus far, this review has focused on the legal-administrative changes introduced by the Salinas government rather than on substantive programs. A brief review of progress in the four priority program arenas previously mentioned—Mexico City's air pollution campaign, forest preservation, river basin remediation, and the IBEP—may flesh out the reaches and limits of Mexico's environmental policy regime.

The Salinas administration's topmost priority in environmental remediation unquestionably was to bring Mexico City's notorious air quality problem under control. As seen previously, little effort was made to control the multiple sources of the city's air quality problem until 1987, late in the de la Madrid administration, which upgraded air quality monitoring networks and began a pilot program of vehicular emissions controls.

Shortly after taking office, in December 1988, the Salinas administration introduced a set of interrelated programs aimed at air pollution. Components included a new municipal traffic system that included a blanket prohibition on driving one day a week; mandatory vehicular emissions testing; introduction of lead-free gasoline, *magna sin*, in the Federal District; replacement of aging bus and taxi fleets; requiring catalytic converters on all vehicles sold after 1990; improvements in sanitation and garbage collection; development of an urban greenbelt; and a reforestation program within the city (*Excelsior* 1988c; American Embassy 1991; Embassy of Mexico 1992). To improve implementation, the Salinas administration assigned industrial pollution control to SEDUE, while giving DDF responsibility for vehicular and other programs. In October 1990, these several programs were incorporated into the Integrated Program for Control of Atmospheric Contamination in Mexico City (PICCA), with an official budget of $4.6 billion supported by credits from multilateral development banks, Japan, the United States, and several other foreign countries (Embassy of Mexico 1992).

Implementation of these initiatives, widely hailed by international observers, predictably encountered numerous obstacles. Lack of technically qualified operators made the vehicular emissions testing program a haven for patronage, thus undercutting performance. Corruption, in the form of payoffs for violations and counterfeited inspection decals, flourished. *Chilangos*, residents of Mexico City, purchased new cars to avoid the "day without a car" regulations (*Christian Science Monitor* 1990; *Excelsior* 1990b). Business interests vigorously opposed the new traffic regime. Academic specialists criticized the "command and control" approach pursued by the government, advocating a less onerous "pollution tax" on gasoline (Eskeland 1992). Moreover, Mexico City's infamous winter pollution worsened in 1991 and 1992, forcing the government to declare multiple air pollution emergencies. On at least one indicator of performance, however, that of public support, polling evidence indicated strong approval of the new regime (*Excelsior* 1990a).

It is still too early to assess the success or failure of the city's new air quality regime, though a number of program adjustments already have been made. The government, for instance, recently has contracted for a new state-of-the-art system of vehicular emissions testing, imposed a limited pollution tax on fuels, and made further adjustments in the "day without a car" program. PICCA's success, however, depends on sustained government investment in regulatory instruments that extends well into the 1994 to 2000 *sexenio*, coupled with policies that restrain the pace of urbanization in the Federal District.

Beyond the Federal District, the Salinas administration undertook several broad programs under the rubric of a new National Program of Ecological Conservation and Environmental Protection (PNCEPA). In the area of forest conservation Salinas introduced a number of reforms that aimed at improving both short- and long-term management. On the substantive side, for example, he declared a limited moratorium on logging and exploitation of forest products in the Lacandon region, extended Mexico's system of protected zones, committed Mexico to enter the Convention on Endangered Species (CITES), and mobilized the Mexican military in a national reforestation campaign (*Excelsior* 1989a, 1989c; *Uno Mas Uno* 1990). These programs, however, were essentially inexpensive symbolic programs that did little to alter the dynamics of resource exploitation that drive the destruction of Mexico's forest. Of greater consequence, Salinas rewrote article 27 of the Mexican Constitution to allow private investment in communally owned property, an unprecedented change in land tenure that was the basis for a major revision of the National Forestry Law in 1992. The new law, employing the logic of privatization, aims to "pave the way for the owners of woodland to earn a living from controlled forestry" by eliminating bureaucratic restrictions on the use of forest reserves (*El Financiero International* 1993; Szekely, Sanchez, and Abardia 1992).

The Salinas administration also directed attention to the nation's polluted rivers and waterways. Particular emphasis was given to the restoration of the Lerma-Chapala River basin, the nation's longest and most intensively used river system. An extensive system of forty-six wastewater treatment plants, collector systems, and reclamation works was proposed (*Excelsior* 1991a; *Uno Mas Uno* 1991) yet the plan remained largely unimplemented when Salinas left office. Lack of direct presidential attention, conflicts among the six basin states, exacerbated by decentralization of policy authority, and limited funding have been cited as contributing problems.

In contrast, the Salinas administration gave considerable attention to Mexico's northern border with the United States. Here, the stresses of rapid urbanization and development generated demands for environmental remediation by U.S. border communities. Though not originally a priority, NAFTA-related criticism in 1990 and 1991 persuaded the Salinas administration to support a bilateral remediation intiative, the Integrated Border Environmental Plan (IBEP)(Environmental Protection Agency 1992). The IBEP focused on sanitation, authorizing sewage treatment facilities at seven sister cities along the border. The Salinas administration allocated $450 million for this purpose, with the support of multilateral bank financing; the Mexican government is cooperating with the United States in developing these joint projects.

The NAFTA initiative also has midwifed several new international institutions, with far-reaching implications for environmental management in the interior and on the border. Specifically, three new bodies have been created (U.S. Congress 1993), a North American Commission on Environmental Cooperation (CEC), a Border Environment Cooperation Commission (BECC), and a new funding facility for border infrastructure, the North American Development Bank (NADBANK), that significantly augment the existing international regime for North American environmental management and heavily impact Mexico (Newman 1994:9–16). For example, the CEC, comprised of the environmental ministers of each of the three subscribing countries, is endowed with supranational authority to invoke sanctions, including trade sanctions, in cases where member countries fail to enforce their domestic environmental laws. The new arrangements open new avenues for environmental groups to influence national environmental policy and introduce new mechanisms of external accountability into the system.

Taken as a package, the Salinas administration's environmental programs chart an ambitious agenda for the future. Their high visibility, their sunk costs, the external accountability built into the new bilateral and trilateral environmental institutions, as well as the international financing components of various domestic programs, make it difficult for Mexico's new president, Ernesto Zedillo, to back away from these reforms.

Even so, policy implementation continues to suffer from the structural problems associated with Mexican public administration described earlier. Critics point to the continuing problems of presidentialism, sexenialism, formalism, and funding uncertainties. The programs themselves remain to be proven. In sum, then, the political context of Mexican environmental policy making continues to be a powerful determinant of Mexico's environmental policy performance.

Politics and Policy in Mexican Environmental Reform: Concluding Assessment

Mexican environmental policy, years of legislative history notwithstanding, is yet in its infancy. Recent administrations, particularly the government of Carlos Salinas, have charted new directions. Salinas' environmental policy reforms are impressive and certainly place Mexico among the frontrunners of developing countries in attempting to address its domestic environmental problems.

However, Mexico's recent reforms labor under the political and institutional structures of Mexico's one-party-dominant, semi-authoritarian political system. The Mexican public has few channels for effective participation in policy making, and most of these are government-dominated forums. Neither the legislature nor the court system provides environmentalists much policy leverage. The print media has been central in exposing government failings in the environmental area, yet remains a relatively weak tool for environmental pressure due to the limited circulation of Mexican newspapers and high levels of functional illiteracy in Mexican society. Opposition parties employ the rhetoric and values of environmental preservation in varying degrees, but they have little policy influence. While the government cultivates a progressive international image, the fact remains that environmental interests have few means by which to hold the regime accountable.

A number of implementation problems are structurally imbedded in Mexican constitutional law and political practice. Mexico's president is, to an exceptional degree, both the source of policy initiative and the driving force in policy implementation. Policy success depends on the executive's personal priorities and willingness to intervene directly in the policy process. Salinas invested his authority in the environmental sphere, and it appears that his successor, Ernesto Zedillo, will follow suit—Zedillo has restored environmental policy to the cabinet level, a development that presages greater efficiencies in environmental administration and more opportunity for public influence in environmental management. Even so, Mexico's unique tradition of no reelection, coupled with its six-year presidential term, historically has produced a good deal of policy discontinuity from one administration to the next, as well as an ad hoc, nonprogrammatic approach to policy implementation that is evident in the environmental arena. Presidential dominance means that formal, statutory commitments are generated easily. Environmental law is no exception. Environmental regulations have in the past performed more of a symbolic function than a regulatory one; only recently has this begun to change. As seen above, officially low-cost, noncoercive approaches to regulation are preferred to sanctions. Environmental policy also suffers from political patronage and the lack of trained personnel in the environmental field. These conditions cannot be remedied in the near future.

If these structural features of Mexican politics dominate the development and implementation of environmental policy, it also may be said that the policy reforms of the de la Madrid and Salinas administrations are increasingly evident in Mexican politics. Mexico's fledgling environmental movement has become an active and periodically influential player in articulating environmental concerns and mediating between government and society on environmental issues. Though lacking institutional power, environmentalists are actively shaping public awareness of environmental problems and are increasingly able to direct attention to government policy failures. The prominence of pollution-related concerns in major urban areas makes the environment a significant political issue the government cannot afford to ignore. A viable green party has yet to emerge as a permanent feature of the national political landscape. But virtually all the national political parties have incorporated the environment in party platforms, an indicator of its political salience.

The 1988 revision of the environmental law and subsequent elaboration of implementing regulations and standards also has opened the door to more effective regulation. It is still too soon to appraise adequately the policy effects of Salinas' recent reorganization of national environmental agencies or their reorganization in the Zedillo administration's new Secretariat of Environment,

Natural Resources, and Fisheries (SMARNP) (Newman 1994:27–29). The new laws prescribe greater rationalization of administration and regulatory functions, though in the Mexican system, the new agencies need sustained presidential sponsorship to become institutionalized and to achieve their intended policy objectives. The Mexican environmental administration's recent focus on strenthening "command and control" regulation also is coupled with a strong emphasis on market forces and economic privatization as an alternate and more decentralized route toward environmental improvement. In the long run, this profound restructuring of Mexico's approach to economic development may hold the key to its' environmental future by altering the incentive structure for pollution and resource management.

In sum, Mexican environmental policy still endures the limitations of its political and administrative system. The wave of recent environmental reforms and the shift in Mexico's approach to economic development have ushered in a new era of regulatory enforcement and resource management. These changes are as yet untested. Ernesto Zedillo, Salinas' successor, has indicated his commitment to deepening recent environmental reforms. Even more may depend on emerging alliances between environmental organizations in the emerging context of NAFTA and their ability to use this new trilateral arena to mobilize public opinion and hold government environmentally accountable. What is certain is that Mexican environmental policy will be scrutinized more rigorously than ever before, both domestically and internationally, and its shortcomings are likely to be attributed to the failings of the political system.

Notes

1. This is the view of a number of Mexican environmental leaders interviewed by this author.

2. Grupo de Cien's Homero Aridjis and Alonso Cipres Villareal of the Mexican ecology movemment are sensitive to cooptation efforts and critical of individuals who had joined the Salinas administration. Both claim the Salinas team offered them lucrative positions in environmental policy administration.

3. Salinas' PFMA director, Sergio Onate Laborde, admitted that his agency lacks the means to investigate citizen-initiated complaints, arguing that building PFMA's capacity to investigate is a major priority (*Uno Mas Uno* 1992b).

4. The Grupo de Cien and Mexican ecology movement, among others, have joined U.S. environmental organizations in efforts to insert environmental provisions in NAFTA.

5. 1323 *convenios* have been signed since 1989 (General Accounting Office 1992).

6. An optimistic appraisal of local government's implementation potential is provided by Wilk (1992).

7. In total, SEDUE's staff increased from 647 to 1,134 personnel between 1989 and 1992 (General Accounting Office 1992:18).

8. To compensate for the lack of qualified inspectors, the Salinas administration has recruited university personnel to help with inspections in the Mexico City metropolitan area (*Uno Mas Uno* 1992c:12).

9. Only two permanent closures were reported by the GAO between 1989 and 1992 (General Accounting Office 1992:19). However, INE Director Sergio Reyes Lujan is on record claiming 100 permanent closures since Salinas assumed office (*La Jornada* 1992b:11; Embassy of Mexico 1992:18).

10. Recently, a number of toxic waste handlers operating along the Mexico-United States border were closed by SEDESOL; in this case the Mexican Justice Department (PGR) reported it had not received a formal complaint from SEDESOL against the offending companies. PGR said PFMA had a separate mandate but that PGR and PFMA were to keep each other informed of actions in the environmental sphere. What this means in practice is unclear (*Uno Mas Uno* 1992c:12).

References

American Embassy. 1991. Unclassified Memorandum to the United States Department of State, 9 April.

Barkin, David. 1990. *Distorted Development*. Boulder: Westview Press.

Belaustiguigoitia, Juan C. 1992. "Case Study for Mexico." In *Structural Adjustment and the Environment*, ed. David Reed, 77–97. Boulder: Westview Press.

Camp, Roderic A. 1993. *Politics in Mexico*. Oxford: Oxford University Press.

Chavez, E. 1991. "El Partido Ecologista se Antiene a la Providencia." *Proceso* 774 (2 September): 22.

Christian Science Monitor. 1990. "VW Beetle Sales Soar in Mexico." (17 July): 8.

Comercio Exterior. 1992a. "Se promulga la Ley Agraria y la Ley Organica de los Tribunales Agrarios." (March): 230.

———. 1992b. "Nueva Ley de Pesca." (July): 622.

Diario Oficial. 1988. "Ley General del Equilibrio Ecologico y la Proteccion al Ambiente." (28 January): 23–57

———. 1992. "Acuerdo Por El Que Se Adscriben Organicamente Las Unidades Administrativas De La Secretaria de Desarrollo Social." (4 June): 32.

El Financiero International. 1993. "Officials pin hopes on new forestry law." (25 January): 10.

El Mercardo de Valores. 1993. "Presupuesto de Egresos de la Federacion para 1993." (1 December): 23.

Embassy of Mexico. 1992. *Mexico Environmental Issues: Fact Sheets.* Washington, D.C.

Environmental Protection Agency. 1992. *Integrated Border Environmental Plan, First Stage, 1992–1994.* Washington, D.C.: February.

Eskeland, Gunnar S. 1992. "Attacking Air Pollution in Mexico City." *Finance and Development* (December): 28–30.

Excelsior. 1988a. "Contaminacion y crimen lo que mas preocupa." (24 January): A1.

———. 1988b. "No solucionara la inficion con medidas coercitivas." (18 February): A4.

———. 1988c. "Anuncia Camacho Solis acciones concretas ante la contaminacion." (15 December): A4.

———. 1989a. "Decreto CSG veda forestal de 3 meses en la Lancandonia." (14 January): En los Estados, 1.

———. 1989b. "Rompamos el ciclo que hace del progreso via de inficion: CSG." (20 January): A1.

———. 1989c. "Ni simulacion ni oferta irresponsable: CSG." (6 June): A1.

———. 1990a. "Nueve de cada 10 automovilistas apoyan que siga Un dia Sin Auto." (12 February): A4.

———. 1990b. "El programa Hoy No Circula provoco un aumento de 137,554 nuevos vehiculos en 89." (17 February): 31A.

———. 1990c. "77 de las cuencas en Nivel Critico." (10 July): A5.

———. 1991a. "Las cuencas mas contaminadas: Lerma-Santiago, Panuco, Balsas, y San Juan." (7 May): A5.

———. 1991b. "Texto integro del tercer informe de gobierno." (2 November).

———. 1992. "Texto integro del quarto informe de gobierno." (2 November).

General Accounting Office. 1992. *U.S.-Mexico Trade: Assessment of Mexico's Environmental Controls for New Companies.* Washington, D.C.: GAO/GGD-92-113, August, 18.

Grindle, Merilee S. 1977. *Bureaucrats, Politicians, and Peasants.* Berkeley: University of California Press.

La Jornada. 1992a. "Financiara el BM trabajos delmedio ambiente en Mexico." (20 September): 11.

———. 1992b. "Inspecciona el Instituto de Ecologia casi 9 mil industrias." (20 September): 11.

Monge, Raul. 1991. "Algunos ecologistas elogian el premio a Salinas; otros loc impugnan por inoportuno." *Proceso* 761 (3 July): 6–11.

Mumme, Stephen P., C. Richard Bath, and Valerie J. Assetto. 1988. "Political Development and Environmental Policy in Mexico." *Latin American Research Review* 23 (1): 7–34.

Newman, Grey. 1994. *Managing Mexico's Environmental Challenge.* New York: Economist Intelligence Unit, Critical Issues for Latin America Series.

Puig, Carlos. 1992. "Se violan los derechos de defensores de la ecologia y de acusadores del gobierno." *Proceso* 816 (22 June): 32–33.

Ranger, Edward M., Jr. 1991. "Environmental Regulation and Enforcement in Mexico." In *Maquiladora Industry Annual Review.* Mexico, D.F.: Seguros de Mexico, S.A.

Secretaria de Programacion y Presupuesto. 1980. *Plan Global de Desarrollo 1980–1982.* Mexico, D.F.: Gobierno de Mexico, SPP.

Spalding, Rose. 1981. "State Power and its Limits: Corporatism in Mexico." *Comparative Political Studies* 14 (July): 139–61.

Stevis, Dimitris, and Stephen P. Mumme. 1991. "Nuclear Power, Technological Autonomy, and the State in Mexico." *Latin American Research Review* 26: 55–81.

Story, Dale. 1986. *Industry, the State, and Public Policy.* Austin: University of Texas Press.

Szekely, Miguel E., M. Angelica Sanchez., and Francisco M. Abardia. 1992. "The Free Trade Agreement and Constitutional Agrarian Reform, Possible Implications for Forest Exploitation." Paper presented at the Latin America Studies Association, 24–27 September 1992.

Tucker, William C. 1956. *Mexican Government Today.* (Minneapolis: University of Minnesota Press).

United States Congress, House. 1993. North American Free Trade Agreement, Texts of Agreement, Implementing Bill, Statement of Administrative Action, and Required Supporting Statements. 103rd Congress, 1st Session. Y1.1/7: No. 103–159, V.1, Doc.

Uno Mas Uno. 1989. "Solicitan que el Ejercito resguarde los recursos forestales del estado de Mexico." (11 March): 12.

————. 1990. "Se aplicaran 5 acciones contra la contaminacion en Mexico: CSG." (6 June): 1.

————. 1991. "La naturaleza se rebela." (28 April): 7.

————. 1992a. "La contaminacion no conoce fronteras." (1 June): Este Pais supplement, 14.

————. 1992b. "Grupos no gobermentales han hecho de ecologia su causa." (7 July): 10.

————. 1992c. "La PGR no ha cebidido denuncia sobre contrabando de desechos toxicos en BC." (8 August): 12.

————. 1992d. "Debera participar la iniciativa privada en el control de la basura del DF: Cuenca Dardon." (10 August): 11.

Vernon, Raymond. 1963. *The Dilemma of Mexico's Development*. Cambridge: Harvard University Press.

Wilk, David. 1992. "The Complementarity between Environmental Plans, Regulations and Lessons from Ciudad Juarez, Chihuahua." Paper given at the Seventeenth International Congress of the Latin American Studies Association, Los Angeles, 24–27 September.

World Resources 1990–91. 1990. Oxford: Oxford University Press.

Wright, Angus. 1990. *The Death of Ramon Gonzales*. Austin: University of Texas Press.

8

POLITICS AND POLICIES IN
VENEZUELA'S ENVIRONMENTAL MANAGEMENT

PABLO GUTMAN

Introduction

Venezuela, sixth in size of the Latin American countries, faces the Caribbean Sea and encompasses approximately 916,000 square kilometers in the northern part of South America. It has a wide variety of landscapes, ranging from high mountains to tropical forests and from coral reef islands to savannas. Venezuela's location near the equatorial line—between 0° 45′ and 12° 12′ north latitudes—results in the dominance of tropical climates, with an average yearly temperature of twenty-seven degrees centigrade at sea level. There are no seasons, and the largest temperature variations result from altitude changes or wind exposure. Rains are heavily concentrated, and the country has a dry period of three to eight months, which disappears in the hyperhumid southern forest but dominates the arid regions along the Caribbean coastline.

Venezuela is also the sixth most populous country in Latin America (a little more than 20 million people in 1992). Population growth rates remain high—2.5 percent annually—but population density is moderate (2,180 persons per square kilometer). Estimates of Venezuela for the middle of the twenty-first century project a population density not greater than that of Mexico in 1990.

This image of a sparsely populated country does not reflect the high spatial and urban concentration of Venezuela's population. Due to climatic and historical reasons, the majority of Venezuela's population chose to settle near the coastline or in the mountain valleys, which have a milder climate and good agricultural soils. Avoiding the areas of endemic tropical diseases was also a major location criteria until the middle of the twentieth century. Rapid urbanization began in the 1950s; by 1990 approximately 90 percent of Venezuela's population was located in 10 percent of its territory, and nearly 80 percent of the population inhabited the urban centers north of the Orinoco River and, in particular, half a dozen cities in the central northern region.

A minor exporter of tropical products during the nineteenth and twentieth centuries (sugar, coffee, cocoa), Venezuela remained a poor country until well into the twentieth century when oil production and export began to soar. Since 1950, Venezuela (see map 8.1) has experienced accelerated economic growth, and in the early 1970s, the country achieved the highest per capita gross domestic product (GDP) in Latin America. After the international oil price boom, Venezuela grew even faster in the 1970s and was ranked among the world's high middle income countries.[1]

Oil and its derivatives plus iron mining and steel and aluminum manufacturing dominate Venezuela's economy. These products account for 85 percent of all export revenues. Together with petrochemical and power production, they account for more than 30 percent of Venezuela's GDP. All other manufacturing activities add another 12 percent to Venezuela's GDP. Agriculture accounts for 6 percent, construction another 6 percent, and services make up the remaining 46 percent of the GDP.[2]

Since the 1980s, Venezuela has faced considerable economic hardship: low or negative growth, inflation pressures, difficulties with its $30 billion external debt (ranking tenth among the world's debtors), and declining social indicators. While growth resumed in the early 1990s, economic performance has been uneven and the country has undergone a period of social unrest.

With a per capita GDP of $2,910 in 1992, Venezuela has good aggregate or average indicators of quality of life compared with other developing countries, and it ranks high in Latin America: life expectancy is seventy years, the illiteracy rate is 13 percent of the adult population, and the daily average supply of calories is 2,500 per capita. Hidden in the national averages, an unequal distribution of wealth and income render a different picture. In 1989, 22 percent of the country's population was classified as severely deprived, and more than 50 percent was considered below poverty lines. Worse, these figures come to almost twice those of the late seventies (World Bank 1991b).

Venezuela is a presidential republic. The country is divided into twenty-two states and more than 280 counties (*alcaldias*). The national executive is organized in sixteen ministries (including a Ministry of the Environment), plus five central offices with cabinet rank. Different lines of authority link this core structure with some 125 autonomous institutes and more than 300 public companies. At the executive level, the most important decision-making forum is the national cabinet or some of the subcabinets.

Until recently, Venezuela's government was highly centralized, both in political and budgetary terms, with almost 85 percent of public revenues coming from federal taxes on oil exports. Before the reforms of 1990, the

MAP 8.1

Oilfields and Topography of Venezuela

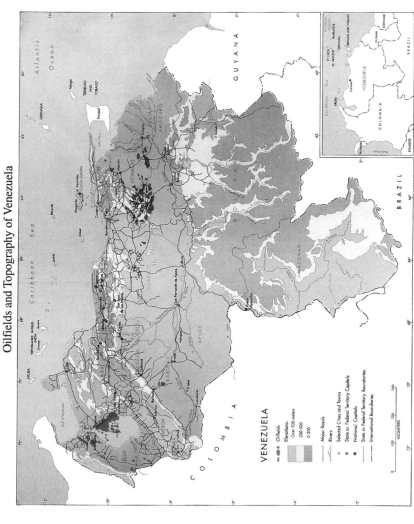

Source: World Bank, 1990, March, World Bank Map of Oilfields in Venezuela (Map #1 BRD 22154).

president appointed state governors and city mayors. States were grouped into regions for development planning purposes, and most of the technical and financial resources were concentrated in the regional development corporations, with authorities also appointed by the president. Some of these corporations, particularly the Venezuela Corporation of Guayana (CVG), control a significant portion of Venezuela's natural resources.

Venezuela is rich in energy resources, particularly oil and hydropower. The country ranks sixth worldwide for its oil reserves and eighth for oil production (2 million barrels a day). Venezuela already captures some 20 percent of its hydropower potential, estimated at 54,700 MW.[3] The country's endowments of iron ore, bauxite, coal, and phosphate also are significant and, together with energy resources, have fostered important steel and aluminum industries.

Agricultural resources are more limited. Good agricultural soils are located mostly north of the Orinoco River where some 9 million hectares are suitable for agriculture and another 22 million hectares are good for cattle ranching. In the early 1990s, little more than 2 million hectares were in farm production, of which 440,000 were irrigated. Another 18 million hectares were devoted to ranching. Almost 60 percent of the country—some 56 million hectares—is covered by natural forests.

One important natural resource of Venezuela is its biological diversity (see table 8.1).[4] Naturally rich biodiversity occurs in different world locations, but it is particularly striking in tropical countries. Venezuela, with less than 0.7 percent of the world's lands, is among the first ten countries in megadiversity. Not only does Venezuela rank high worldwide in biodiversity, but it also ranks high in opportunities to conserve it. Southern Venezuela contains the largest tract of undisturbed tropical forest in Latin America, most of it in national parks and other protected areas, including the largest Amazonian national park, Parima-Tapirapecó, with 3.4 million hectares. On that account, southern Venezuela represents one of the world's five major tropical wilderness areas, and it is the only one with good prospects to remain so in Latin America in the next century (McNeely et al. 1990).

To manage its biodiversity wealth and to protect its natural resources, Venezuela has put more than 54 percent of its territory under different forms of protection (see table 8.2). At the core of the protected areas are Venezuela's thirty-nine national parks and seventeen natural monuments.[5]

Environmental Problems

Several studies[6] have considered Venezuela's environmental problems, pointing to those discussed in this chapter.

TABLE 8.1

Biodiversity in Venezuela

Species	World Number	In Venezuela	% Venezuela	Venezuela Position in the World	Endemic in Venezuela	Endangered
Mammals	4,327	330	7.63	9	9	39
Birds	9,198	1,311	14.25	6	51	32
Reptiles	6,300	283	4.49	10	27	17
Amphibians	4,184	202	4.82	10	76	3
Fish	21,595	1,200	5.56	?	33	10
Angiosperms	?	20,000	?	7		
Plants	250,000	25,000	10	5	4,000	218

Source: Reproduced from Diaz, 1991, table 1. The angiosperms figures are from McNeely et al. (1990), table 14.

TABLE 8.2

Venezuela's Protected Areas

Category	No.	Size (hectares)
National parks	39	12,968,812
National monuments	17	1,751,046
Buffer zones	48	15,929,242
Forest reserves	10	11,367,807
Logging reserves	8	1,009,256
Wildlife reserves	2	244,126
Wildlife refuges	7	76,161
National water reserves	9	1,729,203
Water works buffer zones	2	46,033
Zones for priority reclamation	5	1,621,172
Zones reserved for future dams	2	4,734
Integrated rural development areas	6	3,492,678
Total	155	50,240,270

Source: Minister of the Environment, MARNR.

Environmental Impact of Large Investment Projects

Venezuela's rapid economic growth during the 1960s and 1970s fostered many megaprojects, particularly those involving mining, oil, and heavy industry, with major impacts on the country's natural resources. Although some of these projects went through an environmental impact assessment in the planning stages, there has been little or no control of environmental compliance during construction and operation. Because many of these projects are in the oil and petrochemical sector, they are potential producers of severe air pollution, water pollution, and hazardous wastes.

Environmental Impact of Small-Scale Productive Activities

The adding up of many small activities, particularly deforestation in some rural areas, is a major environmental threat in Venezuela. Soil erosion that results from deforestation is acute in mountain regions. Estimated annual losses of top soil in the Andean region average 300 tons per hectare. In other cases, selective logging has severely impoverished native forest and accelerated the conversion of forest land into ranching areas.

Water Resource Depletion and Pollution

Water supply and water quality both are major environmental concerns in Venezuela. Because most of the population is located in the northern region of the country while most of the water supply is in the south, costly water systems could be necessary in the next decades, if the efficiency of the existing system is not improved significantly. As for water pollution, in 1992 Venezuela began to construct several water pollution treatment plants in major urban centers, with financial support from the Inter American Development Bank. But until now, pollution of river and coastal waters has gone unchecked, resulting in major environmental hazards that afflict particularly poor neighborhoods.

Protected Areas Management

As stated before, with more than 10 million hectares in national parks, Venezuela has one of the most extensive systems of protected area in the world. However, many of these parks are "paper parks" with little or no in-situ management.

Power Consumption and Air Pollution

Per capita energy consumption in Venezuela is less than one-third of that in the United States (WRI 1992). Nevertheless, current levels of energy consumption pose environmental and economic problems. Moderate air pollution problems are present in all major urban and industrial areas. At the same time, low energy efficiency reduces Venezuela's potential GDP. With the same levels of per capita energy consumption as Spain, Venezuela's energy efficiency is four times lower.[7]

The Encroachments

Rapid urban growth since the 1950s, particularly in the central-northern region and the state capitals, has resulted in environmental problems such as (1) urban growth in the industrial corridor, Caracas-Maracay, which has consumed a large portion of the good, middle-altitude agricultural soils of the country (the Aragua valleys); and, (2) uncontrolled construction on hillsides, both by high-income developments and by squatters, which has increased landslides and accelerated water and soil pollution. It also has complicated the task of providing infrastructure and public services. The encroachment of coastal recreational areas, and particularly coastal and marine national parks, fueled by huge tourism developments and a year-round summer, is well represented in Margarita Island and the Mochima National Park.

Gold Mining

Gold mining in the southern tropical forest, carried on by small miners, many of them Brazilian trespassers, *garimpeiros*, results in deforestation (for campsites and landing fields), water pollution (caused by explosions and the use of mercury), and in several cases, conflicts with the local Indian population.

Environmental Policies and Institutions

Environmental Law, the Parliament, and the Courts

Venezuela has some of the best developed environmental legislation of Latin America. Although environmental considerations can be found in many early laws, modern environmental legislation dates primarily from the 1970s and 1980s when the citizens' right to a healthy environment and the state's responsibilities for their protection were incorporated into Venezuela's constitution. A partial survey of Venezuela's main environmental legislation (MARNR 1992b) identifies 10 organic laws,[8] 21 laws, and 171 presidential decrees. In addition, as of 1991, Venezuela had signed 31 international environmental conventions. Venezuela's environmental legislation can be grouped according to the following criteria:

1. Related to the goals and means of conservation: (1) the Organic Law of the Environment (1976) defines goals and instruments for a comprehensive environmental management of Venezuela; (2) the Organic Law of Land Planning (1983) gives the framework for national and regional land use policies; and (3) the Organic Law of Urban Planning (1987) gives the framework for urban development.
2. Related to the management of the environment: (1) the Organic Law of the Central Administration (1976) that reorganized the federal government and created the Ministry of the Environment and Renewable Natural Resources; (2) the Organic Law of the Municipal Regime (1989) that delegates to local governments the management of a good number of environmental issues; (3) the Organic Law of Decentralization (1989) that has put in motion a gradual transfer of responsibilities and resources from federal to state authorities.
3. Related to law enforcement and the courts: (1) the Penal Law of the Environment (1992) defines what should be considered an environmental crime, the role of the court in the prosecution of offenders, and the minimum and maximum sanctions; (2) in order to implement the new penal law, some twenty decrees were passed during 1992 relating to maximum allowable discharges to the environment, environmental impact assessments, and acceptable procedures for such tasks as sampling and assessing.

As for Parliament's environmental concern, in both chambers of the National Parliament there are commissions that deal with environmental issues. Parliamentary commissions not only produce and review law drafts, but they also control the executive branch and pursue parliamentary investigation of conflicting issues. Nevertheless, Parliament's capability to deal with and its interest in environmental issues should not be overstated. By and large, existing legislation has evolved from projects that originated in the executive.

Until recently, courts have played a minor role in Venezuela's environmental issues. In the Roman-Spanish legal tradition, only the law grants a right. So only conflicts based on previously existing laws can be submitted to courts, and the offended party needs to prove that direct damage has been inflicted on that individual or his or her property. This situation surely will change in the near future as courts and the Public Ministry enforce the new Environmental Penal Law, passed in 1992.

Public Environmental Management

Until 1992, environmental management responsibilities in Venezuela were concentrated in the national Ministry of the Environment (MARNR). Established in 1976, MARNR is a federal office with headquarters in Caracas and branches in all state capitals and in other major cities. MARNR's mandate includes environmental research, national and regional planning, and environmental standards setting and enforcement. MARNR also manages several federally owned natural resources, including inland waters, groundwaters, national forest, and protected areas. Finally, MARNR also invested in resource development, particularly in the construction of dams and other water infrastructures for irrigation and urban consumption.

Set up in 1976 with a simple internal structure—research, planning, management, and enforcement—MARNR has gone through several reorganizations. By the end of 1992, MARNR had eight major technical departments with environmental responsibilities: (1) research, (2) watershed conservation, (3) planning and land use, (4) enforcement and control, (5) education, (6) environmental quality control, (7) infrastructure (construction), and (8) the Orinoco-Apure development program. Administrative responsibilities (such as budget and personnel) were handled by eight other departments.

Other institutions are attached to this core structure: eight "autonomous services," including the forest services, national cartography, the management of wildlife, and the environmental management of southern territories. Autonomous services form part of MARNR but can charge for their services and raise funds outside the government budget. Also attached to MARNR are the much more independent "autonomous institutes." They include the National Park Service (INPARQUES); the Institute for the Management of Lake Maracaibo, the National Water Company (INOS), and the Caracas Waste Management Company (IMAU).[9] Also, several foundations linked to MARNR either raise funds for specific purposes (education, fire fighting) or sell services (national laboratories).

This complex structure is replicated in each of Venezuela's twenty-two states where MARNR has its main regional offices. Smaller delegations also are to be found in other cities, giving MARNR national coverage, although in many cases regional offices are poorly equipped and staffed. In 1992, MARNR had some six thousand employees, 30 percent of them in the headquarters. This figure probably understates the number of persons devoted to environmental control in Venezuela, because it includes neither personnel hired under short-term contracts nor personnel outside the core institutions.[10]

Based on the Organic Law of the Central Administration, the Organic Law of the Environment, and the Organic Law of Land Planning, MARNR enjoys an impressive amount of power to define environmental policies and to enforce them nationwide. Any new commitment of a natural resource or the siting of any infrastructure outside a city's limits needs MARNR's approval. As for pollution control, MARNR has the authority to propose all types of national emission standards and to enforce them once Parliament or the cabinet endorsed them. Finally, MARNR directly manages a large portion of the natural resources in public ownership (excluding minerals, oil, and power). Although MARNR has a fairly good reputation among Venezuela's population, community representatives often demand more stringent law enforcement, while the business sector complains about excessive environmental requirements and bureaucratic procedures.

Several other federal institutions have a part in Venezuela's environmental management, among them:

- CORDIPLAN, the central planning office, reviews all major sectorial programs and external borrowing. It also acts as the technical secretariat of the economic cabinet where major economic decisions are made.[11]
- The Ministry of Health (MSAS) has legal responsibility for pollution as a human health hazard, and its mandate overlaps in several areas with MARNR.
- The Agricultural Ministry (MAC) and adjoining agencies such as the Land Institute (IAN) also have major responsibilities for agricultural technology (including agrochemicals use), irrigation, land uses, and fishery, among others.
- A special branch of the army, the "Cooperation Armed Forces" (FAC) cooperates with MARNR in enforcement and surveillance activities.
- Several ministries have a de facto impact on the environment through their sectoral development programs. These include the already mentioned Ministry of Agriculture, the Ministry of Power and Mining, the Ministry of Industry, the Ministry of Urban Development, and the Ministry of Transport.
- Large public holding companies are among Venezuela's major investors in natural resource development, with far-reaching environmental impacts.

Of particular note is Petroleos de Venezuela, the public holding company that controls all of Venezuela's oil and petrochemical industry, and CVG, the holding company that controls hydroelectricity, steel, aluminum, and other heavy industries in Bolivar state.

While some public companies have well-developed and sophisticated environmental departments, particularly in the oil, petrochemical, and hydropower industry, environmental management capability in the public sector is currently very limited outside MARNR.

The Community and the Private Sector

Community organizations, mostly with a territorial base (urban neighborhood or rural town), are common in Venezuela, and in the last decades, many of them have come together to develop into national federations of community organizations. Although each local group has different goals, environment has been a growing concern among them, including environmental education, recycling, appropriate technology, and environmental advocacy.

A 1991 survey by MARNR identified more than 350 NGOs interested in environmental issues. As elsewhere, many NGOs are short-lived, but others are well established and respected institutions. As an example, during 1992 a forum with some fifty NGOs reviewed the Venezuelan document to be presented to the Rio 92, the UN Conference on Environment and Development.

The private sector in Venezuela has reacted to the growing national and international environmental concern in the same vein as those in other developing countries. Industrial associations voice their interest in conservation but warn against its costs. The National Chamber of Industry firmly opposed the Environmental Penal Law during its 1991 congressional debate. Nevertheless, big industry has invested heavily in environmental pollution control and in "green publicity." More recently, several industry-supported foundations have granted funds for environmental projects. Finally, an environmental private sector is growing in Venezuela. Many consulting and engineering companies are working on environmental issues both for the private and for the public sectors. Also, a small but growing industry supplies pollution control devices, in many cases in association with foreign firms.

Environmental Education and Research

Compared to other Latin American countries, Venezuela has devoted considerable resources to environmental education and research. Today, high-level training and research on environmental issues is conducted by (1) a dozen national universities (the best known are the Central University of Venezuela, the University Simon Bolivar, and the University of Los Andes); (2) several national laboratories, such as the Venezuela Institute of Scientific Research (with pioneering works on tropical rain forests), the Venezuelan Institute of Oil Research (with several international patents on oil pollution control), or the Center on Tropical Diseases; and (3) several private institutions and NGOs devoted to research on conservation (Terramar, FUDENA, Bioma, for example).

Environmental concerns have been incorporated on a national scale in elementary and high school programs. Also, public institutions such as MARNR and private foundations and NGOs invest in nonformal education through short training programs and other educational activities and periodic campaigns in the media.

Environmental Policies and Politics

The Forerunners

Why are Venezuela's environmental management and institutions what they are? What is the interplay between politics and environmental policies? How did Venezuela's society become interested in environmental issues? This is an unwritten history. Environment being a minor concern in Venezuela's political arena, there are almost no records of the political debates surrounding environmental issues. In looking at the intellectual forerunners of Venezuela's environmental politics, at least two groups should be mentioned.

From the middle of the nineteenth century through the first half of the present century, the work of natural scientists laid the foundation for Venezuela's interest in conservation. First came the visit of Humboldt and Bonpland and the subsequent publication of their works. A host of European and local naturalists followed Humboldt's pioneering efforts in the study of tropical Venezuela. Early in this century Henrie Pittier, the father of Venezuela's modern conservationism, arrived in Caracas and devoted his life to the study of Venezuela's natural environment. Because of his efforts, the first national park was created in Venezuela in 1937 (now the Henrie Pittier National Park).

Although the influence of naturalists and other "savants" has waned in recent decades, environment has remained a personal interest of several of Venezuela's public figures, whose prestige has helped maintain a public focus on the environment. One of the most respected, albeit eccentric, of these figures was the late Perez Alfonso, known in Venezuela as "the father of the OPEC," due to his involvement in the creation of the international oil cartel during the 1960s.

After 1950, water engineers replaced naturalists as the most influential advocates of conservation, due to their concerns about water supply constraints for the rapidly growing Venezuelan cities. The work of the National Commission for the Planning of the Water Resources (COPLANARH), headed by Pedro Pablo Azpurba during the early 1960s, was remarkably successful, not so much for its planning but for the political awareness that emerged with a new generation of environmentalists. Arnoldo Gabaldon, who later became the first minister of the environment, was at that time a young water engineer closely associated with COPLANARH's director.

Another important political antecedent to modern Venezuela's environmentalism was the nationalization of oil companies and oil fields in the 1960s. The nationalization of the oil industry was motivated by economics and was carried out through careful negotiations that aroused little conflict with its former owners, the international oil companies. Nevertheless, the surrounding rhetoric placed high value on the "rescue of national resources," a concept that later was associated also with natural resource conservation and the emergence of the country's environmental concerns.

As for international influences, Venezuela always has been influenced by U.S. fashions and trends. Environmental issues have been no exception. Both the timing and the shape of Venezuela's environmental initiatives of the 1970s closely resemble other international experiences in general and those of the United States in particular.

As other Amazonian countries, Venezuela has been subject to the pressure of international concern for the rain forest, although never on a scale comparable to Brazil or the Southeast Asian countries. In this framework, some conservation initiatives in the country's southern region also have been spurred by international interest and funds.

Political Parties and the Environment

After independence from Spain in the early nineteenth century, a turbulent succession of dictatorships, both open and disguised, followed. This situation came to an end in 1958. Since then Venezuela has become one of the most stable Latin American democracies, measured by the years of uninterrupted elected governments and the alternation in power of Acción Democrática (AD) and COPEI, the two leading parties (the former affiliated with the international Social-Democrat movement and the latter with close ties to European Christian parties).[12]

Neither AD nor COPEI voiced any significant environmental concerns during the 1950s and 1960s. But in the late 1970s and after, both parties embraced the standard international phraseology related to environmental protection and sustainable development.

Despite similarities in terminology, strong differences exist between the two parties. AD governments are to be credited for establishing most of Venezuela's national parks, for passing the majority of Venezuela's environmental laws, and for creating the first Ministry of the Environment in Latin America. In contrast, COPEI, either in government or in Parliament, has little to show in terms of environmental initiatives. This difference is rooted in the attitudes of the individual parties toward natural resource management. The AD's traditional platform regarding oil nationalization and agrarian reform and its generally more interventionist approach paved the way for its more active environmental politics and policies after the 1960s.

As for the third Venezuelan party, MAS (movement towards socialism), a center-left party, the environment has been an important element in its political platform for the last twenty years. This probably stems from the strong presence of middle-class professionals among MAS party members. Being a minority party, MAS's influence on Venezuela's environmental policy has been limited but not negligible. It has been exerted mostly through support given to the environmental demands of community organizations (in most cases in relation to the provision of public services) and through the presidency of the environment commission of the National Chamber of Representatives, where in the mid-1980s it set up a computer data base to handle environmental complaints from the public.[13]

Long-Run Politics and Short-Run Interests

Although environmental policies can be rooted in distant influences, both nationally and internationally any major political decision combines long-run politics and short-run interests. The creation of the Ministry of the Environment in 1976 is a good example.

After the oil boom of the early 1970s, the Venezuelan public budget rocketed, with the government involved in countless pharaonic projects. Consequently, the then Ministry of Public Works—encompassing power, transport, housing, and water-works—controlled more than 60 percent of the national budget.[14] On the one hand, dismantling this too-powerful ministry was the main short-run reason in 1976 for passing the Organic Law of the central administration, a law that divided the former Public Works Ministry into four new ministries. On the other hand, long-run political changes explain why there was an environmental ministry among these four. But to placate the fears of the oil lobby—both a short-term and a long-term concern—the new environmental ministry was not given authority over Venezuela's oil. Hence, its unusual name: Ministry of the Environment and the "Renewable" Natural Resources.

Recent Political Developments and the Environment

Since 1975, although the environment has been a growing political concern in Venezuela, it is still a minor one. Several examples could be put forward:

- In the congressional distribution of commission control between the leading parties, the presidency of the environmental commissions—seen as matter of limited relevance—traditionally has been offered to the third political force in both chambers of the Parliament.

- A former environmental minister—Guillermo Colmenares F.—survived a change of both government and ruling party. This unparalleled record in Venezuela's political history underlines the limited importance attached to the Ministry of the Environment rather than the unquestionable merits of Mr. Colmenares.
- One of the few cases where an environmental problem has been the center of a political debate that involved all political parties, the army, and the media was the control of illegal gold mining in the southern Amazonian region. But it was always clear that the environmental concerns were a surrogate for geopolitical concerns as most illegal miners were Brazilians who trespassed the international Venezuelan-Brazilian border.

Venezuela's political stability came to an abrupt end in the early 1990s, following a tough stabilization plan enforced by the newly elected government of Carlos Andres Perez, with the advice of the IMF and the World Bank.[15] Severe episodes of rampage ("el Caracazo") followed an attempt to raise transport prices, and the subsequent army repression resulted in hundreds of deaths. Popular unrest gave way to several military upheavals—a development unheard of in Venezuela in the last forty years. The military putsches failed to overthrow Perez, but they succeeded in undermining his power.

Accused of embezzlement, Perez resigned in 1993.[16] Rafael Caldera, a former president and a leading figure of the Christian party, COPEI, broke away from COPEI and headed a coalition of center-left forces that won the 1993 election with promises of undoing Perez's stabilization program. As of 1994, Venezuela's prospects remain uncertain. On the one hand, both traditional parties, but particularly AD, have received a severe blow. On the other hand, Caldera's government is fraught with doubts and dissent, and military and social unrest go on, fueled by an unrelenting economic crisis, that in mid-1994 forced the government to nationalize the banking system to avoid generalized bankruptcy of the financial sector.

The environmental consequences of the structural adjustment policies pursued by Venezuela from 1989 through 1992, and their partial reversal after Rafael Caldera took government in 1993, are difficult to grasp. A recent study (CENDES 1994) yielded mixed conclusions.

- Public budgets have been curtailed, and the environmental agencies—like most other government agencies—have lost well-trained staff. On the other hand, environmental NGOs reported an increasing influx of international aid.
- A survey of the chemical industry found that many firms, blaming economic hurdles, abandoned their pollution abatement programs. But

this was not the case for the larger petrochemical firms whose pollution control programs are driven largely by export considerations and international standards.

- Due to massive currency devaluation, the tourism industry boomed, bringing a manyfold increase in the number of national and international tourists. This trend added pressure to many national parks at a moment when budgets for park management were shrinking.
- On a national scale, slow or negative economic growth reduces the pace of resource depletion and pollution. However, and although information is scant, it seems possible that deteriorating economic opportunities in the urban markets have driven peasants and fishermen to increase their pressure on protected natural resource areas.
- According to the above-mentioned study, the most dramatic problems are related to increasing urban and rural poverty that triggers both deterioration in quality of life and environmental deterioration.

Economic hardships may distract societies from environmental concerns—a process reported worldwide—but it is hoped that Venezuela's setback will be temporary, as it is moderated by several national and international trends that counteract the short-term gloomy perspectives. Among these are the vigorous growth of the NGO environmental movement, particularly in urban areas; the general advance of environmental education, from elementary school through college; and the internationalization of environmental concerns that increasingly challenge national governments. Meanwhile, twenty years of environmental management—and mismanagement—can offer several lessons that are reviewed in the following section.

Environmental Policy Experience

When Venezuela created its National Ministry of the Environment (MARNR) in 1976, few other agencies of that sort existed in the world. Before 1992, no other environmental ministry existed in Latin America. The idea of creating a ministry of the environment was and is criticized by many experts. Critics point out that because environmental management is a cross-sectorial issue, it should be the concern of many, if not all, public agencies.

According to these critics, what is needed is not a sectoral environmental agency, but a coordinating mechanism. This is the approach adopted in 1992 by Chile with its national and regional environmental councils (CONAMA and COREMAs). But this approach does not seem to work. The environment becomes the responsibility of everyone and of no one. Because all member agencies are equals in environmental terms, a simple task such as scheduling a meeting becomes a nightmare. Looking to the rest of Latin America, the approach adopted by Venezuela for its environmental agency ranks among the most successful, and it is beginning to have some followers.[17]

Venezuela's Ministry of the Environment covers environmental control and resource development activities, particularly water resource development. International experience has demonstrated that this is an unhappy marriage. Water development not only has drained MARNR's budget and concern away from environmental protection, it also has made MARNR (or INOS, its affiliated water development institute) one of the country's worst polluters, undermining MARNR's moral and legal right to demand compliance with environmental standards.[18] This situation is changing. In 1990, MARNR began a process of privatization and handing over service activities to state and local authorities.

According to Venezuela's institutional and political traditions, MARNR was created as a highly centralized national agency, to the detriment of state and local governments and local communities. But almost everybody agrees that effective environmental management requires a fairly high level of decentralization. As mentioned elsewhere, in 1990 Venezuela embarked on a major decentralization effort. With the Organic Law of Municipality Power and the Organic Law of Decentralization (both passed in 1989), mayors and state governors are now elected directly by popular vote. Also, a substantial part of the public revenues and responsibilities are being handed over to state and local authorities through a several-year process under the surveillance of a high-level independent commission (COPRE), which gives technical advice to smooth the transition.

Environmental issues rank high among the areas to be decentralized, and in 1991, MARNR was reorganized to reduce the size of its headquarters and to strengthen the regional offices that eventually will be handed over to the states. According to the new laws, local and state authorities will be responsible for environmental enforcement and for providing environmental services (e.g., solid waste management, sewage). MARNR will retain responsibility for national environmental planning and policy, establishing environmental standards, reviewing environmental impact assessments of large-scale developments, and managing nationally owned natural resources.

Land Use Planning vs. Environmental Quality Control

Venezuela's environmental management is particularly strong in resource use management, such as establishing protected areas (currently covering more than half the country) and instituting land use planning, to cover most of the territory with national land use plans, state land use plans, and a system of permits that controls the siting of new activities in rural areas. By contrast, limited attention has been devoted to environmental quality problems such as environmental standards, pollution control, health hazards prevention, biodiversity management, and impact assessment.

There are several reasons for this. First, information on land, land uses, and other major resources was collected in Venezuela for many years. In most cases, this type of information varies little over time, allowing for an incremental approach to data collection (geology, soil quality, and climate do not change often). Thus, MARNR found itself with a wealth of resource information and many professionals trained in using it. Almost the opposite was true for environmental quality, which demands permanent monitoring to update short-lived data. This requires costly equipment and trained personnel, both of which were and are in short supply in Venezuela (and in many developing countries).

Second, it could be argued that in a fast-growing but still sparsely populated developing country such as Venezuela, pollution problems—associated with environmental quality—are minor while resource use problems loom vast. Thus, it pays to concentrate on territorial management and to postpone environmental quality issues. This argument holds true only in part. Pollution problems are already severe in many Venezuelan urban areas. Furthermore, proper resource management requires environmental quality information, the lack of which already hampers the management of water, forest, and protected areas in Venezuela.

Management Capability

In spite of a well-developed legal framework and a highly elaborated institutional system, actual environmental management capability in Venezuela is low. Several factors have been blamed for this situation:

- One factor is limited human, technical, and financial resources devoted to enforcement of the existing environmental norms. To a great extent, environmental management in Venezuela (as in many other countries) is more prone to enact new laws than to enforce existing ones.
- Another factor is limited incorporation of environmental considerations in economic decision making, both in the public and in the private sectors.
- A third factor is a widespread culture of no compliance with public regulations, coupled with slack enforcement and low sanctions to offenders. For instance, the greatest environmental fine up to 1992 was one thousand dollars.[19]

Environmental Impact of Price Policies

Distorted markets or inefficient pricing policies have been blamed as a major source of environmental damages. Most economists argue that if prices do not reflect national opportunity costs or international market prices, they will result in too much or too little consumption of the goods at stake (including environmental goods), which in turn will produce a suboptimal allocation of resources. These price distortions could result from prices that do not take into account positive or negative externalities (market failure) or from government tinkering with subsidies or with nonneutral taxes (government failures).[20]

The theory that an optimal environmental situation could be reached through the correction of market and government failures has several limitations that have been analyzed by many environmental economists (see Daly 1992). It does not take into consideration intergenerational issues and distribution problems. It does not explain why, while the most inefficient markets are in developing countries, the major share of world pollution comes from the more efficient markets of developed countries. Nevertheless, it is sensible to expect that grossly subsidized natural resources and energy prices would foster higher consumption levels (depending on the price elasticity of the goods considered) and low efficiency and would result in negative environmental impacts. Such cases have been reported in Venezuela.

Agriculture used to be a highly subsidized sector in Venezuela[21] (e.g., low interest rate credits, low prices for agrochemicals and irrigation). Most subsidizing policies were abandoned in the early 1990s, following the advice of international credit agencies (World Bank 1992a). Only irrigation water remains heavily underpriced, with current water charges covering as little as 1 percent to 2 percent of maintenance costs. Several studies of Venezuela's irrigated agriculture have found environmental problems such as salinity and waterlogging, which commonly are associated with poor technology and excessive irrigation. They also have reported some cases of resource misallocation (for instance, the use of socially valuable irrigated lands for pastures, probably due to low water prices) (World Bank 1991c, 1992a).

In 1989, Venezuela used 160 kg of fertilizer per hectare of cropland. This is relatively high compared with the world average, although far below European averages.[22] Fertilizer prices used to be heavily subsidized, either through government sales of imported fertilizers at a fraction of their costs or through the provision of low-priced gas to local fertilizer producers. Subsidies were reduced drastically in the 1990s, and by 1993 Venezuela's fertilizer prices were similar to international prices. As a result, fertilizer consumption was slightly reduced and cost increases were passed into food prices. Although this is in complete agreement with orthodox economics, it seems that in this case reducing market distortions has reduced neither fertilizer consumption nor the associated environmental deterioration. In this case of low price elasticity, better rural extension and greater environmental controls of the agrochemical industry could probably help the environment more than a price increase.

Traditionally, the biggest subsidies in Venezuela went to energy consumption. In 1992, the price of a gallon of gasoline was thirty cents, one-half the real cost of production and one-third the sales price in the international market. These low energy prices fostered overconsumption and reduced efficiency. Nevertheless, the fear of social reactions (severe riots and looting came after transport prices increased in 1991) has led Venezuela's government to abandon its plans to increase energy prices. In this area, better and tougher air pollution controls could help reduce pollution and consumption, perhaps with fewer negative social reactions.

Pricing policies for logging activities in national forests have been blamed for deforestation and poor forest management. Until 1989, almost 50 percent of the logging concessions in national forests were on an annual basis, with no reforestation requirement. Stumpage fees did not differentiate between wood qualities, encouraging selective deforestation and forest impoverishment. In the 1990s, Venezuela's authorities are trying to correct these policies, issuing long-term concessions, increasing prices, and requiring reforestation. Nevertheless, poor information on natural forest productivity troubles Venezuela's forest management. A combination of price policy and research is necessary to foster sustainable development of Venezuela's logging resources.

Environmental Impacts of Macroeconomic Policies

Venezuela's economic development has been based largely on its oil wealth, with the government expenditure as the central mechanism for redistribution of the export earnings. Some long-term environmental consequences of this economic system have been

- the concentration of population, wealth, and power in few locations and in a small number of social groups. Hence environmental impacts are also highly concentrated.
- neglect of economic and resource efficiency, resulting in high resource consumption and poor conservation of natural, social, and man-made capital.
- limited capacity to incorporate a large portion of Venezuela's population and environments into the economic model. This has resulted in the subutilization of important regions of the country and the deterioration of rural areas. It also has limited access of the population to the more productive activities and fostered a poor quality of life among a high percentage of the urban and rural populations.

By and large, these problems are not unique to Venezuela. In fact, they are widespread in many developing countries. Venezuela has tried to correct them through political decentralization, economic diversification, and social programs. The outcomes of such policies will become apparent only in the long run.

Conclusions

After accounting for its successes and failures, Venezuela's environmental policy emerges as one of the better and more comprehensive in Latin America. Venezuela benefited from an early start and continuity of institutions and teams. It has enjoyed great visibility among the many other pressing national issues. The weak aspects of Venezuela's environmental management stem from the same problems that hamper all of Venezuela's public administration, and these will take time and effort to correct. But, in contrast to other areas of government, environmental issues attract the interest of many social actors, such as local and international NGOs, community organizations, the private sector, and research and academic institutions. This multiplicity of concerned stakeholders strengthens the opportunities for sound environmental development in Venezuela's future.

Notes

1. More than $2,500 of per capita GDP, according to World Bank classification.

2. These are average figures for the early 1990s.

3. The system of dams on the Gury River, one of the main rivers of the Orinoco basin, concentrates 90 percent of Venezuela's hydropower production.

4. In its larger meaning, *biological diversity* (or biodiversity) refers to all living species and the current and potential functions they perform. In a more restricted sense *biodiversity* refers to the presence of a rich, living environment, which includes a variety of species, gene pools, habitats, and ecosystems. Biodiversity provides the economy with a reservoir of new natural resources, drugs, and chemicals. Beyond its short run economic value, biodiversity is important to the continued evolution of life on earth, and it is part of most biochemical cycles that govern many physical, chemical, and biological parameters of the earth, such as climate, rains, nutrient cycles, and dilution of pollutants.

5. Whereas the goal of the International Union for the Conservation of Nature (IUCN) is to ensure that 5 percent of the world's land surface is turned to national parks, Venezuela has already committed 15 percent of its territory.

6. Among the best known are the country's report to the UN Conference on Environment and Development (MARNR 1992a) and the World Bank review (World Bank 1991a).

7. Overall energy efficiency is a crude indicator because it is highly influenced by the GDP mix. However, there is consensus on the toll imposed by Venezuela's low energy efficiency. One example is lost export earnings (see MARNR 1992a).

8. An organic law in Venezuela's legal system is a law second only to the constitution.

9. The last two institutes were restructured during 1992, with the intention of privatizing provision of services and leaving control in the hands of the states.

10. For example, INPARQUES, not included in the above-mentioned figures, had more than one thousand employees in 1992.

11. MARNR has a chair without vote in the economic cabinet.

12. The alternation of AD and COPEI as majority parties came to an end in 1993; see below the section on recent political developments.

13. Almost half the eighty complaints processed during 1991 resulted in corrective actions by the government environmental agency.

14. This excludes the budget of the regional development corporations.

15. Carlos Andres Perez was Venezuela's president for the first time during the mid-1970s, at the height of the first oil-price boom. Perez's first presidency was both revered and condemned for its lavish social expenditures, its embezzlement and bribe scandals, and its pharaonic projects.

16. Subsequently, Perez was found guilty by Venezuela's supreme court and is serving a mild sentence.

17. In 1993, Colombia promoted its environmental agency to ministerial rank. Recently, the Clinton administration voiced its intention to grant cabinet status to the United States Environmental Protection Agency director.

18. Until recently, MARNR managed the water and sewage systems of the largest cities and, therefore, was responsible for the discharge of untreated raw sewage waters into streams, lakes, and coastal areas.

19. At least the amount of the fines has been raised significantly by the new Environmental Penal Law, passed in 1992.

20. This is standard neoclassical environmental economics; see for instance Baumol and Oates 1975.

21. As it is today in Europe and the United States.

22. See WRI/UNEP/UNDP 1992, table 18.2.

References

Baumol, W. J., and W. E. Oates. 1975. *The Theory of Environmental Policy*. Englewood Cliffs, NJ: Prentice-Hall.

CENDES. 1994. *Case Study for Venezuela*. Caracas: CENDES. [A contribution to David Reeds, ed. 1996. *Structural Adjustment, the Environment, and Sustainable Development*. London: Earthscan.]

Congreso de Venezuela. 1989a. "Ley Orgánica de Descentralización y Transferencia de Competencia del Poder Público." *Gaceta Oficial* 4153, Caracas.

————. 1989b. "Ley de Reforma parcial de la Ley Orgánica de Régimen Municipal." *Gaceta Oficial* 4109, Caracas.

————. 1992. "Ley penal del Ambiente." *Gaceta Oficial* 4358, Caracas.

Daly, H. E. 1992. "Allocation, Distribution and Scale: Towards an Economics That Is Efficient, Just and Sustainable." *Ecological Economics* 6(3):185–93.

Diaz, Romero A. 1991. *Auditoria Ambiental de Venezuela*. Caracas: Bioma.

MARNR. 1992a. *Un Compromiso Nacional Para el Desarrollo Sustentable. Conferencia de las Naciones Unidas Sobre el Medio Ambiente y el Desarrollo 1992 (CNUMAD) Informe de Venezuela*. Caracas: MARNR.

————. 1992b. *Legislación ambiental Venezolana*. Caracas: MARNR.

————. 1992c. *Memoria y Cuenta, Año 1991*. 3 vols. Caracas: MARNR.

McNeely, Jeffrey A., Kenton R. Miller, Walter V. Reid, Russell A. Mittermeier, and Timothy B. Werner. 1990. *Conserving the World Biological Diversity*. Washington, DC: IUCN, WRI, WWF, World Bank.

World Bank. 1991a. *Environmental Issues in Venezuela*. Report no. 8272-VE. Washington, DC: World Bank.

————. 1991b. *Venezuela Poverty Study*. Report no. 9114-VE. Washington, DC: World Bank.

————. 1991c. *Venezuela's Irrigation and Drainage*. Report no. 9221-VE. Washington, DC: World Bank.

————. 1992a. *Venezuela Structural and Macroeconomic Reforms: The New Regime*. Report no. 10404-VE. Washington, DC: World Bank.

————. 1992b. *Venezuela Public Administration Study*. Report no. 8972-VE. Washington, DC: World Bank.

————. 1992c. *World Development Report*. New York: Oxford University Press.

WRI/UNEP/UNDP. 1992. *World Resources, 1992–1993*. New York: Oxford University Press.

9

COMPARATIVE ENVIRONMENTAL ISSUES AND POLICIES IN NIGERIA

OLUSEGUN AREOLA

Introduction

In recent years in Nigeria, a marked positive change in attitude toward environmental issues has occurred, both in government and among the populace. The factor responsible for this is much the same as that which spurred earlier sporadic efforts to mitigate the impact of environmental problems (Areola 1987). A spate of environmental disasters in the recent past has jolted both the people and the government to action. The media, particularly radio and television, and to a lesser extent newspapers, have brought these problems home to the people.

Such environmental problems include (1) recurrent severe dry seasons since the late 1980s during which many farmlands and plantations of tree crops (e.g., cocoa, rubber) have burned in the humid forest region; (2) extensive gully erosion that has swallowed up roads and motorways, buildings, villages, and sections of towns in parts of central eastern Nigeria; (3) desertification that has resulted in widespread land degradation, accompanied by shifting sand dunes that bury *fadama* and other arable farmlands and threaten to consume villages, wells, and livestock watering points in the northeast Sahel zone (Gwandu 1991); (4) the Bagauda Lake Dam burst in Kano State in 1988 that resulted from poor management of the catchment and poor maintenance of the earth dam; and (5) the Koko Port toxic waste incident of 1987, in which an Italian ship covertly brought in drums of toxic and radioactive chemical wastes, to be buried in selected sites in Nigeria.

These experiences have made the government more amenable to the usual prodding by international organizations to take concrete action on environmental issues. Although it is impossible to guess what the current attention span will be for environmental issues, it is obvious that environmental problems cannot be dispensed with easily and quickly, because of their increasing severity and geographical spread. The problem can no longer be ignored or taken lightly, as many Nigerians now realize. It is necessary to discuss some of these environmental and resource problems in Nigeria and the issues that arise from them, in order to have the right perspective on current environmental politics and program formulations.

Overview of Environmental Problems and Issues

The Nigerian ecological environment varies. It consists of (1) a broad coastal belt of mangroves, freshwater swamps, coastal thickets, and lowland tropical forests; (2) a much more extensive hinterland of savannas with a variety of physiognomic types and pockets of upland grassland; and culminates in (3) the semiarid scrub lands of the Sahelian region around Lake Chad.

Because of the long history of human occupation and high population densities every ecological zone in Nigeria has been deeply affected by human activities. Man has destroyed or modified much of the original natural vegetation cover such that there is no true wilderness anywhere in the sense of natural, undisturbed wild land (Onochie 1979) (see table 9.1).

The major environmental issues in Nigeria today stem either from a lack of or an improper appreciation of the dynamic relationship between environmental factors and man's land management practices. These issues can be highlighted under four major subjects: (1) deforestation and vegetation degradation; (2) soil erosion; (3) drought and desertification; and (4) pollution.

Deforestation and Vegetation Degradation

Deforestation, due to outright clearance or the loss or alienation of forest lands to other land uses, has reached alarming proportions (Fair 1992). So also has the degradation of the vegetation in terms of quantity and quality of vegetation cover and the diversity of the flora. High forests that in the early decades of this century covered 10 percent of Nigeria's total land area have been drastically reduced to a little under 2 percent, mainly since the end of World War II (Udo et al. 1991; Areola 1991). The secondary forests have not been allowed to regenerate into maturity but have been cleared on a large scale to make way either for tree crop farms or for plantations of exotic tree species, notably teak (*Tectona grandis*) and gmelina (*Gmelina arborea*). Forest regeneration has become difficult also because of the increasing incidence of bush burning in the forest region, a phenomenon that has been aggravated by the succession of severe dry seasons since the late 1980s (Areola 1990).

Concern about deforestation and vegetation degradation throughout the country has come primarily from two major pressure groups. The first group comprises forest ecologists, forest economists, and forest administrators who

TABLE 9.1

Ecological Status of Nigeria

Land Area	923,773 km²
Coastline	843 km
Total Population (1991 census)	88,814,501
% Under 5 Years	20

National Resources Balance Sheet:

Arable Land as Percentage of Total Land	57[a]
Livestock per Capita	0.56[a]
Production of Fuelwood per Capita	0.92[a]
Average Annual Deforestation	320,000.00 ha[b]
Average Annual Deforestation (% forest area)	2.7[a]
Greenhouse Index (carbon heating equivalents per capita)	0.8[a]
Industrial Round Wood	7,868,000 m²[b]
Fuel and Charcoal	10,735,000 m³[b]

Climate and Biological Diversity:

Climate Type	Tropical
Rainfall	625-4,300mm
Mean Minimum Temperature	25° C
Mean Maximum Temperature	32° C
Vegetation Zones	Tropical wetlands, forest, savanna and sahelian scrubland

Percentage Habitat Loss in:

Dry Forest	76[b]
Moist Forest	83[b]
Savanna	80[b]
Wetlands Marsh	80[b]
Mangrove	50[b]

Number of Threatened Animal Species:

Mammals	5[c]
Birds	8
Reptiles	9
Amphibians	3[b]

TABLE 9.1 (*continued*)

Ecological Status of Nigeria

Protected Areas:	
Number	4[b]
Land Area	960,082 ha[b]
Marine and Coastal Area	0[b]
Biosphere Reserve Area	460 ha[b]

Key:

    a = Human Development Report, 1991

    b = World Resources, 1990–91

    c = First National Rolling Plan, 1990–92, vol. 1

Source: Adapted from Aina and Salau, eds., *The Challenge of Sustainable Development in Nigeria*, NEST, 1992.

are worried not only about the environmental consequences, but also about the economic and social repercussions of the rapid depletion of Nigeria's wood resources and the disappearance of her forest estate (Enabor 1992). Of course, the views of the foresters are not new, and foresters and forestry establishments have been in the forefront of conservation action in Nigeria from colonial times (Adeyoju 1975; Areola 1987). But now their exalted position and their conceptualization of and strategies for conservation are being challenged by another closely related group, the wildlife experts and managers of game reserves and national parks.

Deforestation and vegetation degradation have adversely affected Nigeria's meager wildlife population. Ajayi (1979) drew attention to the drastic decline in the export figures for forest mammals and by-products from southern Nigeria between the 1965/66 and 1976/77 financial years. There was a decline of about 80 percent in revenue. There was no national legislation operative during that period due to the decline in the resource itself. Recent investigations indicate that the nature (forest) reserves that used to provide succor to the beleaguered wildlife have suffered greatly from encroachment (Afolayan 1992). Firewood exploitation, bush burning, and intensive cattle grazing have reduced the vegetation cover of many forest reserves drastically, including those in the Kainji Lake National Park. The degradation of riverine vegetation is particularly serious because the river valleys serve as refuge for wild game from the bush fires and during the dry season when forage and surface water are scarce elsewhere.

The conversion of degraded or secondary forests into plantations of exotic trees, once much favored by forestry experts, is now considered by wildlife experts to be disastrous to the indigenous wild game population. Changes in habitat conditions and indiscriminate killing of wild game by the local people and poaching in the game reserves have greatly depleted the populations of many species and lowered their conservation status. According to Afolayan (1987), some wildlife species, such as the giant eland and the scimitar-horned oryx, have become extinct in Nigeria; the giraffe, elephant, pygmy hippopotamus, gorilla, colobus monkey, drill, and chimpanzee are threatened with extinction; and of the twenty-three varieties of antelope, only two, bushbuck and grey duiker, have population sizes of satisfactory conservation status.

The wildlife experts worry that Nigeria's approach to the management of nature reserves and the conservation of wildlife is too negative, being mainly in the form of edicts and laws prohibiting ordinary folk from entering and removing any resource materials from the nature reserves. This approach does not take cognizance of the fact that the creation of nature reserves constitutes a big loss to the local communities—wild game once provided about 20 percent of the protein consumed by rural Nigerians in the forest region (Charter 1970) and 13 percent for the whole country (Nigerian Environment Study/Action Team 1991). Apart from loss of land, it alienates whole traditional occupational groups as their means of livelihood is cut off suddenly, without any provision for compensation or alternative occupations. Hence, like others elsewhere in Africa with similar experiences (Neumann 1992), the people, in protest, have resorted to such "illegal acts" as poaching, burning, and farming on nature reserves.

A new conservation ethic is being canvassed that emphasizes the full participation of the local people in wildlife conservation programs and ensures that they are the first and major beneficiaries of such programs. This new approach is considered necessary if the government is to realize its dream of developing tourism and recreational travel within the country.

The Natural Resources Conservation Council (NARESCON), about which more will be said later, recently commissioned a study group to develop viable projects on integrated natural resources conservation based on local community participation (Ajayi 1993). One of the projects under consideration is the organization of local hunters into "Indigenous Hunters Associations," to manage wildlife resources in the nature reserves. This is taking a cue from a similar local initiative in Ondo State, in southwestern Nigeria, where an organized hunters association in the Ore and Odigbo local government areas has taken effective control of game harvesting and marketing in the 4,000 square kilometer Oluwa Forest Reserve. Another group of cooperative farmers also is engaged in tree planting and food crop cultivation in the same forest reserve under the *taungya* system (Afolayan 1993).

Soil Erosion

The devastation caused by gully erosion, particularly in the eastern states of Abia, Anambra, Enugu, and Imo, recently has been the subject of public debate. Much has been said and written about the problem of accelerated soil erosion in these parts of Nigeria in the past (Areola 1990). What has made the present debates and calls for action more strident is, perhaps, the fact that while in the past gully erosion was, in a sense, a "rural" phenomenon, since the mid-1980s it has gnawed its way into towns and the roads linking them. The problem no longer looks so distant and remote to the urban elite, the bureaucrats, and other government functionaries, some of whose home communities and towns have been devastated. Gully erosion also has devastated large tracts of such emergent tourist centers as the Mambilla and Jos plateaus.

The problem is so widespread and so enormous, particularly in eastern Nigeria, that both the people and the local and state governments have despaired of arresting the onslaught of gully erosion; everyone is looking to the federal government. Thus far, engineering measures have been favored in the sporadic efforts to check gully erosion. Such measures have great psychological impact because, in panic or emergency situations such as often arise in the affected areas, engineering measures come in handy as a means of quick response; they are highly visible and somewhat reassuring to the panic-stricken population. Biological approaches, including reservation of land, revegetation, and afforestation, take much longer to plan and implement and to achieve tangible results. They also require greater mobilization, involvement, and support of the grassroots population, tasks that have daunted most government planners and administrators.

However, the "quick-fix" engineering measures have not always provided permanent solutions, especially as they have been applied in a piecemeal fashion to check individual or isolated gullies. There is consensus among experts that what is needed is a combination of engineering and biological control measures applied on a regional basis within recognized drainage basins or gully systems. The success of such an erosion control program would depend also on advances in the areas of land zoning, land use control, and town and country planning. Implementation of such comprehensive programs of land use control and inculcation of conservation practices in land use requires strong political and legislative support and a sustained mass mobilization program with the cooperation and active participation of the people.

Unfortunately, even in the present heightened state of public concern about soil erosion, there are doubts about the political will and courage of the ruling elite, both military and civilian, to implement a sustained program of soil erosion control and soil conservation. Even less certain is the extent to which the people are willing to cooperate and accommodate the initial costs and discomfort of soil erosion control and soil conservation programs. The beliefs that environmental problems are the responsibility of government and that solutions to such problems require huge sums of money that only government can provide have tended to make the people underrate the part they can play in environmental management. This situation is partly the outcome of attitudes unwittingly developed during Nigeria's oil boom years of the early 1970s, when the feeling was rife that money could solve all problems. Thus, every disaster was followed by the granting of a relief fund by federal and state governments. The weakness of this practice was that most of the funds were usually expended on rehabilitating the victims, which was justifiable in a sense. But there have not been corresponding efforts and resources directed at finding long-term or lasting solutions to the environmental problems.

The federal government has institutionalized the relief fund approach by endowing an ecological fund to which 2 percent of annual government revenue is contributed. In addition to disaster relief operations, the fund, which is being managed by the Ecological Fund Office (EFO) within the presidency, is used to support research establishments and projects instituted by government on specific ecological problems such as coastal erosion, oil pollution, soil erosion, desertification, and invasion of coastal waters by aquatic weeds.

Drought and Desertification

Drought and *desertification* have become household words in Nigeria in recent years, and the experts and international agencies have succeeded in guiding the discussions and debates to focus on the human factors, that is, the role of human activities in exacerbating the impact of drought and thereby promoting desertification. Such human activities include cultivation, grazing, and fuelwood exploitation in the marginal Sudano-Sahelian zone.

Government largely has sidetracked the problem in that it has not confronted the local land users, farmers, and pastoralists alike, to control and modify traditional land management practices. Density of crop cultivation and intensity of animal grazing and fuelwood exploitation continue to increase in the marginal lands of the Sahel zone (Cline-Cole 1991). Piecemeal ameliorative measures such as constructing dams, establishing shelter belts/windbreaks, and digging wells for livestock watering do not provide effective and lasting solutions because of failure to integrate them with a comprehensive program of total catchment management (Longworth 1988) for the conservation both of water and of land resources.

On the local level, the main concern appears to be the impact of some of the measures taken to combat the problems of drought and desertification. A particularly contentious issue is the construction of dams for irrigation farming along the major rivers that flow into the Sudano-Sahelian zone. It is not that the people do not appreciate the benefits; rather, perhaps, they believe that the benefits are still too little relative to their losses in land and that the benefits affect too small a proportion of the farming population and only a fraction of the cultivated lands in the Sudano-Sahelian zone (Wallace 1979, 1980; Adams 1987; Olofin 1992). Poor management of resettlement programs and delayed and inadequate compensation for loss of land and economic trees led to civil strife during the Bakolori Dam project in Sokoto State.

Perhaps the greatest disaffection about the dam projects is to be found among people in the downstream communities who see their lot as a case of double jeopardy. Not only are they not benefiting directly from the dam schemes, they also must suffer the adverse consequences of damming the rivers. These adverse consequences include (1) channel incision and valley-side erosion (cf. Olofin 1990); (2) deprivation in the fadama lands of the annual flood waters and associated rich silt load; (3) over time, a progressive reduction in the area of fadama; (4) loss of fishing grounds as a result of irregular river flow and reduced inundation of valley floor pools and depressions; and (5) drastically reduced water supply in drought years when water is held back behind the dams.

In addition, the downstream communities now live in constant fear of dam bursts, given the experience of the Bagauda Lake Dam burst in Kano State in 1988. According to Olofin (1992), the flood flow from the Bagauda Dam burst wiped off all the sediments in the downstream channel, breached a road, and in place of the rich silt and clay deposits on the alluvial terraces, deposited the rubble and infertile sands derived from the dam and the upper reaches of the river. If the Bagauda lake, which is less than 5 percent of the nearby Tiga Reservoir in volume, could wreak so much havoc, it is frightening to imagine what failure of the Tiga Dam would bring about.

Both the people and governments in the Sudano-Sahelian zone are sufficiently alarmed by the prospect of dam bursts that studies have been commissioned to assess the danger. Impetus for such studies has come also from the Hadejia-Nguru Wetlands Conservation Project, sponsored by the International Union for the Conservation of Nature and Natural Resources (IUCN) (HNWCP 1991). Understandably, the project managers are concerned about the effects of water impoundment behind the dams on the sustenance of the Hadejia River wetland ecosystem. They are equally worried about the possibility of dam bursts that could result in a deluge that would destroy the wetland ecosystem altogether.

Of course, other strategies are being pursued to combat drought and desertification, but none is on as grand a scale as dam construction for irrigation farming. A few years back, some state governments in the Sudano-Sahelian zone took the initiative to try to reduce fuelwood exploitation by encouraging the local people to use kerosene stoves. The effort was vitiated by the prolonged shortage and high cost of kerosene that occurred in the late

1980s. This program, however, spurred the establishment of research projects on alternative energy sources, for example, at the Usmanu Danfodiyo University, Sokoto (Sambo 1991). The emphasis is on solar energy, but one of the research projects is to develop more efficient wood-burning stoves that would lead to greater economy in the use and exploitation of firewood (Maishanu, Danshehu, and Sambo 1990).

The Federal Department of Forestry also has pilot projects aimed at developing appropriate methods of stabilizing the shifting sand dunes. This is in addition to its much older and successful programs of urban tree planting and the establishment of shelter belts and windbreaks throughout the Sudano-Sahelian zone (Adeyoju and Enabor 1973; Enabor 1977). By contrast, there has been no noticeable progress in the control of grazing and bush burning, two critical agents in the advance of desertlike conditions into the Sudan and Sahel regions.

Pollution

The establishment, by decree in 1988, of the Federal Environmental Protection Agency (FEPA) was a direct fallout of the Koko port toxic waste incident mentioned earlier. The incident, in which lethal wastes were shipped into the country undetected, was a major embarrassment to the government and its security agencies. But for the outcry of Nigerian students in Italy who read about the toxic waste shipments in Italian newspapers, the unethical act would have gone unnoticed and unreported. Furthermore, up to that time, Nigeria had no law at all regarding shipment and disposal of toxic wastes. Thus, the culprits could have been prosecuted only on some other related charges, rather than on shipment of toxic waste. The military government quickly had to promulgate an enabling decree to address future occurrences; the result was the Harmful Wastes (Special Criminal Provisions, etc.) Decree of 1988.

The incident jolted the people out of their almost complete lack of concern about pollution. Communities in the Niger Delta had long complained about the destruction of their land and fishing grounds by oil pollution, but the rest of the country turned deaf ears (Saro-Wiwa 1989). Soon after the Koko waste dump discovery, the widespread rumor that there had been earlier shipments of toxic wastes, buried secretly at different locations in Nigeria, made the general public, perhaps for the first time, listen to the outcry of the delta peoples and begin to appreciate the danger posed by environmental pollution. Then the urban dwellers themselves got a taste of what oil pollution does to the environment: effluents from the Kaduna oil refinery have polluted the Romi River and valley. The public outcry against this oil pollution in the northern heartland, far away from the oil-producing delta region, forced the Nigerian National Petroleum Corporation (NNPC) to commission detailed analytical studies to find ways to stem the problem.

About the same time the public debate over the Koko toxic waste dump was raging, residents of the then federal capital city of Lagos awoke one day to find the lagoons, creeks, and canals covered by water hyacinths (*Eiehhornia crassipes*). The weed spread to the coastal waters of southwestern Nigeria, and the people immediately linked the invasion to the long history of waste and sewage dumping in the lagoon waters. This, in addition to excessive sedimentation, has led to the silting up of the coastal waters and their invasion by aquatic weeds.

Thus, there is now greater public awareness of the dangers of water pollution. Indeed, oil and water pollution and aquatic weed invasion of the coastal waters were the first preoccupation of FEPA at its inception.

Oil pollution and environmental degradation in the oil-producing delta region of Nigeria have become major political issues in Nigeria (Stanley 1990). After decades of passivity, the various communities in the delta region (see map 9.1) have become more militant and vocal in their resistance to the continued devastation of the environment by oil companies. This environmental degradation is the more irksome to the local communities because, in their view, the huge wealth being derived by the country from oil exploitation is not being reinvested to raise their standard of living (Lakemfa 1993). Rather, much of the oil wealth is being used to develop other parts of the country. Hence, some communities have reacted violently by sabotaging the activities of the oil companies. For instance, 31 percent of all cases of oil spill from 1976 through 1983, were due to sabotage (Ikporukpo 1986).

In 1991 and 1992, a number of pressure groups emerged from the oil-producing areas, bent on influencing the choice of presidential candidates by the two political parties, the National Republican Convention (NRC) and the Social Democratic Party (SDP). Two such groups were the Association of Minority Oil Producing States (AMOS) and the Association of Petroleum Producing Areas of Nigeria (ASPAN). Their goals were the same: to ensure the choice of a presidential candidate who would have the environmental health and development of the oil-producing delta region as major programs on his ticket.

Ken Saro-Wiwa, a founding member of ASPAN once wrote:

> I invite academics, students and all Nigerians to pay close attention to the terrible destruction which is going on in the oil-bearing areas and to realize that what is being lost there is far greater than whatever Nigerians can be said to be getting from oil. Of course, oil has been a curse to Nigeria. Unless we realize this, we may lose everything, including the country, before long to oil. (*Daily Times*, 1992:9)

Violent clashes have occurred between local communities and law enforcement agencies in the oil-producing areas over the local people's

MAP 9.1

Oil and Gas Producing Areas in the Niger Delta

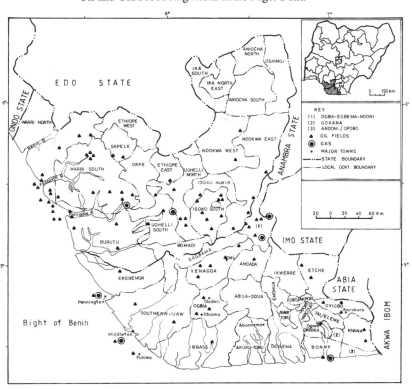

Source: Olusegun Areola, 1996.

relationships with the oil companies and the people's access or the lack of access to the benefits that accrue from oil exploration activities. The most recent bloody clashes occurred from July through September 1993, between the Angoni and the Andoni peoples of Rivers State (Eze 1993:8).

Politics of the Environment: Ideology, Interests, and Institutions

The rather spasmodic nature and the apparent lack of a clear direction in Nigeria's response to environmental challenges, as is evident in the foregoing discussion, reflect the paucity of well-articulated policies and comprehensive programs on the environment. In place of such comprehensive policy and program formulations, edicts, decrees, and legislation exist that address various aspects of the environment and natural resource use and conservation (Okediran 1991). The few tangible policies and programs that exist have not stood the test of time because, being essentially measures taken to deal with "emergency" situations, they lack long-term solutions to the problems addressed. Thus, a recent study commissioned by the newly constituted Natural Resources Conservation Council (NARESCON) identified weak policy and legal framework as major constraints to conservation-conscious resource and environmental management in Nigeria (Ajayi 1991). This is partly a reflection of the politics of environmental management in the country.

Environmental politics in Nigeria, basically, have been the politics of resource allocation, characterized by a struggle between various interests for the nation's resources, a struggle rooted primarily in the primordial ethnic domains that make up the Nigerian state (cf. Ekeh 1989). Public debates and discussions in the literature have not transcended the traditional, right-wing view that sees the environment as a social resource that must be shared between the diverse communities in the country.

Indeed, a significant notion of human rights in Nigerian constitutions is as communal rights or ethnic rights that must be protected by the state in order to promote the general welfare (Jinadu 1989). It is this particular notion of human rights as communal or ethnic rights that constitutes the fundamental basis of federalism as a structure of government in Nigeria. Also, Nigerian federalism sees politics in terms of an adversary process for reconciling rival ethnic claims to and concerns with the exercise of power as in, for example, the allocation of national resources. Resource allocation is referred to euphemistically as "the sharing of the national cake." The politics of resource management and utilization in Nigeria is such that issues of environmental quality and conservation become residual considerations in the struggle for national resources. This, for example, is the main complaint of Ken Saro-Wiwa and his co-agitators for the rights of the oil-producing areas of Nigeria.

The neglect of environmental matters in the past was reflected clearly in Nigeria's first two post-independence national development plans (1962–68 and 1970–74), which made no specific reference to the environment. But, as a carryover from the colonial era, there were provisions for sanitation and for the development of forest and game reserves (Obadan, Chokor and Salau, 1992). The Third National Development Plan (1975–80), was the first to consider seriously the environmental component of economic development and the need to include environmental issues in all aspects of national development planning. The Fourth National Development Plan (1981–85), introduced the provision that an environmental impact statement (EIS) should be incorporated in the feasibility study of any major public- and private-sector projects. Unfortunately, even these few laudable provisions on environment and development in the two plans never were implemented or enforced.

The concern for environmental management in Africa expressed by the Western powers and institutions was long viewed with apprehension by the Nigerian elite, who perceived this concern as emanating from selfish economic and political motives and not from altruistic reasons. In the early 1970s, this concern for environmental quality was interpreted to mean less economic growth and vice-versa (Pearce, Markandya, and Barbier 1989). Hence, Western concern for environmental management in Africa was seen as a ploy to keep African countries economically and politically subservient to Western capitalist and neocolonialist interests.

But attitudes have changed over time. A workshop on environment and development organized in 1989 at the University of Dar-as-Salaam by the Institute for African Alternatives (IFAA), a nongovernmental organization that is highly critical of Western economic and political systems, "acknowledged the existence of a real environmental crisis aggravated by unfair international trade practices, foreign debt, technology gaps, civil wars and autocratic rule, whether military or civilian" (Suliman 1991:5). However, in spite of the change in attitudes and in spite of a greater understanding of the interdependence of the environment and the economy, attempts to promote a conservationist program in Africa have not elicited strong responses in Nigeria. This is due in part to lingering doubts about the true motives of the Western powers; for example, Rees (1990) argues that the concept of 'sustainable development' can turn out to be another cloak for capitalism—"capitalism with a green face"—if we make the mistake of using the strategy of proper pricing of resources as a way of determining rather than of achieving ecological goals or standards. Perhaps it also is because, as Bell (1987) noted, the conservationist program for Africa is a strategy of limitation of resource use and human population increase. This goes not only against the instincts and economic interests of broad sections of the Nigerian hegemonic elite, comprising the intelligentsia and the political-cum-business classes (Dudley 1982), but also against the strong pronatalist values, orientations, and institutions in Nigerian society (Ologe et al. 1992).

Nigeria's federalism, since the mid-1960s, has been characterized by centralizing trends such that the onus for policy formulation and execution has devolved more and more on the federal government (Agbaje et al. 1992). There has been a sharp decline in the size, influence, and fiscal viability and autonomy of the federated states as a result of the successive subdivision of the country into more states and the centralization of the Nigerian federal public finance system. This trend toward centralization has come about partly as a result of the benefits and advantages that accrue to the dominant elements of the hegemonic elite and partly as a result of the continuing involvement in government of the military with its tradition of a centralized command structure (table 9.2).

TABLE 9.2

Brief Summary of Nigeria's Political History, 1960–93

Political Independence (1 October 1960)

Political independence from British colonial rule.

Establishment of a federation of 3 (later 4) powerful regions and a central government under a Westminster type parliamentary system.

First Republic (1960–66)

1960–63	Federal Government of Nigeria under British royalty represented by the governor-general. Sir Abubakar Tafawa Balewa headed a coalition government of the Northern People's Congress (NPC) and the National Council of Nigeria and the Cameroons (NCNC).
1963–66	With the enactment of the Republican Constitution, Nigeria became a federal republic on 1 October 1963 with Sir Abubakar Tafawa Balewa as prime minister and Dr. Nnamdi Azikiwe as president.

First Period of Military Rule (1966–79)

January–July 1966	Unitary system of government under Major General Aguiyi Ironsi caused disaffection among northern leaders and peoples.
July 1966	Counter coup by northern military officers ousting the government of Aguiyi Ironsi and replacing him with Lt. Col. Yakubu Gowon.
1966–75	Military government of General Yakubu Gowon.
1967	First round of creation of states—Nigeria partitioned into 12 states.
1967–70	The Nigerian civil war.
July 1975–February 1976	Military government of General Murtala Muhammed:

    (a) Purge of the federal and state civil service.
    (b) Proclamation of a new Federal Capital Territory (Abuja).
    (c) Second round of creation of states. Nigeria repartitioned into 19 states plus the new Federal Capital Territory.

1976–1979	Military regime of General Olusegun Obasanjo.
1976	Local government reforms—creation of 304 local government areas.
1976	Creation of River Basin Development Authorities.
1978	The Land Use Decree vested all land in the government.
1978	First home-grown constitution drafted and adopted (the 1979 Constitution).

TABLE 9.2 (*continued*)

Brief Summary of Nigeria's Political History, 1960–93

1979	General election to usher in the Second Republic under an American type presidential system of government.

The Second Republic (1979–83)

	Alhaji Shehu Shagari was sworn in as first executive president of Nigeria.
1979–83	Green-Revolution Campaign.
	Unsuccessful attempt to pass a Federal Environmental Protection Bill into law.

Second Period of Military Rule (1984–93)

1984–85	Military regime of General Muhammadu Buhari.
1985–93	Military regime of General Ibrahim Babangida.
1987	Third round of creation of states bringing the number to 21.
1988	Federal Environmental Protection Agency Decree No. 58.
1988	Natural Resources Conservation Council Decree No. 50.
1989	Enactment of a new constitution.
1991	Fourth round of creation of states bringing the number to 30.
1993	End of military regime(?).

The centralizing trend is reflected clearly in the treatment of environmental management in the 1989 constitution, which outlines the jurisdiction of all levels of government—federal, state, and local—in the federation with regard to environmental management. The Nigerian federal structure is made up of a federal government at the center, with the country divided into thirty constituent units called "states," each with its own state government and a Federal Capital Territory (FCT) presided over by a federal minister. Each of the thirty states and the FCT are further subdivided into smaller administrative units called "local government areas" (LGAs), of which there are now 589.

Aspects of parts I and II of the Second Schedule in the 1989 constitution allocate responsibilities for the environment between the federal and state governments (tables 9.3a and 9.3b), while part I of the Fourth Schedule defines the responsibilities of local governments in this regard (table 9.4). The essence

TABLE 9.3A

The Exclusive Legislative List of Federal Government Responsibilities for the Environment in the Nigerian Constitution

1. Arms, ammunition and explosives.

2. Aviation, including airports, safety of aircraft and carriage of passengers and goods by air.

3. Construction, alteration and maintenance of such roads as may be declared by the National Assembly to be federal trunk roads.

4. Incorporation, regulation and winding up of bodies corporate, except cooperatives, local governments and others established directly by state (regional) assemblies.

5. Customs and excise duties.

6. Export duties.

7. Drugs and poisons.

8. Fishing and fisheries other than fishing and fisheries in rivers, lakes, water ways, ponds and other inland waters within Nigeria.

9. Immigration into and emigration from Nigeria.

10. Marine shipping and navigation on tidal waters and the River Niger and its effluents and any other inland waterways designated by the National Assembly as an international or inter-state (regional) waterway, and ports designated by the National Assembly as federal ports.

11. Meteorology.

12. Mines and minerals, including oil fields, oil mining, geological surveys and natural gas.

13. National parks as designated by the National Assembly with the consent of state (regional) governments.

14. Nuclear energy.

15. Quarantine.

16. Identification, collection, preservation and management of ancient and historical monuments and records and archaeological sites and remains identified by the National Assembly to be of national importance.

17. Railways.

18. Trade and commerce, inter-state (regional) and international.

TABLE 9.3A (*continued*)

The Exclusive Legislative List of Federal Government Responsibilities for the
Environment in the Nigerian Constitution

19. Traffic on federal trunk roads.

20. Water from sources deemed by the National Assembly to affect more than one state (region).

21. Wireless broadcasting and television other than that owned by state (regional) governments and allocation of wavelengths for wireless, broadcasting and television transmission.

22. Any other matter on which the National Assembly is competent to make legislation.

Source: Parts I and II of the Second Schedule to the Federal Constitution of Nigeria, 1989.

TABLE 9.3B

The Concurrent Legislative List on which Both the Federal and
State Governments Could Act

1. Antiquities, monuments and archives.

2. Electric power.

3. Exhibition of cinematograph films.

4. Industrial, commercial or agricultural development.

5. Scientific and technological research.

Source: Parts I and II of the Second Schedule to the Federal Constitution of Nigeria, 1989.

of these constitutional provisions is that the federal government is given most of the vital regulatory and supervisory powers over the environment, while the powers and areas of jurisdiction of the state and local governments are greatly circumscribed. Thus, as Agbaje and others (1992) noted, the result of the constitutional framework is the ironical situation in which the level of government that is closest to the people, the local government, has the least constitutional responsibility in the management of the environment.

Because of the centralizing trend in Nigeria's federation and the constitutional provisions on the environment, official efforts at institution building for environmental management have been concentrated at the federal level, to

TABLE 9.4

Constitutional Responsibilities of Local Governments on the Environment

1. Formulating economic planning and development schemes for the local area.

2. Establishing and maintaining cemeteries, burial grounds, and homes for the destitute or infirm.

3. Licensing bicycles, trucks (other than mechanically propelled trucks), canoes, wheel barrows, and carts.

4. Establishing, maintaining, and regulating slaughter houses, slaughter slabs, markets, motor parks, and public conveniences.

5. Constructing and maintaining roads, streets, street lighting, drains, parks, gardens, open spaces, or such public facilities as may be prescribed from time to time by the House of Assembly of a state (region).

6. Naming roads and streets and numbering houses.

7. Providing and maintaining public conveniences, sewage, and refuse disposal.

8. Controlling and regulating out-door advertising, places for sale of food to the public, laundries, and moving and keeping pets of all descriptions.

9. Licensing, regulating and controlling the sale of liquor.

The schedule also enjoins local governments to cooperate with state (regional) governments in the areas of:

1. Providing and maintaining primary, adult, and vocational education.

2. Developing agriculture and natural resources, other than the exploitation of minerals.

3. Providing and maintaining health services.

4. Any other functions as may be delegated to local government by state legislatures.

Source: Part I of the Fourth Schedule to the Nigerian Constitution, 1989.

the almost total neglect of the state and local government levels. The two major institutions for environmental management today are the Federal Environmental Protection Agency (FEPA), established by Decree number 58 of 1988, and the Natural Resources Conservation Council (NARESCON), established by Decree number 50 of 1989. FEPA is responsible for the protection and development of the environment in general and environmental technology, including initiation of policy in relation to environmental research and technology (table 9.5). NARESCON was established with the mandate to

TABLE 9.5

The Functions and Powers of the Federal Environmental Protection Agency

Functions

1. Advise the Federal Military Government on the national environmental policies and priorities and on scientific and technological activities affecting the environment.

2. Prepare periodic master plans for the development of environmental science and technology and advise the Federal Military Government on the financial requirements for the implementation of such plan.

3. Promote cooperation in environmental science and technology with similar bodies in other countries and with international bodies connected with the protection of the environment.

4. Cooperate with federal and state ministries, local government councils, statutory bodies, and research agencies on matters and facilities that relate to environmental protection.

5. Carry out such other activities as are necessary or expedient for the full discharge of the functions of the agency under this decree.

Powers

1. Make grants to suitable authorities and bodies with similar functions for demonstration and for such other purposes as may be determined appropriate to further the purposes and provisions of this decree.

2. Collect and make available, through publications and other appropriate means and in cooperation with public or private organizations, basic scientific data and other information that pertains to pollution and environmental protection matters.

3. Enter into contracts with public or private organizations and individuals in order to execute and fulfill the agency's functions and responsibilities.

4. Establish, encourage, and promote training programs for agency staff and other appropriate individuals from public or private organizations.

5. Enter into agreements with public or private organizations and individuals to develop, utilize, coordinate, and share environmental monitoring programs, research efforts, and basic data on chemical, physical, and biological effects of various activities on the environment and to participate in other environmentally related activities as appropriate.

6. Establish advisory bodies composed of administrative, technical, or other experts in such environmental areas as the agency may consider useful and appropriate to assist it.

TABLE 9.5 (*continued*)

The Functions and Powers of the Federal Environmental Protection Agency

7.	Establish such environmental criteria, guidelines, specifications, or standards on the protection of the nation's air and interstate waters as may be necessary to protect the health and welfare of the population from environmental degradation.
8.	Establish procedures for industrial or agricultural activities in order to minimize damage to the environment from such activities.
9.	Maintain a program of technical assistance for bodies (public or private) to implement environmental criteria, guidelines, regulations, and standards and to monitor enforcement of the regulation and standards thereof.
10.	Develop and promote such processes, methods, devices, and materials as may be useful or incidental in carrying out the purpose and provisions of this decree.

Source: Federal Environmental Protection Decree No. 58, 1988.

formulate a national policy on and coordinate all matters concerning the conservation of habitats, species, and natural resources in Nigeria.

As is common with many government institutions, there had been intense in-fighting between FEPA and NARESCON over jurisdiction. The initial thinking in government seemed to have been that NARESCON would confine itself to the renewable natural resources, while FEPA would deal with only the nonrenewable resources and associated activities. FEPA had a head start over NARESCON, and it fully mobilized for action long before NARESCON got off the ground. It has linked up with research institutes, universities, and nongovernmental organizations (NGOs). The United Nations Conference on Environment and Development (Rio de Janeiro, Brazil, June 1992) also gave FEPA the pride of place in articulating Nigeria's policy and program formulations on the environment (Federal Environmental Protection Agency 1992).

However, NARESCON seemed to have had the greater clout with government and was backed by the group of foresters, wildlife experts, and managers of game reserves and national parks. But happily, the government decided to streamline its institutional framework for environmental management. It decided to repeal the NARESCON decree and merge its salient provisions with the FEPA decree. This was done through Decree number 59 of 2 August, 1992, Federal Environmental Protection Agency (Amendment) Decree 992. Perhaps to reassure the ecologists and ensure that NARESCON programs would be implemented, in August 1993 the government deployed NARESCON's executive secretary to serve as the expanded FEPA's director general. The new decree states that the repeal of NARESCON "shall not affect anything done or purported to have been done under the repealed enactment." The decree makes FEPA an integral part of the presidency and constitutes for the agency a governing council and a technical committee.

At the state level, institution building is limited to the establishment of Environmental Protection Commissions (EPCs) and environmental enforcement agencies such as the Environmental Task Force (ETF). The schedule of work of the task force has been reduced mainly to environmental sanitation in many states, hence the establishment of environmental sanitation task forces. But, in places, task forces have been set up to tackle other specific environmental problems. A typical example is the old Anambra State Task Force on Soil Erosion Control, which made notable achievements before the state was split into two (Anambra and Enugu) in 1991 (Anambra State Task Force 1988). The relationship between the EPCs and ETFs has not been formalized such that each seems to operate more or less independently of the other. The relationship between the EPCs themselves and the government ministries (particularly the Ministry of Works) in each state has been problematic. The EPCs claim they are independent of ministerial control, being responsible to the respective state governors, but the ministries do not agree.

Institution building for environmental management is at its lowest at the local government level, and the scope of environmental action at that level is limited almost totally to the management of solid waste disposal. The Waste Disposal Board, usually a subunit of the health unit in the local government Department of Health and Social Welfare, is the major environmental management institution. The effectiveness of the Waste Disposal Boards is often greatly limited by poor funding, lack of waste collection trucks and facilities, shortage of personnel, and poor remuneration of workers (Bello-Imam 1985).

The institutional framework for the environmental action program has been strengthened somewhat in recent years by the emergence of nongovernmental organizations (NGOs) concerned with environment and development (table 9.6). In some other countries, nongovernmental organizations have played a pivotal role in galvanizing governments and their agencies to take decisive action on the environment. They have helped in mobilizing the people for popular participation in environmental action programs. They have played significant roles in the development of international environmental legislation and in the application and enforcement of international environmental law, through advocacy and litigation (Sands 1992).

Although the overall impact of the NGOs is still low in Nigeria, there are hopeful signs of greater achievements in the future. Part of the problem of the NGOs is the still all-pervasive influence of the federal government in environmental policy and program formulation and implementation. Concentration of environment regulatory and supervisory functions in the federal government and the federal government's sheer financial prowess, compared to that of the

TABLE 9.6

Major Nongovernmental Organizations (NGOs) Concerned with
Environment and Development in Nigeria

---

1. Forestry Association of Nigeria (FAN)

2. The Nigerian Field Society

3. Ecological Society of Nigeria (ECOSON)

4. The Nigerian Environmental Society (NES)

5. The Society for Environmental Management and Planning (SEMP)

6. The Nigerian Conservation Foundation (NCF)

7. The Nigerian Environment Study/Action Team (NEST)

International Agencies

1. World Wildlife Fund (WWF)

2. International Union for the Conservation of Nature and Natural Resource (IUCN)

3. The United Nations Environment Program (UNEP)

4. The African Conservation Foundation

5. The United Nations Food and Agriculture Organization (FAO)

6. The European Economic Community (EEC)

Funding Agencies

1. Ford Foundation, New York

2. International Institute for Environment and Development (IIED) London

3. International Development Research Center (IDRC) of Canada

4. Canadian University Service Overseas (CUSO)

---

state and local governments, have drawn the NGOs inexorably to the ambit of
the federal government and its agencies. Another factor responsible for this
close link of NGOs with the federal government is, of course, the weak
institutional framework for environmental management at the state and local
government levels.

The relationship between the government and the NGOs is cordial,
perhaps too cordial, to the extent that government continues to dictate what the

boundaries of discourse and interaction should be between them. Some of the NGOs have received funding from government and government agencies for some of their conferences, seminars, and workshops. A conference held in 1991 in Kaduna between the government and NGOs in Nigeria under the auspices of the Federal Ministry of Social Development and the United Nations Environment Program (UNEP) identified a mentality of dependence on government for support and funding as one of the major weaknesses of the NGOs. Other weaknesses include lack of awareness or understanding of a broad NGO ideology; weak capacity, particularly in terms of personnel and finance; and low level of awareness of environment and development issues.

The commanding role played by the federal government in the NGO movement was demonstrated clearly in 1991 when it unilaterally selected and declared one of the NGOs, the Nigerian Environmental Society (NES), as the "premier environmental society" with a mandate to function side by side with FEPA as guardians of Nigeria's environment. NES was then made responsible for implementing the federal government project on the creation of three "ecological villages" to serve as models of a sustainable village in Nigeria. NES has been offered accommodation in Lagos and landed property in Abuja, the new federal capital.

The Nigerian Environmental Society's relationship with government has given rise to a novel form of NGO, the government-owned or government-organized nongovernmental organization (GONGO). NES, formed in 1985, has among its members engineers, scientists, and others engaged in environmental control and protection.

NES is funded mainly by the Federal Environmental Protection Agency (FEPA) and the oil companies, which is why there are doubts about its ability to act freely and objectively when environmental issues concerning its powerful patrons arise. It interacts mostly with the federal government and has few or no links with the state and local governments.

It is not possible to discuss in detail each of the other NGOs listed in table 9.6, but we will draw attention to three of them, providing a broad picture of the activities of these organizations in Nigeria in general.

The Nigerian Conservation Foundation (NCF), registered in 1982, is a charitable trust dedicated to the promotion of nature conservation in Nigeria. Its activities cover conservation education (e.g., in Okomu, in Edo State, and in the North-East Arid Zone Development Project), support for wildlife research, and protection of endangered species and habitats (e.g., establishment of wildlife sanctuary and conservation education projects in Okomu Forest Reserve, Edo State, Cross River State, and Lekki Lagoon in Lagos), and lobbying for legislation and policy initiatives that promote nature conservation. NCF's pioneering efforts in the field of environmental education and conservation awareness in Nigeria are well known in Yobe, Borno, Cross River, and Edo and Lagos states (Okali et al. 1992). The foundation played a key role in formulating Nigeria's National Policy on the Environment. It also prepared the draft proposals for a national conservation education strategy that was adopted in 1988. Its basic aim is to make environmental education part of the National Policy on Education and to integrate formal education with the National Conservation Strategy.

The Nigerian Field Society, one of the oldest NGOs in Nigeria, was founded in 1930 to gather, document, and propagate knowledge about Nigeria's natural history, its indigenous cultures, and its cultural artifacts. It organizes talks and field excursions on different themes in the Nigerian environment. It publishes a journal, *The Nigerian Field*, which is a useful source of information about the Nigerian environment.

The Nigerian Environment Study/Action Team (NEST), established in 1987, is a research and advocacy agency dedicated to promoting public awareness of issues regarding the environment and of sustainable development. NEST represents a successful blend of social and earth scientists, ecologists, forestry economists, and administrators. Its objectives are to (1) collect basic and comprehensive information and data on the status of the Nigerian environment; (2) investigate and document areas of potential hazards, with a view to identifying gaps in knowledge and promoting specific ameliorative projects; (3) analyze patterns of human behavior, social relations, and cultural preferences as these affect the environment; (4) stimulate debate and help intensify awareness in Nigeria of the environmental consequences of our socioeconomic activities; and (5) place at the disposal of all relevant groups and governments the information and perspectives that will assist in formulating policies to rejuvenate and conserve the Nigerian environment.

NEST has organized several study programs, conferences, and workshops. These have resulted in five landmark publications on the Nigerian environment and sustainable development.

Besides nongovernmental organizations, two other associations—the Nigerian Tourism Association and the Manufacturers Association of Nigeria—are worth mentioning because of their influence on environmental policy and program formulation and implementation. The Nigerian Tourism Association has played a key role in government efforts to promote tourism and outdoor recreational travel in Nigeria. Tourism was given prominence in the Third National Development Plan (1975–1980), both in the federal program and in various state government programs. The programs emphasized building hotels and improving transport to facilitate local travel. The Nigerian Tourism Association and allied groups such as the travel agencies or bureaus have served as pressure groups to promote action on the development of the nation's tourist resources, particularly the forest and game reserves. These groups played a key role in the creation of national parks and holiday resorts.

The Manufacturers Association of Nigeria (MAN) is important because of its role as a counterweight to the environmental leanings of the NGOs and other associations. MAN is set up primarily to protect the interests of private investors in the manufacturing sector. Understandably, it has shown keen interest in the activities of the Federal Environmental Protection Agency (FEPA) since it was created. It has set up an Environmental Sanitation Committee, ostensibly to promote the observance of set standards and regulations regarding the environment. But it also established a subcommittee on effluent discharge, air pollution, and solid waste to advise the government and its environment-related agencies on the appropriateness of some legislation and regulations.

In spite of pretenses to the contrary, MAN is a pressure group whose goal is to ensure that government does not set environmental standards they would consider unbearable. For example, MAN opposed a proposed Lagos State Environmental Pollution Edict that would have introduced the "polluter-pay-principle" as a measure to control environmental pollution. Nothing has been heard about the edict for some time, perhaps because FEPA claims it has to review all state edicts on the environment before they are enacted.

The almost total lack of official institution building for environmental action programs at the local level was alluded to earlier. Thus far, there has been no sustained effort to mobilize local communities and organizations for popular participation in environmental action programs. This reflects a basic flaw in the system: that of almost total reliance on the state for development and social change. It was the Directorate of Food, Roads and Rural Infrastructures (DFRRI) that took the first decisive steps to remove this flaw. DFRRI tried to identify and map local communities and economic and sociocultural organizations in order to mobilize them as agents of social change and economic development at the grassroots level (Directorate of Food 1987).

Nigeria has a long tradition of people's participation or involvement in local political and socioeconomic affairs through various associations and organizations. Trade or occupational guilds, cooperative societies, and traditional societies whose livelihood and production activities impinge on the environment do exist. These groups are critical to any program of action on environment and development. Such groups, as well as the numerous community development associations (CDAS), need to be strengthened to participate meaningfully in environment and development activities. Environmental awareness campaigns, such as the ones initiated by the Nigerian Conservation Foundation, are needed to sensitize and mobilize local communities to action. Then, it is necessary to develop small-scale community-based resource development projects that can be handled by the local people who should be fully involved in all stages of project planning and implementation. They should be the major beneficiaries of the proceeds from such projects. This, briefly, is the essence of the new conservation ethic being canvased by the Natural Resources Conservation Council (NARESCON), as indicated earlier.

The Hadejia-Nguru Wetlands Conservation Project (HNWCP), Nguru, Northeast Nigeria, has been experimenting with a number of such small-scale, community-based wetlands conservation projects (Mbanyiman 1990; Mathes 1990; HNWCP 1991; Thomas and Kaigama 1992). Similarly, the Forestry Research Institute of Nigeria is experimenting with a tree-planting system based on a modified taungya system that entails full participation of the local people, who have direct control not only over the food crops but also over the tree crops. Since the project intends that the local people would harvest the tree crops on maturity, the local people are fully committed to protecting the tree crops against illegal tree fellers (Adebagbo 1992).

Overall, through their combined efforts, government agencies, the non-governmental organizations, the international agencies, and local institutions have successfully, if inadvertently, achieved in Nigeria the effect of what Chouri (1993) referred to as "the politicization" of global environmental change, which is helping to inject scientific evidence (and uncertainties) into the policy domain. A brief survey of the policy and legal framework for addressing Nigeria's environmental problems would reveal slow but steady progress in this direction.

Policy and Legal Framework

Some of the existing legislation, policies, and programs date back to the colonial period (Adeyoju 1975). The response of the colonial administration to what was considered the primitive and wasteful land-use practices of the natives was to embark on a program of forest reservation through legislation or by persuasion (communal forests). The objective was to protect the land and the forests and to conserve water. The purpose was not to keep large areas of land unutilized, but rather to use and manage the reserves in a rational manner to the benefit of the colonial economy; hence the subsequent use of the forest reserves for logging, plantation forestry, and wildlife preservation.

As Areola (1987) has noted, the policy of forest reservation was an indirect approach to conservation as it largely side-tracked the basic problem of aggravating soil and land degradation by both cultivators and pastoralists. However, in spite of its faults, the colonial forestry policy that has been carried through into postindependence Nigeria is, perhaps, still the only well-focused and sustained natural resource program in the country. For all its faults, such as its archaic content and terminology and its ludicrous penalties against contravention of its provisions, the Forestry Act of 1938, which was further consolidated in 1958, is still the only piece of legislation dealing specifically with forests in Nigeria. The Federal Department of Forestry is still the best organized and most goal-oriented natural resource management unit in Nigeria and has produced tangible results. There are no other units of comparable longevity and national and international standing and with comparable sustained action programs.

This sad situation results from several factors, including the failure of postindependence administrations to sustain resource units inherited from the colonial era and to pursue their well-set-out frameworks for the systematic survey and mapping and management of Nigeria's natural resource base. Such specialized units, which include the Geological Survey of Nigeria, the soil survey units of the regional Institutes for Agricultural Research, and the Federal Survey Department and its Aerial Survey Section, have been starved of funds and modern equipment. In consequence, most units have lost their experienced staff and professionals (Areola 1988).

In the postindependence era, the perception of environmental issues in terms of narrow ethnic and selfish political interests has greatly hampered the development of environmental action plans. For this reason, the record of the two eras of civilian administration (1960–66 and 1979–83) in environmental decision making was dismal. Strangely, in spite of the environmental disasters experienced in Nigeria between 1968 and 1978, such as drought, flash floods, urban floods, and oil well blowouts, environmental questions did not emerge as important issues in the political campaigns of the last civilian era (1979–83). There are no major environmental legislation or action programs that can be attributed to the two brief periods of civilian administration. The executive and the legislative branches of government in 1983 bungled the attempt to pass into law an environmental protection bill (Areola 1987).

It is to the military era and military administrations, then, that we have to look to gain an insight into Nigeria's efforts in the formulation of environment-conscious policies and legislation. Yet, most of the time, the military has acted off-the-cuff, taking on issues as they come. In this regard, it is interesting to note that the 1979 Nigerian Constitution, the most deliberate and comprehensive piece of legislation by the military at that time, gave scant recognition to environment or conservation issues. As Okediran (1991) noted, conservation of renewable natural resources is treated in a fragmentary way in the constitution, although there is implicit recognition of the principle: "In furtherance of the social order, exploitation of human or natural resources in any form whatsoever for reasons other than the good of the community shall be prevented." There is no substantial difference between the 1979 constitution and the new 1989 constitution in this regard.

Furthermore, the Nigerian Constitution dwells more on the exploitation and supply of resources than on their protection and conservation. There are no specific enactments addressing resource conservation in a comprehensive manner. For such legislation, we have to look at the diverse decrees promulgated by the military governments.

The laws fall into four broad categories: (1) international conventions to which Nigeria is a signatory; (2) federal laws that are applicable throughout the country; (3) state edicts promulgated in particular states; and (4) local government by-laws passed by the different local governments in the country.

The international conventions are significant, not only in themselves, but, perhaps more important, because of the lead they have provided to the federal government to enact corresponding laws specific to the Nigerian environment and problems. Pressures for government initiatives in this regard have come from organizations such as the International Union for the Conservation of Nature and Natural Resources (IUCN), the World Wildlife Fund (WWF), the United Nations Environment Program (UNEP), the United Nations Food and Agriculture Organization (FAO), and the European Economic Community (EEC).

The international conventions pertain mainly to water, especially marine, resources; to hazardous wastes; and to endangered plant and animal species. The Prevention of Pollution of the Sea by Oil Convention of 1954 directly influenced the promulgation of the Oil in Navigable Waters Decree by the federal military government of General Yakubu Gawon (1968). The Convention on International Trade in Endangered Wild Species of Fauna and Flora (1974) is aimed at protecting certain wild animals and plants against over-exploitation through trade. It was in pursuance of the objectives of this convention that Nigeria later promulgated the Endangered Species (Control of International Trade and Traffic) Decree of 1985, during the military regime of General Muhammadu Buhari. Efforts made by the Federal Department of Forestry, as well as by wildlife experts, to get this law into the statute books before then did not materialize; it was virtually impossible to get anything tangible done by the civilian administration.

In 1977, during the regime of General Obasanjo, both for strategic and for economic reasons, Nigeria had rallied the republics of Cameroon, Niger, and Chad to sign an Agreement on the Joint Regulation of Fauna and Flora on Lake Chad. Nigeria also ratified the African Convention on Nature and Natural Resources, which seeks to ensure the conservation, rational utilization, and development of the soil, water, flora, and fauna resources to the best interests of the people.

By the mid-1980s, both the Nigerian people and the government had become sufficiently alarmed by the ravages of drought and desertification, forest degradation, bush burning, and gully erosion that there was virtual total agreement on the need to take positive steps to ameliorate the environmental impact of these natural and man-made disasters. Hence, General Ibrahim Babangida's administration can be credited with some of the most decisive and far-reaching legislation and action programs Nigeria had known for a long time. The immediate catalysts for action were, perhaps, the Koko Port toxic waste incident (1987) and the Bagauda Dam burst (1988). Perhaps the most important piece of environmental legislation by the military until then was the Land Use Decree (1978), which was incorporated into the constitution by military fiat (Udo 1990). As noted elsewhere (Areola 1987), the Land Use Act never was conceived as a conservation measure; it was, basically, a law designed to facilitate acquisition of land for public projects and to prescribe the maximum area of land that any individual can obtain both in the rural and in the urban areas (Nwaka 1979; Uchendu 1979).

The yearnings of Nigerian environmentalists to have a national environmental policy was fulfilled partially in 1988 with the promulgation of the Federal Environmental Protection Agency (FEPA) Decree. As indicated earlier, the Koko Port toxic waste incident pushed the government to take action on this piece of legislation, which had been in the making since the Shagari administration (1979–83). The people of the Niger Delta had long agitated for positive action against ecosystem degradation by oil pollution and oil exploration activities. The Oil in Navigable Waters Decree number 34 of 1968 was ineffectual because General Gowon's military government did not want to do anything that might seriously constrain the activities of this vital sector of the economy. The people were mollified somewhat by the designation of the delta as a special development area for purposes of accelerated economic and physical development.

The FEPA decree reflects the circumstances of its resuscitation: that is, the toxic waste dump and its aftermath. The terms of reference of the agency pertain mainly to the environmental impact of the exploitation of nonrenewable resources, particularly crude oil and other minerals as well as of industrial, agricultural, infrastructural, and other development activities. There is great emphasis on pollution prevention or abatement and the specification of quality standards in resource development and utilization (see table 9.5). This probably accounts for the preoccupation of FEPA with oil pollution, water quality, water pollution, and industrial pollution since it began operating in 1988. Two pieces of legislation most recently introduced attest to this: the National Environmental Protection (Effluent Limitation) Regulations (1991) and the National Environmental Protection (Pollution Abatement in Industries and Facilities Generating Wastes) Regulations (1991). They are additional regulations to the Harmful Wastes (Special) Criminal Provisions (etc.) Decree (1988), passed in the wake of the Koko Waste dump incident. FEPA's core staff also consists mainly of environmental chemists and biologists.

The National Policy on the Environment was published in 1989. It reflects the viewpoints of forestry. Its major concern is to focus on the antiforest activities in the country, including cultivation, commercial timber felling, fuelwood exploitation, accidental forest fires, and burning related to farming and game hunting. The policy puts forward strategies for achieving a balance between the need for development and the need to sustain the productivity of the natural vegetation, protect the wildlife, maintain genetic biodiversity, and avoid soil and forest degradation.

A major goal of the National Policy on the Environment is to lend support to the National Conservation Strategy for Nigeria, which is itself patterned after the World Conservation Strategy formulated in 1980 by the International Union for the Conservation of Nature and Natural Resources (IUCN). Bell (1987) has criticized the premise upon which the World Conservation Strategy is based; he questioned the Western view that the environmental problems of Africa are primarily the result of human population increase and that such problems can be solved by constraints to resource utilization, as indicated in a conservationist program such as that of IUCN. Nigerian conservationists, especially the wildlife and national park management experts who were instrumental in establishing the Natural Resources Conservation Council (NARESCON), are laboring to live down this kind of image that portrays conservationists as being against economic growth.

One of NARESCON's functions is to formulate and implement a national policy for renewable natural resources in Nigeria. Thus, it has developed a Natural Resources Conservation Action Plan for Nigeria (Ajayi 1991), based on a new strategy that seeks to (1) target local communities as the focal points for implementing conservation programs; and (2) promote the creation of employment and income-generating activities as essential components of natural resource conservation programs. In order to change the negative perception of conservation both by government planners and by the rural land users, NARESCON realizes the need to reorient conservation ethics toward production of goods and the creation of employment and income-generating activities coupled with conservation of the basic resources on which such production systems and activities are based. It recognizes the need to involve local governments, local communities, and sociocultural organizations, as well as rural development agencies, in the formulation, planning, and implementation of conservation programs.

State edicts and local government by-laws are, invariably, derived from federal laws. But, in general, they usually are tidier and more focused than the federal legislation because they address specific issues or problems of local significance. Furthermore, penalties stipulated against contravening these local laws generally are more adequate and appropriate than those in the federal legislation. However, perhaps more so than federal laws, the edicts and by-laws are negative in their approach to conservation; most are "prohibition" laws. They also often address the issue of conservation from the perspective of nuisance abatement. However, the issues covered are fundamental to the growth of the conservation culture; they include burning, quarrying, fishing, logging, tree planting, erosion prevention, land and water resources conservation, livestock development, animal pests and diseases control, water supply, solid wastes, and environmental sanitation.

Conclusion

Based on the foregoing discussion, there can be no doubt that there is a ferment of activity in Nigeria in the area of environmental management. The immediate challenge is to provide a proper focus and a sense of direction to environmental policy and action programs. Efforts in these directions may be attributed largely to the two major government-established environmental institutions, FEPA and NARESCON, and the nongovernmental organizations and international agencies.

However, much of the environment-related activity has been at the national level, involving efforts to get the federal government to adopt policies and to pass legislation favorable to the environment and also to support resource conservation and habitat protection projects (Chokor 1992). Action at the regional (state) and local levels has been limited by a weak policy and institutional framework aggravated by inadequate constitutional provisions to accord the state and local governments their rightful roles and powers in environmental management.

In order to rectify this situation and move environmental action programs to the grassroots level, new ideas and concepts are being introduced, including the concepts of 'sustainable development' (World Bank 1990; Aina and Salau 1992) and 'integrated natural resources conservation' with local community participation (Ajayi 1993). But there is the big task of operationalizing these ideas and translating them into concrete action on the ground. Experience in other parts of Africa suggests that these are complex issues, difficult to put into operation. This may be illustrated with the example of community-based, integrated natural resources conservation, which is similar to the concept of 'conservation-with-development' (CWD), a way to maintain biological diversity by promoting development and involvement of local people. According to Stocking and Perkin (1992:347), the East Usambara Agricultural Development and Conservation Project in Tanzania demonstrates an essential point: CWD "is difficult to transfer from paper to reality. It is complicated, it requires a large number of skills, it cannot be under-funded and cannot afford to have too many component failures." They also point out that development activities are not always compatible with conservation objectives, even when they are designed by the same CWD team.

What this means, in essence, is that Nigeria still needs to devote more time and attention to thinking through and designing its environment action programs. There is need for more of the kind of learning process now going on in the Hadejia-Nguru Wetlands Project in the northeast Sahel zone where the local land users, farmers, fishermen, and pastoralists are being introduced to simple wetlands management and production systems (HNWCP 1991; Jimoh 1989, 1992).

The issue of funding of conservation-conscious programs is becoming important in discussions on environment and development (Ojo 1992). This is because inadequate funding now constitutes a major constraint to environmental management in Nigeria. The government is virtually the sole financier of conservation projects, and unfavorable fluctuations in budgetary allocations and declines in government revenues make the prospects for environment action programs rather dim (Olomola 1992). Furthermore, the private sector as a whole is investing little in the management and preservation of the environment, which is the resource base for most enterprises. This is due in part to lapses in policy on the economics of resource utilization and conservation. According to Chokor and Obadan (1992), not much has been done, for example, to establish the value of natural scenery and its tourism potential by introducing effective and correct pricing that takes into account the environmental impacts of resource use and the direct and indirect values of the resources to present and future generations. There are no specific charges on damages to natural ecosystems commensurate with the degree of degradation that is caused. There are no standard and established techniques for valuing the cost of environmental damage, nor is there an effective system of national resource accounting (Adamu 1992).

Thus, in conclusion, there are still many unresolved issues and hazy ideas on the environment and development in Nigeria. But as these issues and ideas are discussed and articulated, the country as a whole should benefit. The politics of resource allocation will be elevated above mere interethnic squabbling over sharing the spoils of nature. The rise of politically conscious pressure groups is a sure sign that resource conservation and environmental problems will remain veritable political issues in Nigeria in the Third Republic (Chokor 1992).

References

Adams, W. M. 1987. "Approaches to Water Resource Development, Sokoto valley, Nigeria: The Problem of Sustainability." In *Conservation in Africa: People, Policies and Practice*, ed. D. Anderson and R. Grove, ch. 15, 307–25. Cambridge: Cambridge University Press.

Adamu, S. O. 1992. "Towards a Natural Resource Accounting for Nigeria." In *Proceedings on Mobilizing Finance for Natural Resources Conservation in Nigeria*, ed. J. A. T. Ojo, ch. 3, 27–39. Abuja: National Resources Conservation Council.

Adebagbo, C. A. 1992. "A Critical Appraisal of Taungya Farming Practices in Plantation Establishment in the Sapoba Moist Tropical Rainforest Site of Nigeria." Paper presented at the 21st Annual Conference of the Forestry Association of Nigeria, Uyo, Akwa-Ibom State, 7–12 April.

Adeyoju, S. K. 1975. *Forestry and the Nigerian Economy.* Ibadan: Ibadan University Press.

Adeyoju, S. K., and E. E. Enabor. 1973. *A Survey of the Drought Affected Areas of Northern Nigeria.* Ibadan: Federal Department of Forestry.

Afolayan, T. A. 1987. *Man's Inhumanity to Nature: The Overexploitation of Wildlife Resources.* Akure, Nigeria: Inaugural lecture series no. 3, Federal University of Technology.

———. 1992. "Proposals for the Management of Animal Populations and Vegetation of Kainji Lake National Park." In *Kainji Lake Research Institute: Review of Master Plan for Kainji Lake National Park.* Ibadan: Tuna Consultants Ltd.

———. 1993. "Integrated Natural Resources Conservation Based on Local Community Participation: A Case Study of the Indigenous Hunters Association in Ore and Odigbo Local Government Areas of Ondo State." In *Indigenous Natural Resources Conservation with Local Community Participation*, ed. S. S. Ajayi, ch. 2. Abuja: NARESCON.

Agbaje, A., K. Taiwo, K. Agbaje, and T. Akin Aina. 1992. "The Environment and Institutional Framework." In *The Challenge of Sustainable Development in Nigeria*, ed. T. A. Aina and A. T. Salau, ch. 5, 119–49. An NGO report prepared for the United Nations Conference on Environment and Development, Rio de Janeiro, Brazil, 1–12 June 1992. Ibadan: NEST.

Aina, T. A., and A. T. Salau, eds. 1992. *The Challenge of Sustainable Development in Nigeria.* An NGO report prepared for the United Nations Conference on Environment and Development, Rio de Janeiro, Brazil, 1–12 June 1992. Ibadan: NEST.

Ajayi, S. S. 1979. "Wildlife and the Nigerian Forest Ecosystem: State of Knowledge." In *The Nigerian Rainforest Ecosystem*, ed. D. U. U. Okali, ch. 6, 55–64. Ibadan: Man and the Biosphere Programme.

———. ed. 1991. *Natural Resources Conservation Action Plan Final Report*, vol. 1. Abuja: Natural Resources Conservation Council, the Presidency.

———. ed. 1993. *Indigenous Natural Resource Conservation with Local Community Participation.* Abuja: Natural Resources Conservation Council, the Presidency.

Anambra State Task Force on Soil Erosion Control. 1988. *Guide on Soil Erosion Control*, vol. 1.

Areola, O. 1987. "The Political Reality of Conservation in Nigeria." In *Conservation in Africa: People, Policies and Practice*, ed. D. Anderson and R. Grove, ch. 13, 277–92. Cambridge: Cambridge University Press.

———. 1988. "Systematic Soil Survey and Mapping in Nigeria: Contribution of Ad Hoc Projects." *Nigerian Geographical Journal* 31:115–35.

———. 1990. *The Good Earth.* An inaugural lecture. Idaban: University of Ibadan.

———. 1991. *Ecology of Natural Resources in Nigeria.* Aldershot: Avebury Studies in Green Research.

Bell, R. H. V. 1987. "Conservation with a Human Face: Conflict and Reconciliation in African Land Use Planning." In *Conservation in Africa: People, Policies and Practice*, ed. D. Anderson and R. Grove, ch. 4, 79–101. Cambridge: Cambridge University Press.

Bello-Imam, I. B. 1985. *Institutional Framework for Environmental Management in Nigeria.* Ibadan: Nigerian Institute of Social and Economic Research (NISER).

Charter, J. R. 1970. "The Economic Value of Wildlife in Nigeria." Paper presented at the first Conference of the Forestry Association of Nigeria, Ibadan.

Chokor, B. A. 1992. "Environmental Pressure Groups and Habitat Protection in the Developing World: The Case of Nigeria." *The Environmentalist* 12:169–80.

Chokor, B. A., and M. I. Obadan. 1992. "Environment and Economics in Nigeria: Toward a More Effective Resources Pricing and Conservation." In *Proceedings on Mobilizing Finance for Natural Resources Conservation in Nigeria*, ed. J. A. T. Ojo, ch. 5, 47–62. Abuja: National Resources Conservation Council (NARESCON).

Chouri, N. 1993. "Political Economy of the Global Environment." *International Political Science Review* 14(1):103–16.

Cline-Cole, R. A. 1991. "Sustainable Development and the Fuelwood Problem in the Sudan-Sahel Belt." In *Sustainable Development in Nigeria's Dry Belt: Problems and Prospects*, ed. K. O. Ologe, ch. 5, 27–35. Ibadan: NEST.

Daily Times of Nigeria. 1992. Forum: Re "Oil, the State and Insensitivity," 15 June, 9.

Directorate of Food, Roads and Rural Infrastructures. 1987. *Community Structures of Local Government Areas in Nigeria.* Lagos: Office of the President, Dodan Barracks.

Dudley, B. 1982. *An Introduction to Nigerian Government and Politics.* Bloomington: Indiana University Press.

Ekeh, P. P. 1989. "Nigeria's Emergent Political Culture." In *Nigeria Since Independence: The First 25 Years*, vol. 5: Politics and Constitutions, ed. P. P. Ekeh, P. Dele-Cole, and G. O. Olusanya, ch. 1, 1–9. Ibadan: Heinemann Educational Books (Nigeria) Ltd.

Enabor, E. E. 1977. "The Role of Forestry in the Amelioration of Drought in Nigeria." *Nigerian Geographical Journal* 20:153–64.

———. 1992. *Deforestation and Desertification: The Challenge of National Survival.* An inaugural lecture. Ibadan: University of Ibadan.

Eze, Emeka. 1993. "News Spot: The Facts and Fictions of the Ogoni/ Andoni Feud." *Nigerian Tribune*, 26 October, 8.

Fair, D. 1992. "Africa's Rainforests—Retreat and Hold." *Africa Insight* 22(1):23–28.

Federal Constitution of Nigeria. 1989. Lagos, Nigeria: Federal Government Printing Press.

Federal Environmental Protection Agency. 1992. *Transition to Sustainable Development in Nigeria.* Lagos: FEPA.

Gwandu, A. A. 1991. "The Menace of Desertification in Sokoto State." In *Sustainable Development in Nigeria's Dry Belt: Problems and Prospects*, ed. K. O. Ologe, ch. 4, 19–25. Ibadan: NEST.

HNWCP. 1991. *Hadejia-Nguru Wetlands Conservation Project: The First Three Years, 1987–90.* Nguru, Nigeria: HNWCP.

Ikporukpo, C. O. 1986. "Sabotage and the Problem of Oil Spill Management in Nigeria." *AMBIO—A Journal of the Human Environment* 15(5):306–10.

Jimoh, M. A. 1989. *Fuelwood-Fishery Activities in the Hadejia-Nguru Wetlands.* Nguru, Nigeria: HNWCP.

———. 1992. *Livestock Grazing and Its Production Value in the Hadejia-Nguru Floodplain.* Nguru, Nigeria: Hadejia-Nguru Wetlands Conservation Project (HNWCP).

Jinadu, L. A. 1989. "Theoretical Issues in Nigerian Constitutions." In *Nigeria Since Independence: The First 25 Years*, vol. 5: *Politics and Constitutions*, ed. P. P. Ekeh, P. Dele-Cole, and G. O. Olusanya, ch. 2, 13–37. Ibadan: Heinemann Educational Books (Nigeria) Ltd.

Lakemfa, Owei. 1993. "Vanguard Forum: Ijaws: What They Demand." *The Vanguard*, 25 October, 12–13.

Longworth, L. D. 1988. "Soil Conservation Service of NSW—A History." *Journal of Soil Conservation, New South Wales* 44(1):4–9.

Maishanu, S. M., B. G. Danshehu, and A. S. Sambo. 1990. "Saving Fuelwood with Improved Woodburning Stoves." In *Energy and the Environment*, ed. A. A. M. Sayigh, 1923-27. Elmsford, N.Y.: Pergamon Press.

Mathes, H. 1990. *Report on the Fishery-Related Aspects of the Hadejia-Nguru Wetlands Conservation Project.* Gland, Switzerland: IUCN—The World Conservation Union.

Mbanyiman, E. S. 1990. *Draft Management Plan for Dagona Water-Fowl Sanctuary, Borno State, Nigeria*. Nguru, Nigeria: The Royal Society for the Protection of Birds, UK/Hadejia-Nguru Wetlands Conservation Project.

Neuman, R. P. 1992. "Political Ecology of Wildlife Conservation in the Mt. Meru Area of Northeast Tanzania." *Land Degradation and Rehabilitation* 3(2):85–98.

Nigerian Environment Study/Action Team. 1991. *Nigeria's Threatened Environment: A National Profile*. Ibadan: NEST.

Nwaka, G. I. 1979. "The Nigerian Land Use Decree: Antecedents and Prospects." *Third World Review* 1:193–204.

Obadan, M. O., B. A. Chokor, and A. T. Salau. 1992. "Environment and Economics." In *The Challenge of Sustainable Development in Nigeria*, ed. T. A. Aina and A. T. Salau, ch. 3, 61–92. An NGO report prepared for the United Nations Conference on Environment and Development, Rio de Janeiro, Brazil, 1–12 June. Ibadan: NEST.

Ojo, J. A. T. 1992. *Proceedings on Mobilizing Finance for Natural Resources Conservation in Nigeria*. Abuja: Natural Resources Conservation Council (NARESCON), the Presidency.

Okali, D. U. U., A. E. Akachuku, I. I. Ero, and E. E. Osuji. 1992. "Environmental Education and Public Awareness." In *The Challenge of Sustainable Development in Nigeria*, ed. T. A. Aina and A. T. Salau, ch. 4, 93–118. An NGO report prepared for the United Nations Conference on Environment and Development, Rio de Janeiro, Brazil, 1–12 June. Ibadan: NEST.

Okediran, A. Y. 1991. "Legal Implications of the Action Plans on Natural Resources Conservation." In *Natural Resources Conservation Action Plan Final Report*, vol. 1, ed. S. S. Ajayi, ch. 6, 118–99. Abuja: Natural Resources Conservation Council, the Presidency.

Olofin, E. A. 1990. "Some Effects of the Tiga Dam on the Environment Downstream in the Kano River Basin." Ph.D. Thesis, Department of Geography, Ahmadu Bello University, Zaria.

———. 1992. *The Gains and Pains of Putting a Waterlock on the Face of the Drylands of Nigeria*. An inaugural lecture. Kano: Bayero University.

Ologe, K. O., R. R. Bature, S. Nkom, and D. O. Ogbonna. 1992. "Population and the Environment in Nigeria." In *The Challenge of Sustainable Development in Nigeria*, ed. T. A. Aina and A. T. Salau, ch. 2, 25–60. An NGO report prepared for the United Nations Conference on Environment and Development, Rio de Janeiro, Brazil, 1–12 June. Ibadan: NEST.

Olomola, A. 1992. "Financial Support Policies for the Conservation of Renewable Natural Resources in Nigeria." In *Proceedings on Mobilizing Finance for Natural*

Resources Conservation in Nigeria, ed. J. A. T. Ojo, ch. 10, 109–18. Abuja: National Resources Conservation Council.

Onochie, C. F. A. 1979. "The Nigerian Rainforest Ecosystem: An Overview." In *The Nigerian Rainforest Ecosystem*, ed. D. U. U. Okali, ch. 1, 1–13. Ibadan: Man and the Biosphere Programme.

Pearce, D., A. Markandya, and E. B. Barbier. 1989. *Blueprint for a Green Economy: A Report for the UK Department of the Environment*. London: Earthscan.

Rees, W. E. 1990. "Sustainable Development as Capitalism with a Green Face—A Review Article." *Town Planning Review* 61(1):91–94.

Sambo, A. S. 1991. *Documentation of Solar Energy Systems Developed and Ready for Mass Production*. Sokoto Nigeria: Sokoto Energy Research Centre, Usmanu Dan Fodiyo University.

Sands, P. 1992. "The Role of Environmental NGOs in International Environmental Law." *Development: Journal of the Society for International Development* 1992(2):29–32.

Saro-Wiwa, Ken. 1989. *On a Darkling Plain: An Account of the Nigerian Civil War*. Epsom, Nigeria: Saros Publishers.

Stanley, W. R. 1990. "Socioeconomic Impact of Oil in Nigeria." *GeoJournal* 22 (1): 67–79.

Stocking, M., and S. Perkin. 1992. "Conservation-with-Development: An Application of the Concept in the Usambara Mountains, Tanzania." *Transactions of the Institute of British Geographers (New Series)* 17(3):337–49.

Suliman, M. 1991. "Alternative Development Path for Africa." In *Alternative Development Strategies for Africa*, vol. 2: *Environment. Women*, ed. Suliman Mohammed, ch. 1, 1–10. London: Institute for African Alternatives (IFAA).

Thomas, D. H. L., and A. Kaigama. 1992. *Margadu Tree Nursery and Agroforestry Project. Progress Report*. Nguru, Nigeria: HNWCP.

Uchendu, V. C. 1979. "State, Law and Society in Nigeria—A Critical Assessment of Land Use Decree 1978." *Journal of African Studies* 6:62–74.

Udo, R. K. 1990. *Land Use Policy and Land Ownership in Nigeria*. Lagos: Ebieakwa Ventures Ltd.

Udo, R. K., O. Areola, J. O. Ayoade, and A. A. Afolayan. 1991. "Regional Studies of Transformation: Nigeria." In *The Earth as Transformed by Human Action: Global and Regional Changes in the Biosphere Over the Past 300 Years*, ed. B. L. Turner II, et al., ch. 36, 589–603. Cambridge: Cambridge University Press, with Clark University.

Wallace, T. 1979. *Rural Development Through Irrigation: Studies in a Town on the Kano River Project*. Report no. 3. Zaria: Ahmadu Bello University, Centre for Social and Economic Research.

————. 1980. "Agricultural Projects and Land in Northern Nigeria." *Review of African Political Economy* 17:59–70.

World Bank. 1990. *Towards the Development of an Environmental Action Plan for Nigeria*. Washington, D.C.: World Bank.

10

ENVIRONMENTAL POLICY IN THE CZECH REPUBLIC AND SLOVAKIA

CATHERINE ALBRECHT

Introduction

The establishment of a democratic government in Czechoslovakia in 1990, followed in 1993 by the creation of two independent states, Slovakia and the Czech Republic (see maps 10.1 and 10.2), has had an enormous impact on environmental policy in the two countries. Access to information about environmental problems has awakened public concern about environmental issues. Voters now have the opportunity to express their policy preferences openly, and citizens can organize informal environmental groups more freely than in the past. Appropriate environmental policies are being framed to correspond to the emerging market economy in the Czech Republic and Slovakia. And the two states have established closer relationships with neighboring countries, with which they share many environmental concerns.

All this change makes the policy-making process more complex. The roles of governmental and nongovernmental organizations, political parties, and individuals in addressing environmental concerns are still in flux. The two countries each face distinct environmental problems and are taking different approaches to economic reform. Nonetheless, an examination of some of the most pressing environmental problems facing Slovakia and the Czech Republic may help discern the political forces active in making and implementing environmental policy.

The Scope of Pollution

The complex ideological, economic, and political reasons for severe environmental degradation in Eastern Europe and the former Soviet Union have been studied extensively (Debardeleben 1985; Jancar 1987; Kramer 1983;

MAP 10.1

Topography of the Czech Republic

Source: Central Intelligence Agency, 1994.

Ziegler 1987). Ideologically, Marxism argues that the natural world has no economic value until it is transformed by labor. Therefore, raw materials inputs into production were undervalued, and little account was taken of the costs of pollution until the effects on human health were made apparent by medical professionals and demographers.

Economically, large state-run industrial enterprises were inefficient producers, since economic planning emphasized the quantity of output, rather

MAP 10.2

Topography of Slovakia

Source: Central Intelligence Agency, 1994.

than its quality. State subsidies allowed enterprises to operate unprofitably, while the debts of East European governments made it difficult for them to invest in technology that might have reduced energy consumption or the emissions of their enterprises. Since the Soviet Union supplied oil and gas to its East European neighbors at prices significantly lower than those on the world market, there was little incentive before the 1980s to conserve energy. Agriculture was affected in a similar fashion, as large state and cooperative farms were run inefficiently and were encouraged to increase production by means that have resulted in extensive soil erosion and contamination.

The responsibility for monitoring environmental quality and overseeing the implementation of laws protecting the environment was widely dispersed before 1989. Environmental experts were attached to the various economic ministries and were unable to act independently or to influence economic decision making. Scientific bodies within the Academy of Sciences, such as the Geographical Institute and the Hydrometric Institute, collected data that were not always comparable and were rarely publicized. In addition, enterprises were expected to monitor their own emissions. Although laws regarding emission levels were among the strictest in Europe, they were rarely enforced, and the fines for exceeding the statutory limits were too low to motivate a change in behavior. Their lack of autonomy discredited the government's environmental agencies, while nonchalant enforcement undermined public respect for environmental laws.

Lack of information and restrictions on unofficial organizations in the former Czechoslovakia limited public awareness of the extent or intensity of pollution, which was confined mostly to anecdotes about the most obvious local problems. The unofficial publication in 1983 by the human rights organization Charter 77 of an environmental study undertaken by the Czechoslovak Academy of Sciences sparked growing public concern about the environment (Charter 77, 1983).

Air Pollution

The primary source of air pollution in the Czech Republic and Slovakia is sulfur dioxide. Emissions of sulfur dioxide exceeded 2.4 million metric tons in 1990; the former Czechoslovakia was the fifth largest polluter (in terms of total quantity of sulfur dioxide emissions) in Europe in 1990. In per capita terms, Czechoslovakia's sulfur dioxide emissions were second only to the former German Democratic Republic (Kabala 1991a; Moldan and Schnoor 1992) (table 10.1).

The source of much of the country's sulfur dioxide pollution is brown coal. Sulfur dioxide pollution is concentrated in the most heavily industrialized regions of northwest Bohemia and northern Moravia, part of the "dirty triangle" that includes southern Poland and the former German Democratic Republic. The city of Prague also suffers from heavy air pollution, a result not only of industrial emissions but also of central heating plants, home heating, and automobile exhaust. In all three regions, temperature inversions in the winter months have occasionally caused sulfur dioxide concentrations to exceed 1,000 mg per cubic meter.

Brown coal mined in the Czech Republic has an ash content of 40 percent, and the total suspended particulates in the atmosphere are therefore particularly high (Moldan and Schnoor 1992; Schnoor 1992). Power plants and other factories lack scrubbers or flue gas desulfurization equipment. Brown

TABLE 10.1

Total Emission into the Atmosphere (1,000 metric tons/year)

Year	Particulates	SO$_2$	NOx	CO	CxHy
Czech Republic					
1985	1014	2161	795	899	136
1986	988	2171	850	740	139
1987	950	2163	816	738	139
1988	840	2065	857	737	138
1989	673	1997	919	951	253
1990	631	1875	741	887	225
Slovakia					
1985	357	621	196	339	60
1986	364	611	195	344	62
1987	348	607	192	345	62
1988	304	605	196	353	63
1989	317	565	202	543	66
1990	308	547	246	403	78

Source: Federàlnì vỳbor pro životnì prostředì, *Zpràva o stavu životnìho prostředì v ČSFR*. Prague: Vesmìr, 1991, 9.

coal also contains traces of lead, cadmium, mercury, zinc, and arsenate that, along with emissions from the chemical industry in northwest Bohemia, contribute to contamination of the soil (Schnoor 1992).

Another source of air pollution in the territory of the former Czechoslovakia is automobile exhaust (Boehmer-Christiansen 1990). Obsolete auto emissions technology and the age and mechanical condition of automobiles manufactured in Eastern Europe add to their polluting impact. The driving habits of Czechs and Slovaks are changing because the price of gasoline has reached world market levels. But many Czechs and Slovaks are taking advantage of the market economy to purchase new automobiles from Western Europe. Czechs and Slovaks are driving more, but the newer cars may pollute less.

Water Pollution

Both surface and groundwater are heavily polluted. It is estimated that one-half of all drinking water in the Czech Republic is substandard, and 17 percent of river water is unsuited for municipal water supplies. Only 40 percent of waste water and sewage is treated satisfactorily before being discharged (Kabala 1991a). Seventy percent of the rivers in the Czech Republic and

Slovakia are heavily polluted (World Bank 1992). More than four hundred contaminants have been identified in the Vltava River alone, ranging from heavy metals to nitrates to human waste. The main sources of water pollution are the runoffs of agricultural chemicals, industrial effluents, and municipal sewage.

Less information is available about groundwater pollution, simply because the problem has not been studied thoroughly. Chemical factories such as the Slovnaft oil refinery near Bratislava were notorious polluters of groundwater (Stansky 1988). Contaminants from hazardous waste dumps that are only now being discovered are likely to have leached into groundwater supplies.

Agriculture and Forestry

Food supplies are contaminated from the residue of heavy metals such as lead, arsenic, polychlorine biphenyls (PCBs), and cadmium (Schnoor 1992; Pohl 1988). The overuse of fertilizers, pesticides, and herbicides is also a culprit. Some foodstuffs produced in the Czech Republic (such as canned hams) are prohibited from the European market because they do not meet European Community standards.

Extensive cultivation has resulted in soil erosion and silting of streams, while canalization and irrigation have depleted the flow of fresh water in streams and rivers. Pollutants thus have become more concentrated in surface waters.

Acid rain stemming from automobile exhaust and sulphur-laden coal has decreased the average life span of forests to a mere twenty years, which will have a significant impact on the lumber industry in the future. Clear-cutting has contributed to soil erosion, while monoculture has weakened the ability of forests to withstand environmental pressures and disease.

Energy Consumption

Inefficient industry and low energy costs for household consumers led to overconsumption of energy in the 1970s and 1980s. Czechoslovakia had one of the highest per capita energy uses in Europe. Brown coal supplied 40 percent of Czechoslovakia's total energy needs in 1990. In 1987, Czechoslovakia mined 100 million tons of brown coal, leaving 508 million tons of mining waste. Black coal provided another 20 percent of Czechoslovakia's energy needs, with oil and natural gas, hydroelectric power, and nuclear power supplying the remainder (Kabala 1991a).

Solid Waste

It is estimated that there are over 1,400 unregulated "wild dumps" in the Czech Republic (Kabala 1991b; Bretislav 1991). Hazardous waste dumps have been discovered on the former Soviet military bases. Disposal of nuclear waste from Czech and Slovak nuclear power plants is also an issue, since Russia is no longer accepting the waste that previously had been sent to the Soviet Union.

Illegal transboundary transport of hazardous waste from Germany has been discovered in Albania, Romania, and most recently in the Czech Republic itself. Paint dyes were dumped in northern Bohemia by a German firm in 1992 (RFE/RL, March 17, 1993). Although Germany has agreed to pay for the cost of returning the waste, such dumping reveals the danger of open borders and the vulnerability of East Central Europe to its economically stronger neighbor.

The volume of household trash also has increased. The consumer-oriented society developing in the Czech Republic and Slovakia has produced more extensive packaging. The one-crown deposit on glass bottles is no longer a strong incentive to return the bottles, and more beverages are being sold in aluminum cans and "drink packs," which are discarded after their contents are consumed.

Effects on Human Health

Air pollution has had significant effects on the environment and human health, particularly in the Czech Republic where 54 percent of forests show signs of deterioration (Moldan and Schnoor 1992). Acid rain also has caused deterioration of historic buildings and monuments, particularly in Prague. Life expectancy in the Czech Republic is three to five years below the European average (Federal Committee for the Environment 1991a). In the most polluted areas, northwest Bohemia and northern Moravia, life expectancies are even lower. The incidences of respiratory diseases, heart disease, infant mortality, and cancer are especially high in polluted regions. In the worst affected areas of north Bohemia, the government frequently issues air pollution alerts and children are sent to special health camps in the summer months. Czech women also have high concentrations of PCBs in their breast milk (Schnoor 1992).

Priorities

It will take fifteen to twenty years for the countries of East Central Europe to meet Western European environmental standards, and the cost of environmental cleanup for the Czech Republic and Slovakia has been estimated by the World Bank at $50 to $100 billion (World Bank 1992). The long-range objective is to reach a level of "sustainable development," a level at which both the economic and the environmental needs of the two countries can be met.

Given the range and intensity of environmental degradation in the Czech Republic and Slovakia, it is imperative for both countries to establish clear environmental priorities. The first concern is to reduce pollution in areas that have reached an environmental crisis (Alcamo 1992a). The second goal is to assess the scope of pollution and establish standards and a reasonable structure for the enforcement of environmental laws. The third priority is to reduce emissions across the board by making pollution expensive and requiring new enterprises to install equipment that will keep emissions low. Only later will the Czech Republic and Slovakia be able to tackle the expensive and long-term problem of cleaning up existing pollution (World Bank 1992).

Institutional Structure and Legislative Framework

Environmental protection in the Czech and Slovak Federal Republic developed on a parallel course with changes in the political climate. Just as the "velvet revolution" of November 1989 proclaimed a new, ethical approach to politics, so too were environmental issues placed initially in a moral context. The Czechoslovak Federal Committee for the Environment proclaimed in 1991 "a moral obligation to limit the negative impact of the disrupted environment on people's health," while the Federal Environmental Act listed the environmental rights of Czechoslovak citizens (Federal Committee for the Environment 1991b). In the intervening months, this idealistic vision has given way to a more limited, realistic approach to politics in general and to environmental policies in particular.

In 1990 the Czechoslovak Constitution was revamped to direct power away from the federal government and toward the Slovak and Czech Republic governments. Questions over the authority of the federal government and the governments of the two republics slowed the articulation of new environmental policies in the Czech and Slovak Federal Republic. The Federal Committee for the Environment, headed until its dissolution at the end of December 1992 by Josef Vavroušek, helped prepare federal laws and retained the power to cooperate with foreign countries in developing international environmental initiatives and negotiating foreign aid for the environment.

In addition to the Federal Committee for the Environment, each republic established a separate environmental office in 1990. The Czech Ministry for the Environment and the Slovak Commission for the Environment (which was elevated to a ministry upon independence) brought together technical experts and activists. The republic offices proposed specific laws for each republic that dealt mainly with the implementation of federal laws. They also had the practical responsibility to coordinate and enforce environmental laws and monitor the environment. They collected fines and established environmental funds to pay for the clean-up of existing pollution (Czech Republic 1991).

Since independence, the Slovak and Czech environmental ministries have absorbed the responsibilities of the former Federal Committee for the Environment. They are now charged with establishing the broad outlines of environmental policy, drafting all legislation, and negotiating with foreign governments and international aid organizations, in addition to the practical tasks assigned to them in 1990.

The responsibilities of local government officials and regional environmental offices in both republics are still being defined. Central governments thus far have been reluctant to give much authority to local governments (Vidlaková 1993). Following the lead of the European Community, responsibility for environmental policy initiatives and environmental monitoring may devolve to the "lowest level capable of handling it" (Howe 1991). In Slovakia, District Environmental Offices and Centers for Environmental Information have the authority to monitor pollution. In the Czech Republic, a separate Environmental Inspectorate with regional inspectors has been established under the Ministry of the Environment. District Environmental Offices gather data and prepare policy recommendations but do not monitor or enforce environmental legislation. The District Offices also maintain communication with town councils and environmental offices throughout the country (Czech Republic 1990; Stancíková 1992). It is not yet clear what role the courts will play in interpreting and enforcing environmental legislation.

The federal environmental laws passed before December 31, 1992, were accepted by the two republics upon independence. The federal laws set the policy framework and basic principles of environmental protection. The Czechoslovak government sought advice from international experts, including the United States Agency for International Development's Environmental Law Agency, independent legal counsel from the United States, and representatives of the European Community, in drafting its new federal laws. Such foreign experts advised the Czechoslovak government to draft laws that set realistic standards and used economic incentives to reduce pollution.

The Federal Environmental Act of 1992 (no. 17, 1992 Sb) established a general framework for environmental protection. Article 4 proclaimed the environmental rights of Czechoslovak citizens:

1. Everyone has the right to a favorable environment. . . .
2. Everyone has the right to timely and complete information on the state of the environment and of natural resources. . . .

. . . .

4. Everyone has the right to take part in care of the environment. . . . (Federal Committee for the Environment 1991c)

The Environmental Act also detailed citizens' environmental duties to avoid harming the environment, to remedy damages, to inform public authorities of damage, and to intervene, if possible, to prevent environmental destruction. And, finally, the act also outlined the basic obligations of those whose "activity pollutes or damages the environment" to monitor pollution, select the "best available technologies," renew and conserve natural resources, and assess the environmental impact of their activities (Federal Committee for the Environment 1991c). The Environmental Act thus followed the United States model by establishing "the role of the public in environmental policy making" (Kabala 1991a). The Federal Act on the Environment was accompanied by republic acts to implement its provisions: the Slovak Act on the Administration for the Environment (no. 595, 1990 Sb.), the Act on the State Environmental Fund of the Slovak Republic (no. 128, 1991 Sb.), and the Act on the State Environmental Fund of the Czech Republic (no. 388, 1991 Sb.).

Other federal acts were passed in 1991 to regulate air and water pollution and waste management. These laws are based on European Community standards (Hladík 1991). The air pollution law identifies the obligations of polluters to use "the best available technologies with respect to the costs" and to provide the government and public with information about the extent of their pollution. Air pollution limits are set by the government and will be increased step by step. The maximum fine for polluters who exceed the limits was set initially at 10 million Czechoslovak crowns (Czech and Slovak Federal Republic 1991).

In both the Czech Republic and Slovakia, the new laws are intended to provide a flexible, market-oriented context for environmental protection. The legislation allows emissions to be reduced over time and demands that polluters pay the costs of environmental damage by purchasing appropriate technology and assessing and monitoring the environmental impact of their activities. The laws have been criticized by environmental groups as weak and vague, but they have been accepted by economists more concerned with privatization and fostering investment in new technology. Institutionally, the environmental ministries of the Czech Republic and Slovakia are relatively weak. They are staffed for the most part by technocrats who do not have the public stature to press for further environmental reforms. In addition, the environmental ministries have not yet made the transition from bodies that implemented federal laws to ministries that must set overarching policy.

Political Support for Environmental Reform

The two main sources of pressure for further environmental reform are informal environmental groups within the Czech Republic and Slovakia on the one hand and the international community on the other. On rare occasions local groups and international bodies may work together to effect change in environmental policy. Public opinion is brought to bear on environmental policy making only when local issues become pressing. Because the role of local governments in environmental policy making is still undefined, nongovernmental organizations are the main fora for expressing local concerns.

Informal Groups

Informal environmental organizations in East Central Europe have been studied extensively, not just for insights into environmental issues, but also because they acted as surrogates for real political movements. Influenced by green movements in Poland, Hungary, and Germany, Slovaks and Czechs began to organize independent environmental groups in the 1980s. Informal environmental clubs such as the Defenders of Nature, Slovak Union for the Protection of the Environment and Landscape, Brontosaurus, Green Circle, Ecoforum, Children of the Earth, Rainbow, and others generally focused on local concerns. They organized small local demonstrations even before 1989 to draw attention to the severity of local problems. To illustrate the "power of the powerless," environmental groups emphasized the moral and human rights issues involved in environmental degradation. They highlighted the social dislocation that accompanied pollution and argued that suicide, drug abuse, and depression could be attributed to the effects of environmental degradation (Charter 77 1984; RFE/RL, August 9, 1983). These claims were an indirect attack on the political restrictions of communism, and it is not surprising that environmental groups are credited with spearheading the "velvet revolution" of November 1989 in Czechoslovakia.

Even today, activists argue that environmental degradation threatens to be politically destabilizing, an assertion that underlines the severity of pollution in heavily industrialized areas. The Federal Committee for the Environment argued in 1991 that the deterioration of human health as a result of pollution "has disrupted the social structure of the affected areas and has estranged the individual from this society which is unable to provide the basic and necessary conditions for human existence. In some places . . . the tension is about to explode" (1991b). The latter observation was confirmed in February 1993 during a temperature inversion in northern Bohemia that created an atmospheric catastrophe: sulfur dioxide levels reached 1,200 micrograms per cubic meter and nitrogen oxide was recorded in excess of 1,050 micrograms per cubic meter. Citizens were warned to stay inside, schools were closed, and children and pregnant women were transported to healthier climates outside the affected region. Operation of power plants, the source of the pollution, was restricted, and power had to be imported from Germany and Slovakia. The political repercussions of this incident are profound, as the inhabitants of one of the affected communities, Chomutov, threatened to close the town with a general strike unless the government promised to install pollution control devices within the next two years.

Informal environmental organizations lost a great deal of their momentum after 1989. One of their goals, the publication of environmental data, was accomplished. Some of their proposals were incorporated into official environmental programs adopted in 1991 by the Czech, Slovak, and federal governments (Federal Committee for the Environment 1991b). Many activists were recruited after 1989 into environmental ministries or other governmental positions. Environmental groups also need to learn how to raise money to support their activities, seeking charitable contributions from within their countries and funding from international environmental organizations (Czajkowski 1993). The Regional Environmental Center in Budapest provides grants for environmental NGOs in East Central Europe. An additional hindrance on the activities of environmental NGOs is the fact that the public in both countries is more concerned today with the pressing issues of economic and political reform.

Public Opinion

The public's attention is focused now on entrepreneurial opportunities, the prospects for unemployment and inflation, the erosion of social services, and other consequences of economic reform. Although public opinion polls in 1990 indicated that environmental degradation was considered to be a pressing problem by most Czechoslovak citizens, such concern has eroded in the face of other political and economic issues. A Gallup poll conducted in 1992 showed that in Hungary and Poland less than 1 percent of the population thought that the environment should be their countries' first concern (Dunlap, Gallup, and Gallup 1992).

Local environmental initiatives are still important, however. A lingering distrust of central government means that many Slovak and Czech citizens are more willing to devote their energies to autonomous local organizations. Environmental experts hope that local environmental councils can identify the most pressing environmental problems, establish environmental priorities that appropriately reflect citizens' concerns, and propose solutions to them. Local councils can help build a consensus in favor of environmental measures. In addition, local groups have taken a leading role in organizing educational activities in an attempt to raise citizen awareness of environmental problems (Czech Republic 1991).

Since 1990 data assessing the environment both of the Czech Republic and of Slovakia have been widely publicized (Czech Republic 1991). It is expected that education and data will help Slovaks and Czechs make informed decisions about the environmental consequences of their behavior as voters, consumers, and producers. Data on environmental damage seem to show that pollution has decreased since 1990. This perhaps has lulled Czech and Slovak citizens into thinking that the problem can solve itself. In fact, it has been suggested that the "improvement" in the environment may be simply the result of new methods of collecting data, which make current data incompatible with those collected prior to 1989. In addition, some reduction in emissions is a result of the industrial recession, particularly in Slovakia. Western aid programs have provided new technology to gather environmental statistics and have encouraged the Slovak and Czech governments to collect more environmental data to begin to assess the risks of pollutants.

International Context

Because of the importance of foreign trade and investment, international relations play an important role in establishing environmental policies in Slovakia and the Czech Republic. The Czech Republic in particular is a net exporter of pollution. Although Czechoslovakia signed the Geneva Convention on Long-Range Transboundary Air Pollution in 1979, the republics will fail to meet their commitment to reduce sulfur dioxide emissions by 30 percent by 1995. If the Czech Republic and Slovakia wish to be accepted as equal partners in the European Community (EC), they must meet the European Community's environmental standards and establish a regulatory framework that is compatible with existing EC legislation.

Relations between the two republics and their more powerful European neighbors could be undermined if the republics fail to reduce their emissions. Countries like Germany and Austria that are most affected by Czech and Slovak pollution have been the most willing to offer aid, although much of this aid is directed toward problems that affect the foreign government, rather than problems that are deemed most important by the Czech and Slovak governments themselves (Budnikowski 1992). The desire to "rejoin Europe" in an environmental sense thus raises some questions of sovereignty as well.

Many international organizations have expressed an interest in helping Slovakia and the Czech Republic address their environmental problems. The EC has organized the Polish and Hungarian Assistance for the Reconstruction of Europe (PHARE), which has provided $34 million to the Czech Republic and Slovakia. PHARE aid is being used for research, training, data collection, and policy recommendations to address the hazardous waste problem, water quality, nuclear safety, and sulfur dioxide emissions. It also has supported groundwater testing in connection with the Gabčikovo Dam project (Kabala 1992a).

The World Bank has assessed the region's environmental problems and proposed action plans that it believes will be the most cost-effective in the short, medium, and long term (1992). The United States also has allocated aid for improvements in energy efficiency and environmental clean up. The United States Agency for International Development has established a center for environmental information in Budapest. The United States Environmental Protection Agency has provided technical training and helped develop an integrated information system (Stancíková 1992). And the National Aeronautics and Space Administration has provided satellite images of the Czech Republic and Slovakia. Both republics also have received environmental aid for particular projects from Austria, Belgium, Denmark, France, Germany, the Netherlands, and Switzerland (Czech Republic 1991). Thus, a great deal of aid is available, but the projects proposed by these international bodies need to be coordinated to be most effective.

Regional Cooperation

The problems of the "black triangle" can be solved only by a coordinated effort among Poland, Germany, and the Czech Republic. Long-standing disputes over the environment among the four countries may hinder their willingness to cooperate on environmental issues. Poland still demands compensation from the Czech government for a heating oil spill in the Oder River in 1984. Austria and the Czech Republic are trying to resolve the issue of the nuclear power plant at Temelín. And Hungary and Slovakia are engaged in an acrimonious dispute over the Gabčikovo-Nagymaros dam project. Nonetheless, the Western European countries have made it clear that they expect their neighbors in East Central Europe to cooperate to solve environmental problems, and some financial aid has been available for the Black Triangle, the Danube Basin, and other areas affected by pollution.

The Czech Republic

Since 1990 the main issue in the Czech Republic has been economic reform. In addition, the Czech Republic has sought to enhance its relations with Western Europe. Czech politics were mired for the first few years after 1990 in the process of "lustrace," or screening of political figures who had been officials in the Communist party or who had had connections with the secret police. The process of lustrace affected environmental policy because the investigations discredited some former dissidents (who had at one time been Communist party members) and environmental activists, including the respected scientist Bedřich Moldan, who was forced to resign after one year as the Czech Republic's first minister of the environment. Lustrace also diverted attention from more pressing issues and seemed to have the effect of reducing dissent within the Czech Parliament (Dvoráková 1993). Despite efforts of environmental groups in the Czech Republic, its new constitution does not ensure citizens' right to a clean environment.

Economic Reform

Economic reform is the most important context in which to examine environmental policy in the Czech Republic. Privatization of economic assets has raised questions of liability for past pollution. The introduction of market prices and the "polluter pays" principle mean that the costs of environmental cleanup will be passed on to consumers. A more consumer-oriented society will produce more waste. The Czech Republic has been particularly successful in wooing foreign investment, which also has consequences for environmental policy.

The structural changes that will accompany economic reform are expected to help reduce pollution as older, inefficient, or unprofitable plants are closed. Only those enterprises that attract private investors will remain in operation. However, there is an obvious political cost in suggesting that economic recession and unemployment will benefit the environment. Czech Prime Minister Václav Klaus has promoted rapid privatization to overcome quickly the hazards of transition to a market economy, but he also has been criticized for subordinating social concerns to his vision of a high-tech, Western-oriented economy. In Klaus' view, economic reform must precede any other substantial reforms, including environmental clean-up.

Privatization of large enterprises is being accomplished by two means: the voucher system and foreign investment. Private ownership will make it easier to collect fines for pollution (Hladík 1991). The reverse is true also, however: the threat of fines will undermine the willingness of investors to purchase notorious polluters. In order to overcome this aversion, the government of the Czech Republic has assumed liability for past pollution.

Czech citizens who have invested their vouchers in existing firms may be less interested in the short term in supporting expensive new technology, even though such technology will improve efficiency and enhance the value of their shares in the long term.

In the medium term, foreign investors are expected to import new technology, much of it produced in the West. Czech environmentalists have expressed apprehension that foreign investors may engage in "ecocolonization" and introduce obsolete technology, although the new laws do require the use of the "best available technology." Much of the international aid for the environment is being spent to pay for the technology and services of foreign firms. The United States Department of Commerce has sponsored several environmental trade and investment missions to East Central Europe to encourage American firms to invest in environmental projects and technology. International organizations have provided grants for pollution control equipment imported from the West. The German firm Gottfried Bischoff, for example, is installing scrubbers in the incinerator at Malešovice and in the Prunerov II power plant in the Czech Republic (FBIS-EEU, October 26, 1992).

The State Environmental Policy adopted by the Czech government in 1995 attempts to define the relationship between state regulation of the environment on the one hand and the responsibilities of private owners on the other. The original draft of the policy prepared by the Ministry of the Environment was rejected by the government, which sought greater protection of private ownership. In the final document, the state is defined as having

> a primary obligation to protect those components of the environment where ownership relations are difficult to define and/or those cases where external negative effects are produced which affect the public good. Therefore, State participation in the protection of the environment is essential where the components of the environment represent common goods which cannot be owned and/or where it is impossible to exclude the use of these goods . . . and where international commitments must be observed. (State Environmental Policy 1995)

The State Environmental Policy seeks to transfer costs from the public to the private sector by imposing fees that will be deposited in the State Environmental Fund and to establish limits and standards for pollution that can be realized, given the available technology.

The market economy also has brought some direct environmental hazards. For example, the increase in truck transport from Western Europe has put a great strain on the infrastructure of the Czech Republic, adding to air pollution. Open borders to Western Europe have contributed to the illegal transboundary transport of hazardous wastes.

Policy Initiatives

In addition to general laws on environmental protection, air pollution, water pollution, hazardous waste, and protected areas, the Czech Republic also has adopted some specific environmental policies. Czechoslovakia was the first country in Eastern Europe to introduce unleaded gasoline in 1990, and the Czech Republic will require catalytic converters on new automobiles by the end of 1994. In addition, the Czech Republic introduced in 1994 a special automobile permit that will charge more for drivers who wish to drive more than 5,000 km per year.

Waste management is another concern. In order to handle the increased volume of refuse, incinerators at Malešovice, Prunerov, Vysočany, and other sites are being expanded or completed. Since the existing incinerators are themselves polluters, new technology is needed to reduce their emissions. The Czech government has proposed using foreign technology to build incinerators for some of this hazardous waste (Kabala 1992a). Composting is not an option because of the presence of hazardous materials (Bretislav 1991). Neighborhood efforts to recycle glass and aluminum have yet to yield much response, even though recycling bins have been placed throughout Prague.

Another demand put forward by environmental groups is a ban on freon. In 1993, the Czech Parliament passed a law on the protection of the ozone layer. Environmental groups claim that the law is too vague and have called for a complete prohibition on freon by July 1, 1994, a prohibition that the Ministry of the Environment considers technically unfeasible.

Energy Policy

An important challenge for Czech environmental policy is to find new sources of clean, affordable energy. All the East Central European countries used energy excessively before 1989, with their per capita energy consumption 20 to 40 percent higher than in Western Europe (Kramer 1991; Cooper-Lybrand 1991; Foell 1992). Because of its polluting effect, Czech coal is no longer seen as a viable source of energy. Existing power plants are archaic and do not use pollution control devices. Centralized heating plants in urban areas, previously described as a benefit in East Central Europe, are now seen as a liability because the dilapidated systems are significant local polluters. In some areas, local protests have won a commitment from the government to convert coal-fired heating plants to gas in order to reduce pollution. Low prices of centralized heating and hot water and the absence of meters in most households have contributed to overconsumption of energy.

Oil and gas imports have become more expensive as the terms of trade with Russia have changed. In place of countertrade or trade balanced in convertible rubles, Russia is now demanding hard currency and world prices for its oil exports to East Central Europe. Old trade debts between Russia and the Czech Republic also are hindering the supply of oil. To overcome its reliance on Russian oil and gas, the Czech government advocates the construction of a pipeline from the Adriatic through Germany to East Central Europe. The proposal was blocked for several years by environmental groups in Bavaria, but recently has been approved. The Iraqi invasion of Kuwait in August 1990 and the subsequent embargo against Iraq dramatically increased the cost of imported oil to Czechoslovakia, which had long-standing contracts with Iraq for the delivery of oil.

Higher prices for fuel, the closing of unprofitable plants, and the opening of more efficient enterprises are expected to reduce energy consumption. The Czech government has sought alternative sources of energy, particularly an expansion of its capacity to generate nuclear power (Carter 1986; Polach 1968). Unlike their counterparts in Germany, Czech environmental activists generally had supported nuclear power in the 1980s as the only alternative to coal-fired plants or dependence on imported fuel. The accident at Chernobyl, however, made the hazards of Soviet-designed plants evident. Although radiation levels are recorded and the data now made public, some environmental groups have protested the reliance on nuclear power.

Temelín

Soviet-designed nuclear reactors provide one-fifth of the energy needs of the Czech Republic and Slovakia. The nuclear power plant at Temelín in south Bohemia is of particular concern both to local residents and to the Czech Republic's neighbor, Austria. Construction on the Temelín plant began in 1986. It was suspended in 1990, but in March 1993 the Czech government under the initiative of Prime Minister Klaus reaffirmed its intention to complete the nuclear plant at Temelín. The government sought foreign contracts to introduce the technology needed to make the plant safe (Kabala 1991a). In 1994, the United States Export-Import Bank approved a $35 million loan to enable Westinghouse to provide the technology.

The Temelín controversy has provided a forum for environmental groups and has attracted a great deal of public attention both in the Czech Republic and in Austria. A local group, the Association of South Bohemian Mothers, has organized protests, and sixty communities in South Bohemia have signed petitions protesting the completing of Temelín. The controversy has demonstrated the weakness of the Czech Minister of Environment, František Benda, who abstained from the cabinet vote that decided to proceed with construction in March 1993, and only recently issued a statement giving the conditions for the Environmental Ministry's approval of the project.

Environmental objections to completing the plant are several. First, environmental groups argue that even with Westinghouse's involvement, the technology to be introduced will not meet American or West European standards. Unlike the World Bank, which in any case refuses to finance nuclear power projects, the Export-Import Bank did not have to obtain an environmental impact statement before approving the loan. Second, environmentalists argue that the project does not represent an effective allocation of financial resources. They suggest that it would be more cost-effective to invest in scrubbers and desulfurization equipment for coal-fired plants in north Bohemia. Energy conservation measures also would be less expensive. Third, opponents contend that the government has not made adequate provisions to store nuclear waste. And, finally, environmentalists argue that Prime Minister Klaus intends to export some of the electricity produced by the Temelín plant to Western Europe (Respekt 1994). Greenpeace, Rainbow, and Children of the Earth have challenged the constitutionality of the decision to proceed with the construction of Temelín, arguing that citizens' right to information has been violated in the discussion.

The Temelín controversy shows clearly the primacy of industrial interests in environmental decision making in the Czech Republic. Technological solutions are sought to modernize Czech industry, with the expectation that new technologies will be more efficient and reduce emissions. However, environmental groups argue that not enough is being done to encourage recycling or conservation of resources. The Temelín controversy, however, also may provide the opportunity for refocusing the energies of the environmental movement and awakening public attention to environmental problems.

One objective of Czech Prime Minister Klaus is to reduce the role of the state in all areas of economic and political life. In environmental policy making, decentralization of authority may empower local environmental councils and nongovernmental organizations, which can help create a consensus in favor of local priorities and environmental standards. However, strong national administration and centralized data systems are necessary to ensure enforcement of environmental legislation. Local initiatives must be balanced with the bureaucratic traditions inherited from previous regimes.

Slovakia

For Slovakia, the most pressing issue since independence is establishing the character and institutions of an independent country. Thus, national autonomy receives a high priority in environmental affairs, and the country is less open to outside involvement in its policy making. Independence also has brought to the forefront concerns over ethnic minorities, particularly the large Hungarian minority in south Slovakia. The controversy over the Gabčikovo Dam has a strong political dimension because of the protests of the Hungarian minority living near the dam. Finally, the government of Prime Minister Vladimír Meciar has not been open to criticism in the press, in his own political party, or in Parliament. Meciar on several occasions has accused the press of disloyalty and has not appreciated dissenting opinion, including again protests against the Gabčikovo Dam.

Economic Reform

Economic reform has proceeded more slowly in Slovakia than in the Czech Republic. Privatization of large industrial enterprises has not been accorded a high priority. As a result, there has been significantly less foreign investment in Slovakia. (In 1992 Slovakia received only 10 percent of all foreign investment in Czechoslovakia.) For this reason, the process of introducing new, more efficient technology has been slower. The structure of Slovakia's industry also hinders environmental improvements. Slovakia has a large armaments industry, and its most notorious polluter, the aluminum plant in Ziar nad Hronem, is an important local employer. Slovaks living in the region of Ziar have petitioned the government not to close it, despite its harmful emissions. Instead, Slovakia has received a loan from the European Bank for Reconstruction and Development to reduce emissions at the Ziar plant.

Prime Minister Meciar has supported maintaining a high level of social services and continued government ownership of crucial industries. As a result, environmental policies in Slovakia are likely to rely more on government directives and less on the market mechanisms that are being implemented in the Czech Republic (Nelson, Prizemin, and Prizemin 1993).

Energy Policy

Self-sufficiency in energy policy is a high priority for the Slovak government. Unlike the Czech Republic, Slovakia does not have significant reserves of coal. However, it is likely that Slovakia's trade will be more oriented toward its eastern neighbors (Russia and Ukraine), and it may continue to rely on oil from the former Soviet republics. Slovakia has several nuclear power stations, but as in the case of Temelín, these plants are not considered safe. Slovak environmental groups, following the lead of their Czech neighbors, recently have protested construction of nuclear power plants at Jaslovské Bohunice (where two reactors were shut after accidents in the 1970s) and Mochovec.

Gabčikovo

As an alternative source of electric power, the Slovak government has embraced hydroelectric power. The Gabčikovo-Nagymaros Dam project, which had been discussed since the 1950s, was formally inaugurated in 1977. It proposed to dam the Danube River to create a hydroelectric plant that would provide electricity both to Czechoslovakia and Hungary (Reisch 1992; Okolicsanyi 1992; Binder 1992; Vasarhelyi 1992; Fisher 1993). In 1984, the Danube Circle was formed in Hungary to coordinate protests over the environmental impact of the dam. The Danube Circle argued that important wetlands habitats would be destroyed by diverting water from the banks of the Danube and concentrating it in the large reservoir behind the dam. The lower water level would lead to a rise in water temperature and a greater concentration of pollutants. After the dam was put into operation by Slovakia in October 1992, the Hungarian press reported large fish kills (JPRS-EER-92-163; JPRS-EER-92-170).

Because the dam project was associated with the "gigantomania" of the Communist era, Hungary suspended its participation on the dam project in 1989 and formally withdrew from it in May 1992. Czechoslovakia reaffirmed its commitment to the dam and proceeded with "Variant C," which required the building of a new channel on Slovak territory to divert the waters from the Danube to the reservoir formed between the Little Danube and the Danube rivers.

The Gabčikovo dam project quickly became a contentious issue in relations between the Slovak Republic and the Czech Republic and between

Slovakia and Hungary. The Czechoslovak federal government was paralyzed on the dam issue, since the Slovak representatives supported it while the Czech representatives opposed it. The Czechs argued that proceeding with the dam in the face of Hungarian opposition would damage Czechoslovakia's relations with the EC. They sought to delay any formal action until after the dissolution of the country, so as to minimize the Czechs' association with the controversy (FBIS-EEU-92-210; FBIS-EEU-92-212). Nonetheless, the dam began operation on October 24, 1992, much to the irritation of the Czechs. For Slovakia, the dam became a symbol of its separation from the Czechoslovak federal state and the end of its political and economic subordination to the Czechs.

Relations between Hungary and Slovakia are affected not only by concern over the environmental impact of the dam project but also by questions of territorial sovereignty and national minorities. The Slovak government has accused the Hungarian minority in Slovakia of supporting the Hungarian position on the dam, and it argues that Hungary is using the dam project to arouse Hungarian opposition to the Slovak government, with eventual irredentist aims. The Hungarian government has protested the dam not just on environmental grounds but also on territorial grounds, since Hungary claims that, by diverting the waters of the Danube River, Slovakia illegally has altered the border between Hungary and Slovakia.

In favor of the dam, Slovakia has claimed that even more environmental damage will occur if the dam is not used, since forest land already has been denuded in preparation for flooding. Slovakia also has argued that the faster water flow from the dam will cleanse the Danube of pollutants; that the project is "environmentally friendly"; and that navigation, flood control, drinking water supplies, groundwater quality, and tourism all will improve. Hungary contends that these areas will deteriorate.

Finally, financial issues are involved. Czechoslovakia pursued the construction of the dam much more vigorously than did Hungary. Czechoslovakia spent 6,000 million crowns ($20 million) on the construction of the dam; Hungary spent an equivalent amount, much of which was borrowed from Austrian investors who have a stake in the completion of the project (FBIS-EEU-92-213). If the dam is not put into operation, Slovakia will demand financial compensation from Hungary. Equally important, Slovakia suffers from 12 percent unemployment, and the dam will provide jobs as well as a much-needed source of electricity.

Because the issues involved are so complex, Hungary and Slovakia appealed to the EC to assess the environmental consequences of the dam. In October and November 1992, a Trilateral Commission met in London to propose a compromise under which Slovakia would cease operating the power plant by the end of November. The Trilateral Commission's recommendations that while negotiations were proceeding Slovakia divert only 5 percent of the water in the Danube were not heeded (FBIS-EEU-92-211). In February 1993, Hungary accepted an EC compromise that allows Slovakia to use 50 percent of the water in the Danube in the summer and 20 to 40 percent of the water in the winter (RFE/RL, February 4, 1993; RFE/RL, April 8, 1993).

Hungary has pushed to present the case to the International Court of Justice at the Hague. Here the issues are likely to be legal rather than environmental. Hungary will argue that the diversion of the Danube violates the Paris Peace Treaty of 1947. Slovakia will argue that Hungary unilaterally abrogated its contract to complete the dam, which remains valid. The International Court is not expected to reach a judgment until 1997.

The Gabčikovo dam illustrates the complexity of environmental issues in the international context of East Central Europe. International cooperation is likely only in areas in which there is not a conflict of interest between states. Because Slovakia has thus far received relatively little foreign investment, it may be less subject to pressure from the EC. If a compromise that is satisfactory to Slovakia is not reached, Slovakia may find itself drawing away from Western Europe.

The Gabčikovo controversy also reveals some of the differences between Slovakia and the Czech Republic in environmental affairs. The Czech Republic is more highly industrialized and therefore inherited most of the environmental degradation of the former Czechoslovakia. It is seeking foreign aid and investment to help reduce emissions and eventually clean up existing pollution. Slovakia's environmental problems are more closely associated with particular industrial enterprises, many of which (like armaments plants or obsolete aluminum factories) are unlikely to attract high-technology foreign investment. The Slovak government also is concerned with establishing its sovereignty and will be less likely to accept internationally imposed solutions to its environmental problems.

In Slovakia the state is likely to remain a more active participant in the economy. This may have the effect of hindering local environmental initiatives. Recent conflict between Prime Minister Meciar and the Slovak media reflects an ongoing debate over free criticism of the Slovak government and its policies. Slovakia may be more likely to adopt a "command and control" approach to environmental regulation in place of the market-driven mechanisms proposed for the Czech Republic.

Conclusion

Environmental policies are being made in a context of dramatic change. The political institutions of the Czech Republic and Slovakia have been created anew since 1989; the balance of political forces and parties in the two countries will be in flux for some time to come. Environmental issues will remain subsidiary to economic reform in the Czech Republic and to the development of a stable political system in Slovakia.

Environmental policy making is closely linked to economic reform both in Slovakia and in the Czech Republic. The most important environmental priorities in both countries are to reduce harmful emissions and improve energy efficiency. With foreign aid and investment, both goals may be reached through economic incentives. More difficult will be changing the behavior of consumers and small producers in both countries, whose waste will be much more difficult to monitor. Pent-up consumer demand means that a reduction in consumption is unlikely, and the challenge for environmental policy makers is to integrate environmental control into a market economy. Informal environmental groups will need to work more closely with the public if they are to have an influence on environmental policy.

The international context is crucial to the future of environmental policy making in the Czech Republic and Slovakia. The desire of these two countries to become fully integrated into the European market and accepted as full members of the international community is an important impetus to reform of environmental policy; foreign aid will be necessary to achieve a real reduction in emissions and a cleanup of existing pollution. However, international bodies will need to respect the sovereignty in environmental affairs both of the Czech Republic and of Slovakia.

References

Alcamo, Joseph M., ed. 1992a. *Coping with Crisis in Eastern Europe's Environment.* Pearl River, N.Y.: Parthenon.

———. 1992b. "Emergency Care Needed in Central and Eastern Europe." *Environment* 34(3):44–45.

Binder, Julius. 1992. "Gabčikovo: The case for." *East European Reporter* 5(5): 76–78.

Boehmer-Christiansen, Sonja A. 1990. "Putting on the Brakes: Curbing Auto Emission in Europe." *Environment* 32(6):16–20.

Borsos, B. 1991. "Socio-Political Aspects of the Bos-Nagymaros Barrage System." *International Water Power and Dam Construction* 43(5):57–59.

Bretislav, Thomas. 1991. "The General Plan for Treatment of Municipal Waste in Prague." *Journal of Resource Management and Technology* 19(1):25–28.

Budnikowski, Adam. 1992. "Foreign Participation in Environmental Protection in Eastern Europe: The Case of Poland." *Technological Forecasting and Social Change* 41:147–60.

Carolina. 1993. "Economical Ministers in Favor of Completion of Nuclear Power Station," 18 February.

Carter, F. W. 1986. "Nuclear Power Production in Czechoslovakia." *Geography* 71:136–39.

Charter 77. 1983. "Rozbor ekologické situace v Československu." Document no. 36/83, published as a supplement to *Listy* 14(1).

Charter 77. 1984. "K situace v Severoceském kraji." Document no. 26/83. *Listy* 14(2):17–18ff.

Cooper-Lybrand. 1991. "Energy in Eastern Europe." *Energy Policy* 19(9):818–40.

Czajkowski, Przemyslaw. 1993. "Environmental Organizations: And Now Help Yourself." *The Warsaw Voice*, 30 July.

Czech and Slovak Federal Republic. 1991. *The Law Concerning the Protection of the Atmosphere from Polluting Substances.* No. 309/91, 9 July.

Czech Republic. Ministry of the Environment. 1991. *Životní prostředí České republiky, Ročenka 1990.* Prague: Práce.

———. 1995. *State Environmental Policy.*

Debardeleben, Joan. 1985. *The Environment and Marxism-Leninism.* Boulder: Westview.

Dunlap, Riley E., George H. Gallup, Jr., and Alec M. Gallup. 1992. *The Health of the Planet Survey: A Preliminary Report on Attitudes Toward the Environment and Economic Growth Measured by Surveys of Citizens in 22 Nations to Date.* A George H. Gallup Memorial Survey. Princeton: The George H. Gallup International Institute.

Dvořáková, Vladimíra. 1993. "Political Reform in the Czech Republic." Unpublished paper.

FBIS-EEU-92-207. 1992. "Czech Minister: 'Halt' Further Steps in Dam." 26 October, 5.

FBIS-EEU-92-210. 1992. "Government Divided on Gabčikovo Dam Issue." 29 October, 10–11.

FBIS-EEU-92-210. 1992. "Klaus Doubts Government to Resign over Dam." 29 October, 11.

FBIS-EEU-92-212. 1992. "Trilateral Memorandum Issued on Dam Project." 30 October, 10.

FBIS-EEU-92-212. 1992. "Martonyi Interviewed on Gabčikovo Dam Dispute." 2 November.

FBIS-EEU-92-213. 1992. "Dam Dispute to Move to 'Technical' Level." 3 November.

Federal Committee for the Environment. 1991a. *Zpráva o stavu životního prostředí v CSFR*. Prague: Vesmír.

———. 1991b. *Strategy to care for the Environment* (Prague).

———. 1991c. *Draft Environmental Act*, 16 September.

Fisher, Sharon. 1993. "The Gabčikovo-Nagymaros Controversy Continues." RFE/RL Research Report (September 17): 7–12.

Foell, Wesley K. 1992. "Energy Management in Eastern Europe and the Former USSR: Economic and Environmental Opportunities." *Columbia Journal of World Business* 27/3-4: 175–85.

Hardi, Peter. 1992. *Impediments on Environmental Policy-Making and Implementation in Central and Eastern Europe: Tabula Rasa vs. Legacy of the Past*. Berkeley: Institute of International Studies, University of California.

Hladík, René. 1991. "The Ecological Dimension of Economic Reform in Czechoslovakia." *Czechoslovak Economic Digest* 3:8–10.

Howe, Charles W. 1991. "Environmental Implications of the Single European Market." *Environment* 33/10: 4–11.

Inglehart, Ronald. 1990. *Culture Shift in Advanced Industrial Society*. Princeton: Princeton University Press.

International Energy Agency. 1992. *Energy Policies: Czech and Slovak Federal Republic 1992 Survey*. Paris: OECD.

Jancar, Barbara Wolfe. 1987. *Environmental Management in the Soviet Union and Yugoslavia: Structure and Regulation in Federal Communist States*. Durham: Duke University Press.

Jancar-Webster, Barbara. 1993. *Environmental Action in Eastern Europe: Responses to Crisis*. New York: M. E. Sharpe.

Jennings, Cheri Lucas, and Bruce H. Jennings. 1993. "Green Fields/Brown Skin: Posting as a Sign of Recognition." In *In the Nature of Things: Language, Politics, and the Environment*, ed. Jane Bennet and William Chaloupka, 173–94. Minneapolis, Minnesota: University of Minnesota Press.

Johanisova, Nadja. 1991. "State of Environment in Czechoslovakia." *Forum for Applied Research and Public Policy* 6: 54.

JPRS-EER-92-163. 1992. "Fish Dying 'in Droves.'" 27 November, 1.

JPRS-EER-92-170. 1992. "Effects of Gabčikovo Dam on Residents Described." 17 December, 38–39.

Kabala, Stanley J. 1991a. "Czechoslovakia: The Reform of Environmental Policy." *RFE/RL Report on Eastern Europe* 2 (22 February): 10–14.

―――. 1991b. "The Hazardous Waste Problem in Eastern Europe." *Report on Eastern Europe* 2 (21 June): 27–33.

―――. 1992a. "EC Helps Czechoslovakia Pay 'Debt to the Environment.'" *RFE/RL Research Report* (15 May):54–58.

Kramer, John M. 1983. "The Environmental Crisis in Eastern Europe: The Price for Progress." *Slavic Review* 42: 204–220.

―――. 1991. "Eastern Europe and the 'Energy Shock' of 1990-1991." *Problems of Communism* (May-June): 85–96.

Moldan, Bedřich, and Jerald L. Schnoor. 1992. "Czechoslovakia: Examining a Critically Ill Environment." *Environmental Science and Technology* 26/1: 14–21.

Nelson, Roger H., Jurij Prizemin, and Peter Prizemin. 1993. "Entrepreneurship and Ecology in Slovakia." Unpublished paper presented at the annual meeting of the AAASS, November.

Okolicsanyi, Karoly. 1992. "Hungary: Antall's Government Proves Less than Green." *RFE/RL Research Report* 1/33 (21 August): 65–69.

Paehlke, Robert C. 1989. *Environmentalism and the Future of Progressive Politics*. New Haven: Yale University Press.

Pohl, Frank. 1988. "Impurities in Czechoslovak Meat and Dairy Products." *RFE/RL Background Report* 192 (20 September): 1–5.

Polach, Jaroslav G. 1968. "Nuclear Energy in Czechoslovakia: A Study in Frustration." *Orbis* 12: 831–51.

Reisch, Alfred A. 1992. "The Difficult Search for a Hungarian-Slovak Accord." *RFE/RL Research Report* 1/42 (23 October): 24–31.

Respekt. 1994. "Czechs Selling Electricity to Pay for Temelín." CTK National News Wire, 17 February.

RFE/RL. 1983. "Charter 77 on Ecological and Social Devastation in North Bohemia." *Czechoslovak Situation Report* 14 (9 August).

RFE/RL Daily Report. 1993. "Hungarian-Slovak Talks in Gabčikovo." (4 February).

―――. 1993. "Toxic Waste Found in Czech Republic." (17 March).

―――. 1993. "Hungary and Slovakia Turn to the World Court to Settle Dam Dispute." (8 April).

Schnoor, Jerald L. 1992. "Environmental Strategic Plans in Developing Countries: Czechoslovakia case study, an EPAT case study." Unpublished paper, Center for Global and Regional Environmental Research, The University of Iowa.

Smetana, Susannah A. 1993. "Sustainable Development in the Czech Republic and Slovakia: The Integration of Environmental Protection and Economic Development." *Georgetown International Environmental Law Review* 5/3: 783–814.

Stancíková, Pavla. 1992. "Environmental Information in Czechoslovakia." *Information Development* 8/3: 142–46.

Stansky, Pavl. 1988. "Pollution: The Tale of Bratislava." *East European Reporter* 3/3: 26–30.

Vasarhelyi, Judith. 1992. "Gabčikovo: The Case Against." *East European Reporter* 5(5): 76–78.

Vidlaková, Olga. 1993. "Options for Administrative Reform in the Czech Republic." *Public Adminlstration* 71: 65–74.

Walls, Margaret A. 1993. "Motor Vehicles and Pollution in Central and Eastern Europe." *Resources* 113: 2–7.

World Bank. 1992. *Czech and Slovak Federal Republic Joint Environmental Study.* 2 vols. Washington, D.C.: World Bank.

Ziegler, Charles E. 1987. *Environmental Policy in the USSR.* Amherst: University of Massachusetts Press.

11

POVERTY, GOVERNMENT, AND THE GLOBAL ENVIRONMENT

UDAY DESAI

A driving determination by hundreds of millions of desperately poor men, women, and children to improve their material life is an unmistakable fact of life in poor industrializing countries. Economic growth, seen as the way to improve material conditions, has become the central purpose for most people and public policies in these countries. Whether economic growth is used in reality to relieve the desperate poverty of the millions or to enrich a small elite, the goal of economic growth has become an overwhelming justification for public policies. Whenever a policy is seen as hindering economic growth it becomes suspect or undesirable.

In developing countries around the globe there is a drive for economic growth through industrialization and resource exploitation, even at the expense of environmental degradation. In a choice between economic growth and environmental protection, the environment almost always loses. In India, China, Mexico, Taiwan, and many other countries, the drive for rapid economic growth has been characterized by rapid industrialization and the building of mega projects such as huge dams and irrigation and power projects. In Nigeria, Thailand, and many other resource rich countries, the drive for rapid economic growth often has centered on single-minded exploitation of the natural resources such as oil and forests. In most countries, rapid industrialization, mega projects, and natural resource exploitation have gone hand in hand. All three have been taking place simultaneously. The environment has suffered grievously as a result.

There is widespread distrust in developing countries of all those who oppose rapid economic growth. This distrust is especially strong when the opposition comes from the West. There is widespread belief that the West's opposition to economic growth in developing countries is self-serving. There is the suspicion that the West does not want the poor countries, often excolonies, to become prosperous and powerful. There is widespread belief that the West has become rich and powerful by doing precisely what it now wants others not to do. The West is seen by many in the developing countries as the cause of most of the global ecological problems. There is little sympathy among them for the West's demands that poor countries protect their environment, particularly when that protection is at the expense of economic growth. For many in the poor countries, the environment has become an excuse for the rich Western countries to interfere in their national affairs. The environment, for them, is another instrument of Western neocolonialism.

It seems unrealistic, if not futile, to expect the industrializing countries to sacrifice economic growth and prosperity for the protection of the global environment. It is hypocritical for those in the West, who on average consume twenty to forty times more resources than the people in developing countries, to tell those in the poor countries to stop increasing their resource consumption. This advice is especially ineffective when the rich countries are unwilling to reduce their own consumption and exploitation of global resources and are unwilling to share even a small part of their riches with the poor countries. For a global effort to protect the global environment—that is, to reduce global warming, repair the hole in the ozone layer or protect biodiversity—a willingness to share some of the riches will be necessary. Without such willingness, no global effort to protect the world's environment will succeed. Environmental policy makers both in rich and in poor parts of the world will need to develop and support policies that relieve grinding poverty while protecting the environment.

Environmental issues, as Cribb points out in his chapter, are seldom quarantined from broader social and political issues. They cannot be separated from international trade and aid policies. They cannot be isolated from poverty or global distribution of resource consumption or pollution production. It is now widely recognized that the world "population problem" cannot be quarantined from the problems of women's and children's health, education, and nutrition; similarly it is time to recognize that global environmental issues cannot be separated from the problems of poverty, unemployment, or inequity. Environmentalists must be willing to engage in a broader policy arena if they are to succeed in protecting the global environment. Blaming the poor countries for our global environmental problems is not only inaccurate but is also futile.

It is rather essential to tie environmental protection to the national interest and pride of the poor countries. Environmental protection must be perceived by the people as enhancing their quality of life. To be effective, environmental discourse will have to be grounded in national religious and cultural traditions and myths. This already is beginning to happen. In Thailand, as Rigg and Stott have pointed out in their chapter earlier, wider use of

Buddhism to generate environmental discourse is now commonplace. If it is to take root, environmental protection will have to be grounded in indigenous tradition and history, especially when it requires people to forego material prosperity.

In the West, environmentalism is tied to comfortable and secure middle-class existence. Environmental values in the wealthy countries have been called "postindustrial," "postmaterialist" values. It is suggested that only in a postindustrial society can a majority of the people have the security and comfort necessary for them to be concerned about the global environment and the long term future of the planet (Paehlke 1989). In Inglehart's (1990) influential argument, the source of political discontent in advanced industrial countries, including discontent over environmental issues, has been the economically secure, middle-class professionals. This raises two important issues. First, this secure and comfortable middle-class life in the West has significant environmental costs. It is this comfortable lifestyle that has created and continues much of the global environmental destruction. If postmaterialist values in the West depend on an economically secure middle-class majority, then there is a fundamental contradiction. Postmaterialist values are dependent on a lifestyle inimical to global environmental health. Second, if environmentalism in the poor countries must depend on a similarly secure and comfortable middle-class majority, then the global environment is in grave peril since such a lifestyle for the majority in poor countries would require enormous economic growth, natural resource exploitation, and consequent environmental destruction. Environmentalism in these countries must find some less destructive basis.

Many traditional cultures still vibrant in industrializing countries are based on values comparable to the postmaterialist values and may provide a basis for an alternative to the Western middle-class lifestyle that is so destructive of global environment. Vandana Shiva writing about native communities, especially a community of women, notes that "native cultures and the vast majority of those who have occupied the planet regard nature not as 'resource' to be redefined or mastered, but as 'home' to which care must be given and within which life is regenerated and sustained by interdependence" (quoted in Jennings and Jennings 1993:179). In the current climate of ever-increasing integration of the poor countries and their native communities into the global economy and culture, it is nearly impossible even to conceive of any practical and desirable alternative to the Western middle-class lifestyle. Models of such an alternative most likely will have to come not from outsiders, but from the people themselves in the poor countries. Since there still exist a rich variety of nonmaterialist cultures across the globe, there could be many potential alternatives. However, the allure of material riches associated with the resource-intensive Western lifestyle should not be underestimated. Prospects for development and adoption of such alternative lifestyles in poorer countries are likely to be encouraged by the development of such alternatives in the Western countries, based on their own cultural and religious traditions.

While environmental protection almost always takes second place to economic growth when the two are in direct conflict, there has been no lack of policies to control and mitigate environmental destruction in the industrializing countries. Almost all of them now have a large corpus of policies and programs to control air and water pollution, to protect land, forests, and biodiversity, and to control the environmental impacts of economic activities generally. These policies are the result of international pressures, increasing awareness of the health risks and economic consequences of environmental pollution, and increasing popular demand for protection from the environmental hazards created by economic growth.

While environmental laws, policies, regulations, and programs have proliferated, governmental capacity to enforce and implement them has lagged behind significantly. In most industrializing countries there is, in general, a gap between the government policies and regulations on the one hand and their implementation and enforcement on the other. Environmental policies and regulations are no exception to this implementation gap. They are often especially prone to it. The state's autonomy and its capacity to work its will on the society often are quite limited in these countries.

The highly centralized governmental system in many industrializing countries is often a cause of the implementation difficulties. Centralized decision making, far from the problems on the ground, often fails to take into account the powerful local interests and weakness of local governmental machinery. Comprehensive policies and regulations often are enacted with little consideration for the local reality and without much concern for their actual implementation. They often seem to exist only in the offices and corridors of central or provincial ministries and secretariats. A rigidly hierarchical system of authority often prevents the central officials from learning from local officials, or local officials from sharing their knowledge and experiences with the central officials, so that they could make the policies and programs more realistic in their aims and more effective in their results. For environmental policies and regulations, centralized decision making is especially problematic since environmental protection activities are essentially local in nature. However, decentralizing the decision making and involving local officials in environmental policy design and implementation create different problems. A more highly decentralized system would require more effective coordination. It would require more complex information and monitoring systems. Often these are precisely the capabilities that governments in poor industrializing countries lack most sorely. The decentralized system also would require a spirit of cooperation and mutual trust and respect between central and local officials and administrators. Again, this is often in very short supply in these countries.

Developing effective environmental policies and regulations requires considerable scientific knowledge and technical expertise. Their effective implementation requires much administrative and technical expertise. The development of this knowledge and expertise requires an extensive infrastructure of institutions of higher education and scientific research. Many poor industrializing countries lack this infrastructure and hence face a lack of expertise among the officials and bureaucrats engaged in developing and implementing environmental policies and programs. This has been changing in recent decades. There is a growing number of young people with technical and administrative expertise. International aid and exchange programs have played an important role in the development of local scientific and administrative expertise in these countries. However, limitations of technical and administrative expertise among government officials still remains an important constraint in protecting the environment in these countries.

The lack of expertise is not uniformly distributed between central and local governments or between government and private sectors. There is a higher level of expertise available at the center than at local levels in most industrializing countries. This is partly the result of better pay and working conditions as well as higher prestige attached to the central government positions. This disparity in expertise exacerbates the centralizing tendency discussed earlier. Increasingly, there is a higher level of technical expertise in the private sector than in the public sector. Better pay and working conditions now are found in the private sector. With liberalization of the economy and privatization of previously public enterprises, the lure of private-sector employment has become irresistible for many highly trained technical and managerial personnel. These developments are likely to further aggravate the expertise gap and restrict government's capacity to design and implement environmental policies and programs.

In addition to the scarcity of expertise, widespread official corruption is a major culprit in environmental destruction in many industrializing countries. The corruption often reaches the highest levels of government. In some countries, Nigeria and Indonesia for instance, the corruption pervades even the head of state and his family. The cabinet ministers and senior members of the legislatures, ruling party, and military, as well as senior career civilian administrators are all often involved in schemes that involve kickbacks, bribes, and various other kinds of payments from business and industry as well as from ordinary citizens. In return, these officials help them get special favors, such as government contracts and concessions, or allow them to ignore government policies, such as environmental laws and regulations. Such high-level corruption is principally responsible for much of the destruction of the forests and wildlife in Indonesia and the pollution of land and water by the petroleum industry in Nigeria. Such corruption inevitably seeps down. In many industrializing countries, petty corruption by mid- and low-level officials and bureaucrats both at the center and at the local level is widespread and endemic. Environmental regulations often are observed only in their breach.

Use of market mechanisms to accomplish environmental protection has gained popularity in the West in recent years. The market is considered a more efficient means of controlling pollution and cleaning up the environment than government controls and enforcement. In some industrializing countries, India and China for example, policies of economic liberalization and privatization have created an interest in market-based environmental pollution control policies. However, the institutional infrastructure necessary for effective functioning of the market generally is underdeveloped in poor industrializing countries. The colonial heritage of centralized government, lack of information and expertise, widespread corruption, and restrictions on the free flow of available information further limit the functioning of the market. Several other factors also make it unlikely that market-based instruments will play a significant role in environmental protection in these countries in the near future, including a popular distrust of the market and the widespread belief in many poor industrializing countries that environmental problems, like any other major social problem, are the responsibility of the government. Government controls and programs are likely to remain the major instruments for environmental protection.

The responsiveness of governments to citizens' demands for environmental protection may prove to be the most critical factor. Demands for environmental protection in poor industrializing countries come from two distinct sources. The urban, professional middle class is becoming an important source of these demands. The urban middle class is increasingly affected by air, water, land, and noise pollution. These well-educated people have become more knowledgeable about the costs of environmental degradation to their health and their quality of life. In industrializing democracies these middle-class professional groups have organized to become important sources of pressure for environmental policies and for rigorous enforcement of existing environmental regulations.

Indigenous tribal, hill, and forest communities have become the other major source of demand for environmental protection. These people have depended from the beginning of time on nature: the forests, rivers, oceans, and all nature's creatures who live among them. Destruction of nature by unchecked exploitation of natural resources, the building of mega projects, and increasing industrial waste threaten the very survival of these communities. These communities, however, are becoming increasingly assertive about protecting the very basis of their livelihood and identity. They are finding support for their cause among the international environmental community as well as among urban professionals in their own countries. But there remains strong opposition or indifference by the large majority to environmentalism. The involvement of international agencies and environmental groups often increases the majority's opposition to demands for environmental protection, especially if they threaten projects for economic growth. However, both in industrializing democracies and in nondemocratic countries, the growing awareness of the costs of environmental destruction should create increasing pressure on governments to protect and clean up the environment. In the nondemocratic countries, open organization and protest against environmental destruction are less likely, though, considering the severe repressive consequences to anyone engaged in such organization or protest activities. While authoritarian systems are in theory conducive to long-range environmental planning since the regime does not expect to be removed at election time or by civil unrest, they rarely do so. On the contrary, they often show complete disregard for the environment and engage in wanton environmental destruction to enrich themselves and their friends.

Whether democracies are more likely to be environmentally friendly is not entirely clear. It may be that democracies with small, organized minorities of urban professionals and indigenous people demanding environmental protection and a large majority of those indifferent or opposed to environmentalism may be more friendly to the environment. Or it may be that dictatorships with little or no opposition may be more effective environmentally if they decide to act. In the long run, with collaboration between the urban professionals and indigenous minorities and with the help of international environmental organizations and pressures and aid from other democracies, and with a bit of luck, the industrializing democracies perhaps have a better chance of protecting their environment for the benefit of their own people as well as the global community.

References

Inglehart, Ronald. 1990. *Culture Shift in Advanced Industrial Society.* Princeton: Princeton University Press.

Jennings, Cheri Lucas, and Bruce H. Jennings. 1993. "Green Fields/Brown Skin: Posting a Sign of Recognition." In *In the Nature of Things: Language, Politics, and the Environment*, ed. Jane Bennett, and William Chaloupka, 173–194. Minneapolis: University of Minnesota Press.

Paehlke, Robert C. 1989. *Environmentalism and the Future of Progressive Politics.* New Haven: Yale University Press.

CONTRIBUTORS

Uday Desai is professor of political science at Southern Illinois University at Carbondale. He was director of the MPA program for six years before becoming chairman of the department in 1995. His last book, *Moving the Earth*, was published by Greenwood Press in 1993. He also has published six book chapters and over two dozen articles in refereed journals. He has been the co-editor in chief of *Policy Studies Journal* since 1990. He currently is working on a volume to accompany this one on environmental policy and politics in industrial countries, which will be published by State University of New York Press next year.

Catherine Albrecht is associate professor of history at the University of Baltimore. Her specialty is history and contemporary affairs in East Central Europe. In addition to articles on environmental policy, Dr. Albrecht also has published extensively on the history of economic nationalism and the development of the economics profession in the Bohemian crownlands of the Habsburg monarchy.

Olusegun Areola is professor of geography at the University of Ibadan, Nigeria. He served as a member of the Expert-Group of UNEP Global Environment Monitoring System. He was a Fulbright scholar at the University of South Carolina and the University of Iowa from 1990 to 1991. In 1983, he was a visiting associate professor at the University of Florida.

Robert Cribb has written on many aspects of modern Indonesian history, including contemporary politics and the revolution of 1945 through 1949 against Dutch colonialism. His books include *Gangsters and Revolutionaries* (1991) and, with Colin Brown, *Modern Indonesia: A History Since 1945* (1995). He is presently a research professor at the Nordic Institute of Asian Studies in Copenhagen, where he is writing a history of environmental politics and policies of Indonesia in the twentieth century.

Pablo Gutman is an Argentinean environmental economist, currently at the Center for Urban and Regional Studies, Buenos Aires, and a member of Argentina's National Science Council. He has been a lecturer and consultant on environmental issues in almost all Latin American countries and has published widely in Spanish and English. He was senior economist at

Venezuela's Ministry of Environment from 1976 through 1983. After 1983, he returned several times to Venezuela as consultant to the United Nations Development Program, the World Bank, and the Food and Agriculture Organization.

Stephen P. Mumme is a professor of political science at Colorado State University where he specializes in a comparative environmental politics with an emphasis on Latin America and Mexico. His published work appears in various books and monographs and in a wide range of journals, including *Environment, Journal of Environment and Development, Environmental Management, Natural Resources Journal*, and *Latin American Research Review*, among others. He also serves as the Americas regional editor for the *Boundary and Security Bulletin*.

Jonathan Rigg is reader in geography at the University of Durham. He has worked in Thailand since the early 1980s, particularly in the northeastern regions where he has developed a particular interest in rainfed agriculture, livelihood strategies, and rural-urban interactions. He is author of *Southeast Asia: A Region in Transition* (London: Routledge, 1995) and recently has edited a collection of papers on Thailand's environment, *Counting the Costs: Economic Growth and Environmental Change in Thailand* (Singapore: Institute of Southeast Asian Studies, 1995). He also has edited with Philip Stott and Raymond Bryant a special triple issue of *Global Ecology and Biogeography Letters, The Political Ecology of Southeast Asian Forests: Transdisciplinary Perspectives* (1993, vol. 3, nos. 4–6).

Lester Ross is an attorney in the Beijing office of Paul, Weiss, Rifkind, Wharton & Garrison, where he focuses on international banking and finance, project finance, and corporate and environmental law matters. He has a JD *cum laude* from Harvard Law School and a Ph.D. in political science from the University of Michigan. He has been a visiting scholar at the Chinese Research Academy of Environmental Sciences in Beijing and has studied Chinese at Taiwan National University. He currently is a participant in several projects relating to Asia with the Council on Foreign Relations and the American Academy of Arts and Sciences.

R. K. Sapru is chairman and reader in the department of public administration at Punjab University in Chandigarh, India. He has written and published widely on development administration and public management in India. He has published articles in *Indian Journal of Administrative Science, Indian Journal of Public Administration, Indian Economic Journal*, and *Indian Journal of Political Science*, among others.

Philip Stott is professor of geography at the School of Oriental and African Studies at the University of London. He has been working in Thailand since the early 1970s and has a particular interest in the evolution of the Thai *mu'ang*, in human-land relationships in the Sukhothai period, and in indigenous views of the environment. Trained as a physical geographer and ecologist, he has published widely on the links among culture, history, and environment of Thailand and Southeast Asia. He is the editor of *Nature and Man in South East Asia* (London: SOAS, 1978) and has recently co-authored *Ancient Capitals of Thailand* with Elizabeth Moore and Suriyavudh Sukhavasti (London: Thames & Hudson, 1996). He also has edited with Jonathan Rigg and Raymond Bryant a special triple issue of *Global Ecology and Biogeography Letters, The Political Ecology of Southeast Asian Forests: Transdisciplinary Perspectives* (1993, vol. 3, nos. 4–6).

JuJu Wang is an associate professor jointly appointed both at the Graduate Institute of Sociology and Anthropology and at the Center for General Education, National Tsing Hua University in Hsinchu, Taiwan. Professor Wang is teaching and doing research in an interdisciplinary spectrum ranging from environmental justice issues, social impact assessment, paradigm shifts, community-based environmental management, ecological wisdoms, to soundscape. In August of 1996, Dr. Wang became engaged in a two-year appointment as associate dean of general education to carry out an experimental program of core curriculum at the National Institute of Technology at Kaohsiung.

INDEX

Thai names are indexed by first name.